ESSENTIAL ISRAEL

PERSPECTIVES ON ISRAEL STUDIES

*S. Ilan Troen, Natan Aridan, Donna Divine,
David Ellenson, and Arieh Saposnik, editors*

Sponsored by the Ben-Gurion Research Institute for the
Study of Israel and Zionism of the Ben-Gurion University
of the Negev and the Schusterman Center for
Israel Studies of Brandeis University

ESSENTIAL ISRAEL

ESSAYS FOR THE 21ST CENTURY

Edited by
S. ILAN TROEN AND RACHEL FISH

Indiana University Press
Bloomington & Indianapolis

This book is a publication of

Indiana University Press
Office of Scholarly Publishing
Herman B Wells Library 350
1320 East 10th Street
Bloomington, Indiana 47405 USA

iupress.indiana.edu

The paper used in this publication
meets the minimum requirements of
the American National Standard for
Information Sciences—Permanence
of Paper for Printed Library Materials,
ANSI Z39.48-1992.

*Manufactured in the
United States of America*

*Library of Congress
Cataloging-in-Publication Data*

Names: Troen, S. Ilan (Selwyn Ilan), 1940-
editor. | Fish, Rachel, editor.
Title: Essential Israel : essays for the 21st
century / edited by S. Ilan Troen and
Rachel Fish.
Description: Bloomington, Indiana : In-
diana Unviversity Press, 2017. | Series:
Perspectives on Israel studies | Includes
bibliographical references.
Identifiers: LCCN 2017001783 (print)
| LCCN 2017003426 (ebook) | ISBN
9780253027009 (cloth : alk. paper) |
ISBN 9780253027115 (pbk. : alk. paper) |
ISBN 9780253027191 (Ebook)
Subjects: LCSH: Arab-Israeli conflict. |
Arab-Israeli conflict—Peace. | Israel—
Politics and government. | Zionism. |
Israel—Civilization.
Classification: LCC DS119.7 .E86 2017 (print) |
LCC DS119.7 (ebook) | DDC 956.9405—dc23
LC record available at https://lccn.loc.gov
/2017001783

1 2 3 4 5 22 21 20 19 18 17

Your elders will dream dreams,
your youth shall see visions.

Joel 2:28

To Lynn and Paul with gratitude
Your dreams and visions guide and
inspire ours and future generations

CONTENTS

ACKNOWLEDGMENTS

This book was conceived in the unique environment of the Schusterman Center for Israel Studies at Brandeis University, where we were confronted with a fundamental question: What does it mean to be literate about Israel in the twenty-first century? This manuscript is the product of a series of collaborations and ongoing conversations that we initiated several years ago when we embarked on our search for an answer.

We gratefully acknowledge and thank colleagues in the Brandeis community from the Schusterman Center for Israel Studies, the Cohen Center for Modern Jewish Studies, the Mandel Center for Jewish Education, Hadassah-Brandeis Institute, the Hornstsein Program in Jewish Professional Leadership, and the Near Eastern and Judaic Studies department, who have been our partners in developing and significantly enriching this project.

Our consultants under the rubric of what came to be termed the "Israel Literacy Project" came from Brandeis and elsewhere. Practitioners teaching about Israel in the community, educators deliberating on how this teaching could best be done, and scholars engaged in researching and teaching Israel in the university came together to address each other and plumb the question. Together we debated which topics to examine and what issues were key to a basic grounding in the complexity of Israel today. These individuals, from Brandeis and beyond, included Yaakov Ariel, Cheryl Aronson, Ofra Backenworth, Marci Borenstein, Abi Dauber, Sharon Feiman Nemser, Sylvia Barack Fishman, Steve Bayme,

Jan Darsa, Shira Deener, Donna Divine, Alan Dowty, David Ellenson, Rachel Fish, Sylvia Fuks Fried, Lisa Grant, Rachel Harris, Alex Joffe, Annette Koren, Jon Levisohn, David Makovsky, Daniel Marom, Ranen Omer-Sherman, Zohar Raviv, Joe Reimer, Shula Reinharz, Len Saxe, Ellen Smith, David Starr, Yedidia Stern, Norman Stillman, and Gil Troy.

Each author who contributed to *Essential Israel: Essays for the 21st Century* was tasked with writing accessible narratives for readers seeking knowledge without polemics and advocacy. Our authors engaged with us to frame their ideas and arguments for nonacademic audiences without sacrificing the sophistication and rigor appropriate to the academy.

Carol Troen's skill as an editor and knowledge of the subject matter contributed to making these individual essays into a coherent whole. She also created and imagined the organization for the glossary, worth reading in its own right as an introduction to Israel literacy.

The staff of the Schusterman Center for Israel Studies have been indispensable from the beginning to the conclusion of this complicated project. JoAnn Leavitt, Anina Selve, Keren Goodblatt, Kristin Shulman, Rise Singer, and Abby Huber ably coordinated and integrated the work of a diverse set of experts meeting at specially convened conferences, in focus groups and seminars in an undertaking that spanned time and space. Special thanks are due to David Ellension, who became director of the Schusterman Center for Israel Studies after participating in formulating the project and contributing one of the chapters. David has appreciated the significance of the project and has given it unstinting support. We are grateful to these colleagues for their commitment to producing this book. They have attended to myriad details while maintaining an inviting, friendly, and generous working environment.

We gratefully acknowledge the Central Zionist Archives and Yad Yizhak Ben-Zvi of Jerusalem for generously permitting the use of photos that we have reproduced here. We thank, too, Noga Yoselevich of the Department of Geography and Environmental Studies at Haifa University for her expert preparation of the maps.

We thank Dee Mortensen of Indiana University Press, who took on this book, and deeply appreciate her special combination of acuity, sympathy, and critical expertise.

Finally, we are glad to acknowledge Terri Kassel and Carrie Fillpeti of the Paul E. Singer Foundation not only for their financial support from the beginning of this project but also for their appreciation and encouragement for what we aimed to achieve. Likewise, the Judy and Michael Steinhardt Foundation provided indispensable support for developing instruments to measure literacy among different sectors of the public, a crucial step that helped us determine where we should place our emphasis.

Ilan Troen and Rachel Fish
Schusterman Center for Israel Studies
Brandeis University, Waltham, MA
December 2016

ESSENTIAL ISRAEL

ONE

An Invitation to Israel Literacy

S. ILAN TROEN AND RACHEL FISH

What does it mean to be literate about Israel, and what does this have to do with you?

American academics, educators, community and religious leaders, students, laypeople, Jews, Christians, and Muslims are regularly confronted with conflicting reports on Israel in newspaper, radio, TV, or online news. Often complex situations are reduced to oversimplified sound bites, and even longer accounts focus on the immediacy of events and invite us to form opinions and take sides on issues we actually know very little about.

One important reason for this is that Israel was not a significant area of study in university curricula until very recently; only within the last decade have courses on Israel been offered on American campuses. As a result, most Americans are ill-prepared to engage seriously in the increasingly serious public debates about Israel as a beleaguered democratic state in the Middle East and its relation to the United States. *Essential Israel: Essays for the 21st Century* examines a wide variety of complex issues and current concerns in an essential historical context, and it does so in a single volume that highlights their interconnectedness.

This unique collection of voices develops a grounded, multifaceted mosaic of Israel's dynamic society and culture and addresses both Israel's struggle to be a Jewish and democratic state with a place in the Middle East, and US ties to Israel. A highly readable and maximally informative volume, it includes a series of autonomous essays that range

1

from the Arab/Israeli conflict and the role of American diplomacy in peace negotiations to Israeli cinema and literature, questions of personal status, religion and state, and relations with American Christian and Jewish communities.

The essays in *Essential Israel* are not meant to be a typical chronological history. Although you will find it a useful introduction to the study of Israel, this collection is not a conventional text, and the essays were not written as opinion pieces or policy papers. Rather the essays are meant to be maximally engaging, informative, accessible, and usable for American audiences who have questions about Israel—its history, society, culture, and people—and their relationship to it.

The essays were invited in response to what our research revealed contemporary readers wanted to know more about:

- What is the Arab/Israeli conflict and why hasn't it been resolved?
- What explains the failure of American diplomatic efforts to bring about peace in the Middle East?
- What is Zionism, and why are people saying such terrible things about it?
- Can Israel be both a Jewish and a democratic state?
- What are the relationships of different groups of American Jews and Christians with Israel?
- How is Israel dealing with questions of personal status and non-Jewish citizens in the Jewish state?
- What are Muslim and Christian views and concerns about a sovereign Jewish state in the land all consider holy?
- What accounts for the changing perceptions of Israel in world public opinion?
- What are the facts concerning Israeli identity including tensions among Israeli Jews and Arabs, immigrant groups, Sephardi and Ashkenazi and secular and religious Jews?
- What can we learn about Israel and Israelis (and many of the preceding questions) from Israeli literature, music, dance, and film?

As should be clear, our approach in this project is not advocacy. Rather we intend the informed and nuanced analyses of Israel's internal and external conflicts to enable you to interrogate the issues in their complexity and to engage in grounded and more fruitful deliberations about them.

Israel Studies and the Design of the Volume

The academic staff of the Schusterman Center for Israel Studies at Brandeis University is probably the most significant agent in the rapid spread of Israel studies in the academy worldwide. Formally established in 2007 to advance the newly emerging field of Israel studies in the university, the center runs an annual Summer Institute for Israel Studies that has been attended by 270 academics from two hundred universities, largely from the United States—including the Ivy League, state universities, US military academies, denominational schools, and so forth—but extending to China, India, Eastern and Western Europe, and South America. To date, the Summer Institute alone has resulted in six hundred new courses on Israel ranging from political science to film and anthropology, which have attracted more than twenty thousand students in the United States and worldwide. Brandeis itself is an important laboratory that offers graduate and postgraduate programs and courses designed for professionals in the Jewish community. Its publications program produced Anita Shapira's 2014 National Jewish Book Award winner, *Israel: A History*, and publishes the most widely read journal in the new field, *Israel Studies* (Indiana University Press). This experience includes detailed yearly evaluations and has provided us with extensive and invaluable data on what diverse populations know, do not know, and want to know about Israel.

Ongoing systematic research into levels of knowledge about Israel among young adults conducted by the Schusterman Center for Israel Studies and the Cohen Center for Modern Jewish Studies, both at Brandeis University, further confirmed this need. Unlike other surveys, these have not focused on what people say they *feel* about Israel but on what they *know*. Even highly educated university students often lack substantial background knowledge and base their opinions on misinformation. In other words, when it comes to Israel, they tend to be illiterate.

As you will see when you consult the brief biographical notes, the authors of the essays for *Essential Israel* are outstanding scholars and acknowledged experts. Except for one, they do not live in Israel, although they have extensive relations with the country and its peoples. We selected "outsiders" to ensure that the questions that animate their curiosity and thinking come from viewing Israel from the outside. They do not assume American readers are privy to the codes of the initiated. A popular Israeli saying, based on a line from a song by Yaakov Rotblit, is that "what you can see from *here* can not be seen (i.e., understood) from *there.*" Perspective makes a difference. The essays are meant to illuminate differences between American perspectives and those of Israel, and to help readers recognize how their own assumptions, for example, about the individual and society or religion and state, may differ substantially from those of Israeli "Others."

By design, then, the essays in *Essential Israel: Essays for the 21st Century* are accessible and readable narratives with few footnotes. They can serve as the intellectual anchor for personal and professional development and for educational forums and are not intended to provide a "final" word. Rather, they allow readers to explore current debates on key issues embedded in a richly evoked sociohistorical context. For interested readers, we provide suggestions for further reading.

CONTENTS AND STRUCTURE

Essential Israel examines fourteen topics critical to being literate about the State of Israel. They were developed through a yearlong series of conversations with scholars engaged in the study of Israel and teachers and community leaders who regularly use and transmit such information in a variety of settings. The essays may be read singly or in clusters according to interest or purpose, and the volume does not have to be read in any necessary sequence or even in its entirety.

Nevertheless, the ordering of the essays is not random. The opening essay, by S. Ilan Troen, Maoz Azaryahu, and Arnon Golan, is an overview of Israel: its geography, who lives there, when they came, what they did, and what the country produces (chapter 2). For example, some readers will be surprised to discover that the country's population was only five hundred thousand in 1900. It increased about twenty times to ten million just in the twentieth century as Palestine under the Ottomans and British became Israel, and the population is continuing to grow at a rapid rate. This information prepares the way for Michael Brenner's essay on the history of Zionism (chapter 3). His account of sometimes conflicting, powerful, and motivating ideas and how they developed into an ideological movement makes clear that the land that loomed large in the collective imagination of Jews was an underdeveloped entity on the margins of contemporary history. Zionism utterly transformed it into a successful modern state, a player in the world economy, and the focus of international attention.

From the history of Zionism and ideological theory, the third essay moves to praxis, as S. Ilan Troen analyzes Jewish settlement of Ottoman and British Mandatory Palestine and then Israel (chapter 4). Many decisions were made in the tension between what settlers imagined and wanted and the realities they encountered. The Zionists' successful efforts to return and reclaim the land and make the desert bloom have been appreciated and even celebrated. They have also been met with increasingly bitter opposition and a century-old conflict with neighboring Arab nations and local Palestinians that feature regularly in the headlines and are topics of ongoing debate.

Three essays deal with the Arab/Israeli conflict. Alan Dowty traces the history of the conflict over the course of the past century, detailing both Jewish and Arab perspectives and delineating four distinct stages in the evolution of the conflict (chapter 5). In the first stage, he examines the origins of a conflict between two peoples from the end of the nineteenth century until the 1947 UN decision for partition of Palestine into a Jewish and an Arab state. The second stage moves from Israeli independence in 1948 through the late 1980s, when the conflict was largely one between the Jewish state and neighboring Arab states. The final two stages involve a conflict with Palestinian Arabs and, more recently, with external interventions rooted in ideological rejection.

The international community invested considerable efforts to enable the establishment of a Jewish state in the Arab and largely Muslim Middle East, and the search for peace has involved sustained and frequent US diplomatic interventions in recent decades. David Makovsky charts the role of the United States in negotiations between Israel and neighboring Arab states and between Israel and the Palestinians (chapter 6). He interrogates both the success and failures of this complicated and ongoing process primarily in the aftermath of the 1973 October/Yom Kippur War through the 1993 Oslo Accords and up to Secretary of State Kerry's efforts in the recent past. In the last essay in this set, Gil Troy covers much the same period but focuses on when and how the establishment and existence of Israel became an object of heated controversy in the United Nations and the international community (chapter 7). The essay traces changes in Israel's image in largely Western public opinion from general favor through the 1967 War, to increasingly negative criticism and hostility from the 1970s to the present. By covering the topic from three distinct angles, the three essays provide an invaluably rich and nuanced account of the conflict on the ground, in diplomatic efforts to resolve it, in the United Nations, and in public opinion.

The United Nations and supporters worldwide celebrated the establishment of Israel as a Jewish and democratic state. Yet working out what a Jewish state means in practice, and in the context of the Middle East, has created frictions among the Jewish citizens of Israel, between the State and its non-Jewish citizens, and between the State and both Jews and non-Jews living abroad.

Four interrelated but distinct essays expose the dilemmas inherent in creating a Jewish society that is also democratic. Yedidia Stern explores the complexities of identifying a shared vision among divergent groups of secular and religious Israeli Jews, including ultra-Orthodox Jews who reject Zionism, and the daunting challenges of organizing public space to accommodate these groups with very diverse beliefs as well as Arab citizens (chapter 8). During a hiatus of two millennia, Jews were not sovereign and had no territory. Thus, the establishment of Israel poses an unexpected and as yet unresolved challenge to national cohesion. The secular, democratic state must find and maintain the uneasy balance between the particular yet highly diverse Jewish aspects of the nation-state and its universal, democratic values.

From the perspective of political science, Donna Robinson Divine juxtaposes the hard realities of praxis and what has actually emerged (chapter 9). She examines Israel's political system with particular attention to degrees of inclusion—and inequalities—among Arabs, Jewish immigrant groups and women, and inequalities regarding access to land, and elaborates on the competing demands of the obligations of citizenship and the personal rights of individuals. Both Stern and Divine highlight tensions inherent in the novel challenges posed by territorial sovereignty and the complexity of negotiating conflicting demands on the State, a dilemma that increasingly confronts other multicultural democratic states today.

However, the question of identity raised by Israel's establishment as a sovereign Jewish state is not limited to citizens of Israel but engages Jews and others from outside. Steven Bayme examines the notion of Jewish "peoplehood" now that there is a Jewish state and delineates how questions it raises about Jewish identity impact relations between Jews in Israel and those in the Diaspora, particularly in the United States (chapter 10). Given Israel's identity as the Jewish homeland, Bayme asks how the American Diaspora and Israel interact for mutual benefit, what happens when they disagree, and how close or "distant" these communities are from one another. In a complementary essay, David Ellenson highlights the impact of the Jewish state on Judaism itself, as distinct from ethnicity or "peoplehood" (chapter 11). He contextualizes and explains the basis of state support for Jewish religious institutions and inquires into the institution of the Chief Rabbinate and the State's relationship to Jewish law: Who supervises conversion? Who has authority over the rites of passage in general? Who determines the right to be identified as a Jew? What limits the right to express Judaism in ways other than state-sanctioned orthodoxy? Conflicts generated by such issues are regularly headline news. The essay reveals their complexity and cautions against the simple assumption that the American system that separates church/synagogue from state can and should be imposed in Israel. These essays amply illustrate the complex demands of creating a multiethnic and multicultural "Jewish" democracy.

The attitudes of different Christian denominations and Muslims toward the Holy Land must also be appreciated as diverse rather than imagined as monolithic. Two essays, valuable for non-Jewish readers as well as for Diaspora Jews, investigate the evolution of attitudes among Christians and Muslims and correct a tendency to imagine that "Others" have a monochrome attitude to the Jewish state by demonstrating their enormous internal divergence. Christians and Muslims were unprepared for the unexpected emergence of Jewish sovereignty in the land each considers sacred. Yaakov Ariel traces differences among Christian denominations in their attitudes and relationships to Israel—both support and antagonism—that have continued to evolve, and touches on repercussions for American politics and policies in the Middle East (chapter 12). Norman A. Stillman examines the relations between Jews and Muslims in historical perspective and explores the reasons Islam has found it so difficult politically and ideologically to come to terms with a Jewish state (chapter 13). He points out that while it is true that Islam has found it difficult to accommodate Jewish sovereignty theologically, it is also true that the independent Jewish State of Israel was established on Islamic lands. One cannot be literate about Israel without such basic knowledge of the views of Christians and Muslims in the United States and the Middle East and their impact on Israel.

The last two essays in the volume deal with culture as written and performed in Hebrew. Each provides a window through which to view the main tensions and currents in Israeli society that are examined from different perspectives in the preceding essays. The artistic works they describe add an essential personal and individual dimension to the complexity of Israeli society. At the same time, the reviews provide an invaluable context for readers who encounter the many works of Hebrew culture available in translation and widely distributed.

As with other national movements, the national language and literature in Hebrew became the carrier of the movement's hopes, conflicts, and frustrations. Theodor Herzl, the founder of international Zionism, believed that modern Jews would inevitably express themselves in a modern European language, specifically German. Today there are more Jews and non-Jews who speak Hebrew than there are speakers of many European languages. However, "Hebrewism" was not an obvious outcome. Rachel S. Harris narrates the intriguing story of the development of modern Israeli Hebrew song, music and dance, and theater and cinema and how these have registered, expressed, and performed the excitement and also the clashes inherent in the birth of the new Jewish state: between the often idealized past enshrined in history and memory and the realities of the present; between the individual's needs and dreams and the contributions required for building a secure and just society; between ensuring a home for diverse national selves, defining a unifying national self, and including the Other as equal (chapter 14).

Finally, Ranen Omer-Sherman's overview and analysis of Hebrew literature, the national literature of a new state written in an evolving vernacular, takes the reader into the interiors of Israeli society and politics and reveals something of the Israeli psyche as glimpsed through Hebrew poetry and prose (chapter 15). The works examined exhibit the hopes invested in Zionism from its beginnings and the protagonists' struggles with the impossibility of fully realizing the dream in all its dimensions. The Hebrew literature surveyed up to the present deeply and often poignantly interrogates the moral, social, and political complexities of creating and maintaining a Jewish state. The essay includes an annotated contemporary bibliography for further reading. It is a fitting way to conclude this volume.

UNIQUENESS AND INNOVATIONS

American readers who seek an introduction to Israel's history, politics, culture, and relations with the United States in order to engage in a more fully informed, literate discourse on Israel can do no better than *Essential Israel: Essays for the 21st Century*. There is no comparable volume available. The essays are not focused on key dates, facts, and names of people or places to memorize. Our primary purpose is to expose issues crucial to understanding the current situation, richly contextualized in the present and in history. For example, to interrogate the role of the Chief Rabbinate in Israeli society, one should know the following:

- Israel developed in the context of the millet system of the Ottoman Empire (in place for centuries), which meant that different "confessional" or religious groups lived in separate and not entirely equal communities and followed their own distinctive laws.
- Israel does not have an American-type separation of church and state.
- The leadership of the secular Zionist movement and the ultra-Orthodox religious groups reached an accommodation manifested in the Status Quo Agreement of 1947 that remains in force.
- A variety of issues from personal status of Israeli Jews (marriage, divorce, and burial) to relations between the Conservative and Reform movements and Israel, are affected by the institution of the Chief Rabbinate.

The essays illuminate such notions as "partition," "armistice lines," and "bi-nationalism" that regularly feature in the ongoing debates over the political disposition of the land between the Jordan River and the Mediterranean. The glossary at the end of the volume elaborates such concepts and names of individuals for convenient reference and to ensure that information and facts do not congest the text. A list of items glossed follows each chapter to make it easier for readers to fill information gaps.

The Schusterman Center for Israel Studies at Brandeis University has and will continue to develop a website that can be readily accessed by readers, as we are aware that this collection of essays is neither static nor complete. Over time, other topics will be made available, ranging from environmental issues to the economy and entrepreneurial environment of Israel as the "Start-up Nation." We see this volume as a beginning and anticipate incorporating additional materials via the e-book and the internet.

We invite you to use the website of the Schusterman Center for Israel Studies at no additional cost. The center has consistently developed and updated this site since the inauguration of its Summer Institute for Israel Studies in 2004. Go to http://www.brandeis.edu/israelcenter/ and you will find links to a rich variety of supporting material and updates. You are likely to find http://israelresources.brandeis.libguides.com/content.php?pid=25580 of particular value.

For interested readers, the section designed for the Fellows of the Summer Institute includes links to recommended websites on a wide variety of topics including politics, art, religion, and minority issues. Syllabi and bibliographies from courses offered by our Summer Institute participants are also available and address a range of topics such as the Arab-Israeli conflict, the impact of the Holocaust on Israeli society, Israeli literature and film, national politics, and Israel in its regional context. We will continue to update the growing archive of podcasts and webinars related to the subjects in the volume.

Finally, we welcome reactions of readers to *Essential Israel: Essays for the 21st Century*. We envision *Essential Israel* as a living, dynamic, and ongoing project.

S. Ilan Troen is the Karl, Harry, and Helen Stoll Chair in Israel Studies and founding Director of the Schusterman Center for Israel Studies at Brandeis University. He is founding editor of *Israel Studies* (IUP). His publications include *Imagining Zion: Dreams, Designs and Realities in a Century of Jewish Settlement* and (with Jacob Lassner) *Jews and Muslims in the Arab World: Haunted by Pasts Real and Imagined.*

Rachel Fish, PhD, is an expert in issues of binationalism and their impact on the construction of a Jewish state. She is Associate Director of the Schusterman Center for Israel Studies and teaches Israeli history at Brandeis University. She is committed to and deeply engaged in developing programs that bring a balanced and fully informed understanding of Israeli history and society to scholars, community professionals, and the public.

TWO

Israel: Geography, Demography, and Economy

S. ILAN TROEN, MAOZ AZARYAHU, AND ARNON GOLAN

Introduction

Located on a narrow strip of land where the Mediterranean meets mountains and desert and where caravan routes once connected Africa and Asia, Israel has been the venue for events and ideas recorded in an extraordinary biblical and postbiblical literature that is regarded as a shared world heritage. Although small, Israel is also one of the most sensationalized locales in the contemporary world. The intense spotlight of the media on the Arab/Israeli conflict and the volatile Middle East in conjunction with romantic and literary views of the past both shape and distort the image of modern Israel, which is too often represented in isolation and without reference to context. Our challenge is to provide this missing context in a grounded overview of the country as it has developed through the Zionist experience. To do this we have to place in context subjects that may be simple elsewhere but not in Israel. Israel comprises different and often contending nationalities and religious cultures. It has two official languages—Hebrew and Arabic—but English is increasingly used in the public sphere, and information in Russian is often included on signs and packaging. Many if not most Israelis speak more than one language. This extreme diversity extends to matters of politics and history. Israel's citizens contest interpretations of its past and future. They dispute the names of places, the marking of borders, and even who can be counted as an Israeli. We invite you to follow us into this complex and fascinating territory and to develop a fuller understanding of Israel by exploring with us the basic characteristics of Israel's geography, demography, and economy.

Geography

In 1948 the United Nations established Israel as a "Jewish state" in a portion of the British Mandate of Palestine, as shown in map 2.1. This decision actually reiterated the British Mandate's position in the Peel Commission Report of 1937. In addition to a Jewish state, the international community intended that an Arab state would be established in another portion of Palestine. A third part, including Jerusalem, was to become an independent sector under international control. The Arab state was never established because of the 1948 War between the Jews and the Arabs of Palestine and their allies from neighboring Arab states who invaded the newly declared state of Israel. In the aftermath of the conflict, the non-Jewish areas were absorbed by Transjordan, an Arab state initially on the eastern side of the Jordan River, and Egypt, which controlled what came to be known as the Gaza Strip. The international portion, including Jerusalem, was divided between the Jewish state and Transjordan, which shortened its name to Jordan to reflect its expansion to both sides of the river following the war.

When we consider Israel's size, it is important to remember that during its first thirty years, Israel did not have internationally recognized borders. Rather it developed within armistice lines. Israel signed peace treaties with Egypt in 1978 and with Jordan in 1994, but the borders with the Palestinians in the West Bank or Judea and Samaria, and those with Lebanon and Syria are still not resolved. If we count only the uncontested territories, the area of Israel totals 20,770 square kilometers, or 8,019 square miles. This means that in terms of size it ranks 153 among 230 sovereign states and territories around the world, between Slovenia and El Salvador. If we include the Golan Heights (approximately 1,200 square kilometers) and East Jerusalem—annexed as state territory under Israeli law, though not recognized as such by the international political system—the total area of Israel is approximately 22,070 square kilometers, or about the size of New Jersey.

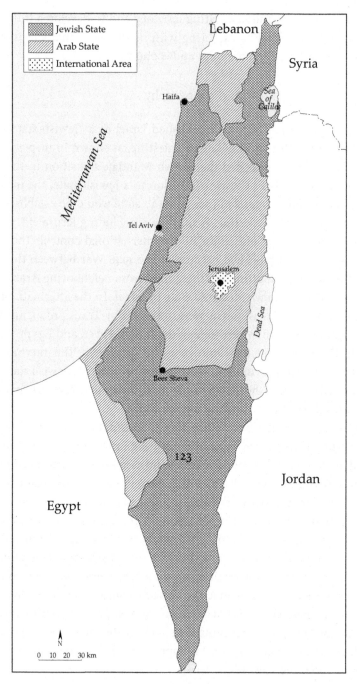

Jewish State
Arab State
International Area

Lebanon

Syria

Haifa

Sea
of
Galilee

Mediterranean Sea

Tel Aviv

Jerusalem

Dead Sea

Beer Sheva

123

Jordan

Egypt

N

0   10   20   30 km

MAP 2.1. UN partition plan for Palestine, November 29, 1947

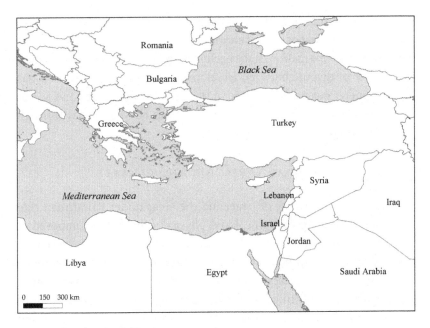

MAP 2.2. Israel and neighboring states

Adding to the difficulty of determining size, Israel also has control over some 60 percent of the West Bank/Judea and Samaria, now designated Area C, which constitutes approximately 5,900 square kilometers. The remaining areas called A and B are under the full or partial control of the Palestinian Authority. Israel's unilateral withdrawal from the Gaza Strip in 2005 removed approximately 360 square kilometers from Israeli control.

However we measure its territory, Israel is a small to modest-sized country. Yet as map 2.2 indicates, its various borders and demarcation lines are extensive, spanning 1,017 kilometers (632 miles). To complicate matters further, Israel's land borders often defy divisions indicated solely by geographic logic. Rather, they have been determined with and without international agreement and in the aftermath of conflict.

Israel also has borders along the sea. The coastline along the Mediterranean extends for some 190 kilometers. This coastal border grants Israel rights in waters within its exclusive economic zone as delineated alongside those of Egypt and Gaza in the south, Lebanon in the north, and Cyprus in the west. These rights gained significance with the 2010 discovery of the first of several enormous natural gas fields in economic-zone waters. Demarcation of the exclusive and lucrative economic zones is a matter of dispute between Israel and its neighbors. Israel also has a 12-kilometer coastal borderline in the Gulf of Eilat that allows access to the Red Sea and the Indian Ocean without having to pass through the Suez Canal.

REGIONAL VARIATION AND CLIMATE

The territory of the State of Israel and the areas under Palestinian rule constitute a single geographical and physical unit that is composed of three main lengthwise strips. As map 2.3 shows, in the west the coastal plain spreads downward, following the shoreline of the Mediterranean Sea, only a few kilometers wide in the north and widening as we move southward, then splitting into different subregions: the western Galilee shore, the Zevulun Valley, the Carmel coastal plain, the Sharon, and the southern coastal plain. In the center is a strip of mountains that are split by valleys that divide them into subregions. Moving from north to south you will see the hills of Galilee, the Samarian hills, the Judean Mountains, and the Negev plateau. The third strip is the Jordan Valley, which also divides into subregions north to south: the Upper Galilee through the Kinneret [Lake of Tiberias, Sea of Galilee] to the Dead Sea and another region that spreads from the Dead Sea through the Aravah until the Gulf of Eilat.

Although it covers a relatively small territory, Israel has very different climate zones shown in map 2.4. If we were walking across it we would see it clearly as a region of transition between the Mediterranean climate characteristic of the seashore and the desert climate of the area to the southeast into Jordan and Saudi Arabia. The northern and western parts of Israel are characterized by a Mediterranean climate: hot summers with little precipitation, erratic seasonal changes, and rainy winters. The southern and eastern parts of the country—the Negev and the Judean Desert—are characterized by a hot and dry climate with little precipitation year-round. Israel's extensive desert constitutes part of the global range of subtropical deserts.

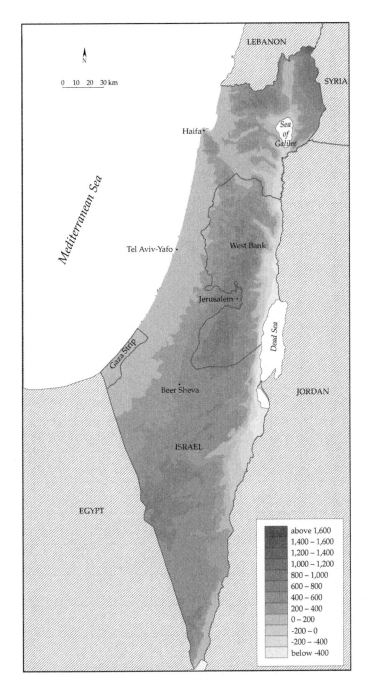

MAP 2.3. Israel topographical map

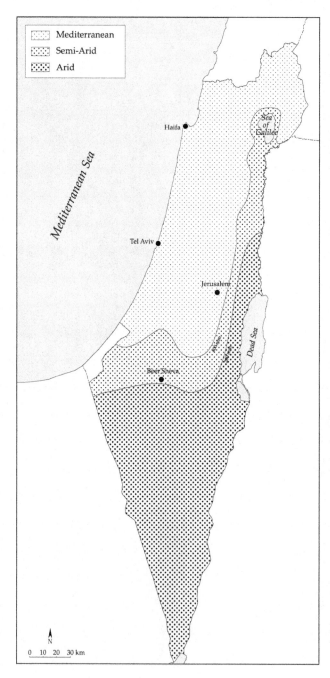

MAP 2.4. Israel climate map

OLD-NEW HOMELAND

The 1922 League of Nations Mandate for Palestine used the term *Reconstitution* to describe what the Jews were going to do in Palestine. This word expressed what was then common wisdom. The mandate's preamble affirmed that it was going to reestablish "a national home for the Jewish people" in Palestine. This intention was explicit. The preamble declares that "recognition has thereby been given to the historical connection of the Jewish people with Palestine and to the grounds for *reconstituting* [our emphasis] their national home in that country." The emphasis on *re*-constitution is also found in other key words used to describe the Zionist enterprise during this period. The Jews were going to *re*-turn, *re*-claim, *re*-build, *re*-store. It is important to notice the crucial common denominator *re*-, which means "again." It is evidence that this generation fully acknowledged that the relationship between Eretz Yisrael and Jews was never lost and was now being renewed. This identity with the Land of Israel figured prominently in early Zionism. Through their language and labor, building, writings and songs, the pioneers proclaimed that they were one with the land. Their offspring, termed *sabra* by the 1930s, were the fulfillment of this longing to return, literally natives in the reconstituted historic homeland.

In the most general terms, the Zionist project was about the "ingathering of the exiles," and a primary goal of this process was to create a Zionist geography. Perceived, experienced, and promoted as a project of restoration, this re-formation of the Zionist landscape entailed both rediscovering and recovering the landscapes of the ancient national past and reshaping the landscape through contemporary resettlement and development. Understood as a restorative measure, the project of creating the Zionist landscape articulated a tension between old and new that was fundamental to Zionist ideology. The notion of this creative tension was succinctly formulated at the outset by Theodor Herzl, the founding father of modern Zionism, in the title of his seminal book *Altneuland* [*Old-New Land*, 1902].

NAMING THE LAND

Names tell us a lot about ideology, culture, and history. It is not surprising, therefore, that names and naming practices played a major role in the drama of Jewish restoration and in the formation of a Zionist geography. During the British Mandate the abbreviation *E.I.* or Eretz Yisrael [Land of Israel] appeared regularly on government documents in connection with Palestine. More prosaically and pertinently, road maps bore the title *Palestine (E.I.) Road Map*. This was a practical expression that the 1917 Balfour Declaration and the 1922 League of Nations Mandate recognized the rights of Jews to Palestine.

The name of the state was set forth in the Declaration of Independence as Israel. This reflected that Jews had long been called "the children of Israel" and that the country had been designated as "the Land of Israel" (Eretz Yisrael or E.I.). The committee charged with drafting the Declaration considered other possibilities including Judea, Zion, and Herzliya. The names Judea and Zion were rejected because they were associated with territories and sites that were then in the Arab portion of Palestine. Herzliya did not evoke the deep and historic resonance of the land with the Jewish past and imagination. It was David Ben-Gurion, the country's future prime minister, who put forward Israel, and it passed by a vote of 6–3.

Yet there are other names for this territory. For Jews it is also the Holy Land, Eretz Hakodesh; for Catholics, Terra Sancta; and for Muslims, Al-Ard Al-Muqaddasah. All three monotheistic religions have holy sites scattered across the countryside that reflect significant events in their traditions. The overlap and proximity of sites holy to all three, particularly in Jerusalem, explains at least in part why it is such contested territory today, even as it has been so often in the past.

THE LANGUAGE OF THE LANDSCAPE

Road signs in contemporary Israel are usually multilingual with a clear hierarchy: Hebrew, the majority language, above; Arabic, the minority language, in the middle; and an English transcription of the name below. Street signs, on the other hand, reflect local conditions. In Jewish cities or mixed cities with a Jewish majority such as Jerusalem, Haifa, and Tel Aviv-Yafo, Hebrew is above Arabic. In Arab towns, such as Umm el Fahm or Kafr Kassem, Arabic is above Hebrew. English also often appears and serves as the meeting ground between the two distinct and often competitive cultures.

The land is marked chiefly in Hebrew. From the Zionists' perspective, reclaiming Eretz Yisrael and repossessing it meant suppressing both Palestine's past under Ottoman rule and their own European past, the "exile" they left behind. They gave new names to the land and its settlements in a visible and significant part of this process. Secular Zionists recovered names like Rehovoth, Arad, and Eilat that are found in traditional, sacred texts, particularly the Bible and the Talmud. They chose names to celebrate leaders of the Jewish people during the long exile, like the great medieval scholar Rambam (Maimonides) or the American Zionist leader Justice Brandeis, remembered for their roles once the Jews returned home. Metaphorically, but not merely figuratively, names functioned like ornamentation, a fundamental part of the style that emerged during decades of frantic state building. There were rules and principles for selecting names. These were diffused and informal from the 1880s and institutionalized during the British Mandate. Following the War of Independence, demographic and political changes gave much wider scope for this process of naming, which continues whenever new settlements are established or roads built.

It is perhaps surprising that some of this renaming of Palestine began in anticipation of actual settlement. From the 1880s, Zionist societies were organized across Europe to establish villages and cities in the Holy Land. The names chosen, whether in Europe or in Eretz Yisrael, reveal how the early Zionists imagined their project; they planned to reinhabit the land and rebuild it in terms derived from Jewish texts, history, and traditions. Thus, the names are worth considering in some detail.

- Rosh Pina, an early settlement founded in 1882 at the base of the Upper Galilee, means "cornerstone." The name derives from a verse from Psalms 118:22, part of the Hallel prayer service, that celebrates national salvation: "The stone which the builders rejected has become the chief cornerstone."
- Rishon Lezion, "a harbinger to Zion," was founded on the coastal plain also in 1882. Its name is based on a biblical verse: "The things once predicted to Zion—Behold, here they are! And to Jerusalem a messenger of good tidings" (Isaiah 41:27).
- Tel Aviv, "Hill of Spring," was founded in 1909. The name was suggested by Nahum Sokolov's Hebrew translation of the title of Herzl's book *Altneuland* (*Old-New Land*) that indicates in a poetic

form the creative tension between the old and the new within the
Zionist return to the homeland.

- When Holocaust survivors founded their kibbutz, Ha'ogen (The
  Anchor) on the coastal plain in 1947, they chose a name to indicate
  that after their sufferings and wanderings, they had come home and
  were anchored in this land.
- An earlier kibbutz, Ramat Rachel (The High Place of Rachel)
  was founded south of Jerusalem in 1926, overlooking the city of
  Bethlehem and the traditional burial site of the matriarch Rachel.
- Named after Yosef Trumpeldor, the Zionist hero-martyr killed in
  Tel Hai in 1920, Kibbutz Tel Yosef (Hill of Yosef) in the eastern
  Jezreel Valley was founded in 1921 by followers of Trumpeldor.
- A final example is 'Usha, a kibbutz in the Lower Galilee, founded
  in 1937. The kibbutz is located two miles west of the ruins of its
  namesake, 'Usha, an important town from the period of the Mishna
  and Talmud where the Sanhedrin, comprising seventy sages of the
  rabbinic court, resided in the mid-second century CE.

Already before Israel was established, some three hundred cities,
towns, and villages were placed across the map of Palestine with new
or recovered Hebrew names. Landscape features were also assigned Hebrew names, with reference, whenever possible, to the original biblical
place-name. Thus, the Sea of Galilee became the Kinneret (Joshua 13:27)
and an early kibbutz of that name was established on its banks. Importantly, the Hebrew names of landscape features were not made official in
the maps produced by the British Mandate in the 1940s. However they
adorned Hebrew maps of E.I. and were used in the autonomous Hebrew
educational system.

The Zionists were not interested in preserving Arabic place names.
They regarded them as corruptions of ancient Hebrew names and replaced them with what was taken to be the original. Thus present-day
Lod in the Hebrew biblical text replaced al-Ludd in Arabic and Lydda in
Greek and Latin. This practice of recovering the biblical name was first
instituted by Christian archaeologists who, from at least the 1840s, were
eager to uncover Palestine's biblical—that is, Hebrew—past, buried just
beneath the ruins of a land then largely desolate. The biblical place name
appeared to validate the Zionists' understanding of their own sacred
and historical texts. European place names and those associated with

the Diaspora were similarly excluded. In the New World names often echo the "old country": New England, New Brunswick, New Orleans, New York and New Madrid recall an earlier homeland. In Israel there is no New Vilna, New Bialystock, New Warsaw, New Minsk, New Pinsk, or New Plonsk. Nor is there an Oxford, Cambridge, Paris, Berlin, and so on.

With the arrival of the British after World War I, naming became part of the effort to assert control over Palestine. During the 1920s, Jewish advisors urged the Mandate to officially recognize Hebrew names. These were numerous since during the Ottoman period Jews were allowed to assign names to their agricultural colonies and to the new city of Tel Aviv. Throughout the development of the Yishuv, hundreds of names were given to settlements, large and small; to their neighborhoods and streets; and occasionally to topographic features. Signs in Hebrew signaling the return of Jews to Eretz Yisrael were everywhere, at the entrance to communities and at the corners of streets and on the blueprints of planners. They also appeared on Hebrew maps and in official documents, newspaper stories, literature, and song.

When Israel was established, a committee was set up in the prime minister's office to systematically assign Hebrew names to the landscape. Two of its members had served in a similar capacity as representatives of the Zionist authorities during the British Mandate and brought that experience to the project. In the shaping of the Hebrew map of Israel, two related concerns converged. One was fixing Eretz Yisrael as the homeland of the restored Jewish nation. The other was privileging Hebrew culture and language as primary features of the national revival. In what became a major program of cultural engineering, the committee assigned Hebrew names in official maps. By 1960, some five thousand Hebrew names had been affixed to maps and signposted throughout the country. The Hebrew map made manifest the transformation of Palestine into the Jewish homeland; alternative maps prepared by Palestinian nationalists both eliminate Hebrew place names and entirely efface Israel's existence.

Naming streets was yet another aspect of imprinting the Jewish presence on the land. Since the eighteenth century, street names have been a feature of urban modernity. In addition to facilitating orientation, commemorative street names inject national and local history into the cityscape. The new Jewish neighborhood of Tel Aviv was the first to introduce official street names. In 1910, within a year of the city's founding, a neighborhood committee discussed how to name the street in a small and as yet only partly built neighborhood. To honor the Zionist visionary who had died in 1904, the committee decided on Herzl Street. In the 1920s, after British rule was established, commemorative naming of streets was extended to Jerusalem and Haifa, though mainly in the new Jewish neighborhoods. Many new streets commemorated Jewish and Zionist history and made it integral to Israel's urban experience. Since the 1990s, Arab towns have also introduced street names, most of which commemorate Muslim history and Arab heritage.

Who are the individuals memorialized in these names? According to a "popularity survey," fifty-six Israeli towns have streets named for Vladimir Ze'ev Jabotinsky, the founder of Revisionist Zionism; fifty-two towns have a Herzl Street; forty-eight have streets commemorating David Ben-Gurion, Israel's first prime minister; and forty-seven have named a street for Chaim Weizmann, the Zionist leader and Israel's first president. Herzl's name echoes in the town Herzliya, and implicitly in Tel Aviv, named after his utopia, Altneuland. Ben-Gurion is also commemorated in the name of numerous neighborhoods and significantly gives his name to Israel's international airport. Chaim Nahman Bialik, the Hebrew national poet, is inscribed in the street names of forty-three towns, including two in Tel-Aviv. Following the assassination of Yitzhak Rabin in 1995, thirty Israeli towns and cities named streets after the slain prime minister.

Nevertheless, the "popularity survey" of street names demonstrates that the most popular names of streets in Israel are not those honoring Zionist leaders, national office holders, or local politicians but rather trees. Most of these "natural" or "landscape" street names appear in rural locales and reflect Zionism's attachment to the homeland's landscape. Ha-Zayit (The Olive Tree) is first on the list and appears in 124 towns, followed by Ha-Gefen (The Grapevine) in 105 towns, and Ha-Te'ena (The Fig Tree) in 95 towns. With similar logic, names of the country's flora, fauna, and topography have been widely incorporated in the personal and family names of Israelis.

POPULAR SONGS AND "KNOWING THE LAND"

The spiritual reconnection with Eretz Yisrael was also expressed in other cultural forms—music, art, and literature. Songs, in particular, fuse popular with patriotic culture in a Zionist mold. Since the 1880s, genres of songs have recounted details of building the country and the accompanying social transformation. Many melodies were European, particularly Eastern European, but the words were in the old/new language of the old/new land. Popular songs included *"Mi yivneh hagalil?"*— "Who will build the Galilee?" and *"Mi yivneh bayit be-Tel-Aviv?"*—"Who will build a house in Tel-Aviv?" A tradition of composing songs for new settlements began with early pioneers and was carried on for decades. The meaning commonly expressed by such songs was epitomized in a favorite, *"Anu banu 'artza livnot 'u'lehibanot bah"*—"We have come to the land to build and to be rebuilt in it."

Many songs were connected with rural, agricultural settlements, but there was no less a repertoire connected with the building of the modern, bourgeois city of Tel Aviv. Poets and musicians in this center of nascent national culture celebrated what was taking place around them. They sang of hammers, crushing stones, whitewash, steel, and concrete. Another theme that excited the imagination was building the port of Tel Aviv in 1936. Songs were composed under the rubric of the "conquest of the sea" even as other songs spoke for land-based pioneers in the interiors of the "conquest of labor," "redeeming the land," and "making the desert bloom." In other words, these early songs celebrated the collective rejuvenation of the Zionist project, an avowed desire to turn the sand dunes into a thriving metropolis and master the Mediterranean to serve the new Jewish city.

By the 1950s popular songs resounded with love for the land, and words and music evoked the exotic landscapes of the Negev, such as the awe-inspiring beauty of Ein Gedi on the shores of the Dead Sea, or the "wild south" unfolding through the desert on the road to Eilat. "Jerusalem of Gold," Naomi Shemer's *"Yerushalaim shel zahav"* first performed in 1967, shortly before the Six-Day War and the reunification of Jerusalem, expresses longing for the pine-scented air, sounds, views, and light of the traditional Jewish sites of Jerusalem, inaccessible to Israelis after this part of the city came under Jordanian control in 1948. As a secular prayer that resonates with Jewish liturgy and Zionist sentiments, the song has remained popular. In 2008, when Israel celebrated its sixtieth anniversary, "Jerusalem of Gold" was voted Israel's most popular song.

The intimate relationship between the people and the land was also fostered by school texts from preindependence Israel on. The subject termed *yedi'at ha'aretz* (knowing the land) carries the biblical connotation of the verb "to know" and connotes deep and intimate knowledge rather than mere geographical information. "Knowing the land" was also an important aspect of regular school *tiyulim*, or field trips. As a patriotic ritual and educational experience, *tiyulim* figured prominently in the curricula of Hebrew schools and the activities of Zionist youth movements. Guided hikes conflated personal experience of place and firsthand knowledge of the landscape with historical and literary sources to instill love of homeland and a deep sense of belonging. Through *yediat ha'aretz* and *tiyulim*, youngsters came to know the historical landscapes of Eretz Yisrael and to appreciate and know that they were part of the country's contemporary development.

Demography

The creation of the State of Israel on May 14, 1948 (the fifth day of Iyar, 5708, in the Hebrew calendar) signaled that the Jewish people could act with sovereignty in their own land rather than as a minority at risk in states governed by others. Jews from all over the world recognized the significance and opportunity of this millennial event; they came in remarkable numbers both because the gates of the country were finally open to them and because of intense pressure, including violence, in Europe, the Middle East, and North Africa. On the eve of independence, only about 650,000 or between 5 and 6 percent of the Jews of the world lived in Palestine. By 2013, ten times as many, or approximately 6,000,000 Jews, lived in Israel. They constitute more than 40 percent of contemporary world Jewry, with Israel moving toward becoming the largest Jewish community in the modern world and in the long history of the Jewish people.

At the start of the nineteenth century, Palestine had an estimated total population of 250,000–300,000. At that time the country was nominally a part of the Ottoman Empire and poorly served by the local officials the Ottomans appointed. Palestine's inhabitants endured considerable instability that inhibited the emergence of a functional economy. Lack of security on the roads prevented the development of a trade network; wars and Bedouin raids repeatedly devastated the villages and the lands on which the inhabitants' livelihood depended.

In 1800 most of the country's population lived in villages in the Galilee and in the hills of Judea and Samaria, which were easier to defend and were near enough to water sources and tracts of land to enable farming. The Jordan Valley, the cross-cutting valleys, the coastal plain, and the southern and Negev areas were almost devoid of inhabitants except for nomadic Bedouin tribes who used these areas for grazing and occasionally for small-scale farming. Urban settlements were small, with only a few thousand inhabitants, and served mainly as administrative centers or market towns for surrounding villages. Acre, a port city that largely served the northern part of the country, had a population of about ten thousand. A similar number lived within the walls of Jerusalem, a small and derelict city that served Muslim, Christian, and Jewish pilgrims. To enhance security, cities had to be surrounded by walls, and this too inhibited development.

During the course of the nineteenth century, the political reality in the country changed. This was due to Egypt's independence after Muhammad Ali, a transplanted Ottoman official from Albania, seized control during the 1830s. European powers, stating that they needed to protect their citizens, began to intervene in Ottoman lands. Their deep interest in the eastern Mediterranean was already evident in the cultural sphere, with visits by growing numbers of tourists, explorers, and pilgrims and the establishment of schools and other charitable institutions. This opening of Palestine to European influence had a dramatic effect. Increased security and services for European visitors and institutions improved the overall security situation and strengthened the local economy. Agriculture expanded, trade increased, and cities grew beyond their walls. In midcentury, Ottoman authorities initiated a series of reforms to improve their control over the country and encourage its development. With these improved circumstances, Palestine's population steadily increased to about 715,000, including 85,000 Jews, on the eve of World War I.

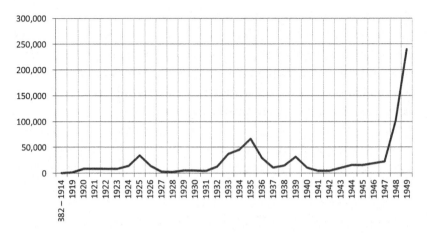

FIGURE 2.1. Immigration, 1882–1949. Naor, Mordechai, and Dan Giladi, *Eretz Israel in the 20th Century: From Yishuv to Statehood, 1900–1950* (Tel Aviv: Ministry of Defense, 1990), 462–463.

When the British conquered Palestine toward the end of World War I, they established a modern civil administration that further stimulated the country's growth. The Jewish population, which had already begun to increase substantially during the nineteenth century, was a major beneficiary. Until the 1880s, Jews had immigrated primarily for religious reasons and settled in Jerusalem. Thereafter, a new wave and type of immigration began. This was largely motivated by national aspirations and catalyzed by the economic and political upheavals that were taking place in Eastern and Central Europe. Motivated by Zionism, Jewish immigrants swelled the population of cities and agricultural colonies. Most of the newcomers settled in cities, particularly in Jaffa, whose garden suburb, Tel Aviv, was transformed during the 1920s and 1930s into the premier city of Mandatory Palestine and Zionism's cultural and commercial center. Many also settled in Jerusalem, the capital of British Mandatory Palestine, and in Haifa, a deep-water port that served as the center of heavy industry and a terminus for a petroleum pipeline from Iraq.

Zionist historiography delineates successive waves of immigration in the pre-state period, as shown in figure 2.1. These are called *aliya* (ascent), since in Jewish tradition this is the term used to designate immigration to Eretz Yisrael. As a result of the first two waves—the First Aliya (1882–1903) and the Second Aliya (1904–1914)—the Jewish communities grew from 27,000 in 1882 to approximately 85,000 by World War I. After renewed immigration in the 1920s—the Third Aliya and the Fourth Aliya—the Jewish population more than doubled to 175,000 out of a total of some 1,039,000 inhabitants, most of whom were Arab. The Fifth Aliya in the 1930s and subsequent illegal and unnumbered waves resulted in a community of 450,000, who constituted 30 percent of Palestine's population on the eve of World War II. By the establishment of the State of Israel in 1948, there were 625,000 Jews, or one third of the country's population of 1,850,000.

The upheaval caused by the War of Independence significantly changed the balance between Jews and Arabs. Some 650,000–700,000 Arabs emigrated from within the armistice lines that marked Israel's boundaries after the conflict. And as noted earlier, the creation of the Jewish state enabled massive Jewish immigration. By late 1951, the Great Aliya—the name given to the immigration that began with the founding of the state—brought Israel's population to 1,577,000, 89 percent of whom were Jews.

Over the course of only sixty-six years, from 1948 to 2014, Israel's population increased about tenfold, as shown in table 2.1. This remarkable growth is primarily the consequence of immigration, although natural increase has been high among both Jews and Arabs. Through the end of the Great Aliya in 1951, immigrants included Holocaust survivors and other Jews from Europe, together with Jews forced to leave their ancient communities in Arab countries such as Iraq and Yemen. The majority of North African Jewry arrived during the latter half of the 1950s and early 1960s. After the 1967 June War and through the early 1970s, there was a wave of *aliya* from the Soviet Union, and nearly one million Jews immigrated with the collapse of the Soviet Union in 1989 and during the 1990s. Significant numbers of Ethiopian Jews immigrated during the 1980s and 1990s.

By the end of 2012 Israel's diverse population totaled approximately eight million, roughly the same as the population of Virginia: 75.4 percent of Israelis are Jews from disparate countries of origin; 20.5 percent are Arab Muslims; and 4.1 percent are "others." This last category includes Christians who do not identify as Arabs, Christians who accompanied

TABLE 2.1. The population of the State of Israel, 1948–2016
(demographic development)

YEAR	POPULATION	JEWS	% OF THE POPULATION	ARABS	% OF THE POPULATION	OTHERS
1948[a]	872,700	716,700	82.2	156,000	17.8	—
1951	1,577,800	1,404,400	89	173,400	11	—
1961	2,234,200	1,981,700	88.7	252,500	11.3	—
1972	3,225,000	2,752,700	85.4	472,200	14.6	—
1983	4,118,600	3,412,500	82.9	706,100	17.1	—
1997[b]	5,900,000	4,701,600	79.7	1,069,400	18.1	129,000
2012	7,984,500	5,999,600	75	1,647,200	20	337,800
2014	8,296,900	6,219,200	75.2	1,720,300	20.8	357,500
2016[c]	8,522,000	6,377,000	74.8	1,771,000	20.8	374,000

Source: Central Bureau of Statistics, the State of Israel (www.cbs.gov.il).
[a]November 8, 1948.
[b]Since 1995, the categories have changed.
[c]May 9, 2016.

Jewish family members who emigrated from the former Soviet Union, and individuals who did not list any religious affiliation.

Zionism has celebrated this influx of Jews as a contemporary miracle, a realization of the prophetic dream of "The Ingathering of the Exiles." Yet not surprisingly, actually absorbing such diverse communities has been an ongoing and major challenge. The results have included successes but also disappointments, frustration, and tension. With hindsight, at least, it was naïve to imagine it could be otherwise. For two thousand years, or since the destruction of the Second Temple and the consequent dispersion, Jews were spread through different countries and over five continents. They came back to reclaim their home with distinctive cultures and patterns of behavior, and diverse and sometimes contrasting political experience, education, needs, and expectations. After living apart for so long, reconstituting themselves as a people with a unifying identity and culture within the homeland was and continues to be a daunting task.

The result of this extraordinary population growth in a relatively small area is that Israel is becoming one of the most densely populated countries in the developed world, with approximately 355 individuals per square kilometer. Most of the Jewish population is concentrated along the Mediterranean coastal strip, primarily within the Tel Aviv metropolitan area (in Hebrew, Gush Dan, or the Dan Block), which is also the hub of economic activity. The unusual diversity and density of its population make for an extraordinary intensity that infuses Israeli society, culture, and politics.

Economy

As we have seen, less than a hundred years ago, Palestine was a poor backwater in the Ottoman Empire. Today, the standard of living in Israel is distinctly Western. Israel's macroeconomic indicators tell a remarkable success story. Its gross domestic product (GDP) is nearly $243 billion with a per capita income of $32,000. It is well known that Israel has a technologically advanced market economy. In 2012, Israel became the thirty-second country to join the Organization for Economic Co-operation and Development (OECD), the exclusive club of the world's wealthy, developed, and progressive states. Its economy is fully integrated into the world economy as a leader in high tech and other knowledge-based sectors.

To gain some perspective on this economic achievement, consider what you would have seen at the British Empire Exhibition of the World's Fair in London (1924–1926). The booth for Palestine displayed the products of various companies that advertised what the economy then had to offer: there was citrus fruit, notably Jaffa oranges; bottles of wine and olive oil and bars of soap; chocolates and sweets; and lace embroidery from a Jerusalem orphanage. The image was of a rather primitive and faltering state that, lacking a modern economic infrastructure, yielded mainly agricultural products. What passed for manufacturing was primarily based on craftsmanship and cottage industry, although a modern textile industry had begun to develop.

An important reason for this low level of development is that under Ottoman rule infrastructure was neglected. Although the first railway in Eretz Yisrael was built in 1892 to connect Jaffa and Jerusalem, transportation within Palestine and to and from the world beyond was grossly inadequate. At the end of the nineteenth century there was still no real port. Ships and the passengers and goods they conveyed had to anchor offshore at Jaffa until small boats transported them to what passed for the city's harbor. It was the British who inaugurated a network of paved roads in the 1920s and developed Haifa as an international port. Nevertheless, it is telling that during the winter rainy season people preferred to travel from the coastal cities Acre/Haifa in the north to Jaffa/Tel Aviv in the south by boat rather than hazard the land route of muddy roads.

The arrival of Jews with technical expertise, industrial experience, and the ability to access capital contributed to a radical transformation. Pinhas Rutenberg, a Russian Jewish immigrant, organized the Palestine Electric Company, which in 1923 began to electrify both the country and the imagination with Palestine's possibilities. In 1930, Rutenberg built a hydroelectric plant on the Jordan River. Also during the 1920s Moshe Novomeysky, another immigrant from Russia, discovered how to extract minerals by evaporating the chemical-laden waters of the Dead Sea, and based on this discovery he founded the Palestine Potash Company. By the time Israel gained independence, Novomeysky's company had become the largest nonpetroleum-based industry in the Middle East. There were other advances in different areas from textiles to optics. Agriculture, too, was transformed through the application of modern methods. Industrialization proceeded so rapidly that by World War II, when the British could not get supplies through the Mediterranean past the Germans and their allies, the Yishuv (the Jewish community in Palestine) became the primary supplier for the British army.

The Hevrat Ha'ovdim (Society of Workers) of the Histadrut (General Federation of Jewish Workers), organized in 1923, played a crucial role in establishing the base for a modern industrial society. Histadrut enterprises included food and construction companies as well as a bank and an insurance company. Both private and public capital supported the country's transformation. Toward the end of the Mandate, more than half of the Jewish community's domestic product was in the service sector. Notwithstanding the prominence of working the land in the Zionist ethos and the crucial importance of farming settlements in establishing a Jewish presence in the countryside, most of the Jewish population resided in cities and urban areas, and agriculture accounted for no more than a sixth of the domestic product of the Jewish economy. By the time Israel's first national plan was drawn up in 1950, it was clear that a modern industrial economy, not a predominantly agricultural one, was essential to the success of the Zionist project. Only such an economy could absorb waves of immigrants and provide a standard of living that would keep them and their children in the country. Ideology and sentimental attachments alone could not compete with the lure of foreign lands that offered a higher standard of living, better employment opportunities, and greater economic security.

When the British Mandate ended, the Jewish economy was strong enough to support the war that followed the declaration of the state. However, independence posed serious challenges to the fledgling Israeli economy. In keeping with the social-democratic ideology of the Labor movement, to meet these challenges the government favored a centralized, socialist-style economy in which the Histadrut's Society of Workers played a central role. Through the first decades of statehood, the government continued to direct the economy and formulate policy. Only in the 1980s and beyond did a capitalistic system familiar to Western democracies emerge that diminished the role of the government and Histradrut industries or replaced them, allowing private actors to become key players in the nation's economy.

Development of infrastructure and industry during Israel's early years depended on revenues from "independence" government bonds directed at citizens and local investors, loans from the United States, traditional contributions as well as loans from Diaspora Jewry in the form of Israel Bonds, and reparation payments from Germany for its responsibility for the Holocaust. The government also invested these resources to establish industries such as textiles and food in new towns where immigrants had been directed to populate the country's long borders and empty spaces.

While growth was generally steady, there were intermittent periods of recession and high unemployment, as before and after the 1967 War. On the other hand, prior to the 1973 Yom Kippur War, there was a surge in development occasioned by investments in infrastructure and the security sector. Developing an arms industry was essential after France placed an embargo on military supplies to Israel in 1967 and given the ongoing and active hostility of Israel's neighbors in the region. After the near disaster of the 1973 Yom Kippur War, the pace of growth slowed significantly with increased military expenditures and the global economic downturn resulting from the energy crisis.

An abrupt change in the orientation of Israel's economic policies was heralded by the political upheaval of 1977 when Menachem Begin and Revisionist Zionists replaced Labor at the head of government and as shapers of economic policy. Until then, the bourgeois and capitalist streams of Zionism had been kept in a secondary position. Now, a free market with an unabashed capitalistic ethos increasingly took shape. Following a period of hyperinflation in the early 1980s, a stabilization program was enacted in 1985 and led to economic reforms that liberalized the economy by reducing government intervention. That has been the dominant policy ever since through years of often spectacular growth. It appears that however appropriate government intervention in the economy of the new state may have been during its early decades, Israel's economy has come to benefit from a radically different approach.

As the Israeli economy matured and prospered, it has moved into new areas. In contrast to the 1950s through the 1970s, when light industry, especially textiles and diamond polishing, was the mainstay, since the 1980s there has been a concerted effort to develop information technology (IT). The emphasis was naturally on military-related products but also on computer engineering, programming, electronic communications, medicine, medical and scientific equipment, and pharmaceuticals. The massive immigration of professionals and researchers from the former Soviet Union during the 1990s—and the high level of education and experience of many of these immigrants—contributed substantively to the development of a high-tech economy. The very size of this *aliya* spurred construction and stimulated economic growth in other ways as well.

National prosperity was further enhanced and encouraged by a positive political environment. Following the 1993 Oslo Peace Accords and the peace treaty with Jordan in 1994, foreign investment increased substantially. Privatization of government companies and general prosperity provided the impetus for Israel's integration into the global economy. We have traced how from a small and primarily socialist economy based on agriculture and traditional industry in the early 1950s, Israel was transformed into a capitalist economy with a developed financial sector and export-oriented high-technology industries.

In 2012 the workforce in Israel included about 3,500,000 individuals, with over 80 percent working in the service sector, only 2 percent in agriculture, and the rest in industry. Although the percentage of agricultural employees is very small, this is a highly efficient and innovative sector of the economy as evident through the constant development of new products for export. The Israeli agricultural sector provides the local population with fruits and vegetables, poultry and eggs, and dairy products, while grains and oils are imported from abroad. There has also been spectacular growth of new industries such as tourism. In 2013, some 3,500,000 tourists visited the country, including 600,000 from the United States.

For all this progress and the egalitarian socialist values of the early Zionists, the enormous wealth generated by the economy has not been evenly distributed. In the early decades, the gap in income between various sectors was among the lowest in the Western world. At present, the difference is among the highest. The consequence of inequality is compounded by a high cost of living as compared with other Western states. One can appreciate the significance of this growing problem by comparing the amount spent on security and defense, about 13 percent of the national budget, with the approximately 10 percent allotted for social security. About a quarter of the population is below the poverty line. This is a systemic problem resulting from the fact that two sectors contribute little to the economy: Ultra-Orthodox men and Arab women. For this reason Israel was ranked only fifty-fourth in workforce participation in 2011. Because both the Ultra-Orthodox and Arabs tend to have more children per family, they are also overrepresented among families below the poverty line.

Despite these problems, there is considerable optimism about the country's future and confidence that social and political challenges can be addressed. Bloomberg Innovation Index 2015 ranked Israel fifth, after South Korea, Japan, Germany, and Finland and before the United States and Sweden. A 2011 international survey ranked Israel fourth in technological infrastructure. Israel's universities, research centers, and military research and development (R&D) units play an essential role in the development of advanced technologies. These depend on a sophisticated infrastructure of higher education. Forty-six percent of its population in 2010 had an academic degree (BA or higher), so that Israel ranked second among OECD countries. This placed Israel just after Canada (51 percent) and ahead of Japan (45 percent) and the United States (42 percent). This emphasis clearly contributes to a dynamic and innovative information

technology sector. Indeed, from the very beginning the Zionist movement understood that science and higher education would be essential to
developing the country. The Technion in Haifa and the Hebrew University in Jerusalem were planted in locales they were intended to develop;
they were not merely outgrowths of mature societies. The commitment
to education has produced extraordinary results. From a country whose
primary export in 1948 was oranges, Israel had turned into a state with
a vibrant economy in which more start-up companies have been created
than in large, established countries such as Japan, Great Britain, Canada,
and South Korea. Dan Senor and Saul Singer have aptly and popularly
characterized Israel as a "start-up nation."

In contrast with many of its Middle Eastern neighbors, Israel is not
rich in minerals or energy resources. Its greatest wealth is its population.
The raw materials produced in Israel, primarily for export, are phos-
phates from the Negev, and potash and bromine, which are extracted
from the Dead Sea. This is likely to change as the natural gas reserves
recently discovered off shore in the Mediterranean are exploited. Even
then, the economic vitality of the country will depend on its commitment to quality education and its capacity to develop and use the talents
of its rich and diverse human capital.

In addition, Israel will have to monitor and deal with the unprecedented challenges to the environment caused by the country's intensive
repopulation and development. For example, aside from citrus and other
fruit groves, the Jewish National Fund has planted approximately 250 million trees over the last century and has thereby utterly transformed the
appearance of the country. Israel is one of the few countries that support
substantially more forests at present than even a century ago. A national
water system has been established that enables settlement, agriculture,
and industry in much of this largely semiarid land, but it is under such
severe strain that only extensive development of saltwater desaliniza-
tion plants can provide this essential resource in the future. At the same
time, an extensive national park system has been set in place as nature
preservation has emerged as a significant public concern that merits a
special cabinet post.

National development has had its costs. Perhaps the most noteworthy
was the attempt in the decade after independence to reclaim marshland
for much-needed agricultural development in the Hula Valley of the

Upper Galilee in the far north. The land proved unsuitable for its new purpose and is being returned to its original state so it can again sustain vast populations of local and especially migrating birds flying the route between Africa and Europe. Another troubling problem has emerged far to the south, in the Dead Sea, more accurately termed the "Salt Sea" in Hebrew [Yam Hamelach]. This body of water is largely dependent on the flow from the Jordan River and its tributaries such as the Yarmuk. However, the vastly expanded draw by Israel as well as Syria and Jordan, which share the Jordan's watershed, have seriously diminished the flow entering the Dead Sea. At the same time, both Israel and Jordan extract valuable chemicals from this body of water, further contributing to a reduction in its area and dangerously lowering its level. The Dead Sea is already the Earth's lowest elevation on land; its future is in peril, and multiple proposals have been made for building canals from either Eilat or Aqaba on the Red Sea or from the Mediterranean to replenish its waters and perhaps produce hydroelectric power. Should such a sea-to-sea canal be built, it would represent a realization of a plan first put forward by Theodor Herzl in *Altneuland*, the utopian novel that inspired the imagination of the first generation of Zionists with a vision of a society based on a productive, modern economy.

Conclusion

Our purpose is to provide background to contextualize some key elements in the Zionist narrative rather than immerse the reader in data. It is clear that the Land of Israel has been transformed. Just a century ago the typical view of Jerusalem depicted an observer looking toward the walled city with the Temple Mount area prominently featured from the distance of Mount Scopus. There was very little to be observed outside the walls of that ancient city. The landscape was picturesque but barren and the observer usually stood near a tree. In fact, it was the only tree in the picture. The depiction was of a relic. The countryside surrounding it was desolate. We know that far more people had inhabited the country two thousand years earlier, in the times of the Temple and of Jesus. But in subsequent centuries, the landscape became sparsely populated with large areas uncultivated and unproductive. The picture today is radically different. In the past century, the Jewish National Fund has planted nearly a quarter billion trees. There are large areas of green that represent productivity and provide venues for recreation and regeneration. The same territory with the same sun, earth, and water now supports a population nearly twenty times as large as in 1900 and at a standard of living found in only the more advanced states in the world.

These dramatic developments are a direct result of the Zionist revolution, whose primary objective is neatly summarized in a traditional and popular song: *"Anu banu artzah livnot 'u'lehibanot bah"*—"we have come to the Land to build it and be rebuilt by it." In this essay we have invited you to examine contemporary Israel against the complicated background of this unparalleled and difficult transformation. The Zionist revolution demonstrates the extent to which geography has been not only a constraint but also a challenge. The remarkable transformation of the landscape has been directly related to changes in demography that, in turn, have influenced and transformed the country's economy. Through the labor and commitment of Jews who came, many as exiles and refugees from disparate lands, Zionism has succeeded in "reconstituting" the Jewish people and the country they call Eretz Yisrael. Zionism not only returned the Jews to history as sovereign actors, it has turned Eretz Yisrael into a thriving center of contemporary Jewish life and an actor in human affairs.

RECOMMENDED READINGS

Ben-Porath, Yoram, ed. *The Israeli Economy: Maturing through Crises.* Cambridge, MA: Harvard University Press, 1986.
Efrat, Elisha. *Geography and Politics in Israel since 1967.* London: Frank Cass, 2005.
Goldscheider, Calvin. *Israeli Society in the Twenty-First Century: Immigration, Inequality, and Religious Conflict.* Waltham, MA: Brandeis University Press, 2015.
Gradus, Yehuda, Eran Razin, and Shaul Krakover. *The Industrial Geography of Israel.* New York: Routledge, 2006.
Rebhun, Uzi, and Chaim Waxman, eds. *Jews in Israel: Contemporary Social and Cultural Patterns.* Waltham, MA: Brandeis University Press, 2003.
Senor, Dan, and Saul Singer. *Start-up Nation: The Story of Israel's Economic Miracle.* New York: Twelve, 2009.
Survey of Israel and Department of Geography. Hebrew University of Jerusalem. *The New Atlas of Israel—The National Atlas.* Jerusalem: Hebrew University of Jerusalem, 2011.

GLOSSARY TERMS

Aliya: First Aliya; Second Aliya; Third Aliya; Fourth Aliya; Fifth Aliya;
    the Great Aliya
Balfour Declaration
Histadrut
Oslo Peace Accords
Peel Commission Report
Revisionist Zionism
War: 1948 War, War of Independence; 1967 June War, 1967 War; 1973
    (Yom Kippur) War
West Bank, Judea, and Samaria (Area C)
Yishuv

S. Ilan Troen is the Karl, Harry, and Helen Stoll Chair in Israel Studies and
founding Director of the Schusterman Center for Israel Studies at Brandeis
University. He is founding editor of *Israel Studies* (IUP). His publications in-
clude *Imagining Zion: Dreams, Designs and Realities in a Century of Jewish
Settlement* and (with Jacob Lassner) *Jews and Muslims in the Arab World:
Haunted by Pasts Real and Imagined*.

Maoz Azaryahu is Professor of Geography at the University of Haifa, Israel. He
is the author of *Tel Aviv: Mythography of a City*.

Arnon Golan is a historical geographer and Associate Professor in the Department of Geography and Environmental Studies, University of Haifa, Israel.

THREE

From Zionism to Zion

MICHAEL BRENNER

Precursors

Even though Zionism emerged as a political movement at the end of the nineteenth century, the roots of Jewish longings for Zion—actually a mountain in Jerusalem often identified with the city or the land as such—reach back several millennia. Long before the dissolution of ancient Jewish statehood under the Romans, Jews were dispersed in Babylonian, Egyptian, and other exiles. Psalm 137 expressed one of the early and better-known yearnings of the Jewish return to Zion:

> By the rivers of Babylon we sat and wept
> when we remembered Zion.
> There on the poplars
> we hung our harps,
> for there our captors asked us for songs,
> our tormentors demanded songs of joy;
> they said, "Sing us one of the songs of Zion!"
> How can we sing the songs of the Lord
> while in a foreign land?
> If I forget you, Jerusalem,
> may my right hand forget its skill.
> May my tongue cling to the roof of my mouth
> if I do not remember you,
> if I do not consider Jerusalem
> my highest joy.

After the Romans destroyed the Temple and transformed Jerusalem, the urge to rebuild the city and restore the Temple became part of a daily prayer ritual. Similarly, the call "Next year in Jerusalem" has become the concluding sentence after the Passover Haggadah as well as after the Yom Kippur service. Medieval Spanish-Jewish poets like Judah Halevi and philosophers like Nachmanides not only articulated this longing in their writings but actually went to the Land of Israel themselves to settle and to be buried there. In the sixteenth century, many prominent Jewish mystics (Kabbalists), both Ashkenazi and Sephardi Jews, left Europe and established a center of learning in the Galilean town of Zefat (Safed). In 1700, a group of Eastern European Jewish mystics set out on their voyage to the Holy Land. Later, Jews from Yemen came to settle in Palestine. Pious Jews often went to Jerusalem not to live their lives there but to be buried in the holy ground.

Political action was not part of their plan, as according to traditional religious Jewish thought the return of all Jews to Palestine and the reestablishment of a Jewish state would have to wait until messianic times. Most religious Jews considered any attempt to hasten the messianic scheme by political means as sacrilegious. Thus, when Napoleon briefly flirted with the idea of establishing a Jewish state in Palestine, the religious Jewish leadership showed little enthusiasm.

This negative attitude toward the establishment of a Jewish home in the land of their ancestors changed gradually in the middle of the nineteenth century among small groups of religious and secular Jews. Several developments contributed to this change of mind. European Jewry had undergone tremendous transformations throughout the nineteenth century. In France they had become "French citizens of the Jewish faith," enjoying equal rights since the days of the Revolution. In the Netherlands and Great Britain, they were in almost every respect de facto equal citizens. In the German states they had integrated rapidly into society, even though formal equality would only be achieved with the new constitution in 1871. In Eastern Europe, where most Jews lived, restrictions remained in force, but there as well changes were beginning to take shape. By the late nineteenth century, there were Russian and Polish-speaking Jews in the big cities, and a growing Jewish proletariat, which was becoming increasingly secular, emerged.

At the same time, European Jews witnessed and often participated in the struggles for unity and independence of European nations, from the Polish rebellions against the Czarist Empire to the Italian Risorgimento and the struggle over German unification. Nationalism was a characteristic trait of life in nineteenth-century Europe, and Jews were right in the middle of it. It is thus no coincidence that the most significant precursors of Zionism came from the much-contested border areas of Europe or explicitly mentioned the fight for sovereignty of European nations as an inspiration of their own (proto-)Zionist writings.

Yehuda Alkalai (1798–1878) was born in Sarajevo and served as a rabbi in Serbian Semlin, today part of Belgrade. Alkalai grew up in the multicultural Habsburg Empire, very well aware of the often heated debates and fights among Serbs, Croats, and Bosnians. Alkalai himself was, like most Jews in Sarajevo, of Sephardi background (meaning that his ancestors had come from the Iberian peninsula). Although he remained observant in every respect, he found an argument that made it possible to circumvent religious opposition to an activist attitude toward the establishment of a Jewish state in Palestine. He pointed to a precedent in the traditional Jewish idea of a first, temporary Messiah from the house of Joseph who would lead a militant struggle to open the way for the final arrival of the real Messiah from the house of David. For Alkalai, Zionism took the role of a collective Messiah of the house of Joseph. He thus legitimized the return of the Jews and the establishment of their state in Israel by his quite original theological interpretation. The immediate political activity of other nations, including Serbians and Croats, striving for their own independence, was undoubtedly an important incentive for him to arrive at his innovative theological conclusion.

Alkalai's contemporary, Rabbi Zvi Hirsch Kalischer (1795–1874), was born in West Prussian Thorn (Torun) and served as rabbi in Posen (Poznan), both eastern border regions of Prussia with populations composed of Poles, Germans, and Jews. Like Alkalai, he too witnessed contentious national battles in his lifetime that affected his religious beliefs. In his treatise *Drishat Zion* (*Seeking Zion*, 1862) Kalischer argued that one should not passively wait for the messianic times. Instead, he called for human intervention to hasten the coming of the Messiah. The colonization of the Land of Israel was one measure he suggested.

A third precursor of Zionism in the middle of the nineteenth century was a secular political thinker and early comrade-in-arms of Karl Marx. Moses Hess, born in German Bonn, was an early theoretician of socialism and had moved away from Judaism. But seeing the influence of the Italian national movement and its success, he was convinced that the Jews could follow the example that the Italians had just set: to return to become a nation after many centuries. "With the liberation of the Eternal City on the banks of the Tiber begins the liberation of the Eternal City on the slopes of Moriah; the renaissance of Italy heralds the rise of Judah. The orphaned children of Jerusalem will also participate in the great regeneration of nations, in their awakening from the lethargy of the Middle Ages, with its terrible nightmares."

Hess's *Rome and Jerusalem*, written under direct influence of the Italian Risorgimento, predicted the gathering of the Jews in their "ancestral homeland" after being in exile for two thousand years. The subtitle of this book, written in epistolary format, was "The Last Nationality Question" and touched upon the very substance of his argument. He first had to convince his German-Jewish readers that they were not, as many of them claimed, "German citizens of the Jewish faith" but actually belonged to a Jewish nation.

A similar argument was brought forward by another German-Jewish intellectual, the historian Heinrich Graetz. In his magisterial eleven-volume *History of the Jews* he refused to follow his predecessor Isaac Marcus Jost in claiming that the Jewish people ceased to exist and that Jews only formed a religion. He held the idea of Jewish peoplehood in high esteem, and he appreciated Israel as the center of the Jewish people. In 1872 he set out on a journey to Palestine and returned inspired by the ideas of modern Jewish settlement. Although it would be wrong to claim him as a proto-Zionist, his writings, in their numerous editions and translations, influenced many Jews of the importance of Jewish peoplehood and of the Land of Israel.

Meanwhile, Eastern European enlightened thinkers (in Hebrew, *Maskilim*) like Abraham Mapu and Moses Leib Lilienblum began reviving the Hebrew language and published articles and books in Hebrew praising the Land of Israel. They and other writers implanted the longing for a return to Israel through literature. As a leading member of the Committee of the Hebrew Language, Eliezer Ben-Yehuda was instrumental in creating a modern Hebrew dictionary. He moved to Jerusalem in 1881, just as the great exodus of Eastern European Jews began, triggered by the assassination of Czar Alexander II in 1881 and the subsequent accusation that Jews were behind it. Pogroms spread in large parts of the Russian Empire, and during the next three decades over two million Eastern European Jews left the continent.

While most Jews went to the United States, the wave of violence led also to the first modern organized movement of Jewish immigration to Palestine. Inspired by the pamphlet *Auto-Emancipation*, the activist call by Leon Pinsker, a Jewish physician from Odessa, small groups of Hovevei Zion (Lovers of Zion) spread in the Czarist Empire. They propagated the idea that the Jews should emigrate not to America but to the Land of Israel. And indeed, by the end of the century, about twenty-five thousand new Jewish immigrants from Eastern Europe had settled not only in Jerusalem and the few other cities of Palestine but in new agricultural colonies, partly established by Jewish philanthropists like Baron Edmond de Rothschild. Rishon Lezion, Zichron Ya'akov, and Rosh Pina were among the early agricultural settlements that came under the wing of the *Nadiv ha'yadua* (the known benefactor), as he was generally known.

This wave of emigration, usually referred to as the First Aliya, began fifteen years before there was a well-organized universal Zionist movement. It implanted a new drive for political autonomy and economic autarky among the Yishuv, the Jewish population of Palestine, which hitherto had been almost entirely dependent on money collections from the Diaspora communities. But many of the new immigrants realized that they had entered a new dependence, this time on the *Nadiv*'s administration in Paris and his emissaries in Palestine.

1897: Jewish Politics in a New Key

Zionism set out to normalize the situation of the Jews by creating a state for the Jews, "like for all other nations." What normalization meant differed widely, however, and in 1897 four distinct paths were publicly proposed. To put the year 1897 in context of European Jewish history, let us remember that in 1893, the Central Association of German Citizens of the Jewish Faith was established to counter the emergence of modern political anti-Semitism in Germany. In the same year, several candidates had entered the Reichstag, the German parliament, on an explicitly anti-Jewish ticket. While German Jews reached formal legal equality with the constitution of the new German Empire in 1871, they remained excluded from certain areas of society, such as officer ranks and government posts. While in France Jews could become officers, their participation as full members of French society did not go unchallenged. When in 1894, a Jewish officer, Alfred Dreyfus, was accused and convicted of high treason, anti-Jewish sentiments could be heard all over the streets of Paris. After being banished for years on a remote island, Dreyfus was finally cleared of the false accusations and rehabilitated, but the damage to the French-Jewish community could not be cleared overnight. In 1897, Karl Lueger was appointed mayor of Vienna, after Kaiser Franz Joseph had repeatedly refused to comply with the voters' support of this populist anti-Semitic politician.

Despite these worrisome developments in the last decade of the nineteenth century, most European Jews held firm in the belief of their social and economic progress. In Western and Central Europe they could look back to an almost unprecedented transformation over the last century and were full of hope that the last bit of social integration would follow suit. But they also became increasingly aware of what historian Fritz Stern so aptly called "the burden of success." Many began to realize that their integration into society was not complete.

One path to normalization was put forward by Walther Rathenau, heir of the largest German electricity company, soon to become a much-esteemed political theorist, the mastermind of the German war economy, and, at the end of his career, German foreign minister. In 1897 Rathenau published his first article titled "*Höre, Israel*" ("Hear, O Israel"). The short essay appeared in one of the leading intellectual journals of the time, *Die Zukunft (The Future)*, edited by Maximilian Harden, a Jewish convert to Protestantism and a major intellectual force in imperial Germany. Although it appeared anonymously, the identity of its author was not much of a secret. The article was so provocative that Walther Rathenau's father, Emil, went so far as to buy all the copies of the essay he could lay his hands on—only in order to burn them! What did Rathenau say that seemed so provocative? He argued that the Jews could become "normal" only by becoming even more like the Germans. His essay reads at times almost like an anti-Semitic tractate:

> Smack in the middle of German life is an isolated exotic race of men,
> shining and strikingly dressed, hot blooded and constantly in motion.
> An Asiatic horde on the sands of the Mark Brandenburg. . . . Thus they
> live in a semi-voluntary, invisible ghetto, not as a living limb of the
> nation, but as an alien organism within its body.

Rathenau was convinced that if Jews were staying in Germany, they had to completely assimilate. They had to adjust their professions, modify their religious practices, and even change their physical appearance. Conversion, however, was not a real solution but only appeared to change their situation at the most superficial and insincere level. He knew early on that "a baptized Jew is never the same as a baptized Christian."

A second path emerged in Eastern Europe, where anti-Jewish pogroms and a profound economic crisis not only triggered the largest movement of Jewish emigration in modern history but also initiated the search for new political solutions to the situation of the Jews in the places in which they lived. In 1897, the same year that Rathenau published *Hear, O Israel*, the Russian-Jewish historian Simon Dubnow published the first of his *Letters on Old and New Judaism* in the Russian journal *Voskhod*. This was to become the theoretical foundation of the Jewish movement for Diaspora nationalism. A few years later he established the Jewish People's Party (Yidishe Folkspartey), which would fight for Jewish national autonomy in Eastern Europe. Dubnow was convinced that the Jews were a nation, but he believed that this did not mean they were bound to live in one territory. In fact, he argued that the Jews had reached the highest level a nation can reach—a level where they would not need a territory anymore.

For the autonomists, normalization meant what was commonly conceived as the future path for all "small nations" in the multinational empires in which most European Jews lived at the time. They felt that Jews should have the same rights as Czechs or Slovaks, Poles, and Ukrainians, even though their situation was different because they had no clearly designated territory. In other words, by receiving not only individual rights as citizens, but collective rights as Jews, their emancipation would be completed. They did not have to leave Europe, they could continue to speak their Yiddish language, and they would enjoy the same rights as all other citizens.

The third path to normalization was also officially launched in 1897. On October 7, Eastern European Jewish socialists met in Vilna (Vilnius) to establish the General Jewish Labor Bund of Poland and Russia (Algemeyner Yidisher Arbeter Bund in Poyln un Rusland), commonly known as the Bund. Their aim was to unite all Jewish workers among a rapidly increasing proletarian population. Initially, the Bund only wanted to take into account the fact that Jewish workers spoke Yiddish and therefore needed to be represented in their own language. Gradually, though, the Bund developed its own ideology as a movement representing a national minority, which fought both against the Jewish bourgeoisie and against anti-Semitism.

Just as for the autonomists, the future vision of the Bund presupposed that the Jews would stay where they lived, continue to speak the same language they spoke, and enjoy the same rights as everyone else. However, it predicted that real normalization was possible only as the result of a successful class struggle. Only with the dissolution of capitalist society and the establishment of the rule of the proletariat could anti-Semitism be uprooted and Jews lead a normal life. Most importantly, only then would they normalize their occupational structure and transform themselves from a bourgeois merchant-class society into a society of workers, artisans, and peasants.

A few weeks before the Vilnius meeting, the first Zionist Congress was convened in the Swiss city of Basel between August 29 and 31, 1897. The delegates to this congress also strove for normalization of what by then was commonly referred to as the Jewish Question. Their path differed substantially from the three others described so far. Certainly, like the autonomists and the Bundists, the Zionists too regarded the Jews as a nation. But in their view the Jews were a nation with a distinct territory, namely their ancient homeland. Thus, for the Zionists, normalization actually meant the Jews would have to leave the places they lived in and "return" to Palestine or the Land of Israel.

Theodor Herzl: Founder of Political Zionism

Theodor Herzl, who was almost single-handedly responsible for convening the first Zionist Congress was an assimilated Jewish Austrian journalist who—like Walther Rathenau—had striven for complete assimilation but realized it was not possible within a hostile society. He concurred with Rathenau's diagnosis that Jews had to be transformed, but he rejected his remedy. Thus, Herzl wrote about Rathenau's essay: "If he is advising the Jews to adopt a different bone structure, I will happily accompany him to this future of selective breeding. I am not poking fun at it, as any typical Jew would, but wish to concur with him. It is just that I think that the Jews will only be able to absorb the phosphorus for these new bones from a single source, namely from their own."

When Herzl first appeared on the scene of Jewish politics, he did not say much that had not been said before. But he said it in a different time and in a different way. These two circumstances made all the difference, allowing him to succeed where Hess and Pinsker had failed. Herzl had read neither *Rome and Jerusalem* nor *Auto-Emancipation* when he wrote *The Jewish State* (*Der Judenstaat*, literally "The State of the Jews") in 1896. His message was the same as theirs, but the messenger was quite different.

Born in Budapest in 1860, Herzl moved with his German-speaking family to Vienna in 1878. He grew up in a fairly assimilated family and adhered to the same kind of assimilation until his discovery of Zionism. He neither had his son circumcised nor did he make him a Bar Mitzvah ceremony. At first he thought to solve the Jewish Question by a mass conversion of all Viennese Jews, whom he would lead in a solemn ceremony into St. Stephen's Cathedral. Later, when he realized that modern racial anti-Semitism could not be solved by religious conversion and asked to present the ideas of his still-unpublished *The Jewish State* to the chief rabbi of Vienna in December 1895. It did not occur to him that Rabbi Moritz Güdemann might be immediately offended the minute he walked into the Herzls' living room. As Herzl noted in his diary: "I just lit the candles of the Christmas tree with my children, when Güdemann walked in. He seemed upset about the 'Christian' custom. Well, I won't let him dictate me what to do. I don't mind, if we call it Chanukah tree—or the solstice of winter."

As this telling anecdote makes clear, Herzl's Zionism was a by-product of anti-Semitism. Had European society welcomed the Jews, he would have been happy as a journalist and writer, or as he once wrote in his diary, would have ideally been a Prussian nobleman. Anti-Semitism was not unfamiliar to the boy growing up in Budapest, and it became a constant reminder that he was an outsider when he lived in Vienna. Shortly after he joined the student fraternity Albia, he witnessed how his new comrades decided to let no further Jews join as members. Herzl's pride was hurt, and he quit Albia. A few years later he saw Karl Lueger, the outspoken and anti-Semitic Vienna politician, win the mayoral elections. To Herzl's dream—to continue on the road to assimilation his parents had taken and become an accepted writer of plays to be performed at the most popular Vienna theaters—this was a decisive setback.

Nevertheless, Herzl rose to some fame as the cultural editor of the liberal Viennese newspaper *Die Neue Freie Presse*, the leading German-speaking paper of its time. His position was so elevated that young writers who wanted to get published regarded him almost as a literary half-god. Here is how the young writer Stefan Zweig described his first encounter with the editor of the cultural section, the *"Feuilleton-Redakteur"* Dr. Herzl:

> The editor of the feuilleton received visitors only once a week between two and three o'clock, because the constant succession of famous and established collaborators seldom left space for the work of an outsider. It was not without a beating heart that I walked up the iron circular staircase which led to his office and had myself announced. After a few moments the attendant returned and said that the feuilleton editor would see me and I walked into the small narrow room. The feuilleton editor of the Neue Freie Presse was Theodor Herzl, and he was the first man of world-importance whom I had encountered in my life.

Zweig's description gives us a sense of Herzl's stature at the time he became engaged in Zionist politics. The editor of the feuilleton of the most respected German-language newspaper was a person held in highest esteem at the time. Some of his plays were performed in the Burgtheater. Herzl was a successful man. What caused him to jeopardize all his achievements as a leading German journalist?

The anti-Semitism in Vienna undoubtedly played a crucial role in Herzl's turn to his new mission. It inspired him to write a play called *The New Ghetto*, in which he described the partially self-inflicted invisible ghetto of Vienna's Jewish middle class. But the decisive turn came when he was sent to Paris as the correspondent for *Die Neue Freie Presse* during the Dreyfus trial. Herzl was less shocked by the unjust verdict of the alleged traitor Dreyfus than by the noise surrounding the trial. He could hear that it was "the Jews" and not one Jewish officer who were held responsible.

If even France, the motherland of the equality of mankind and of Jewish emancipation, was vulnerable to anti-Semitism, there was no other way out than to leave Europe. The Jews needed their own state, as the title of his book *The Jewish State* had it. It was not entirely clear to him yet where this state would be. He mentioned two options, Argentina and Palestine, and for some time seemed to have favored the Argentinean option. Only when he formed a movement did he realize that more important than the rational circumstances of the new territory were the emotions of the people. As he had to concede years later, after he played with the British suggestion of a Jewish home in East Africa (the Uganda Plan), the hearts of his adherents would not follow him to any place but the Land of Israel.

In *The Jewish State*, Herzl combined utopianism and realism, universalism and particularism, modernism and tradition. It was this unique combination that made him succeed. He proposed a Society of Jews that was Jewish only in the composition of most of its members. He did not speak about Jewish religion and culture in his book but rather focused on the practical organization of emigration and on economic principles in the new home. It was no coincidence that he did not refer to a "Jewish Society" but to a Society of Jews and that the correct translation of his book was not *The Jewish State* but *The State of the Jews*.

He did not want to change the lifestyle of middle-class European Jews but simply transplant them to the Middle East by leaving as much as possible as it was: their language (German or French or English but no Hebrew or Yiddish) and their culture, their food and their "little habits" (to which he devoted a whole chapter). "There are English hotels in Egypt and on the mountain-crest in Switzerland, Viennese cafés in South Africa, French theatres in Russia, German operas in America, and best Bavarian beer in Paris. When we journey out of Egypt again we shall not leave the fleshpots behind. Every man will find his customs again in the local groups, but they will be better, more beautiful, and more agreeable than before."

Herzl emphasized this line of thought even more in his second book, the novel *Old-New Land* (*Altneuland*), published in 1902. In his utopian depiction of Palestine in 1923 he described a European society in the

Middle East. One could attend an English boarding school in the morning, sip a Viennese "Coffee Melange" in the afternoon, and choose from the "German, English, French, Italian, or Spanish theater" at night. He mentioned neither Arabic nor Yiddish, and certainly not Hebrew—a language that Herzl did not understand and in which, as he famously claimed, one could not even obtain a train ticket.

Old-New Land spelled out in the form of fiction many ideas he had already developed in his much shorter and more pragmatic *The Jewish State* six years earlier. But there was an important twist. In 1902 Herzl no longer spoke of the Society of Jews but just of a New Society. Non-Jews could join the New Society, but radicals and fundamentalists of all sorts would not be allowed as members. He reserves the most negative description for Jews who denied that non-Jews could be equal members.

Among the decisive characteristics of the New Society were its social and technological achievements. Already in *The Jewish State*, Herzl referred to the new state as the "Seven-Hour-Land." By this he meant that every citizen would work only seven hours a day. This idea was so important to him that the flag he designed for his New Society contained seven stars symbolizing the seven working hours of the day. In this society, women had the right to vote (a right not yet granted to them in any European state). He also listed numerous technological innovations, including electric streetlights, an elevated monorail, and telephone news.

Herzl did not believe that his utopia was unrealistic. When he sent a copy of the novel to Lord Walter Rothschild, Herzl wrote in an accompanying letter: "There will, of course, be stupid people who, because I have chosen the *form* of a Utopia which has been used by Plato and Thomas More, will declare the *cause* to be a Utopia. I fear no such misunderstanding in your case." In another letter to German chancellor Bernhard von Bülow, he emphasized: "I wrote the Utopia only to show that it is none."

Herzl could not imagine that the Arab population would reject so much progress. In *Old-New Land*, he has the noble Arab Reshid Bey participate in all these achievements and welcome the Jewish immigrants. Nothing was further from reality, even then.

In the six years between *The Jewish State* and *Old-New Land*, much had changed. In 1896 Herzl was known as a gifted author. A few years later he became to be known as an exceptional organizer and a char-

ismatic leader of a new movement. Right after publishing his call to
establish a Jewish state he went on to take concrete measures. In 1897 he
convened the first Zionist Congress in Basel. While he did not gain the
support of the wealthy Jewish philanthropists like the Rothschilds or
Baron Maurice de Hirsch, he established a mass movement in Eastern
Europe.

Here conditions had deteriorated and the misery was exacerbated by
pogroms and economic hardship. The call to return to the Holy Land
was well heard in the east but made Herzl a butt of ridicule among his
Western friends. In France and Germany, and in Austria and Italy, most
Jews saw themselves as "French or German, Austrian or Italian citizens
of the Jewish faith." When Herzl wrote, "We are a people. One people,"
they objected. Their Jewishness was defined in terms of religion, not
nationality. In contrast, Eastern European Jews saw their Jewishness as
both a religious and ethnic identity.

The opposition within the Jewish communities of the West was substantial. The Jewish editors-in-chief of Herzl's own paper, *Die Neue Freie
Presse*, declined to mention Zionist ideas or activities even with a single sentence. The Rothschilds refused to listen to him when he wanted
to present his ideas. The Jewish cultural critics in Vienna and Berlin,
among them the provocative Karl Kraus, ridiculed him as the "King of
the Jews." When he began to organize the first Zionist Congress in Munich, both the Munich Jewish community and the Rabbinical Council
of Germany (which consisted of both Reform and Orthodox rabbis) protested and made the meeting impossible. He changed track last minute
and convened the meeting in Basel, where there was only a small and
largely Eastern European Jewish community.

But also in Eastern Europe, Herzl had detractors as well as followers.
There were Orthodox Jews who resisted any man-made endeavor to lead
the Jews back to the Land of Israel. This was the task of the Messiah.
The days to come must not be hastened by a man, and certainly not by a
secular person like Herzl. As we have seen, there were also socialists and
Diaspora Autonomists who both refused to leave Eastern Europe and
adhered stubbornly to their Yiddish culture and language.

Finally, there were those who regarded themselves as Zionists even
before Herzl founded the Zionist movement. While some were happy
to see a new type of leader arise, others were less enthusiastic. The best

known among these detractors was Asher Ginsberg, better known as Ahad Ha'am, a journalist and writer from Odessa.

Ahad Ha'am and Cultural Zionism

Ahad Ha'am did not become a Zionist because of anti-Semitism but because of the fear that Jews would assimilate or lose their sense of cultural creativity if they did not establish a spiritual center in Palestine. The revival of Hebrew was one of the pillars of this kind of cultural Zionism, and one of its heroes was Eliezer Ben-Yehuda, who was instrumental in reviving the Hebrew language for everyday use.

If Karl Kraus and other Western critics ridiculed Herzl as too Jewish, Ahad Ha'am and other proponents of a new Hebrew culture objected that he was not Jewish enough. After all, they argued, what was Jewish about the society he proposed? Besides the fact that it was a place of asylum for persecuted Jews, everything remained as it was in Europe for the assimilated Jews. Ahad Ha'am suggested that what Herzl had in mind was nothing but assimilation on a national scale.

While Herzl wanted a Society of Jews, Ahad Ha'am proposed a Jewish society. This should not be confounded with a religious society, as both were decidedly secular. But the Jewish society should not just be a little Europe transplanted into the Middle East, a Switzerland in the Levant—it should develop modern Hebrew culture and thus help revive Jewish culture in the Diaspora, where according to Ahad Ha'am the majority of Jews would remain.

Ahad Ha'am did not believe Herzl in another important respect. Already years before Herzl appeared on the Zionist stage, he had written several articles in which he warned against the illusion that the Arab population would welcome the new immigrants with open arms. He believed Herzl to be naïve in this, as in other respects.

Ahad Ha'am turned away from the organized movement and did not participate in the Zionist Congresses. Other Zionists founded new factions and parties within the movement. Adherents of Ahad Ha'am's concept of cultural Zionism were among the founders of the Democratic Faction, established at the fifth Zionist Congress in 1901. A year later, religious Zionists established the Mizrachi movement, which combined Orthodox Jewish thought with Zionist ideology.

In 1904, Herzl died at age forty-four. He had neglected his own health when he single-handedly organized the Zionist Congresses, when he spoke to the Jewish masses on behalf of Zionism, and when he tirelessly tried to convince world leaders, from the kaiser to the sultan, from the czar to the pope, of the Jewish right to return to Israel.

Herzl and Ahad Ha'am came to their conclusion from two different perspectives: the Zionism of Theodor Herzl and most Central and Western Europe Zionists was a direct response to anti-Semitism. They had tried hard to be integrated as Austrian or German citizens of the Jewish faith, but when they realized that this was a fruitless endeavor they looked for alternatives. Herzl first wanted to lead all Viennese Jews into St. Stephen's Cathedral to have them baptized and thus to normalize what he termed the "Jewish problem." Once he recognized that it was not a problem of their religion but of their alleged race, he changed his plan. Jews, he now reasoned, would never be recognized as equal Europeans, even if they had changed their religion. The only way out was—literally—a way out—of Europe!

Herzl's Zionism was a plan to make the Jews into a nation like any other nation, and in the language of the turn of the twentieth century this could only mean that they deserved their own state. If the often-quoted saying that "Jews are like anyone else but a bit more so" contains a grain of truth, then Herzl's *Judenstaat* was like any other state, just a bit more so: a model society, a light unto the nations. But also a bit less so: when read closely, Herzl's *Judenstaat* was actually neither a state nor was it Jewish. For Ahad Ha'am, such a society was simply aping European Christian culture and transporting a (Western European) Jewish society to the Middle East.

Eastern European Zionists like Ahad Ha'am were dedicated to the cause of Zion long before Herzl appeared on the stage. Although anti-Semitism was certainly one motif for their national Jewish awakening, other factors were much more important.

For Eastern European Jews, Zionism meant not only that Jews should have their homeland like all other nations, where they would continue to speak German or English or French, or Yiddish for that matter, and live their lives just as before, but rather that they would create a Hebrew-speaking society based on physical labor and the fertilization of the land. The Zionist thinker Jacob Klatzkin thought that the "Jews would regain their norm in Eretz Israel." And Aaron David Gordon wanted to transform "a people that had been distant from nature for centuries, a people that was used to all kinds of occupations with the exception of the natural ones" into a "living, natural, working people." Once they were rooted in their ancient soil again, they would also develop a "normal" occupational structure.

Vladimir Ze'ev Jabotinsky, the emerging leader of Revisionist Zionism, summarized the Zionists' deep desire not only for a geographical removal from Europe but also for a physical transformation into a "normal" people of suntanned peasants and Hebrew-speaking soldiers: "Only after removing the dust accumulated through two thousand years of exile, of *galut*, will the true, authentic Hebrew character reveal its glorious head. Only then shall we be able to say: This is a typical Hebrew, in every sense of the word."

Diplomatic Breakthrough

The Zionist movement entered a power vacuum in the decade after Herzl's death. The best-known Zionist at the time was the second-ranking man in the movement, the prolific writer Max Nordau. Like Herzl, he came from Budapest and initially favored assimilation as a solution to the Jewish Question." He even changed his Jewish-sounding name Südfeld, which literally meant "southern field," into "northern meadow" (Nord-Au), which symbolically meant orienting himself toward Europe and not the Middle East. But Nordau, who had risen to fame with his books critical of modern culture and lashing out against what he termed "Degeneration" (*Entartung*, a term later misused by the Nazis), was prevented from claiming leadership because he was married to a non-Jewish woman. He understood that this would not come across well with the Zionist movement and would make him vulnerable to attacks. He even admitted himself that he was against mixed marriages and would not have married her if he had to marry within the last two years. It is worth noting that Herzl never condemned his marriage. Moses too, he told Nordau, was married to a Midianite.

With Nordau out of the race to be Herzl's successor and Ahad Ha'am having distanced himself from the movement, the person chosen was David Wolffsohn, a self-made wealthy Eastern European Jew living in

German Cologne. Wolffsohn had been a close aide of Herzl and immortalized in Herzl's *Old-New Land*, where the main protagonist (and
later president of the New Society) David Littwak is clearly modeled on
David Wolffsohn (who was a "Littwak," a Lithuanian Jew).

The real Wolffsohn lacked both Herzl's charisma and his intellectual
abilities. He certainly was a bridge between East and West, but he had
little luck in shaping the movement and giving it a new direction. He
stepped down in the midst of conflicts within the movement in 1911.
Wolffsohn's successor, the botanist Otto Warburg, was a respected Zionist but did not approach Herzl's organizational talent and political
skills.

During World War I, the Zionist offices moved to neutral Copenhagen. But the real center of the movement relocated elsewhere. As the
British prepared to take over control in Palestine, the Zionist leadership
realized that from now on London, and not Berlin or Istanbul, would be
the decisive place where decisions in the region were to be made. Chaim
Weizmann, a young and dynamic Russian Zionist who found work as
a chemist in Manchester, rose as the main player behind the scenes.
His invention of synthetic acetone proved critical for the British war efforts and opened the doors to British politicians. Maybe more than his
scientific genius, his rhetoric and his enormous talent to persuade even
experienced politicians of his ideas propelled him to the forefront of the
Zionist leadership.

Weizmann's ability to open doors was crucial in the development
of the most important document for the diplomatic recognition of the
Zionist movement. Just when the British were about to conquer Palestine, Foreign Secretary Lord Arthur James Balfour wrote to Lord Walter
Rothschild. His letter, usually referred to as the Balfour Declaration,
states:

> His Majesty's Government view with favour the establishment in Pal-
> estine of a national home for the Jewish people, and will use their best
> endeavors to facilitate the achievement of this object, it being clearly
> understood that nothing shall be done which may prejudice the civil
> and religious rights of existing non-Jewish communities in Palestine
> or the rights and political status enjoyed by Jews in any other country.

Of course, much remained unclear in this document: What exactly
was the legal meaning of a national home? Which area is intended for es-

tablishing this home "in Palestine"? What about the rights of the Arabs if they objected to the establishment of such a national home? Despite these and other open questions, the Balfour Declaration was the first official document issued by a government in charge of Palestine that made an undeniable promise for the Jewish rights to at least part of the land the Zionists claimed for themselves. While it was still a long way to statehood, the Balfour Declaration helped make Zionism a much more respected movement in the eyes of those who had been indifferent or even hostile to the movement before the war.

The implementation of the Balfour Declaration was the major task of the Zionist leadership in the two decades to come. In the San Remo Conference of 1920, the new League of Nations gave Britain the Mandate over Palestine, and the British treated it not much differently than they would treat their colonies.

Zionist Parties

With the growth of the Zionist movement came fragmentation. In the 1920s, one was not just a Zionist but a Socialist Zionist, a Revisionist Zionist, a General Zionist, or a Religious Zionist. Moreover, one was not only a Socialist Zionist but a Marxist-oriented Poalei Zion adherent or a less ideological Hapo'el Hatza'ir supporter. And the split went deeper: one could define oneself as a right-wing Poalei Zion or a left-wing Poalei Zion supporting the Bolshevik revolution in Russia.

Weizmann adhered to the main stream, which was also called General Zionists. Liberal in their economic vision and moderate in their political outlook, they formed the political center of the emerging party landscape. But the majority of Zionists, especially in Palestine, soon identified with socialism. Influenced by the early theorists of this movement—Nachman Syrkin (1868–1924), Ber Borochov (1881–1917), and Berl Katznelson (1877–1944)—they aimed at creating a classless society. The idealization of workers and peasants was widespread among the Eastern European Zionists, whose goal was to leave the merchant society behind in Europe. In 1930, the main factions of the Zionist left merged to form the Palestinian Labor Party Mapai under the leadership of David Ben-Gurion. Two smaller groups, however—the left wing of the Poalei Zion and the Hashomer Hatza'ir—did not join. Several Russian members of the left-wing Poalei Zion had cast their lot with the communists. Although the socialist direction would dominate the Zionist Organization and later the State of Israel for many decades, it was unsuccessful in forming a truly unified party out of the diverse ideological camps.

Revisionism came on the scene as a final major ideological direction within Zionism. It represented middle-class, antisocialist, and nationalist elements within the movement. The dominant figure of Revisionism right up to his death was Vladimir Ze'ev Jabotinsky (1880–1940), one of the most dazzling presences in Jewish politics in the first half of the twentieth century. He had made a name for himself in the literary world of Russia as a journalist, writer, and translator. His brilliance as an orator soon secured him a large following, the primary basis of which was the mainstream middle class of Polish Jewry of the interwar period. Jabotinsky considered himself the true successor of Herzl, whom he admired greatly, and he initially tried to influence the Zionist movement from within. Like Herzl, he gave higher priority to political and diplomatic efforts than to cultural goals. He also emphasized the necessity of military battle and was successful in establishing a Jewish Legion in the British Army during World War I. The youth organization Betar also had the character of a paramilitary group. It was not until 1925 that Jabotinsky created his own Revisionist party. Ten years later, he and his party left the Zionist Organization because of its allegedly conciliatory line toward the British and Arabs, and Jabotinsky founded his own New Zionist Organization. Jabotinsky and his Revisionists had a very strong base among middle-class Polish Zionists as well as among some smaller Jewish communities, especially the one in South Africa.

The religious Zionists rallied around the Mizrachi party, which remained a small minority among the Zionist parties and had to fight against the non-Zionist *haredim* (Ultra-Orthodox). All efforts to unite the Orthodox Jews under one umbrella failed. It was the British authorities, which forced a Chief Rabbinate (with one Ashkenazi and one Sephardi Chief Rabbi) upon the community (with a significant part of the *haredim* refusing to cooperate). While the secular Zionist leadership welcomed any attempt to unify the Yishuv, it was less enthusiastic over the growing influence of the Chief Rabbinate. The role of the Chief Rabbinate was due in good part to the constitution of the Jewish community approved by the British authorities, which recognized the Jews as a religious but not as a national community. The new position received much of its recognition through the authority of the first Ashkenazi Chief Rabbi of Palestine, Rabbi Avraham Isaac Kook, for whom the establishment of a Jewish state played a major role in the messianic process and the redemption of the Jewish people.

The fragmentation of the Zionist political scene was well under way in the interwar period and constitutes the basis both for the deep rifts and for the common goals in later Israeli society. The main structure of Israel's political system was in place under the Mandate, but it developed further after the establishment of the State of Israel. The main difference is the rise of ethnic parties in addition to the ideological camps. Ethnic parties representing Yemenite or Bukharan Jews were already represented in the first Assemblies of Representatives in Mandatory Palestine, and the Aliya Hadashah Party (the New Immigration Party), formed by immigrants from German-speaking countries, became the third-largest party in the fourth Assembly elections in 1944. But only since the 1980s have ethnic parties, mainly representing Jews from Arab countries and from the former Soviet Union, emerged as major players in government politics. Despite the political dissonance within Zionism and the aggressive style of debate, the political culture in Israel has remained largely nonviolent. The Knesset, the Israeli parliament, provided an inclusive tent for a broad variety of political opinions. The political diversity in the pre-state Jewish society helped lay the foundation for a multivocal democratic state in the Middle East.

Conclusion

Israel was not born ex nihilo in 1948. Zionism, conceived well before the appearance of Theodor Herzl and formed into an organized political movement in 1897, provided the ideological basis and some of the practical and organizational apparatus for hundreds of thousands of people to leave their homes in order to reconstitute themselves in a Jewish state. The society of the Yishuv was in many ways already a state in the making. The Jewish Agency, established in 1929 as the successor of the Palestine Office of the World Zionist Organization (WZO), acted as a pre-state government body during the British Mandate. The cause of recreating a Jewish home in Palestine won prominent Jewish supporters, when Nobel Prize winner Albert Einstein, French prime minister Léon Blum, and the first High Commissioner of Palestine, Lord Herbert Samuel, joined the board of the enlarged Jewish Agency. With the aid of the Jewish National Fund, the agency purchased land for Jewish settlement in Palestine. Educational and cultural matters were organized autonomously and on the basis of the renewed Hebrew language. The political structures of the Jewish state were well in place before the Holocaust.

The Jewish state was always, although not exclusively, thought of as a refuge for Jews who would not live securely in the Diaspora. The pogroms in Russia, the Dreyfus Affair, and the election of an anti-Semitic mayor in Vienna gave rise to the Zionist movement in the late nineteenth century; the anti-Jewish violence in the wake of World War I, the discriminatory policy in Eastern Europe in the 1920s and 1930s, and finally the rise of the Nazi state in Germany legitimized the Zionist enterprise in the eyes of many skeptics. But not even the most pessimistic Zionists could foresee the catastrophe that struck the Jewish people during World War II. The Holocaust might have been decisive to convince the world of the necessity of a Jewish state but at the same time it almost buried the Zionist dreams. As Israel's first prime minister, David Ben-Gurion, observed in Israel's Government Yearbook of 1951: "For hundreds of years the Jewish people offered up a question-prayer: can a state be found for the people? No one considered the horrifying question: will there still be a people found for the state once it is established?"

RECOMMENDED READINGS

Avineri, Shlomo. *The Making of Modern Zionism.* New York: Basic Books, 1981.
Brenner, Michael. *Zionism: A Brief History,* 2nd ed. Princeton, NJ: Wiener, 2011.
Hertzberg, Arthur. *The Zionist Idea: A Historical Analysis and Reader.* Philadelphia: Jewish Publication Society, 1997.
Herzl, Theodor. *Altneuland—Old-New Land.* Haifa: Haifa Publishing, 1964.
Herzl, Theodor. *The Jewish State.* New York: Dover, 1988.
Laqueur, Walter. *A History of Zionism: From the French Revolution to the Establishment of the State of Israel.* New York: Schocken Books, 2003.
Shimoni, Gideon. *The Zionist Ideology.* Hanover, NH: Brandeis University Press, 1995.
Stanislawski, Michael. *Zionism and the Fin de Siècle: Cosmopolitanism and Nationalism from Nordau to Herzl.* Berkeley: University of California Press, 2001.

GLOSSARY TERMS

Ahad Ha'am
Aliya: First Aliya
Balfour Declaration
Betar
British Mandate for Palestine
Chief Rabbinate
David Ben-Gurion
Ha'poel Hatza'ir
Haredim
Hashomer Hatza'ir
Jewish Agency
Jewish National Fund
Mapai (Palestinian labor party)
Mizrachi party
New Zionist Organization
Poalei Zion
World Zionist Organization (WZO)
Yishuv
Zionism: Cultural Zionism; General Zionism; Religious Zionism;
    Revisionist Zionism; Socialist Zionism

Michael Brenner is the Seymour and Lillian Abensohn Chair in Israel Studies and Director of the Center for Israel Studies at American University. He is also Professor of Jewish History and Culture at the Ludwig-Maximilians University of Munich. His books have been translated into ten languages and include *A Short History of the Jews*; *Prophets of the Past: Interpreters of Jewish History*; *Zionism: A Brief History*; *The Renaissance of Jewish Culture in Weimar Germany*; and *After the Holocaust: Rebuilding Jewish Lives in Postwar Germany*.

FOUR

Zionist Settlement in the Land of Israel/Palestine

S. ILAN TROEN

Introduction

The Land of Israel/Palestine again became an actor in world affairs and a focus of wide attention with Zionism's successful effort to ensure a place for Jews among the nations of the world with a Jewish state. Ottoman Palestine was a woefully underdeveloped country with but 250,000 inhabitants in 1800 and only 500,000 in 1900. By 2000, that same land from the Lebanon to the Sinai and from the Jordan River to the Mediterranean accommodated a population that had grown twentyfold to nearly ten million people. The engine for this remarkable transformation has been the skills, initiative, and capital largely provided by the Zionist movement and the State of Israel. How Jewish settlement changed this largely undeveloped territory is a major topic in the history of the region.

During the Ottoman period growth was slow, with small communities of Jewish farmers settling in the Galilee, along the coast on the Sharon plain and in the Jezreel Valley. The expansion of European trade and tourism to the Holy Land through the nineteenth century contributed to the development of cities particularly along the coast, such as Haifa across the bay from historic but dormant Acre and historic Jaffa, and to the subsequent establishment of its dynamic suburb Tel Aviv. The population of Jerusalem grew from a mere fifteen thousand in 1840 to fifty thousand in 1900 and to around seven hundred thousand a century later. By 2010 there were fourteen cities in Israel with more than a hundred thousand residents, according to the country's Central Bureau for

FIGURE 4.1. Jerusalem in the 1870s from Mount Scopus in the east. The Old City at that time was encompassed in its historic walls with minimal population beyond. Jerusalem in 2016 has well over eight hundred thousand inhabitants and is the largest city in Israel. Photo by Felix Bonfils, 1870s. Courtesy of Nadav Mann of Merhavia and Yad Yitzhak Ben-Zvi.

Statistics (CBS). Of these, six—Jerusalem, Tel Aviv-Jaffa, Haifa, Rishon Lezion, Ashdod, and Petach Tikva—have more than two hundred thousand residents. At Israel's founding in 1948, sixty-three years earlier, only Tel Aviv alone had more than a hundred thousand residents.

This process of change is well documented in travelers' accounts, official documents, and reports of explorers. It is also evident in the work of photographers who recorded the country to provide postcards and souvenirs for the growing tourist market. Consider, for example, the two photos by Felix Bonfils, a Beirut based photographer who catered to this trade. Figure 4.1 shows a view of Jerusalem and figure 4.2 shows Haifa, both from the 1870s.

Both scenes record a largely empty landscape that today is filled with vigorous and productive urban cityscapes that support large, new populations.

FIGURE 4.2. A Druze on a donkey on the site where modern Haifa is now situated with the Carmel Mountains in the background. Metropolitan Haifa has a population of nearly six hundred thousand (2015). It is Israel's main port and has a significant industrial area. Photo by Felix Bonfils, 1870s. Courtesy of Nadav Mann of Merhavia and Yad Yitzhak Ben-Zvi.

The same relative barrenness characterized the largely uncultivated countryside. The areas around the Upper Galilee and near Hadera on the coast were marshy and produced more malaria than crops. As B. Z. Kedar's brilliantly illustrated volume of World War I aerial photographs demonstrates, vast areas of the country were desolate or sparsely inhabited, in dramatic contrast with the present. Walid Khalidi, a Palestinian historian who documents the loss of Arab lands and the flight and expulsion of the Arab population, uses photographs of the Palestinian countryside prior to the 1948 war that typically show scattered, small or modest-sized villages and their replacement by Jewish villages, towns, and cities. Whether one celebrates or laments the transformation of Palestine in the course of the twentieth century, it is obvious that a dramatic and radical change has taken place.

The manifest success of Zionist settlement and the extraordinary growth it has occasioned have been met with appreciation and recognition, but also by an animus toward it among many Arabs within and outside Israel and among their sympathizers beyond. Alongside those who regard the Zionist undertaking to make the desert bloom and reclaim the ancestral Jewish homeland as laudable and inspirational, contemporary critics increasingly label Israel a pariah and an apartheid state and call for BDS—boycott, divestment, and sanctions—against the State and its citizens and institutions. Such virulent condemnation including outright rejection of the Zionist project is also addressed in other chapters. It is significant if not central for understanding a host of topics related to Israel. This is also true of Jewish settlement.

I have therefore divided this chapter into two related parts. The first section examines Jewish settlement: how Zionist ideas were modified by pragmatic attention to realities, including Arab opposition, and how they were implemented in creating an extraordinarily vibrant society. The second outlines the arguments used both to justify Jewish settlement and to demand its eradication.

Rural Pioneering

In 1900, about 90 percent of Russia's population was rural and engaged in agriculture. The Jews of czarist Russia mirrored this reality, but only about 10 percent worked the land. Imbued with the ideal of the noble peasant as the essential and fundamental unit of society, Zionists embraced the idea of normalization and imagined transforming themselves and fellow European Jews by returning to the land of their forefathers as farmers. The imperative to return to "the Land" was taken literally; it entailed not merely moving to a new venue but personal and national transformation, and it energized the growing Zionist movement. The first pioneers who came from Eastern Europe in 1881 were young, idealistic, and inexperienced. They struggled to establish small agricultural colonies and to transform the land and themselves into what they had imagined prior to emigration.

What they imagined took several forms: in the *moshava*, independent farmers owned their own land and acted individually; in the *moshav* or cooperative agricultural community, members worked individual farms of generally equal size and sometimes pooled labor as well as machinery and marketing; in the kibbutz or *kvutza*, a collective community, land and even tools and clothing were owned jointly and all decisions, even personal ones, were made by the community. But all these settlements shared a common underlying commitment to living communally. Unlike the pioneers who settled the frontiers in the United States, Argentina, and Australia, Zionist pioneers were not individuals acting alone to establish detached homesteads, large plantations, or ranches. The Zionist frontier was settled by communities through the concerted effort of small *groups* of young newcomers who explicitly organized *villages*. The crucial significance of this distinction can best be understood by a more detailed comparison.

In both the American and Zionist frontier experience, ex-Europeans created societies designed to serve primarily the interests and needs of settler populations. Zionist colonization was highly centralized. It often supported socialist and communist forms of settlement, and its ideology called for individual and collective self-sacrifice for the good of the nation. This is in contradistinction to the private "pursuit of happiness," articulated in the Declaration of Independence, that was the guiding ethos and purpose of the American pattern. Over the course of several centuries, the United States became a continental nation committed to individualism and to furthering and protecting personal rights in a new land that had been foreign to the settlers. In marked contrast, Zionist settlement realized the goals and needs of the Jewish people with deep historic roots in the land.

Thus, during the twentieth century, about seven hundred rural communities were established by groups of Zionists to serve the interests of the Jewish people. From the inauguration of Zionist colonization in the 1880s through the present, there has been almost no homesteading, or farms established by private individuals. Nor have towns or cities been organized and developed by boosters, that is, individual entrepreneurs seeking profit. Israel has virtually no examples of "the little house on the prairie," nor are there Levittowns. Instead, there are various forms of village settlement—of which the *moshav* and the kibbutz are the best known.

It is also useful to compare how pioneering has been idealized and stereotyped in the American and Zionist frontier experience. In the American experience, pioneers are remembered as rugged individualists, whether mythic frontiersmen like Davy Crockett or Daniel Boone or courageous and self-reliant families who left the comforts, culture, and security of established settlements to stake their claim to the land and build their own "little house on the prairie." The equivalent of "pioneer" in Hebrew connotes service and is derived from the biblical *chalutz*, one who went before the people and on their behalf. It derives from biblical passages describing how the Israelites overcame Jericho upon entry into the Promised Land:

> And he [Joshua] said unto the people: "Pass on, and encircle the city, and let the chalutz pass on before the ark of the Lord." And it was so, that when Joshua had spoken unto the people, the seven priests bearing the seven rams' horns before the Lord passed on, and blew the horns; and the ark of the covenant and the Lord followed them. And the chalutz went before the priests that blew the horns. (Joshua 6:7–9)

While the root of the word *chalutz* contains the meaning of "armed soldier," it also and more popularly came to mean one who goes before, or the avant-garde. While the word virtually disappeared from use in Hebrew during the Middle Ages, Zionist writers at the beginning of the twentieth century rediscovered the term and employed it extensively to describe pioneers (*chalutzim*) and pioneering (*chalutziyut*). The initial connotation was fulfilling a divine mission, but secular Zionists readily appropriated the term and the concept to emphasize the necessity for leadership on behalf of a national, secular movement.

In a related phenomenon, land too is a social resource to benefit the group, tribe, or nation. This notion is foreign to the American experience, with the notable exception of at least partial and belated recognition or adjudication of the claims of Native Americans to their ancestral lands. Land was available to individuals through purchase or settlement, and land ownership was regarded as a right and initially guaranteed as an essential liberty. On the other hand, under both the Ottomans and the British Mandate, Jews in Palestine were limited in where they might purchase land and were often deprived of this elementary right because they were Jews. The process of purchase was cumbersome, and few individual pioneers had the ability and means to negotiate the difficulties. Only the national Zionist institutions or an extraordinarily wealthy philanthropist such as a Rothschild had the financial resources, legal expertise, and connections to acquire land by oblique means such as employing Arabs as intermediaries. Land was usually acquired from large landowners, often resident abroad or distant from the area farmed by local peasant farmers who were dispossessed as Jewish pioneers took their places. Once acquired, land was held in trust for the national movement in the name of the Jewish people, not made available to individuals. Even today, Israelis "own" their property through long-term and renewable leases from the Israel Lands Authority or the Jewish National Fund. Hence, it is a longstanding tradition that land is referred to as Jewish or Arab throughout historic Palestine, and that Jewish settlement is undertaken on behalf of the Jewish people.

Changing Preferences in Rural Settlement

The earliest Zionist villages, *moshavot* established from the 1880s to World War I, proved economically unsustainable. In order to maintain themselves they depended on external subsides, primarily from Baron Edmond de Rothschild from France, and consequently could not expand fast enough to absorb the pioneers who wanted or needed to immigrate. By 1910, members of the Second Aliya (1904–1914) were imagining alternative forms of colonization, primarily the *moshav* with a collective, communal approach that blended private ownership with cooperation and was much preferred by the bourgeois leadership of the World Zionist Organization (WZO). Nahalal, the prototype *moshav*, was finally established at the eastern end of the Jezreel Valley in 1921, delayed by World War I when Palestine became a battlefield where the Ottomans with their German allies fought the British. By the mid-1930s, the same bourgeois leadership of the WZO made the communistic kibbutz the prime instrument of settlement. Economic and ideological considerations notwithstanding, by this point security had become a priority.

Realities necessarily modified intentions and ideologies; the national struggle with the Arabs now dictated both the form of settlements and their locations as the need for Jewish self-defense grew in response to growing hostility. The loose organization of watchmen (Hashomer) that was adequate before World War I became more tightly organized and was subsumed by more sophisticated organizations, precursors to the Israeli army established at independence. While the watchmen were primarily concerned with the scattered depredations of Bedouin marauders intent on theft, the attacks organized by a Muslim urban elite in the 1920s reached a watershed in the riots of 1929 that began in Jerusalem and spread to other cities and the countryside. The extended Arab uprising against Jewish settlements and the British from 1936 to 1939 brought about radical transformation in the organization of Jewish settlement. A coordinated policy of colonization was designed to protect not only individual settlements but also the Zionist enterprise as a whole.

In response to the 1929 attacks, Zionist planners developed the concept of the "N" of Jewish settlement, a pattern that emerged from the clustering of Zionist settlements from the 1880s on. The First Aliya pioneers had settled on the plains of Eretz Yisrael: the Sharon or coastal plain, the Jezreel Valley, the Beit She'an Valley below the Sea of Galilee, and up into the finger of the Upper Galilee. This became the "N" of settlement. The Arab population largely inhabited the hills and the mountains of Palestine, but land could be purchased and settled in the valleys where absentee landlords were willing to sell to Jews. Thus, while some Palestinian Arabs initiated violence against Jews, others, members of leading families including that of the Mufti, Muhammad Amin al-Husseini, sold land for Zionist settlement. Moreover, all the lands on which Zionists established these settlements were purchased from Arabs; none were acquired by conquest or international treaty.

As seen in map 4.1, the shaded areas within the "N" of settlement represent land purchased or settled by Jews prior to independence in 1948. The map also indicates selected purchases and settlements outside this region: near Jerusalem, the northern Negev, and the Western Galilee near the Lebanese border. Zionist planners consciously invested their resources outside the West Bank until after the 1967 war. Their policy effectively established which areas would become part of the Jewish state after independence.

The form of village settlements within these areas also changed. As suggested earlier, the earliest settlements through World War I were built

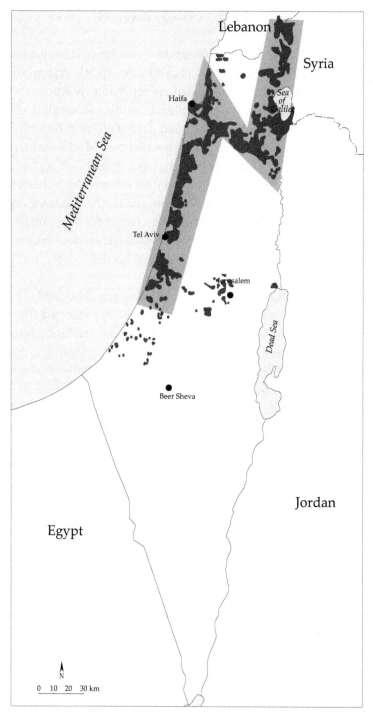

MAP 4.1 The "N" of Zionist settlement

FIGURE 4.3. Kibbutz Tel Amal in the Beit She'an Valley, the first of the "Stockade and Tower" settlements, 1937. Courtesy of the Photograph Collection of the Central Zionist Archives.

without regard to defense. There were no walls around the *moshavot*. In 1921, the buildings in Nahalal were placed in an inner circle with paths leading to the outlying fields like spokes in a wheel, a design meant to increase security, but still, there was no wall and usually no fence. However, after the first Arab attacks of 1936–1939, kibbutzim, particularly those in vulnerable areas, took the form of a stockade with an observation tower known as *homa u'migdal*. Usually prefabricated, they were erected literally overnight to establish "facts" in a hostile landscape, as in figure 4.3, a photograph of Kibbutz Tel Amal, erected in the Beit She'an Valley below the Sea of Galilee in December 1936. It was the first of fifty-seven such settlements founded during this three-year period.

Concern for security also informed settlement after Israel was established in 1948, when the Arab world declared it would not accept the presence of an independent Jewish state in its midst and was preparing for a much publicized "second round" to destroy Israel. As a consequence, the logic of the "N" of settlement continued to shape the defense of the state's borders. This is readily illustrated by the placement of new development towns and of the rural settlements in the 1950s. Such strategic thinking has continued through the present. Security considerations continue to exert a highly centralized control over resources and permits to access land from the Golan Heights down through the Negev and Eilat.

The United Nations partition plan for Palestine of November 1947 established a Jewish and an Arab Palestinian state and designated a significant area around Jerusalem and toward the Mediterranean as an international zone. As the conflict developed, both the Arabs and Jews established lines that ignored the creation of an international zone, and the final battle lines became de facto borders between Israel and Jordan. Similarly, when the conflict ended, additional areas of the Galilee as well as the Negev had been incorporated into the new state. The war ended with armistice lines rather than peace treaties, that is, with a suspension of active hostilities but without agreed international borders, so defense of those armistice lines was essential. As with earlier Zionist settlement, communities were established to defend the borders, and the priority given to security determined how and where Israel absorbed and dispersed a large influx of immigrants.

New villages, whether *moshav* or kibbutz, were placed all along the borders and in other strategic areas, notably the Lachish region between the center of the country and the northern Negev near where the city of Kiryat Gat was later established, that were largely devoid of Jewish populations. In effect, these rural and later urban settlements were needed to secure Israel's border with Jordan and the Egyptian-controlled Gaza Strip. In the absence of such settlements, movement between Jordan and the Gaza Strip would have been unimpeded and the Negev could have been readily cut off from the main body of Israel.

As table 4.1 shows clearly, the kibbutz became the prime instrument of rural settlement in the decade *before* the creation of the state, and it still had a measure of popularity in the few years after independence. However, after 1953 few kibbutzim were established, and the overwhelming choice was again the *moshav*, where individuals farmed privately owned land cooperatively.

The kibbutz, based on the ideological commitments of highly motivated and often still single youth, was essential for defense when there

TABLE 4.1. Establishing settlements 1943–1967 (by five-year periods)

PERIOD	KIBBUTZ	MOSHAV	TOTAL
1943–47	56	24	80
1948–52	79	213	292
1953–57	15	66	81
1958–62	3	17	20
1963–67	2	8	10
Total	155	328	483

Note: Calculations derive from Alex Bein, Immigration and Settlement in the State of Israel (Tel Aviv, 1982), 260–298. The data for 1967 include only until June, when the war broke out.

was no state army to define and hold future borders. But it proved less popular among family-oriented immigrants from cultures that were not imbued with collectivist and radical ideologies. Whatever form they took, whether *moshav* or kibbutz, new settlements continued to be planned and were meant to serve national purposes.

Urban Settlements

Another significant trend one can see in table 4.1 is a decline in agricultural settlements. There are many reasons for this. Zionist ideology did not anticipate the fact that most Jewish immigrants to Palestine would prefer to live in cities. Indeed, there was never more than 20 percent of the population engaged in agriculture. Without the commitment of *chalutzim* who built the settlements of the countryside, the state could not have been established. However, many of Zion's immigrant pioneers who had been tradespeople, artisans, or professionals in their home countries expected to do much the same in their new land. Theodor Herzl's utopian novel *Altneuland* (1902) depicts middle-class immigrants transplanted from a European city to a new city in Palestine with comparable commerce, industry, and arts, including an opera house. In fact, many immigrants were bourgeois or expectant bourgeois intent on achieving a satisfactory European standard of living in their new country. Zionist ideology included a commitment to working the soil and making the desert bloom, and the early history of the state is typically remembered in agrarian terms. But Israel's exceptionally successful advanced modern economy developed in tandem with innovations in agriculture and was crucial to the realization of the Zionist project.

The foundation for urban Israel was laid already in the pre-state period with Tel Aviv and Haifa. Built on the sands just north of Jaffa, Tel Aviv, the first new Jewish city in nearly two thousand years, was home to about one third of the population of the Yishuv by the 1930s. Rapidly expanding Haifa was a substantial second. In contrast, in 1947 no more than 7 percent of the population had ever lived on a kibbutz. This should not be surprising given that Israel is located in a semiarid zone where over centuries much of the soil had been degraded by abuse and rendered unsuitable for productive and profitable agriculture. The wonder is how successful Israel became in developing not only citrus but a whole range of flowers, vegetables, and fruits that it exports to the rich European market and a strong dairy and even meat industry for domestic consumption. However, as with most successful economies, the leading modern states such as the United States, Germany, and Japan are based on advanced urban-industrial economies with fewer than 5 percent of the population engaged in agriculture. The *chalutz* as farmer is celebrated in Zionist ideology and iconography and is a prominent part of collective memory, but the urban component was essential to Zionist settlement.

Contemporary Israel's prominence as a start-up nation with an economy based on high tech, biotechnology, pharmaceuticals, and other sophisticated products was made possible by a settlement program whose ideology included a commitment to education and the application of scientific knowledge to solving human problems. Well before the creation of the state, the WZO supported the establishment of research-oriented universities such as Haifa's Technion (1924), the Hebrew University of Jerusalem (opened in 1925), and the Weizman Institute for Science (1934). In keeping with this tradition, Ben-Gurion University of the Negev was founded in 1969 in the Negev frontier to develop the region and anchor the growth of Beer Sheva, which would become its major city. The development of the country by an educated population was envisioned and intended by Herzl, who portrays the hero of *Altneuland* as a well-educated chemical engineer.

Paradoxically, perhaps, the transformation of Palestine into a state with a modern economy exacerbated relations with the country's Arabs. In addition to the competing religious and national differences between Jews and Arabs, scholars have identified a "dual" economy in which, as early as the 1930s, the Jewish sector was far advanced in economic achievements, literacy and education levels, and civic and economic institutions. This gap still exists despite substantial changes in educational and economic achievement of many Arabs, primarily those who have integrated into Israel's economy. However, even as differences in relative income have diminished, expectations of manifest political equality have grown, giving rise to political and social tensions that aggravate relations between Jews and Arabs.

Post-1967 Settlements

The aftermath of the June War of 1967 marked a watershed in Jewish settlement of Palestine. No longer was any part of Palestine under Ottoman, British, or Jordanian control, nor was it partitioned. For the first time in nearly two millennia, Jews had effective control over the whole country. This unexpected situation paradoxically created a complex challenge to realizing a modern Jewish state that would be both Jewish and democratic.

Immediately after the war, there were conflicting ideas of how the Israeli victory should be exploited. The possibilities initially appeared limited since the Arab League, in the infamous Khartoum resolutions of September 1967, declared the "Three No's": no peace with Israel, no recognition of Israel, no negotiations with Israel. The avowed intention was not merely to regain control of the territories but to eliminate Israel. Some Israelis held to a diametrically opposite view. From the left as well as the right, they joined in the Greater Israel Movement, which was committed to holding all the land west of the Jordan River and, for others, even lands to the east. They claimed that the war was a historic opportunity and argued against relinquishing captured territories, particularly the West Bank. Initially, many were secular Jews. Only after the 1973 Yom Kippur War did settlement expansion come to be identified with Religious Zionism. However, most Israelis accepted United

Nations Resolution 242 of November 1967, which established a formula
for a peace agreement with the neighboring Arab states and was based
on negotiating "land for peace." This was implemented for the first time
only after two further conflicts: a War of Attrition (1967–1970) that in
varying degrees of intensity involved an ongoing conflict between Israel, Jordan, and the Palestine Liberation Organization (PLO), and the
Yom Kippur War of October 1973 between Israel and Egypt and Syria.
Effective American mediation between Egypt and Israel led to a peace
agreement in 1978. As a result, Israel uprooted settlements in the Sinai
and withdrew from the region entirely by 1982. In 1994, a similar agreement that involved minor border adjustments was reached with Jordan.
Further American mediation produced the Oslo Accords between Israel
and the PLO in 1993. They were to affect the West Bank and Gaza. In
sum, it appeared that peace was at hand and that many of Israel's border
issues would soon be resolved. Israel 2020, an effort involving more than
four hundred planners, politicians, military experts, and other professionals, is a plan that envisioned a normal country unburdened by the
threat of conflict.

The stage seemed set to resolve further territorial disputes, but that
did not happen. Negotiations with the Syrians failed and, with the current reality of Syria as a disintegrating state in chaos, claims to the Golan
Heights are likely to remain in dispute. Given the strategic value of the
high ground used by Syrian gunners to rain down fire on Israeli settlements in the valley of the Upper Galilee during the first two decades of
the state, Israeli governments cannot risk reducing the terms for return
of any of these highlands. In an ultimately failed effort to stem continuing conflict with the Palestinians, in 2005 Israel withdrew unilaterally
from Gaza. Nevertheless, with the area under the control of Hamas, a
radical Islamic movement dedicated to the destruction of Israel, violence continues intermittently and, sometimes, on a significant scale.
This leaves the West Bank as the major area requiring negotiation to
fulfill the promise of UN Resolution 242; also termed Judea and Samaria,
it is the area where Israel continues to expend enormous resources and
political capital to maintain control.

The forms of settlement Israel has established given its relationship
to the West Bank is a topic best discussed in two parts: the disposition
of East Jerusalem and the settlements of the West Bank.

Jerusalem

Policy regarding Jerusalem initially enjoyed support within the country and even a measure of sympathy abroad. The popularity of Naomi Shemer's song "Jerusalem of Gold" after the 1967 war reflects the welling up of emotion when the Israel Defense Forces (IDF) took control of East Jerusalem. Jews once again gained access to Mount Scopus, which housed the Hebrew University and the Hadassah Hospital but had been isolated within Jordanian Jerusalem and unusable from 1948 to 1967, and the longed-for Western wall of the temple. Indeed, in the Israeli narrative, the Old City was not *conquered* in 1967 but *recaptured*. There had been a Jewish plurality in East Jerusalem from the mid-nineteenth century to when it was lost to the Jordanians in 1948 and the Jewish population killed, captured, or expelled. The new or western portion of the city was retained after 1948, but at great cost to citizens and the military alike. After the war, Israel built its capital outside the walls of the Old City in those western suburbs. Thus the return to the Western Wall in 1967 and to Mount Scopus was experienced as an unexpected and miraculous event even by the avowedly secular.

Nevertheless, East Jerusalem had become entirely Arab from 1948 when the Jews were expelled during the 1948 war, and it retained a majority population of Arabs after the 1967 war. This population continues to grow with a steady, if often unauthorized, influx of Palestinians from other areas of the West Bank due to the relative economic vitality of the city. A small proportion of the expanding population have chosen to accept the offer of Israeli citizenship, which requires swearing allegiance to Israel and renouncing other citizenships. Most have the status of legal residency, which permits voting in local elections, holding office, and receiving Israeli social security and health benefits, and requires the resident to pay taxes. The proportion of legal residents has recently declined as hope for a Palestinian state has similarly declined or is viewed as less attractive. The close proximity of several populations—Jewish Israeli citizens and two classes of Palestinians—highlights inequalities and raises painful and difficult questions of identity, especially among Jerusalem's Arab residents.

Those responsible for the city after 1967 had experienced or remembered the siege of Jerusalem during the 1948 War and had also recently experienced the Jordanian bombardment at the beginning of the 1967 War. In other words, Jerusalem's vulnerability was abundantly clear, and their effort to secure and fortify the capital dictated post-1967 planning. In addition to formally annexing the Old City at the end of June 1967, the government expanded Jerusalem's borders into the metropolitan area. This reflected a conception developed by Zionist planners following nationwide Arab attacks in 1929 of how to defend vulnerable territory. "Thickening" (*iybu'iy*) involved placing Jewish settlements not only in the areas around the city but along the entire route from the coastal plain up through the mountains to the city's borders. This defensive thinking also involved massive quantities of concrete used for apartment complexes positioned so that they would be difficult to attack and relatively easy to defend. It was, in a sense, the transfer of the "stockade and tower" experience to an urban setting.

Jerusalem is not typical of how contemporary cities have been planned. Jerusalem was intended to serve religious and political purposes, as it did when it was first established by King David three thousand years ago. With the city's function so defined, the economic and strategic irrationality of developing a modern metropolis in the Judean mountains was a problem that had to be overcome. In the ancient world as in the modern one, the Mediterranean coast is where great cities developed far more naturally. Centers of ritual and political capitals were removed from the coast and thereby from the dangers of attack from the sea. Such was the case with Athens and Piraeus, Rome and Ostia. This has not ensured the security of modern Jerusalem during the Arab-Israeli conflicts. As a result, contemporary Israeli planners are as sensitive to fortifying their mountain capital and securing its hinterland as were their ancient predecessors.

Nevertheless, even if unified Jerusalem is now more defensible as a whole, the fundamental pattern of residence in neighborhoods with distinct and clear national and religious characteristics divides the city internally. So long as there is relative calm, the appearance of a united city is maintained. But with the eruption of civic and political tensions, as in the outbreak of violence in the fall of 2015, walls, checkpoints, and fear divide the city functionally. Military and police actions and legislation by the Knesset can do little to ensure peaceful coexistence in Jerusalem's crowded and complicated urban reality.

In other vulnerable areas such as the Galilee with a substantial Arab population, defensive planning called for "rurban" settlements. Initially planted on Galilean hilltops in the 1960s to safeguard areas where Arabs were or were likely to be a majority, these were essentially white-collar rather than farming communities and inhabited by residents who usually commuted to industrial zones in the area or to nearby cities like Haifa. Aptly termed *mitzpim*, these "lookout" communities, located in the elevated parts of the region, doubled as observation posts. These rurban settlements later provided the model for the colonization of the West Bank, with similar "urban" communities set in a "rural" setting scattered across its hilltops.

West Bank Settlements (Judea and Samaria)

West Bank settlement began slowly. The first sanctioned settlement was in the Etzion Bloc (Gush Etzion) south of Jerusalem and near Bethlehem. It reestablished a community that had been settled well before independence and was destroyed just before the 1948 War by Arab forces that killed or took captive inhabitants who did not manage to escape. The resettlement of Gush Etzion met with widespread approval, but the planting of additional settlements encountered opposition.

Contemporary arguments for and against settlements largely focus on the West Bank, including Jerusalem, where intense and extensive development was undertaken particularly after 1977 with a Likud government under Menachem Begin. In the first decade after 1967, fifteen thousand Israelis settled in the West Bank. Under Begin, plans were drawn to settle as many as a million Jews in this area. Although that number has not been reached, with uneven but steady growth under both Likud and Labor governments, by 2010 there were about three hundred thousand, aside from two hundred thousand Jews relocated to East Jerusalem.

Secular as well as religious arguments support settling the West Bank. Many secular Zionists viewed Jerusalem and the West Bank as the historic patrimony of the Jewish people, a matter of momentous historic importance. Others referenced their strategic necessity. Even the influential moderate Yigal Allon, a war hero from 1948 and key Labor leader, argued in a well-publicized plan that bears his name that military bases in the West Bank hill country and along the Jordan River were essential for defense.

The spectacular victory of the IDF that routed the attacking armies of Syria, Jordan, and Egypt in just six days in 1967 rekindled messianic hopes among Religious Zionists. Under the aegis of Gush Emunim and with arguments based in theology, they successfully challenged the government and prior to 1977 established illegal outposts that later gained official recognition as settlements. They saw themselves as patriotic idealists, successors to the nationalistic commitments of Zionism's earlier secular pioneers.

The arguments over settlements grew more complicated in the aftermath of the First Intifada (Palestinian uprising) in 1987, which demonstrated that the Arab population in the occupied territories did not view Jewish control as benign, but as a terrible yoke they were determined to throw off. Based on demographic projections, opponents argue that a Jewish majority in historic Eretz Yisrael cannot be maintained. In 1900, one in ten of Palestine's population was Jewish; in 1947 one in three was Jewish and there was a clear majority toward the end of the twentieth century, particularly with the immigration of a million Jews from the former Soviet Union. However, whether one projects that Arabs in Palestine will become the majority by 2020 or perhaps by 2050, Jews may eventually be a minority if the borders of Israel encompass all of the land between the Jordan and the Mediterranean. Hence pragmatists propose withdrawal to earlier borders where a certain Jewish majority will allow the State to maintain its identity as both Jewish and democratic. If the Arabs between the Jordan and the Mediterranean had the vote, Greater or Historic Israel might be democratic but it would no longer be manifestly Jewish. Moreover, critics contend that permanent control over large Arab populations will necessarily result in human rights violations and have deleterious moral effects on Israeli Jews. At the same time, relinquishing total control to a Palestinian entity that overlooks the coastal plain where most Israeli Jews live as well as Israel's international airport could compromise Israeli security. These religious, strategic, secular, historic, pragmatic, and moral arguments contend vociferously and passionately today, while world opinion, including supporters in the United States, urges Israel to relinquish all or most of the area to a future Palestinian state. Yet nearly seventy years after the 1947 UN vote on partition and nearly fifty years since Resolution 242, Mandatory Palestine has yet to be shared between a Jewish and an Arab state.

The Legitimacy of Zionist Settlement in International Discourse

In the early twentieth century the international community formally affirmed the legal and moral right of the Jews to *re-constitute* themselves as a modern people in Palestine, and to *re*-turn and *re*-claim the land. The *re*- suggests "again," and the language acknowledges the Jewish past and its enduring significance through the continuity of the Jewish people. Research from a wide variety of disciplines including biblical scholarship, archaeology, theology, history, and social sciences supported the Jews' deep and vital historical connection to the Promised Land even as it is used today to argue competing Jewish and Arab claims to Palestine.

In order to understand why this view enjoyed such wide currency and why it is increasingly challenged, we first need very briefly to review the history of nationalism. In the early twentieth century, the nation-state dominated international affairs. The right of nations to self-determination and to independent states was declared in Wilson's Fourteen Points. There were numerous movements for "national" liberation in nineteenth-century Europe and twentieth-century non-European worlds, and at least from the French Revolution on, the nation-state was the accepted instrument for advancing and securing both national and personal rights. These could not be achieved and protected in a vacuum, and they could not just happen. They had to be implemented by political communities organized around distinct peoples. For these reasons nationalism was considered a progressive ideal that would enhance the dissemination of the Enlightenment's highest political values.

When the Ottoman Empire dissolved at the end of World War I, the League of Nations invented the mandate system to nurture national development in large areas of the region the Ottomans had ruled for about five hundred years. Mandates were intended to nurture the formation of new states until independence, including for Jews and for the Arab peoples of Syria and Iraq. In this context, when the League of Nations affirmed the right of the Jewish people to "reconstitute" itself, it recognized the Jews as a people that like other nations was entitled to a state in the part of the world where they had originated and had continued to reside. In other words, defining Jews as a modern people affirmed that they belonged in the region, including in Palestine, where they had a vital presence. The converse of this is that denying Jewish peoplehood denies the legitimacy of the Jewish state.

But formal recognition by such international bodies as the League of Nations or the United Nations was not enough. In other words, the Zionist right to a National Home for Jews was legitimated through evidence of successful reconstitution. A decade later, in November 1947, the thriving agricultural and urban settlements that had been built and populated over such a relatively short period, no less than the prevailing consensus, made UN recognition of Israel possible.

RECONSTITUTION OF THE NATIONAL LANGUAGE

Perhaps the most manifest evidence was the revival of Hebrew. Preserved in texts and prayer over two millennia, Hebrew as a living language reasserted the Jewish people's historic connection to the landscape and the energetic re-creation of a flourishing indigenous culture testified to the vitality of the people's literal roots in the ancient past.

The revival of Hebrew reminds us that the society re-created by Zionism was unlike other European "imagined communities." Zionists explicitly distanced themselves in crucial ways from the European exile they left behind. They never imagined their polity as a satellite or offshoot of a European state, nor did they simply aim to transplant European culture. Rather, they consciously and overtly rejected much in their European past. Their singular success in restoring Hebrew and using it to create a vibrant popular literature, modern media, scientific scholarship, commerce, and politics is a prime example. No other ancient language, even if maintained in the recitation of liturgy or in the study of sacred texts, has been so revived in the modern world. More than eight million people can now use Hebrew as a modern living language if we take into account the Jewish and Arab citizens of Israel, Palestinians on the West Bank and neighboring states, and Jews in the Diaspora. This is more speakers than for many contemporary European languages such as Finnish, Norwegian, and Albanian. There were opponents who insisted that European languages be maintained, and even Herzl expected German to be the language of the Jewish state. However, a vigorous *kulturkampf* decisively defeated that possibility before World War I, and Hebrew became the vehicle for the ingathering of the exiles.

RECLAIMING BY NAMING

Christian explorers, archaeologists, and Bible scholars from Europe and the United States who visited Palestine when it was under Turkish rule from the midnineteenth century tried to recover the original place designations from sacred texts and other historical sources and to derive them from contemporary Arab adaptations or corruptions. As they re-imagined or re-constituted the country's landscape, Zionists continued this process in a deeply personal reattachment to the land of their ancestors. Thus they consciously ignored or set aside many of the physical, social, and cultural markers of both their European origins and Arab neighbors. In Israel there is no New Vilna, New Bialystock, New Warsaw, New England, New York, or Oxford, Cambridge, Paris, Berlin, and so on. Instead, Zionists celebrated the return to history of biblical Rehovoth, Beer Sheva, and Ashkelon. Jerusalem, of course, did not require a new name. In addition, thousands of streets, public squares, and places were named for Jewish historical figures, with signs in Hebrew everywhere. Names like Zichron Ya'akov and Tel Aviv, Rambam Street or Kibbutz Galuyot (the Ingathering of the Exiles, a major thoroughfare in Tel Aviv) announced that the settlements manifested the national revival of the Jewish people. They were neither foreigners nor conquerors but natives legitimately reclaiming their land. For centuries Jews had been strangers. In Eretz Yisrael they expended enormous creative energy to rebuild and resettle their home. It was this remarkable rejuvenation, including in language, that persuaded a majority of the family of nations that the Jewish people deserved an independent state and were entitled to determine their future in the land they had so successfully settled and marked.

Counterproofs/Countertheses

The majority was persuaded, but obviously not everyone agreed. An influential and prominent opponent was George Antonius, a leading Lebanese/Palestinian Christian intellectual, scholar, and public servant who served under the British in Palestine and spent much time in London.

Antonius's views, systematically argued in the period's most influential pro-Arab volume, *The Arab Awakening* (1938), remain central to the discourse prevalent in the Arab world. This discourse, which has become increasingly strident since the 1970s, repudiates Zionism as but another form of European colonization and Zionists as proponents of colonialism. It culminates in the charge that Zionism is racism, comparing it to Nazism and labeling Israel an apartheid state. In keeping with this position, some sociologists, historical geographers, and political scientists assert an identity between Zionist settlement and settler societies, charging the former with the injustices perpetrated by the latter. Thus, while an earlier generation of social scientists supported, even celebrated Jewish settlement of Palestine, some publicly repudiated it as a destructive phenomenon with negative consequences. Current campaigns to delegitimize the Zionist enterprise are based in large measure on this radically different historical paradigm that has been methodically disseminated and now permeates public discourse.

This counterclaim is rooted in an analysis that compares settler societies established during the four hundred years of colonialism beginning with Columbus and ending with Zionism. This analytical framework faults Zionism a priori. To use a phrase: one cannot be a little pregnant. Either one is or is not. Comparing Jews to the Portuguese, Spanish, Dutch, French, and English is to view them exclusively in the European historical framework and to assume their case is identical. Zionist settlement may be more or less benign, but like the starting point of the analysis, the foregone conclusion is that it is colonialist.

A closer examination of the comparison shows that the Zionist project does not fit the rubric established for the Dutch, British, French, Spaniards, Portuguese, Germans, and Italians. During its first forty years, Jewish colonization took place in the Ottoman Empire; it was never a means of imperial expansion or a search for power and markets; it was not a consequence of industrialization and financial interests. Indeed, as numerous scholars have noted, Jewish settlement was so unprofitable that it was judged then, and at times still is, to be economically irrational. As noted earlier, Zionism did not establish plantations or other large units of capitalistic agriculture. Instead, the land was settled by groups with small truck farms or by modest-sized collective colonies. These forms of settlement were suited to homogeneous communities and distinctly unlike the large plantations managed by European settlers and operated by exploiting native labor. Ideologically and practically, Jews worked the land themselves. The traditional economic argument of Zionism as a form of colonialism does not hold.

The misuse of the concept of "settler society" distorts in another crucial way. "Settler societies" were construed as "replicas" of the home society and intended to transplant and reproduce European society. In the case of Algeria, the French even tried to incorporate the colony into the home country. In sharp contrast, Zionist settlements were at once distinct from Europe and different from Arab society. While European and American technology, political ideas, and other aspects of modern culture were transferred to Palestine, Zionist society consciously recast and transformed them in a unique mold dedicated to creating the "new Jew." This was, as we have seen, at the core of the idea of "reconstitution."

Furthermore, when they define Zionists as colonizers, critics implicitly claim that Jews occupy a land where, by this same definition, they do not belong. Underlying this argument is a hidden claim: that Palestine is the legitimate home of one and only one indigenous or native people, the Palestinians. Extreme accounts actually insist that contemporary Palestinians are the direct descendants of the Canaanites, peoples who preceded the ancient Hebrews in populating the land. In an inventive anomaly in the history of colonialism, this new scholarship constructs Palestine as having been occupied by two imperial powers—the British and the Jews. Considering the multitudes of refugees from the Holocaust and from Arab lands who desperately and often unsuccessfully sought entry into Palestine prior to independence, this characterization of Jewish power appears as a cruel joke.

Finally, it is a sad irony that charges that the Zionist enterprise was racist have emanated from the determination of the ideologically self-reliant *chalutzim* to undertake the manual labor entailed in both building and agricultural work themselves. The young pioneers sought redemption in labor and eschewed the exploitative practices of the bourgeoisie. Their insistence on Jewish labor expressed their commitment to live as equals to their Arab neighbors. They did not want to cast themselves as their masters. Nevertheless, contemporary critics hold Zionist ideology and praxis responsible for deliberately creating the economic and cultural separation between Jews and Arabs. The indictment of Israel as an apartheid state follows from this charge. As with the argument that Zionist settlement was a form of colonialism, here too examination of the historic context leads to a different conclusion. During the many centuries that Jews resided in Arab lands, Muslims defined them as *dhimmis*, tolerated but second-class members of the community. This normative separation between Jews and Muslims throughout the Arab Muslim world was imposed by the Muslim Turks and their predecessors after the rise of Islam in the seventh century and has continued through the present. It is absurd to expect a handful of Jews living in remote agricultural colonies under Turkish rule to rebel against such deeply ingrained and accepted practices, or to delegitimize their efforts because they failed to create an egalitarian and integrated civil society that had yet to be actualized even in the United States. Unfortunately, this malevolent fantasy is recognizable as this generation's operative paradigm.

Conclusion

This survey of arguments for and against Jewish settlement leaves us with a paradox. Impelled by ideological and religious yearnings, compelled by tragic circumstances, and through personal risk and sacrifice, Jews of the modern period realized a promise they held fast to and cherished for nearly two millennia. Their state is recognized by more than 150 countries. The achievements of Israeli culture are widely disseminated and appreciated. Its scientific and technological innovations are sought after internationally. Its economy and political system are among the most advanced and progressive, earning Israel membership within the select thirty-plus countries of the OECD (Organisation for Economic Co-operation and Development). Yet Israel must maintain a strong and vigilant military in the face of external and internal threats. The Jews' identity as a nation is questioned, there are continuous moves to delegitimize the State, and it is often treated as a pariah. Voices that remain silent when outrages occur all too frequently elsewhere declare Zionist settlement of Palestine a crime that should never have been allowed to happen.

Nevertheless, Jews continue to immigrate to the country. Despite the many serious problems the country faces and the citizenry's noted rituals of both self-criticism and griping, the rates of outmigration are low. Enlistment in the army's elite units is high. Israel's intellectual and academic life is vital and world-class. Throughout the country there is vigorous building but not enough to keep up with demand. The roads are filled even as construction of highways and the transportation network continually expand. The Zionist settlement project is flourishing in the face of hostility and rejection. This is a difficult tension to bear. Nevertheless, commitment to maintain and improve on what has been achieved by the Jewish resettlement of Zion appears deep and firm. Settlement continues to develop as a work in progress whose complex problems and alluring prospects could not have been readily imagined.

RECOMMENDED READINGS

Avineri, Shlomo. *The Making of Modern Zionism: Intellectual Origins of the Jewish State.* New York: Basic Books, 1981.

Bein, Alex. *The Return to the Soil: A History of Jewish Settlement in Israel.* Jerusalem: Youth and Hechalutz Department of the Zionist Organization, 1952.

Gorenberg, Gershon. *The Accidental Empire: Israel and the Birth of the Settlements, 1967–1977.* New York: Times Books, 2006.

Kark, Ruth, ed. *The Land That Became Israel: Studies in Historical Geography.* New Haven, CT: Yale University Press, 1990.

Katz, Yossi. *The "Business" of Settlement: Private Entrepreneurship in the Jewish Settlement of Palestine, 1900–1914.* Jerusalem: Magnes Press, 1994.

Kedar, B. Z. *Looking Twice at the Land of Israel: Aerial Photographs of 1917–18 and 1987–91.* Tel Aviv: Yad Yitzhak Ben-Tzvi, 1991.

Khalidi, Walid, ed. *All That Remains: The Palestinian Villages Occupied and Depopulated by Israel in 1948.* Washington, DC: Institute of Palestine Studies, 1992.

Near, Henry. *The Kibbutz Movement: A History,* 2 vols. Oxford: Oxford University Press, 1992–1997.

Neumann, Boaz. *Land and Desire in Early Zionism.* Waltham, MA: Brandeis University Press, 2011.

Rotberg, Robert I. *Israeli and Palestinian Narratives of Conflict: History's Double Helix.* Bloomington: Indiana University Press, 2006.

Senor, Dan, and Saul Singer. *Start-up Nation: The Story of Israel's Economic Miracle.* New York: Twelve, 2009.

Shafir, Gershon. *Land, Labor, and the Origins of the Israeli-Palestinian Conflict, 1882–1914.* Cambridge: Cambridge University Press, 1989.

Shapira, Anita. *Land and Power: The Zionist Resort to Force, 1881–1948.* New York: Oxford University Press, 1992.

Shimoni, Gideon. *The Zionist Ideology.* Hanover, NH: Brandeis University Press, 1995, chap. 8.

Stein, Kenneth. *The Land Question in Mandatory Palestine, 1929–1939.* Chapel Hill: University of North Carolina Press, 1984.

Troen, S. Ilan. *Imagining Zion: Dreams, Designs, and Realities in a Century of Zionist Settlement.* New Haven, CT: Yale University Press, 2003.

GLOSSARY TERMS

Aliya: First Aliya; Second Aliya
Hamas
Hashomer
Husseini, Mufti Muhammad Amin al-
Intifada, First
Jewish National Fund
Labor
Likud
Oslo Peace Accords
Partition Plan
Religious Zionism
UN Resolution 242
War: 1948 War; June 1967 War; 1967 War; 1973 Yom Kippur War; War of Attrition (1967–1970)
West Bank, Judea and Samaria
World Zionist Organization (WZO)
Yishuv

S. Ilan Troen is the Karl, Harry, and Helen Stoll Chair in Israel Studies and founding Director of the Schusterman Center for Israel Studies at Brandeis University. He is founding editor of *Israel Studies* (IUP). His publications include *Imagining Zion: Dreams, Designs and Realities in a Century of Jewish Settlement* and (with Jacob Lassner) *Jews and Muslims in the Arab World: Haunted by Pasts Real and Imagined.*

FIVE

The Arab-Israeli Conflict

ALAN DOWTY

Introduction

Let's begin by disposing of a common myth about this conflict over what Arabs call *Palestine* and Jews regard as the *Land of Israel*. It is not an "age-old" conflict; it began in the 1880s when Jewish settlers arrived in the area to reestablish a national presence. At its core, it was and is a clash between two peoples over one land. Jews point to a unique 3,200-year historic tie to the Land of Israel, a bond unmatched in human history and widely recognized internationally. Palestinian Arabs point to the predominantly Arabic character of Palestine in the centuries since the Islamic conquest.

In the beginning, neither side recognized the existence of the other as a people with national historic ties to the land. Arab inhabitants and Turkish rulers regarded Jews as a religion and not as a people, and saw the Jewish settlers as European colonialist intruders. The Jewish settlers, for their part, saw the Arabs in Palestine as individuals who would benefit from the development of a Jewish homeland, and not as a people with a collective identity and collective rights. Neither side even considered that there was a counterpart with whom to negotiate.

The conflict has passed through four distinct stages in its evolution. The first stage, from its origins in the 1880s to 1948, was a collision between two communities in Palestine over land and political control. The second stage, from 1948 to the late 1980s, was an interstate conflict between Israel and neighboring Arab states, with the Palestinians temporarily eclipsed. The third stage, which began after the First Intifada in the late 1980s and early 1990s, was the reemergence of the Palestinians as the major actor opposite Israel. And in the early twenty-first century the conflict entered a fourth stage marked by a resurgence of ideological rejectionism and the intervention of new outside parties.

First Stage of the Conflict:
Jews and Arabs in Ottoman Palestine

On March 1, 1881, Czar Alexander II of Russia—home to half of the world's Jews—was assassinated. Within weeks a wave of violent attacks on Jewish communities began to sweep the country. Thus began a dark period in Russian Jewish history that led to the massive flight of four million refugees over the next four decades. Of these a small trickle, about 2 percent, chose to return to Zion (Zion, a hill in Jerusalem, had since biblical days served as a poetic reference to the Land of Israel).

The achievements of the first two decades of Jewish settlement were not impressive. Jews, from Russia and elsewhere, still constituted less than 10 percent of the population, and of this number only a few thousand were in the new "Zionist" settlements. This first wave of immigration (*aliya*, or "ascent," in Hebrew) failed to put the Return to Zion on the world's agenda. Subsequently the first Russian Revolution of 1905 triggered another massive wave of anti-Jewish persecution. The resulting exodus from Russia in the decade before World War I brought about thirty-four thousand Jewish settlers to Ottoman Palestine, a wave of newcomers known as the second *aliya*.

When Jews motivated by the Zionist vision entered Palestinian areas of the Ottoman Empire during this period, they encountered a population already in place. Only those imagining Palestine from afar could describe it as an "empty" land, and such fantasies did not survive actual settlement experience. But early Zionist settlers did not see the presence of Arabs in the Land of Israel as a problem. In the first place, as they saw it, Jewish religious and historical ties to the Holy Land were undeniable; both Christianity and Islam recorded a Jewish history in Palestine as part of their own scriptures. As for the existing residents of Palestine, the introduction of a modernizing population would raise the level of the entire country, bringing the blessings of modern civilization to all its inhabitants. It was sufficient, in this view, to better the welfare of non-Jewish residents as *individuals*, since they had not (yet) laid claim to a national identity, and *collective* rights, as a people. The early Zionists saw themselves as "Europeans," a self-reference that occurs often in their writings, and the Arab populations they encountered agreed, and regarded them as Europeans. This was an age in which the spread of European ideas and techniques was not questioned, as the benefits seemed beyond dispute. Achievement of the Zionist program would ensure justice on both sides.

Ahad Ha'am, Zionism's most vigorous internal critic, wrote a series of articles titled "Truth from *Eretz Yisrael*" in 1891, which is often—inaccurately—regarded as the first serious Zionist recognition of an "Arab problem." In fact Ahad Ha'am shared the general view that the success of the Zionist enterprise would resolve any conflict by bringing the blessings of European civilization to the local population. Only in 1907 did a Zionist writer suggest that the relationship with the Arabs of Palestine was "a question that outweighs all the others." Yitzhak Epstein, a teacher who had settled in Rosh Pina in 1886, published an article titled "A Hidden Question," arguing for a negotiated solution that would make the Arabs partners and beneficiaries in the Zionist enterprise, though Jews would remain the senior partners. Opposed to Epstein's integrative approach, separatist or confrontational approaches argued that Zionism had to maintain its distance from alien cultures, and that in any event a clash with the local population was inevitable.

The Ottoman government attempted to prevent European Jews from establishing a toehold in its Palestinian provinces. In addition to trying to bar the entry of Jews, it also forbade the sale of land to those who managed to enter anyway, and refused to issue building permits to those who managed to buy land. Given that, how did the Zionists succeed to the extent that they did? By 1914, there were an estimated ninety-four thousand Jews (about 14 percent of the population) in what became Mandatory Palestine. Determined Zionists found ways around or through the obstructions: as religious pilgrims, through the land frontiers with Egypt or Lebanon, or by bribery (*baksheesh*). Once in Palestine, the new settlers could invoke the protection of their consuls to prevent deportation.

How did the Arab population react to the early Zionist settlers? Where they settled, Zionists encountered local hostility and opposition.

This was often dismissed as a natural xenophobic response to strangers; the incidents were isolated and sporadic and did not signal (Zionists reassured themselves) any general pattern of opposition to the idea of a Jewish home in Palestine. But over time resistance to Zionism grew as Zionism itself grew. Every new Jewish settlement had property disputes with neighbors. A major source of conflict was the displacement from purchased land of tenant farmers who had lost rights to land cultivated by their families for generations. Offers of generous compensation, beyond that required by law, did not always work; some disputes dragged on for years. The pattern was that of an established population reacting to newcomers as aliens. This did not require a modern sense of national identity as "Arabs" or "Palestinians"; it required only a sense of being threatened by new settlers.

Arabs from neighboring villages attacked Petach Tikva in 1886, Gedera in 1888, Yesod Hama'ala in 1890, Rehovoth in 1892, 1893, and 1899, Kastina in 1896, Jewish Jaffa in 1908, and Sejera in 1909. In every case there were specific triggers to the attacks, but the general pattern speaks for itself. In June 1891 some five hundred notable Arab figures in Jerusalem sent a petition to Constantinople demanding a halt to all Jewish immigration and all land sales to Jews. The Ottoman government responded by forbidding the entry of Russian Jews in August of that year, and of all Jews in October. Such decrees violated an Ottoman pledge of nondiscrimination on the basis of religion or race and evoked sharp counterpressure from European powers.

In the last decade before World War I, Arab nationalism became a significant force in the region. In 1905 Najib Azuri, a Lebanese Christian who had served in the Ottoman bureaucracy in Jerusalem, published in Paris *Le Reveil de la Nation Arabe* (*The Awakening of the Arab Nation*), the first "textbook" of secular Arab nationalism. Palestine received considerable attention; Azuri predicted that "the fate of the entire world" would depend on the outcome of the Arab-Jewish struggle, which would continue until one side had won a total victory. This was a rather remarkable projection, given that both national movements were still in an embryonic stage.

In July 1908 Ottoman army officers forced Sultan Abdul Hamid II to restore the constitution of 1876, which he had suspended in 1878; in the following year the sultan was deposed. This Young Turk Revolution brought out into the open both the growing Arab nationalist movement and the growing conflict over Zionist settlement in Palestine. Palestinians and other Arabs, by this time, had reached a consensus about the project of a Jewish return to their ancestral homeland. They were opposed to the establishment of a non-Muslim state in the heart of the Arab and Islamic worlds, and so long as this was the Zionist goal, they saw the conflict as irreconcilable.

THE BRITISH MANDATE

When the Ottoman government chose to side with the Central Powers in World War I, Great Britain instigated an Arab Revolt within the Ottoman Empire in order to hasten its demise. The British promised Hussein bin Ali, Sharif of Mecca, to support the establishment of an Arab state or states under Hashemite rule in the Arabian peninsula, Syria, Iraq, and—in the Hashemite interpretation—Palestine. Clearly the British were going to have some trouble reconciling this commitment with a previous agreement with France on the division of the Middle East. But they also made another commitment, known as the Balfour Declaration (November 2, 1917), favoring the establishment of a Jewish "national home" in Palestine.

The Balfour Declaration became legally relevant when it was written into the British Mandate for Palestine by the League of Nations. Zionists welcomed the statement as a major victory, and the establishment of a Palestine Mandate conferred international legitimacy on the Zionist enterprise. Britain organized the territory east of the Jordan River (77 percent of the total area) as a semiautonomous emirate named Transjordan, under the rule of Abdullah, son of Sharif Hussein. This left 23 percent of the original territory, lying west of the Jordan River, as the final Palestine Mandate. These borders became the generally accepted definition of "Palestine."

Within the new Palestine, the British had a built-in conflict to resolve. They were mandated both (1) to help build a Jewish national home and (2) to prepare the population (still overwhelmingly Arab) for self-government. Since Arabs in Palestine opposed the idea of a Jewish national home there, the task facing the British was daunting. In particular, on the issue of immigration there was not and could not be any middle ground. Immigration was the core issue in the dreams and fears of both sides. Thus each new *aliya* triggered Arab demonstrations and riots, and each wave of protest and violence produced the instinctive British response: an investigating commission. Five such royal commissions were established during the Mandate. Typically, each pointed out that the guidelines of the Mandate were contradictory and recommended backing down a little on the commitment to a Jewish national home. Typically, both sides rejected such a compromise. Each community developed its own communal institutions and governing bodies, deepening the deadlock.

Because of deportations and hardships, the Jewish population had fallen during the war years by as much as one third, but by the 1922 British census, it was back up to 83,790, or 11 percent of the total. This increased to 174,606 (17 percent) in the 1931 census and to an estimated 630,000 (32 percent) at the end of 1947 (not including an estimated 100,000 illegal immigrants). Once again, the waves of immigration reflected anti-Semitic pressures in countries of origin: the Third Aliya, 1920–1923, from Russia; the Fourth Aliya, mid-1920s, from Poland; and the Fifth Aliya, mid-1930s, from Germany and other countries threatened by Nazism.

But were Jews any more secure in Palestine? Given Arab attacks in 1920, 1921, 1929, and 1936–1939, wasn't history simply repeating itself? Not at all, in the Jewish view. There was a critical difference in Palestine: in their homeland, Jews were free and able to organize in their own defense. Following the first attacks in 1920, a Jewish defense organization—Haganah (Defense)—was established to protect Jews and Jewish settlements from threatened violence. In the course of time, this became the foundation of the military force with which the Jewish community was able to secure its existence.

By the early 1930s Labor Zionists were the dominant force in the Jewish community in Palestine, and the Labor Zionist leader, David Ben-Gurion, made several attempts to reach an overall accommodation with moderate Arab leaders. However, the dominant Palestinian Arab leader in this period, al-Haj Amin al-Husseini, was known for his unbending opposition to any compromise with Zionism or any accommodation that would include official recognition of a Jewish community in Palestine. In 1921, the British appointed al-Husseini, from a prominent Jerusalem family that had long held key religious offices in the Muslim community, as Mufti of Jerusalem, the top Muslim post in Palestine. In the following year he was also elected head of a new Supreme Muslim Council. In 1936–1939, when Arab unrest erupted into what was termed the Great Revolt, the mufti fled to avoid arrest by the British for his role in the uprising and later discredited himself by collaborating with the Nazi regime in Europe.

By the mid-1930s Zionist Jews and Palestinian Arabs both recognized the seriousness of the conflict between them. This did not mean, however, that either side had yet abandoned its exclusive claim to Palestine. Most Zionists still looked forward to achievement of a Jewish majority in an undivided Palestine. On the other side, Palestinian Arabs were determined to maintain an undivided Palestine as an Arab and Muslim state. David Ben-Gurion put it very simply: "We and they want the same thing. We both want Palestine."

The other major alternative—dividing Palestine—was first proposed in 1937 by the British Peel Commission, which was appointed to investigate the causes of the uprising. Partition has been at the center of most international initiatives and resolutions since then; it was the de facto situation during 1948–1967. In its final report, the Peel Commission concluded that "an irrepressible conflict has arisen between two national communities within the narrow bounds of one small country. . . . There is no common ground between them." The only workable solution, the commission concluded, was to establish two sovereign states: an Arab state of about 80 percent of Palestine united with Transjordan, and a Jewish state in the other 20 percent of Palestine (basically the coastal plain from Tel Aviv north and the Galilee). A majority of the Jewish leadership accepted the principle of partition, though not the specific borders in the Peel proposal. Palestinian Arabs, however, resisted partition and even autonomy for the Jewish minority.

After introducing the idea of partition as a solution, the British quickly retreated. In 1939 they issued a White Paper, stating with finality that there would be no Jewish state and projecting independence for undivided Palestine in ten years. Jewish immigration would end after five years, and the Jewish share of the population would be stabilized at about one third. Further sale of land to Jews in Arab areas would also end. The bottom line was that Palestine would stay undivided and predominantly Arab; for Zionists it was a total calamity. But how could

Jews openly oppose Britain when it was facing a showdown with Nazi Germany? Ben-Gurion's response was to walk a fine line: the Zionists would fight the White Paper as if there were no war, and fight the war as if there were no White Paper.

From the Jewish perspective, the Holocaust—the meticulously planned killing of one third of the Jewish people, the largest mass murder in history—created an unanswerable humanitarian case for a Jewish state. As the Zionist leader Chaim Weizmann told the Peel Commission in 1936, for tyrannized Jewish refugees the world "is divided into places where they cannot live and places into which they cannot enter." The Nazi Final Solution was implemented only after it became clear that mass deportation, the first Nazi "solution," would not work because there was nowhere for Jews to go. If a Jewish state had existed, Zionists lamented, some or most of the six million could have been saved.

In early 1947 the British dumped the Palestine problem in the lap of the new United Nations (UN), successor to the now-defunct League of Nations. The UN formed a United Nations Special Committee on Palestine (UNSCOP), consisting of eleven nations, to investigate. A seven-member majority of UNSCOP returned to the principle of partition, recommending the creation of both Arab and Jewish states, with economic union and the internationalization of Jerusalem. On November 29, 1947, the UN General Assembly adopted the partition plan by a vote of 33 to 13, with 10 abstentions (GA Resolution 181). The borders proposed were more favorable to the Jewish state than the Peel plan had been, giving it 56 percent of Palestine. But the UN Security Council made no move to enforce the General Assembly plan. Instead, as the British proceeded to withdraw from Palestine, fighting between the two sides broke out and grew apace as the British presence dwindled.

Palestinian Arab leaders complained that the proposal gave the Arabs, who still constituted two thirds of the population, only 44 percent of the land, while leaving a large Arab minority of about 42 percent in the Jewish state. But since Palestinian Arabs opposed the principle of a Jewish state, more favorable borders would not have changed this opposition. Palestinian Arabs also felt they were in a better position than in 1936–1939 with strong and growing vocal support from seven independent Arab states, the departure of the British, and a Jewish community of only about three quarters of a million with little military training or experience.

Second Stage of the Conflict: The Emergence of Israel

Fighting between Jews and Arabs in Palestine began after adoption of the partition plan at the end of November 1947. This first phase of fighting, while British troops were still in nominal control, was largely irregular warfare between local Palestinian Arab forces and the military organizations of the Jewish community: the mainstream Haganah and the more radical Etzel (Irgun) and Lehi movements of the Revisionists, who had opposed division of the Land of Israel and had advocated military action against British as well as Arab forces. In the first few months Arab attacks on convoys and settlements within the area allotted to the Jewish state threatened to make its establishment untenable. But in early April Haganah launched an offensive (Plan Dalet, or D) aimed at creating contiguous territorial control over the area of the Jewish state. By the time of the final British withdrawal on May 15, 1948, Jewish forces had managed to hold on to most of the territory allotted to the Jewish state, plus a corridor to Jerusalem.

On May 14, a Provisional State Council of Jewish leaders declared the independence of the Jewish state, to be named Israel. The new state promised "full social and political equality of all its citizens, without distinction of religion, race, or sex," and called on neighboring states to make peace. The following day, as anticipated, five Arab states (the four neighbors and Iraq) sent military forces into Palestine. The war that followed was fought episodically. In the first month, Israeli forces stopped the Egyptian army on the coast twenty miles south of Tel Aviv, kept a corridor to Jerusalem open despite occupation of the West Bank by the Arab Legion of Transjordan, and held the Syrians to minimal gains in the north. This was followed by a monthlong truce imposed by the UN, followed in turn by The Ten Days of fighting (July 8–18), during which Israeli forces took the offensive and captured strategic areas beyond the partition lines. A second, unlimited truce was imposed on July 18; it was punctuated by isolated outbreaks of hostilities on the Egyptian front in mid-October and late December, and battles with Palestinian forces in Galilee in late October.

During the early months of 1949 four separate bilateral armistice agreements were negotiated between Israel and Egypt, Transjordan, Syria, and Lebanon. Like all armistice agreements, these accords ended the military conflict but did not address underlying political issues or final borders; these problems were reserved for the projected peace treaties that were to be negotiated (but were reached only decades later with Egypt and Transjordan, and never with Syria and Lebanon). Egypt clung onto a narrow strip of the southern coast, today's Gaza Strip; Transjordan's Arab Legion, the most effective Arab fighting force, occupied the central region that became known as the West Bank; Syria withdrew from its remaining toehold in Palestine in return for demilitarization of that area; and Lebanon had never been more than a symbolic participant in the fighting. This left Israel in possession of about 78 percent of the former Palestinian Mandate, as opposed to the 56 percent allocated to the Jewish State in the 1947 partition resolution.

The agreements also established a new context for the Arab-Israeli conflict, marking its passage from a conflict between two communities within Palestine to a second stage as a conflict between states. For Jews, coming so quickly after the greatest tragedy in their history, the reemergence of an independent Jewish state after two thousand years was one of their greatest historical moments; for Palestinians it was al-Nakba, The Catastrophe.

The 1948 War transformed the confrontation in a number of other ways as well:

- *The 1949 armistice lines became de facto borders.* Although the armistice lines were explicitly *not* final borders, which were to be settled by projected peace treaties, in the absence of such treaties they acquired great legitimacy. Transjordan annexed the West Bank and renamed itself Jordan.
- *Israel achieved general international recognition.* Israel was admitted to UN membership and established diplomatic relations with most other independent states, apart from Arab and Muslim regimes.
- *The Arab state projected in the partition plan was never created.* Arab states and the Palestinians had rejected the partition of Palestine and did not establish an Arab state.
- *The new Jewish state acquired a substantial Arab minority.* Most of the Arabs in areas that became part of Israel fled or were expelled, but about 150,000 remained in place, constituting about 19 percent of the new state's population (a figure that scarcely changed over the years).

- *The war created a massive Palestinian refugee issue.* Over seven hundred thousand Palestinian refugees fled Israel and rejected resettlement as a solution. As a result, the UN did not deal with them through its normal refugee machinery but instead created a separate body, the United Nations Relief and Works Agency (UNRWA), to address their humanitarian, social, and educational needs. UNRWA was not delegated to deal with long-term solutions to their plight.
- *The war sparked a massive Jewish exodus from Arab and Muslim lands.* Whether they were expelled or left voluntarily, the bulk of the Jewish population in other Middle East countries, estimated at one million, fled Arab lands in the years after the war; about six hundred thousand found refuge in Israel.

NASSER AND ARAB NATIONALISM

During the two decades between the 1948 War and the 1967 War, the Palestinians were temporarily eclipsed as a player. The Middle East stage was dominated by Egypt's charismatic Gamal Abdel Nasser, the prime mover in a 1952 military coup that overthrew the Egyptian monarchy, and the key figure in Arab nationalism until his death in 1970. There were moments when it appeared that Nasserism might sweep all before it, including the new and vulnerable Jewish state on its eastern border.

Three important changes were taking place in international politics during these years. Asian and African states threw off colonial rule and formed a bloc of nonaligned states tied to neither side in the Cold War, giving rise to the Third World. The Arab world was radicalized, with coups not only in Egypt but also in Syria (1949), Iraq (1958), Sudan (1958, 1969), Yemen (1962), and Libya (1969). Finally, the Soviet Union used the fight against imperialism and colonialism to gain leverage in the Cold War competition throughout the Third World, including the Middle East.

All of these new dimensions and dilemmas can be seen in the 1956 Suez Crisis. Threatened by the new Soviet-supplied weaponry in Egypt, Israel was simultaneously beset by increased cross-border raids by *fedayeen* (self-sacrificers) from the Gaza Strip and by Nasser's decision to close the Strait of Tiran, an international waterway at the southern tip of the Sinai peninsula, and bar Israeli sea and air traffic. This last move, in September 1955, closed Israel's only outlet to East Africa and Asia.

When in July 1956 the United States abruptly withdrew promised funding for the Aswan Dam, centerpiece of Egypt's development plans, Nasser retaliated by nationalizing the Suez Canal from its British and French owners. Britain and France were ready to reverse this move militarily but were held back by US president Dwight Eisenhower and secretary of state John Foster Dulles, who felt that such neocolonialism might push the entire Third World into Soviet hands. Finally despairing of the US diplomatic moves on Suez, the two European powers secretly negotiated with Israel to create a conflict in which they could intervene and, incidentally, reoccupy the Canal Zone. Israel did its part at the end of October, invading Sinai and advancing to within a few miles of the Canal Zone; the British and French began their intervention but were forced by immense international and domestic pressure to back down before their goal was achieved. Israel held on to the Sinai and the Gaza Strip for a few weeks, finally withdrawing in return for the stationing of a UN Emergency Force (UNEF), the first UN peacekeeping force, to stabilize the Egypt-Israel border and ensure free passage through the Strait of Tiran. Israel gained a stable border with Egypt and the opening of its access to the East, at least for the next ten years.

During these years, doctrines of guerrilla warfare and popular resistance were resonating throughout the Third World. A number of Palestinian fighting groups were established, most importantly the Palestine Liberation Movement (Fatah, from its Arabic initials in reverse order). Fatah was founded sometime in 1957–1962 (sources differ), was supported initially by Syria, and was headed by Yasser Arafat, a scion of the Husseini family. The Egyptians, trying to stay in front, sponsored the 1964 creation of the Palestine Liberation Organization (PLO), designed to serve as an umbrella organization for all Palestinian factions.

Despite sporadic cross-border attacks by Palestinian organizations after 1965, the period before 1967 was relatively quiet and stable; it did not appear that any of the parties was likely to challenge the status quo within the foreseeable future. This, however, turned out to be an illusion.

THE 1967 WAR

The bare outline of what happened in May and June 1967 is not complicated. The Soviet Union warned Egypt that Israel was about to launch a major strike on Syria; in response, Egypt moved troops into the Sinai peninsula toward its border with Israel and requested the withdrawal of UNEF forces separating the two sides. After reoccupying the position at Sharm el-Sheikh that controls the maritime passage to the Gulf of Aqaba, on May 22 Egypt announced its renewed closure to Israeli ships. As the crisis intensified, Egypt, Syria, and Jordan concluded mutual defense agreements. After a period of futile diplomacy, Israel launched an air and land attack on June 5, and in six days of fighting it conquered the Gaza Strip and Sinai from Egypt, the West Bank from Jordan, and the Golan Heights from Syria.

From the Arab perspective, every Arab move was defensive. Egypt moved forces to its eastern borders to offset Israel's escalation, both as a measure of prudent self-defense and to deter an Israeli attack on Syria. Egypt claimed a legal right to evict UNEF, stationed on Egyptian territory, and asserted that the Strait of Tiran was Egyptian territorial waters. But from the Israeli perspective, every Israeli move was also defensive. Israel had not mobilized forces on its Syrian border, as the Soviet Union charged. The Strait of Tiran was legally an international waterway over which Israel had already fought one war. Moreover, Egypt had declared its hostile intentions openly, with Nasser announcing that he had initiated the crisis deliberately and that "our basic objective will be to destroy Israel."

The 1967 War demonstrated the potential for unintended collisions, and the limits of rationality, in such confrontations. The miscalculation by the Soviet Union showed that outside powers have greater capability to set events in motion than they have to control the consequences. The failure of UN peacekeeping underlined the limits of cooperative international frameworks when local parties believe that vital interests, and perhaps their very survival, are at stake. The 1967 War was, in short, a cautionary tale that is still studied for its lessons by both analysts and practitioners.

Israel's attack began early on June 5 with a massive aerial bombing of Egypt's airfields that successfully crippled the Egyptian Air Force. When the Jordanian army opened fire on Jewish Jerusalem, honoring its commitment to Egypt, similar attacks were carried out on Jordanian and Syrian air bases. Within days the Israeli army had captured all of the West Bank from Jordan, as well as the Gaza Strip and the Sinai

Peninsula, up to the Suez Canal, from Egypt. At the end of the week, a short and sharp campaign wrested the Golan Heights, which dominate the upper Jordan Valley, from Syria.

To Israelis this conflict, labeled triumphantly the Six-Day War, represented deliverance from the dread of destruction and the dawn of a new reality in which Arab states would surely have to sue for peace. Israel's strategic position was enormously improved; instead of Egyptian forces sitting less than fifty miles from Tel Aviv, Israeli troops now deployed on the Suez Canal. To Arabs, this was simply the June War, and the unfortunate culmination of the long Jewish campaign to control all of Palestine. Israel now occupied all of former Mandatory Palestine, as well as Egyptian and Syrian territory that had never been part of Palestine. In a word, the 1967 War turned the Arab-Israel conflict upside down.

What the war did, above all, was to derail the process of de facto partition and to reopen competing options. In Israel, a unitary state again seemed realistic to some, as old territorial ambitions were rekindled. The war brought to life contentious issues that had been locked in cold storage for twenty years, involving not just the future of the territories occupied but also the very nature of Israel itself: a compact and relatively homogeneous state, or a state of two peoples?

Among Palestinians, the war sparked a resurgence of revolutionary radicalism, as it was apparent that Nasser and the Arab states could not defeat Israel. Yasser Arafat's Fatah took over the PLO in 1968 and rewrote its 1964 charter, reaffirming the goal of a unitary Arab state in which only Jews who had resided in Palestine "before the beginning of the Zionist invasion" (variously interpreted as the 1880s, 1917, or 1948) would be permitted to remain. As support for the PLO in the West Bank and Gaza grew over the years, the door to a negotiated settlement based on partition seemed to close; Jordan might have eventually formalized its division of Palestine with Israel in an agreement, but it was unrealistic to expect the same from an organization whose historic base of support came from refugees seeking to return to homes in Israel itself.

Paradoxically, the 1967 War also created a new basis for negotiation. After 1967 Israel could offer withdrawal from territories occupied in the war in return for Arab recognition and a final peace treaty: a "land for peace" formula embodied in UN Security Council Resolution 242 of 1967, which became the point of departure for all subsequent Arab-

Israeli diplomacy. The problem, with the rise of the PLO and the eclipse of Jordan, was the momentary absence of a credible partner willing and able to negotiate within this framework.

Third Stage of the Conflict: Reemergence of the Palestinians

Although it was not apparent at first, the post-1967 period marked the beginning of disengagement by Arab states from the Arab-Israeli conflict, parallel to the reemergence of the Palestinians. The conflict over the next two decades became less of an interstate confrontation and gradually entered a third stage: a renewed clash between Jews and Arabs within historic Palestine.

In the immediate aftermath of the war, Israel pressed for changes in the prewar armistice lines. East Jerusalem, including the Old City and its Jewish Quarter, was quickly annexed. Other claims were on sites where Jewish settlements had existed before 1948, such as the Etzion Bloc south of Jerusalem, and strategically important spots: the Jordan Valley, the Golan Heights, and the Egypt-Gaza border. Accordingly, Labor governments of the late 1960s and early 1970s, under prime ministers Levi Eshkol (1963–1969), Golda Meir (1969–1974), and Yitzhak Rabin (1974–1977), opposed Jewish settlement outside these areas. From 1968 this stance was challenged by the emergence of a settler movement dedicated to establishing a renewed Jewish presence throughout the homeland. Identified informally as Gush Emunim (Block of the Faithful), this movement was inspired by strong religious and historical nationalism and enjoyed close ties with religious and right-wing parties.

On the Arab side, the extent of the 1967 defeat was a psychological barrier to negotiation. Arab leaders convened in Khartoum, the Sudanese capital, at the end of August 1967, to consider their next move, and in the final communiqué called for "no recognition of Israel, no peace and no negotiations with her." The "Three No's" of Khartoum were seen in Israel as total rejection of a diplomatic solution. Arab observers, however, argued that Khartoum did not close the door to political compromise, so long as it did not involve direct contact with Israel or a formal peace agreement.

After succeeding Nasser in October 1970, Egypt's Anwar Sadat became convinced that Israel would not withdraw from Sinai unless Egypt demonstrated that it still had military options. Sadat did not seek a total military victory; his aim was to show that Egypt could inflict heavy costs on Israel so long as it continued to occupy Sinai. Egypt coordinated an attack with Syria, and on October 6, 1973—the holy day of Yom Kippur in the Jewish calendar—their armies struck across the respective cease-fire lines on the Suez Canal and the Golan Heights. Achieving both strategic and tactical surprise, Egypt established a firm foothold east of the canal, and Syria reoccupied most of the Golan Heights before being thrown back a few days later by hastily mobilized Israeli forces. By October 19, Egyptian forces were threatened by an Israeli counterattack across the canal, and fighting ended on October 24 to the background accompaniment of a threatened confrontation between the United States and the Soviet Union.

Following the war, Egypt reversed its entire orientation and forged close ties to the United States, becoming the second-largest recipient (after Israel) of American assistance. The United States also took a more active diplomatic role, as secretary of state Henry Kissinger carried out rounds of "shuttle diplomacy" among the various parties. The first official face-to-face diplomatic meeting since 1949 took place shortly after the war, in December 1973, when Egypt and Jordan (but not Syria or the Palestinians) sat at the table with Israel at a two-day conference in Geneva. But Kissinger's shuttles soon became the central diplomatic pivot and produced disengagement agreements between Israel and Egypt (January 1974) and Israel and Syria (May 1974). A second-stage Interim Agreement, returning an additional slice of Sinai to Egyptian control, was reached in September 1975.

In 1977 half a century of Labor domination ended with an electoral victory for the right-wing Likud party, led by Menachem Begin. Begin was the successor of Vladimir Ze'ev Jabotinsky, the founder of Revisionist Zionism and advocate of militant Jewish nationalism. Begin's government was unswervingly committed to the expansion of Jewish settlements beyond the Green Line (the 1949 armistice lines). In 1977 there were still only about four thousand Jewish settlers in these territories, but thereafter the number grew quickly.

Having been excluded from UN Resolution 242 and even from the Khartoum summit, Palestinians ceased to rely on the Arab states for their deliverance and began to take over their own cause. Arab states could not defeat Israel in an all-out war; furthermore, they were focused on their own occupied territories rather than on the issues of 1948. Palestinians would have to fight their own fight, and the then-popular theory of revolutionary guerrilla warfare provided a ready model. As they lacked an army, direct military confrontation was impossible, so PLO groups turned to surprise attacks on unprotected—usually civilian—targets. By most definitions this was terrorism, but PLO spokesmen argued that in wars of national liberation all of the oppressor's institutions and population were legitimate targets. The attacks did little or nothing to weaken Israel, but Palestinian political and diplomatic offensives were achieving significant gains. In October 1974, with the coerced acquiescence of Jordan, the Rabat Arab summit meeting declared the PLO to be the sole legitimate representative of the Palestinian people.

Against this backdrop, Anwar Sadat made his second unexpected move. Israel still occupied most of the Sinai peninsula. To overcome this impasse, Sadat announced in the Egyptian People's Assembly that he was willing to go anywhere, including Israel, to achieve a settlement. He was immediately invited by Israeli prime minister Menachem Begin to come to Israel and address the Israeli Knesset. In November 1977 this dramatic visit took place and the leaders' declaration that there would be no more war, no more bloodshed, was followed by renewed negotiations between the two nations.

At the Camp David summit meeting in September 1978, US president Jimmy Carter mediated a settlement: there would be two agreements, one for Egypt-Israel peace and the second a framework for a West Bank/Gaza resolution, but they would not be formally linked. Consequently an Egypt-Israel peace treaty was signed in March 1979. Within three years Israel had withdrawn from Sinai, which was demilitarized, and normal diplomatic relations were established between the two nations. The Egypt-Israel peace treaty proved to be durable, but agreement on the West Bank and Gaza was never reached. Conceptions of autonomy—the first projected stage—were far apart, and neither the Palestinians nor Jordan were willing to participate or cooperate.

The Egypt-Israel peace treaty was, beyond all doubt, a singular breakthrough in the Arab-Israel conflict. The military calculus was radically altered: without Egypt, Syria could not seriously contemplate a full-scale war with Israel. Since the peace treaty with Egypt, there has been no full-scale war between Israel and any Arab state. On the everyday level, peace between the two nations made less of an impact. Egypt observed the minimal requirements of normalization to the letter, but no more; social, cultural, and even economic relationships remained stunted. To Israelis it was a "cold peace," not the friendly amity that many had anticipated.

If there was peace, albeit a cold peace, on the border with Egypt, the buildup of a PLO base in southern Lebanon presented a new threat from the north, and terrorist incursions were on the rise. When Ariel Sharon became defense minister after Begin's reelection in 1981, he sought a radical and far-reaching solution: Israel would help anti-Palestinian factions in Lebanon expel PLO and Syrian forces from their country, and the new Lebanon would make peace with Israel. Sharon failed to get cabinet approval for this plan but won consent for a scaled-down version in which Israel would clear the PLO from a zone extending forty kilometers (about twenty-five miles) into Lebanon. The campaign, known as Peace in Galilee, was launched in June 1982 and won strong public backing at first. But Israeli troops did not halt at the forty-kilometer line, moving instead—on Sharon's orders—to besiege PLO forces in the heart of Beirut. Sharon explained each further advance of the Israeli army as a matter of military necessity, but it eventually became clear that he was implementing his original, more ambitious design.

Whatever Sharon's plans, they were dealt a lethal double blow in September. First, Bashir Gemayel, Israel's favored Lebanese ally and newly elected president of Lebanon, was assassinated. Immediately afterward, Lebanese Christian forces entered the Palestinian refugee camps of Sabra and Shatila, in Israeli-controlled Beirut, and massacred an estimated seven hundred to eight hundred Palestinian civilians before being stopped by Israeli forces. This triggered a vociferous international reaction. In Israel itself, the Sabra/Shatila massacre transformed growing opposition to the war into a massive protest movement. An investigating body—the Kahan Commission—concluded that Israeli commanders bore indirect responsibility for the atrocities committed, and Sharon was forced to resign as defense minister. Israel withdrew from southern Lebanon in two stages, in 1983 and 1985, leaving behind a buffer zone patrolled by an Israeli-supported Lebanese force, the Southern Lebanese

Army. But radical Islamist groups, principally Hezbollah, soon took the place of the PLO, harassing the Southern Lebanese Army and attacking across the buffer zone into Israel.

For Palestinians, frustration boiled over in late 1987 with the sustained period of unrest known as the First Intifada (an Arabic word meaning literally "shaking off," but also used to denote a political uprising). The grassroots uprising in the occupied territories helped shift the Palestinians' focus from the events of 1948 to the occupation. In addition, the Intifada convinced King Hussein that it was time to withdraw any remaining Jordanian claim to the West Bank, which he did in July 1988. The Intifada also catalyzed the emergence of radical Islamist groups. In mid-1988 a new group named Hamas (the initials of Islamic Resistance Movement) was formally organized. Its charter seeks "to raise the banner of God over every inch of Palestine," since Palestine is an Islamic trust (*waqf*). The Hamas charter strongly rejects "so-called peaceful solutions" and describes Jews in the language of classic anti-Semitism.

In response to the Intifada, Israeli opinion moved very gradually in a dovish direction on basic issues of readiness for territorial compromise. The focus for resolving the conflict also shifted from Jordan to the Palestinians. In fact, the First Intifada created, for the first time, an apparent majority among both Palestinians and Israelis in support of a two-state solution to the conflict. Within a year the PLO officially accepted UN General Assembly Resolution 181—the Partition Plan of 1947—and UN Security Council Resolution 242 of 1967. By these steps the Palestinian mainstream formally endorsed the "two-state solution" to the conflict, envisioning a Palestinian state alongside the Jewish state rather than in place of it.

With much fanfare, the first all-inclusive peace conference on the Arab-Israel conflict—the first gathering in which credible representatives of all parties met face to face—convened in Madrid on October 30, 1991. After intense negotiation, it had been agreed that non-PLO Palestinians approved by the PLO would form a joint delegation with Jordan. Following the script that had been painstakingly hammered out, the ceremonial sessions in Madrid were adjourned after three days of frequently vituperative speeches, and the actual negotiations began in a number of bilateral and multilateral forums. The five multilateral forums (on water, refugees, economic development, arms control, and the environment) were an innovative effort to build a more cooperative context for bilateral negotiations. Yet despite some initial progress, the multilateral tracks became inactive as the general atmosphere worsened by the end of the decade.

The joint Jordanian-Palestinian delegation was soon revealed as a fiction, and de facto, separate talks took place. Negotiations between the Shamir government and the Palestinian delegation made little progress. However, in June 1992 when Yitzhak Rabin led Labor to its first election victory since 1973 and formed the first Israeli government without Likud since 1977, the stage was set for new departures, and a secret direct channel between the Israeli government and the PLO was created. After months of secret negotiations in discreet Norwegian venues, agreement on mutual recognition and a framework for a comprehensive peace treaty were achieved and dramatically unveiled on the international scene. A festive ceremony was held on the White House lawn on September 13, 1993, to mark the occasion.

An exchange of letters between Rabin and Arafat established mutual recognition between Israel and the PLO, which committed itself to a peaceful resolution of all outstanding issues, assumed responsibility for preventing acts of violence by "all PLO elements and personnel," and promised to drop from the Palestinian Covenant all provisions that denied Israel's right to exist. The Declaration of Principles committed the two parties to creating a Palestinian Interim Self-Governing Authority in the West Bank and the Gaza Strip for a five-year period, during which time "permanent status" negotiations would take place until agreement was reached on all issues of a final peace treaty: Jerusalem, refugees, settlements, security arrangements, and borders.

Implementation of the Oslo framework was plagued by problems and delays from the start. The negotiation of the first step, Israeli withdrawal from about 80 percent of the Gaza Strip and from the Jericho area, was to have been completed within two months; it actually took almost seven months. Nevertheless, the return of Yasser Arafat and the PLO leadership from Tunis on July 1, 1994, and the establishment of the first-ever Palestinian administration on Palestinian soil, was a dramatic event that temporarily revived some of the initial enthusiasm, at least on the Palestinian side.

The next step, an Interim Agreement covering all aspects of the transition period, was to have been completed within nine months after the Oslo Declaration; it actually took two years, until September 1995. This agreement, known as Oslo II, established the Palestinian Authority (PA) and gave it immediate jurisdiction over the major cities of the West Bank and civil jurisdiction with shared security control over most of the towns and villages. These areas together initially comprised about 28 percent of the West Bank, but together with territory controlled in Gaza this put most of the Arab population, outside Jerusalem, under PA jurisdiction. The remaining 72 percent of the West Bank consisted of sparsely inhabited areas, Israeli settlements, and military reserves, all of which remained under Israeli control. Elections were held in January 1996 for president and for the Palestine Legislative Council; Arafat was elected president by an 87 percent majority, and his Fatah party supporters won fifty of the eighty-eight council seats.

Conclusion of a final peace treaty with Jordan was less complicated. Israel and Jordan had long enjoyed a furtive relationship, given their common opposition to the PLO and their common pro-Western orientation. In October 1994 they concluded a peace treaty that covered all outstanding issues; the fact that Jordan no longer claimed the West Bank meant that there were no significant territorial issues to resolve.

Syria had attended the Madrid conference and had participated in bilateral talks with Israel—the first direct talks between the two states. When Labor came to power in Israel, the possibility of applying the "land for peace" formula was revived. But Israel understood full withdrawal to mean withdrawal to the international border between the Palestinian Mandate and Syria that was established by Great Britain and France after World War I. Syria, however, demanded a return to "the lines of June 4, 1967," since Syria had occupied small pockets of Palestinian territory (primarily ten meters on the northeast shoreline of the Sea of Galilee) between 1948 and 1967. The issue remains unresolved.

When on November 4, 1995, an Israeli religious extremist assassinated Prime Minister Rabin, the entire process was thrown into a period of turmoil from which, in many ways, it never recovered. The wave of support for the peace process in the wake of Rabin's murder declined in the following months as Palestinian terrorists launched a series of attacks on Israeli civilian targets inside Israel. A string of four attacks in nine days, during the 1996 election campaign, helped tip the balance against Shimon Peres, Rabin's successor as leader of the Labor party and prime minister. The new leader of Likud, Benjamin Netanyahu, defeated Peres in a direct contest for the prime ministership by 1 percent of the vote. In the past, Netanyahu had opposed recognition of the PLO, rejected anything beyond autonomy for the Palestinians in Judea and Samaria, and insisted on the right of Jews to live anywhere in the historic Land of Israel. Nevertheless, Netanyahu's government maintained the peace process and even pushed it forward in some respects.

In January 1997 Israel and the PLO concluded an agreement on Israeli redeployment from most of Hebron. In September 1998 Netanyahu's government concluded another agreement, the Wye River Memorandum, which provided for Israeli withdrawal from a further 13 percent of the West Bank. With these further redeployments, 41 percent of the West Bank came under Palestinian civil control with 59 percent remaining under Israeli control. The areas under the jurisdiction of the Palestinian Authority now included an estimated 96 percent of the Palestinian population in the West Bank.

But the Wye agreement was too much for some of Netanyahu's coalition, leading to defections that brought down his government and forced early elections in 1999. In the second Israeli election featuring a separate vote for prime minister, new Labor leader Ehud Barak soundly defeated Netanyahu and launched an ambitious effort to get the peace process back on track. After trying without success to revive the Syrian track, and withdrawing Israeli forces from the last stretch of Lebanese territory that they held, in early 2000 Barak sought to leap over the remaining loose ends of Oslo II and go straight for a peace treaty to end the conflict. At Barak's strong insistence, US president Bill Clinton and (much more reluctantly) Yasser Arafat agreed to a summit meeting at Camp David in July 2000, dedicated to overcoming all remaining differences.

The Camp David talks were a spectacular failure, with each side blaming the other. Palestinians argued that Israeli proposals would not produce a viable Palestinian state and pointed to the expansion of Israeli settlements in the West Bank and Gaza as evidence that Israel was not serious about a two-state solution. Israeli accounts emphasized the extent of Barak's substantive concessions at Camp David, especially on territorial issues including Jerusalem. They cast doubt on Arafat's commitment to a two-state solution, claiming that his identification with the refugee population made him incapable of accepting a permanent settlement without a sweeping "right of return" that would transform the demography of Israel. Also, despite commitments to end Palestinian attacks on Israelis, such attacks had continued with apparently little PLO effort to prevent them.

In January 2001 representatives of the two sides met again in Taba, the Egyptian resort town on the Gulf of Aqaba, for negotiations based on proposals made by President Clinton during his last days in office. The establishment of a Palestinian state was taken for granted; the June 4, 1967, lines (i.e., the 1949 armistice lines) would be the "basis" for the border between Israel and Palestine. Israel proposed to annex 6 percent of the West Bank, incorporating most of the Jewish settlements, and to give Palestine the equivalent of 3 percent of the West Bank in territory elsewhere. Palestinian negotiators proposed a straightforward land swap of 3 percent of the West Bank for an equivalent piece of land elsewhere. In Jerusalem, Arab neighborhoods would be part of Palestine, and Jewish neighborhoods would be part of Israel. There was consensus that Palestine would be subject to arms limitations, but no specifics were agreed upon. Less progress was made on the refugee issue, with Palestinians stressing the right of refugees to choose freely between return to their original homes or compensation, and Israel stressing that it could not absorb more than a small fraction of the four million refugees without threatening the Jewish character of the state.

All in all, the Taba negotiations closed the gap between the two sides considerably in some areas, while leaving many issues unresolved. They indicated the contours of any future negotiations that might take place and are thus useful as a guide. But they were overshadowed by a new convulsion that threatened to reduce all diplomacy to irrelevance.

The outbreak of the Second Palestinian Intifada at the end of September 2000, just a few months before the Taba negotiations began, had come as a shock to most of the Israeli public. The Intifada revealed not just a chasm between Israelis and Palestinians on issues but also diametrically opposed conceptions of the peace process itself. For Israelis, the peace process was a *negotiating model*. In this negotiation, each side trades off assets that it considers less valuable for more valued concessions from the other side. A corollary of the negotiating model is that negotiation and violent confrontations are mutually exclusive, if not contradictory. The Palestinian conception of the peace process was quite different. Palestinians argued that negotiations should not reflect the "military imbalance of power" between the two sides, and put forward an *implementation model*, rejecting equal concessions on both sides and demanding that Israel implement international resolutions on withdrawal from occupied territories.

The first pass at peace, in short, produced some changes in the Israeli-Palestinian conflict that are unlikely to be reversed: mutual recognition, majority consensus on a two-state solution, the sense that a Palestinian state is inevitable, and the further disengagement of Arab states. It ended, however, in a quagmire from which neither side seemed able to extricate itself.

Fourth Stage of the Conflict: Ideological Rejectionism

The thunderous collapse of the Oslo peace process was, in a real sense, the tunnel at the end of the light. Since then, the conflict has entered a fourth stage. The central arena has been occupied by proponents of ideological rejectionism reminiscent of the rigid rejectionism of the first stage. Israel has faced its own challenges from its religious extremists who claim divine sanction for acts of violence to protect what they see as the rights of the state (as in the murder of Yitzhak Rabin). But the major icons of the fourth stage have been Hezbollah and Hamas, backed by the theocratic regime of Iran.

Iran had been a peripheral player in the Arab-Israel conflict. Now the Islamic Republic of Iran was sponsoring the Palestinian cause, building up Hezbollah—a non-Palestinian radical religious movement within the Shi'a Arab population of southern Lebanon—as a military force on Israel's border. Given Iran's military experience and expertise, and its considerable resources as a state, this added a new dimension to the conflict. Even Israel's 2000 withdrawal from southern Lebanon did not temper the anti-Israel agenda of Hezbollah and its Iranian sponsor. Hezbollah was an important model in the rise of Hamas in the late 1980s.

Indeed, the fourth stage of the conflict can be dated from January 2006, when Hamas won a solid majority of seats in the Palestine National Council. The victory should not be overstated: Hamas received only 44 percent of the direct party vote against 41 percent for Fatah, and a large part of the support was a reaction to the corruption and mismanagement within the Palestinian Authority. Nevertheless, the election put the legislative powers of the PA, and most of its executive powers, in the hands of a movement that in principle rejected recognition of Israel and any permanent agreements with the Jewish state.

In June 2007 Hamas seized physical control of Gaza in a quick blitz campaign, and in response President Mahmoud Abbas dissolved the unity government that had been formed. The West Bank and Gaza were now effectively divided, and the prospect of a Palestinian negotiating partner able and willing to implement a two-state solution with Israel was delayed indefinitely.

In 2006 a new kind of war was a further signal of a fundamental change in the structure of the conflict. In response to the kidnapping of two Israeli soldiers, Israel launched a campaign, primarily from the air, that proved inadequate either to inflict a decisive defeat on Hezbollah forces or to stop the rain of rockets on northern Israel. Nearly all parties saw the war as a Hezbollah victory, even though it sustained heavier losses, since the organization had survived to fight another day. That both sides claimed victory or defeat according to their predispositions reveals the extent to which the very definition of victory or defeat had come to be questioned and disputed. The Gaza War of December 2008–January 2009, though different in some respects, raised many of the same questions.

The fourth stage has left both sides in great confusion. In Israel it produced the quick emergence and even quicker demise of the shortest-lived school of thought in Israeli strategy: the move toward unilateral disengagement from Palestinian territories. During the Second Intifada, support had grown for unilaterally drawing lines between Israel on one side and the West Bank and Gaza on the other. Behind this was a growing realization that demography was working against Israel, and that there would soon be an Arab majority in Israel and the territories taken together. In order to remain both Jewish and democratic, Israel would have to get out of the West Bank and Gaza.

On this basis, Prime Minister Ariel Sharon, his reputation as a superhawk notwithstanding, carried out the evacuation of Israeli settlements and forces from Gaza in late 2005. Disengagement—or "consolidation"—was the declared objective of the government formed under the new Kadima party after elections in early 2006. But as attacks and threats from areas that had been evacuated intensified—Lebanon in 2000 and Gaza in 2005—support for further unilateral withdrawals evaporated.

The Israeli elections of 2009 and, to a lesser extent, 2013 confirmed that a significant shift to the right, first seen in 2003, had been associated with events of the fourth stage. This turn to the right was set in motion by the Second Intifada, the rise of Hamas as the pivotal Palestinian player, the intrusion of Iran, and what is seen by many Israelis as the failure of unilateral disengagement in Lebanon in 2000 and Gaza in 2005. In essence, the new configuration erased the impact of the 2006 election that followed Ariel Sharon's establishment of the new centrist party Kadima.

But despite all in the setbacks and disappointments of recent years, a majority of both Palestinians and Israelis continue to support negotiation and a two-state solution in principle. In the Israeli case, greater support for rightist parties is paradoxically offset by the move of the entire political spectrum toward greater acceptance of political options that were anathema in an earlier period. There was a time when only a tiny radical minority of Israelis was willing to recognize the PLO or accept the idea of a Palestinian state—just as the PLO rejected the very idea of a Jewish state alongside a Palestinian state. In June 2009, following his return to the prime ministership, Benjamin Netanyahu announced his conditional acceptance of a demilitarized Palestinian state alongside Israel, thus putting even the Likud—Israel's right-wing party—on record behind the two-state model.

In the meantime the guiding concept of two states for two peoples has come under renewed attack. One model that has attracted attention was the idea of a binational state, a state that would be neither Jewish nor Arab but in which the two peoples would share power in a neutral framework. The vision of Israelis and Palestinians living together cooperatively, with neither side dominating the other, is undeniably attractive. But close observers ask if such a design is workable in intense ethnic conflicts. Binational states have a very poor track record, outside of the two Western liberal democracies of Canada and Belgium, and there are no ready examples of successful power sharing between parties still at war. Why would parties that have been unable to negotiate terms of separation suddenly be able to agree on intricate cooperation in all the minute details of public life? Most important, how would a binational state allow both sides the self-determination and national identity that each has defined as the core of their aspirations over the last century?

Conclusion

I have argued that what has been called the Arab-Israeli conflict is actually an evolving conflict that has changed through four distinct stages. Initially a struggle over land and political control and then, until the late 1980s, a conflict between Israel and the neighboring Arab states, the conflict changed significantly when, after the First Intifada in the late 1980s and early 1990s, the Palestinians emerged as the major actor opposite Israel. Finally, in the early twenty-first century the conflict entered a fourth stage marked by a resurgence of ideological rejectionism and the intervention of new outside parties.

Today, the likely terms of a settlement of the conflict are actually fairly clear to most observers. Although serious negotiations over the basic issues—the "final status" questions—have taken place only for a few months in 2000–2001, 2007–2008, and once again in 2013, these talks show the emerging contours of what a final resolution might look like. There would be a Palestinian state alongside the Jewish state, with borders based on the pre-1967 armistice lines with minor changes. The status quo on the holy sites would remain, with the Muslim mosques (Al-Aqsa and the Dome of the Rock) under Muslim control and the Western Wall under Jewish control, with formal sovereignty left vague. A token number of Palestinian refugees might be reunified with families in Israel, but the right of return would be exercised primarily to Palestine. Palestine would have forces to maintain law and order, but not to threaten Israel. An international presence would probably be needed to guarantee the agreement.

It is much easier to predict the likely content of a settlement, however, than to predict when it will be achieved. The general trends of the last century and a quarter give us a certain degree of confidence that, sooner

or later, the majorities on both sides that favor a compromise will prevail. But the events of the early twenty-first century remind us that this
denouement is not imminent.

RECOMMENDED READINGS

Bar-Siman-Tov, Ya'akov. *Justice and Peace in the Israeli-Palestinian Conflict.*
New York: Routledge, 2014.
Caplan, Neil. *The Israel-Palestine Conflict: Contested Histories.* Malden, MA:
Wiley-Blackwell, 2009.
Dowty, Alan. *Israel/Palestine*, 4th ed. Cambridge, UK: Polity Press, 2017.
Khalidi, Rashid. *Palestinian Identity: The Construction of Modern National
Consciousness.* New York: Columbia University Press, 1997.
Laqueur, Walter, and Barry Rubin, eds. *The Israel-Arab Reader: A Documentary
History of the Middle East Conflict.* New York: Penguin, 2008.
Mandel, Neville. *The Arabs and Zionism before World War I.* Berkeley: Univer-
sity of California Press, 1976.
Tessler, Mark. *A History of the Israeli-Palestinian Conflict*, 2nd edition. Bloom-
ington: Indiana University Press, 1994.

GLOSSARY TERMS

Ahad Ha'am
Aliya: Second Aliya
Balfour Declaration
British Mandate for Palestine
Camp David Summit
Etzel
Fatah
fedayeen
Haganah
Husseini Haj Amin al-
Intifada, First
Irgun
Labor Zionism
Lehi
Madrid Peace Conference
Nakba al-
Nasser, Gamal Abdel
Oslo Peace Accords
Oslo II
Partition Plan

Peel Commission
Revisionist Zionism
Weizmann, Chaim
West Bank

Alan Dowty is Professor Emeritus of Political Science at the University of Notre Dame. His numerous publications include *The Middle East Crisis: U.S. Decision Making in 1958, 1970, and 1973*; *The Jewish State: A Century Later*; and *Israel/Palestine*, now in its fourth edition.

SIX

History of the Peace Process

DAVID MAKOVSKY

Following the 1967 War, the international community put forward a template that would guide diplomacy aimed at ending the Arab-Israeli conflict for decades to come—*land for peace*. This was the core concept of United Nations Security Council (UNSC) Resolution 242 in the wake of the June 1967 War, a concept reaffirmed after the October 1973 War in UNSC Resolution 338.

The idea that Israelis and Arabs might agree on terms for peace sounded downright futuristic until these resolutions proposed that in return for peace with its Arab neighbors, Israel should yield land won in the 1967 War, which had more than tripled the size of the country. The idea was rejected by the Arab world at the 1967 postwar conference in Khartoum, where the Arab League issued its infamous resolution declaring "Three No's"—no negotiations, no peace, no recognition of Israel. Despite this unequivocal rejection and arguments over the wording of Resolution 242, whether it meant yielding all the territories or only a slice, the resolution provided an important paradigm for a series of negotiations in what has come to be known as "the peace process." Over a period of five decades this process has engaged a variety of US administrations and different parties and regimes in the effort to resolve the Arab-Israeli conflict. As we will see by considering this history, the conflict has not yet been resolved, but its nature has evolved over time.

The first major breakthrough achieved by diplomatic activities was the 1979 Egypt-Israel Peace Treaty. Egypt wanted to recover its Sinai Desert land, and the price was ultimately peace with Israel. Since Egypt

118

was the most populous Arab country, the peace with Cairo signaled an end to the Arab-Israeli Interstate War. This was followed by a new stage of the conflict, as nonstate actors took up the struggle against Israel in an altogether different type of war. Even as agreements have been reached between Egypt and Jordan to secure borders, other tensions have erupted, suggesting that the initial paradigm of "land for peace" will have to be adjusted to address the complex issues that now confront the parties to the conflict.

In the aftermath of the 1967 War, different US views emerged regarding Arab goals and Middle East diplomacy in general. While some assumed the Arabs were taking comprehensive steps to maximize their leverage and force Israeli concessions, but with minimal, if any, reciprocity, others thought the Arab states were essentially focused on furthering their own domestic interests and would be willing to engage. One school in the United States almost always assumed the former, but developments in the 1970s made it increasingly clear that key players in the Arab world were indeed following their national self-interests. Moreover, while there was broad agreement that US involvement in the Mideast should be viewed in the context of relations with the Soviet Union, there were differences about how to assess US-Soviet ties. Those who thought the United States should work with the Soviets to ease regional tensions argued that Middle East conflict resolution would limit Soviet mischief. Others considered Soviet involvement in regional disputes dangerous and sought to halt the Soviets from supporting Syria and Egypt, among others. These opposing assessments within the Nixon administration hampered US diplomatic efforts.

At the start of his presidency, Richard Nixon seemed to lean toward the first approach, favored by secretary of state William Rogers, and he gave Rogers permission to try a comprehensive approach to the Middle East. The term *comprehensive* came to mean dealing with all the different fronts of the 1967 War, that is, resolution with Egypt, Syria, and Jordan, at least until 1974, when Arab states insisted that Jordan yield its negotiating authority to the Palestinians. The division of authority between Jordan and the Palestinians remained controversial even after Jordan's King Hussein severed ties to the West Bank in 1988. The plan ignored two significant parties—the Arabs and the Israelis—an exclusion that raised suspicion about the viability of the approach since it was drawn up without consulting anyone in the region. Israelis saw that it required virtually nothing of the Arabs, and the Arabs were not interested in peace with Israel even if minimalistic.

Predictably, the Soviets wanted to know how the United States viewed a final settlement. Rogers relayed that it involved returning to the prewar 1967 borders with minor territorial adjustments. In other words, the basis of the Rogers Plan put forward on December 9, 1969, was essentially a standstill cease-fire. There were no direct talks between the Arabs and Israelis, no Arab normalization with Israel, no peace treaty, and no detailed focus on security. Major parties—Egypt, Israel, and the Soviet Union—were opposed to the Rogers Plan. In his memoirs, Henry Kissinger blames the plan's failure on the mistaken assumption, which he opposed, that the United States could curry favor with radical regimes by making concessions:

> I believed that a steady stream of American concessions would increase Soviet temptations to act as the lawyer for Arab radicals. Proponents of an active policy wanted to win the radicals to our side by making generous offers. I argued that the radical regimes could not be won over; their moderation was more likely if we insisted on a changed of course as a precondition of major American involvement.

The Sadat Factor

Diplomacy was deadlocked, but the realities in the region were changing. When Egypt's iconic nationalist leader Gamal Abdel Nasser died in 1970, his vice president, Anwar Sadat, was installed. Some ridiculed Sadat as a lightweight who could not possibly fill Nasser's shoes. However, the new Egyptian leader made it clear from the outset that he was different from other Arab leaders in at least three distinct ways. First, he would not count on others to put forward diplomatic ideas, but would initiate them. Second, if Israel took a meaningful step, he would reciprocate. Finally, he recognized that there were serious disadvantages to linking diplomacy to the goal of achieving a comprehensive peace. This linkage would create a lowest-common-denominator effect and encourage regional spoilers such as Syria, so that the different parties could not proceed to separate agreements with Israel. In other words, Egypt could only reach agreements with Israel if the far more recalcitrant Syria were moving toward Israel at a comparable pace. Sadat saw this as a trap that would make Syria the arbiter of Egypt's diplomatic moves.

Moreover, Sadat gave primacy to Egyptian interests over those of the Palestine Liberation Organization (PLO). In retrospect we can recognize that Nasser's death marked the end of pan-Arab nationalism and Sadat's revised priorities shook the Arab world. While Arab states continued to pay lip service to the idea of pan-Arabism, in practice each country, like Sadat's Egypt, was beginning to prioritize its own national agenda.

In February 1971, Sadat delivered a speech to the Egyptian parliament that echoed an idea being floated by Israeli defense minister Moshe Dayan. As a first step toward breaking the military deadlock, Israel would move its troops away from the Suez Canal. Sadat made clear that he was not offering peace in return. However, his proposal introduced two new ideas, *gradualism* and *nonbelligerency*, that would follow Israeli withdrawal from all the territories won in 1967. That is, peace would come gradually but there would be an end to war. Egypt was not ready for a peace treaty with embassy relations with Israel, and certainly the Arabs were not. Instead, Sadat proposed nonbelligerency, a phase short of peace.

This proposal could be seen as path-breaking, since this was the first time an Arab leader broke with the rejectionism of the Khartoum Conference. Yet it is difficult to assess its impact. Kissinger wrote years later that he was skeptical of the proposal. Had it led to energetic diplomacy in 1971, could this have prevented the outbreak of the 1973 War? Sadat's move may have been a chimera. Among other things, there was no guarantee that the ten thousand Soviet technicians who had been based along the canal during the War of Attrition would actually leave if Israel withdrew, or that Israel was prepared to consider the idea.

The point is that in the absence of diplomatic activity, by the spring of 1973, Sadat was planning to go to war with Israel as the only way to break the deadlock. Sadat's national security advisor returned from secret meetings with Kissinger only to report that the United States would not urge Israel to withdraw from the Sinai. Unwilling to accept the status quo, Sadat held secret talks with Syrian president Hafez al-Assad to decide the dates for the war. At the same time, in public speeches he called 1973 the "year of decision" and advocated using oil as a weapon. But his threats were ignored. Kissinger later admitted publicly, "we did not take

Sadat very seriously," adding that this was because Egypt "was (always) making terrible threats, which he [Sadat] never implemented."

The 1973 War began with a joint Egyptian-Syrian surprise attack on Yom Kippur, the Jewish calendar's holiest day. Earlier that year Sadat had mobilized Egyptian troops twice to deceive Israel into mobilizing its own, reserves-based army. The third time, Israel dismissed the move—but this time it was for real.

The United States expected an Israeli rout, recalling the lightning victory of 1967. However, Egypt used the advantage of surprise to blitz across the Suez Canal and used Soviet surface-to-air missiles to shoot down Israeli planes. Believing it could preserve a very nascent détente with the Soviet Union, in a controversial move, the United States withheld supplying heavy weapons to Israel. Golda Meir was so concerned about Israel's military position she proposed coming incognito to the White House, but the United States demurred, hoping to shape the psychology of postwar diplomacy by enabling the war to end with Egyptian forces on the Israeli-controlled side of the Canal. Emboldened by the lack of Israeli progress and US inaction, Sadat rebuffed a UN Security Council Resolution calling for a cease-fire. But with the Soviet Union's plan to resupply Egypt, the United States saw its prioritization of détente as unfairly exploited and began its delayed airlift of heavy weapons to shift the military dynamics on the ground. The battle subsequently turned in Israel's favor, with Ariel Sharon parachuting troops behind Egyptian lines on the Egyptian side of the canal.

Though it faltered on the battlefield, Egypt effectively mobilized broad Arab support in a successful effort to force US diplomatic involvement. On August 23, 1973, Sadat made an unannounced visit to Saudi Arabia's King Faisal in Riyadh and notified the Saudi monarch of his decision to go to war. Faisal promised Sadat to use oil in support of Egyptian interests. When he met with four visiting Arab foreign ministers led by Saudi foreign minister Omar Saqqaf on October 17, Nixon pledged that then Secretary of State Kissinger, who had soured on prospects of peace since the Rogers Plan, would now be personally enlisted to mediate peace. It was the first time Nixon made such a postwar commitment, and not coincidentally, he made his statement on the very same day that oil ministers met in Kuwait City to discuss raising the price of oil. Bluntly, the United States was trading peace diplomacy for favorable oil prices, a rationale the United States would use several times in the future. On October 18, Nixon expressed optimism that the worst was behind him, reporting to his cabinet:

> [In] meeting with the Arab foreign ministers yesterday, I made the point that we favored a cease-fire and movement towards a peace settlement based on UN Resolution 242. Arab reaction, thus far, to any resupply effort [benefiting Israel] has been restrained and we hope to continue in a manner which avoids confrontation with them.

But his optimism soon proved unfounded. October 20 brought the announcement of an Arab embargo that involved a cut in oil production, a move Kissinger would call "political blackmail." The Arabs had made halfhearted efforts toward an embargo in 1967, but it had gone nowhere. Six years later, rising oil consumption, a lack of US spare capacity, and new rules in Arab ownership of oil revenues enabled Arab states to unilaterally set prices. Whereas in 1947 the United States had imported only about 8 percent of its oil, by 1973 this figure had skyrocketed to 36 percent. The oil embargo sharply affected the world economy, leading to a sustained recession, which ended only in 1975.

But did the oil embargo have much of a political impact? It is worth reflecting on what actually transpired. Arab leaders intended to maintain the embargo until Israel withdrew from all the territories taken in the 1967 war, including East Jerusalem. In fact, the oil embargo lasted only five months. It spurred the United States to push for an Israel-Egypt disengagement agreement—part of which was concluded in January 1974, leading to Israeli troops withdrawing a few miles from the Suez Canal. The embargo also influenced Kissinger's decision to initiate an Israel-Syria disengagement agreement. However, in neither case were the terms dictated by the embargo. The second and more extensive Israel-Egypt agreement occurred that August, as a result of a key US package of quid pro quos, not the embargo. Israel withdrew from the majority of the Sinai only in the wake of Sadat's historic trip to Jerusalem in 1977 and the subsequent Egypt-Israel peace treaty of 1979. In short, the oil embargo did not materially affect the peace negotiations.

Five factors explain why the embargo ended after only five months and show the limits of linking oil to foreign policy. On a purely economic level, an embargo would not be effective over time because while Arabs cut shipments to the United States, they continued to provide to others, and these third parties then shipped oil to the United States, mitigating the embargo's impact. Production cuts could have been effective, but this would have required Organization of the Petroleum Exporting Countries (OPEC) discipline to maximize its profits. OPEC members liked higher oil revenues but were often reluctant to cut production. Thus, Arab production cuts were limited to 9 percent of the fifty million barrels per day of international production. Moreover, oil is a double-edged sword. The Arab states understood that undermining the US economy could have destabilizing economic implications globally, including for them. Indeed, a recession in 1974 and part of 1975 dampened the demand for oil and drove down Saudi revenues. As Saudi oil minister Sheikh Ahmed Zaki Yamani told counterparts, "If you went down, we would go down." It is possible Yamani feared that a fourfold rise in oil prices would lead the United States to pursue alternative energies. Kissinger observed that oil prices reflected economic rather than political conditions. Indeed, oil fluctuated over subsequent decades, so that the price was occasionally lower in real terms than it had been before the embargo.

A second reason the Saudis were not inclined to maintain an embargo strategy is their reliance on the US military for defense and arms acquisitions. So long as there was an embargo, the United States would not sell weapons or enhance other forms of defense cooperation. On January 7, 1974, defense secretary James Schlesinger publicly mentioned the prospect of reprisals against those who perpetrated the embargo. Since the Saudis ultimately counted on the United States as a guarantor of their security, they had an interest in ending the embargo. Thus, national interests took priority over pan-Arab loyalties and Arab-Israeli concerns.

A third reason is that the United States held diplomatic cards in the Mideast, not just military ones. Ultimately, the other Arab states wanted Kissinger to pursue a disengagement agreement with Syria in addition to a first disengagement with Egypt. In principle, Kissinger was keen to do this anyway, to avoid Sadat being exposed as the only Arab leader signing a cease-fire with Israel. Having a more radical Syria engaged would provide Sadat with political cover until the embargo was lifted. A compromise had Kissinger begin an early round of disengagement talks with Damascus before the embargo was lifted on March 18, but in fact his Syria shuttling only began April 29 and ended May 31.

A fourth factor is that the embargo could not be fine-tuned to the bilateral specifications of the Saudis. It was relatively easy to impose an embargo, but a collection of states was required to end it. When some Arab states wanted to lift it in February, Damascus insisted it continue until Kissinger started his new diplomatic mission. Moreover, it became clear that the embargo helped Riyadh's rival, Tehran, since with high oil revenues Iran could buy more weapons and challenge the Arabs, shifting the balance of power in the Persian Gulf. Iraq, another Saudi rival, also benefited from the rising oil prices. Iran's oil revenues jumped from $4.1 billion in 1973 to $17.4 billion in 1974, and Iraqi oil revenues grew from $1.5 billion in 1973 to $6.8 billion in 1974.

Lastly, once the first disengagement agreement was signed, Egypt, the biggest Arab country and the one leading the war effort, lost interest in the embargo. It was Sadat who had first proposed the oil embargo before the war, but his view began to change as his relationship with Kissinger and the United States matured. Nixon insisted that Sadat intercede with Saudi Arabia to have the oil embargo lifted. In December 1973, Kissinger convened the ceremonial opening of the Geneva conference, an international conference co-chaired by the United States and the Soviet Union, as a cover for US-Egyptian bilateral diplomacy, per Sadat's wishes. Nixon wrote Sadat, "Our nations stand at the threshold of a great turning point in history [but] in order to make it possible for me to move decisively it is necessary that the discrimination against the United States which the oil embargo represents be brought to an end." Nixon added, "It is essential that the oil embargo . . . be ended at once. It cannot await the outcome of the current talks on disengagement."

Sadat was not merely responding to US pressure in entering its orbit. The Soviets had no leverage with Israel, and only the United States could help him regain the Sinai. Since the Soviet Union had cut ties with Israel in 1967, in 1974 only Washington had that special relationship with Jerusalem that might persuade Israel to relinquish the land Egypt wanted. At different times, Sadat would say that the United States held "99 percent of the cards" necessary to regain Egyptian land. In short, the linkage idea that the Arab world could leverage their oil power to force the United States to use diplomacy to obtain Israeli military withdrawal was at its zenith for a few short months in 1973–1974 period, but its impact was limited, a short-lived window of opportunity, and not to be repeated

once key Arab states such as Egypt and Saudi Arabia began to prioritize national interests—political and economic—over the multilateral
regional strategy demanded by pan-Arabism. Indeed, since 1974, Egypt
and Saudi Arabia have repeatedly demonstrated that they will always
prioritize their own national security concerns.

Thus, while advocates of linkage saw the Arab states as a bloc, in reality they were divided by rivalries among themselves and with Iran. Saudi
Arabia and Egypt needed a strong United States and a strong domestic
economy. Riyadh feared that high oil revenues—even if sustainable for
only a short time—would disproportionately favor Tehran. The Arab
embargo might put pressure on the United States, but it could also back-
fire and produce an American reaction against the Arabs.

In short, US-brokered disengagement agreements with Egypt led simultaneously to a partial return of the Sinai, much closer ties with the
United States, and a further Egyptian pivot away from the Soviet Union.
This paved the way for Sadat's historic trip to Jerusalem in 1977, which
accelerated his recovery of Egyptian territory. The Egypt-Israel peace
treaty of 1979, the first between Israel and an Arab state—the biggest of
them all, no less—thus originated with Kissinger's diplomacy.

Kissinger's postwar diplomacy succeeded because he recognized and
seized on Sadat's willingness to leave the Soviet orbit. He saw in Sadat an
Arab leader willing to make a move, albeit incremental, toward peace,
and thereby able to diminish the Soviet role in the region. As a result,
the United States moved closer to Egypt and Israel simultaneously, and
the terms of the second Sinai disengagement of 1975 created a de facto
alliance between the United States and Israel.

The Road to Sadat's Visit to Jerusalem and Beyond

President Jimmy Carter's administration, like that of his predecessor,
was solicitous of the Arab states. It was also the first to deal directly with
the Palestinian issue. However, like Nixon, Carter also failed to grasp
underlying regional dynamics—including inter-Arab rivalries. The comprehensive approach his administration tried to impose failed to account
for national interests, especially Egypt's. The plan did not accommodate
Sadat, who jettisoned Carter's comprehensive Geneva conference framework and, without consulting Carter, headed to Jerusalem. That trip,

highlighted by Sadat's speech in the Knesset, remains the emotional high-water mark of Israeli-Arab relations. Golda Meir, who as prime minister led Israel during the 1973 War against Egypt, observed when Sadat visited Israel that it was "as if the Messiah had almost arrived."

To understand this historical moment in the peace process, it is important to recognize that Sadat's visit to Israel came not as a result of Carter's efforts, but in spite of them. To be fair, President Carter shifted gears following Sadat's lead, both to support Sadat's move and to test if he could engage other Arab players. Carter's involvement proved critical in securing the Egypt-Israel peace treaty of March 1979. But American diplomatic failures through much of 1977 prompted Sadat to go off on his own. So how did US strategy fail? Why did Carter miss Sadat's signals that he disapproved of the US approach?

President Carter came to power wanting to change many of the features of Henry Kissinger's Middle East diplomacy. Carter aimed to end gradualism and bilateralism and the marginalization of the Soviet Union, and to open a new focus on the Palestinians. Whereas Kissinger had set up a negotiating track with incremental moves such as disengagements, Carter sought to grapple with all the core issues in order to make peace immediately. His plan comprised the following goals:

- One aim was to replace bilateralism with a comprehensive Middle East peace conference. Kissinger had convened a Geneva conference, co-chaired with the Soviet Union, in December 1973, in theory, to demonstrate superpower cooperation. In practice, Geneva only convened for one day, and Syria was not in attendance. Kissinger believed Geneva served little function except to rubber-stamp what was already agreed upon with the parties separately. Carter's reinvigorated approach to Geneva was more to the liking of Arab states because it provided collective Arab bargaining. This meant that all peace tracks were linked and subject to the lowest common denominator. In other words, any agreement between Israel and its neighbors—Egypt, Jordan, Syria, and the Palestinians—could be blocked by the objection of any one participant. No peace agreement with Israel could be complete until each individual agreement was concluded.
- Another aim, shared by Carter and secretary of state Cyrus Vance, was that the United States should work closely with the Soviets as part of a broader détente policy between the two countries.

While Kissinger had wanted to sideline the Soviets in the Mideast, Carter and Vance viewed détente as a more extensive enterprise of cooperation without regional caveats. They thought the United States could coordinate Middle East policy with Moscow, and wrongly believed that Moscow could deliver Syria and the PLO to negotiations with the Israelis.

- Carter was also the first American leader to call for a Palestinian homeland (in the spring of 1977) some three years after the 1974 Arab summit shifted responsibility for negotiations from Jordan to the PLO. Israel viewed this change in US policy negatively. It believed bilateral diplomacy had a better chance of success and that overly ambitious goals would emphasize collective Arab bargaining to Israel's disadvantage. Moreover, Israel saw the Soviets as a radicalizing force since Moscow had cut ties with Israel in 1967 and armed its enemies. Consequently, Carter's relations with Israel in 1977 were fraught. In his first nine months in office, Carter sparred with top Israelis of both moderate and conservative governments— prime minister Yitzhak Rabin, prime minister Menachem Begin, and foreign minister Moshe Dayan. Dayan famously remarked to Carter during a particularly contentious conversation, "Mr. President, I only have one eye, but I am not blind."

Carter thought Sadat would approve a comprehensive peace conference. After all, Arab leaders had told the United States that they sought such a solution. But Geneva was never reconvened. Apparently the turning point for Sadat was Carter's October 1, 1977, joint US-Soviet communiqué outlining the president's blueprint for a comprehensive Middle East peace conference. There had been no prior give-and-take with Egypt or Israel, and the joint statement that William Quandt, who worked in the Carter White House, later called a "political error, showing considerable amateurishness" startled both parties.

Paradoxically, their objections to the joint communiqué and Carter's attempts to reinstate the Geneva conference were driving Israel's leaders and Sadat together. Yitzhak Rabin, Begin's predecessor, read the joint communiqué as "the beginning of a process aimed at political solution imposed by the two powers, with the coercion directed primarily against Israel. It is known today that the Soviet and American positions are identical, that is, withdrawal to the lines of 4 June 1967." Sadat was keen on making rapid progress on the Egyptian-Israeli negotiating track and had already told Carter privately, in their initial meeting in April 1977, that Egypt was ready to sign a peace agreement with Israel. At US behest over the summer, Egypt had also drafted a peace treaty. Remarkably, three days after the US-Soviet October 1 statement, Sadat sent Carter a personal note urging the United States to do nothing "to prevent Israel and Egypt from negotiating directly." Sadat still did not reject the Geneva conference in his October 4 note but stated clearly that Geneva should be used merely to ratify what the parties had already achieved on their own, as was the case in Kissinger's time.

What accounts for Sadat's negative reaction to the joint communiqué? Carter's national security advisor, Zbigniew Brzezinski, later speculated that Sadat veered after seeing Carter seemingly retreat from the joint communiqué following a tough meeting with Moshe Dayan on October 4. However, Brzezinski's theory that Sadat viewed Carter as unreliable in the face of Israeli pressure is not supported by the facts. As Carter noted in his diary that day and later recorded in his memoir, *Keeping Faith*, foreign minister Ismail Fahmy delivered Sadat's October 4 letter before Carter and Dayan met in New York that evenng. Carter notes that Fahmy, who resigned when Sadat announced his trip to Jerusalem, did not like the message. It was not Carter's retreat from the joint communiqué that soured Sadat on Carter's peace initiative, but three other factors.

First, a secret Egypt-Israel bilateral negotiating track had started a few weeks earlier, and Sadat apparently worried that Carter's initiative might preempt its prospects. With the intervention of Morocco's King Hassan, secret talks were launched between Israeli foreign minister Moshe Dayan and Egyptian deputy prime minister Hassan Tuhami in the Moroccan capital of Rabat on September 16. In his memoirs, Dayan records that Tuhami viewed Geneva as merely a place to sign an agreement. King Hassan hoped to use the meeting as a prelude to a Sadat-Begin private session. While there is no evidence to suggest that Tuhami and Dayan cut a deal in Rabat—indeed, neither was empowered to do so—it seems that Tuhami's report to Sadat was enough to convince him that a breakthrough was possible. Indeed, according to Muhammad Heikal, authoritative chronicler and confidant to both Sadat and Nasser, Sadat raised the private talks with Dayan when the two met on the first evening of Sadat's historic visit to Jerusalem. However, although Dayan informed Vance of the secret channel two weeks before the joint communiqué was issued, the United States proceeded on October 1 as if this groundbreaking negotiation had never occurred. At best, Carter ignored the back channel that Egypt and Israel had opened up for direct communication. And while there is little evidence that Carter intended the Geneva framework to thwart the Egyptian-Israel diplomatic effort, the proposed framework did give Syria a de facto veto. As Carter envisioned it, the Geneva summit would allow Syria not merely to set the pace of progress but to determine whether there would be any progress at all. In Sadat's view, al-Assad was not committed to peace, and the proposed negotiations' format spelled disaster for Egypt. As Nicholas Veliotes, a senior State Department official responsible for Arab-Israeli affairs and subsequently ambassador to Egypt, commented later, "Sadat possessed the fundamental and unalterable preference to keep control of all negotiating decisions in Cairo's hands, and not let them fall into the Syrian preference for a unified Arab delegation." US Ambassador to Egypt Hermann Eilts emphasized Sadat's displeasure with Syria's procedural procrastination when he addressed the Carter administration's preliminary questions about Geneva before October: "To [Sadat's] horror and distress, there was no response from the Syrians. Weeks went by, and Sadat began to say, 'Peace is slipping through my fingers for procedural reasons.'"

A second factor that contributed to Sadat's disquiet with the Carter approach embodied in the joint communiqué was his fear of Soviet Union reentry into Middle East diplomacy. Sadat understood Soviet interests as more aligned with the USSR's client in Damascus and less with its erstwhile proxy in Cairo, which had spurned Moscow. Having made the transition toward closer ties to the United States, he was skeptical that the Soviet Union had any useful role to play. In Veliotes's assessment, "Sadat had just expelled the Soviets out of Egypt and now Carter was letting the Soviets back in. Sadat surely did not like that." The other diplomats in the State Department's Bureau of Near East Affairs were similarly unhappy that the Carter administration was bringing the Soviets back after Sadat had sidelined them as part of Kissinger's diplomacy. Carter's move made the United States appear unreliable and untrustworthy. Veliotes's comments reflect Heikal's claim that the October 1 statement "angered Sadat, who did not want the Soviet Union to be involved." Heikal quoted Sadat as complaining, in the days after the statement was issued, "We kicked the Russians out of the door and now Mr. Carter is bringing them back in through the window."

Third, as indicated in his letter to Carter on October 4, Sadat wanted to pursue his own national strategy and wanted to avoid a format that would give Syria and the Soviet Union leverage over decision making. But Carter still adhered to Geneva. He wrote to Sadat on October 21 and, in his own handwriting, urged Sadat to publicly endorse the Geneva conference. President Carter referenced the current impasse, declaring: "The time has now come to move forward and your early public endorsement of our approach is extremely important—perhaps vital—in advancing all parties to Geneva."

Some have seen this as a plea to Sadat to do something dramatic to break the stalemate, and thus as inspiring his trip to Jerusalem. Heikal recalls the exchange with Romanian leader Nicolae Ceausescu, when Sadat wanted to know if Begin was willing and strong enough to make peace. Ceausescu insisted Begin had that strength. On that same trip, Sadat also visited Saudi Arabia. According to Heikal, Sadat "explained to Crown Prince Fahd that he felt American efforts were stuck and that some form of negotiation with Israel would be necessary. Not knowing what Sadat was planning, Fahd could only give general encouragement, wishing the Egyptian president luck in his effort."

Sadat notified Carter of his decision to go to Jerusalem on November 8, just one day before his dramatic public announcement in Egypt's parliament. This was the full extent of US-Egyptian consultation between the leaders on the eve of Sadat's historic trip. Carter's initial response was hostile. According to Stuart Eizenstat, Carter's top domestic aide, Carter said he was "very upset" and wanted to criticize Sadat publicly for "ripping apart" the possibility of a comprehensive settlement. Fortunately for Carter, he held his tongue. According to Veliotes, State Department officials were delighted but feared making public statements because of White House commitment to Geneva.

Clearly President Carter misread the mistrust between Egypt and Syria, Egypt's antipathy toward the Soviets, and Sadat's interest in a bilateral channel with Israel. Above all, he failed to recognize that after the 1973 War, Egypt concluded that it had done its duty for the Palestinian cause and would now give Egyptian national interests priority over pan-Arabism. As Heikal explains, food riots had occurred across Egypt earlier that year protesting a rise in prices. With the Egyptian military demobilized in 1977, Sadat could not meet rising economic expectations. Heikal insisted that as a result of these riots and a failed grab at Libyan oil that spring, Sadat felt a need by mid-1977 "to negotiate a new relationship with Israel."

Nor did Carter understand that Sadat was a proud Egyptian nationalist above all. When asked if he feared being isolated by other Arabs, Sadat replied that the Arabs could only isolate themselves, not Egypt. Sadat's electrifying visit to Jerusalem and his break from the Carter framework demonstrated that Egypt, the largest Arab state, was intent on pursuing national, rather than regional, Arab interests.

To be fair, Carter recognized the value of an Egypt-Israel peace treaty, once he realized that a comprehensive peace was not possible. He agreed with Begin and Sadat at Camp David that the parties should create a framework for Palestinian self-government before tackling Arab-Israeli territorial solutions. Carter was relentless in making the summit a success and promised that if reelected in 1980, he would reengage on the Palestinian issue.

The first peace treaty between Israel and an Arab country produced its share of ironies. Among them, a few stand out. Carter opposed Sadat's separate approach that he saw as torpedoing his comprehensive Geneva initiative but was key to the signing of the Egypt-Israel peace treaty on March 26, 1979. Begin, a known hardliner on territorial issues, was the father of the first Israel peace treaty that led to Israel yielding the entire Sinai. Begin's willingness to give up 100 percent of the Sinai created a precedent for Arabs interpreting Resolution 242 to mean yielding all or some of the land for peace. Finally, Sadat—initially viewed as unworthy to fill the shoes of the renowned Nasser—put diplomacy in play as a result of his trip to Jerusalem. He reclaimed every inch of Sinai territory and by removing Cairo precluded a viable war coalition against Israel. The idea of land for peace, as envisioned by Resolution 242, was vindicated.

The Aborted London Agreement

The 1982 War in Lebanon and its aftermath shaped much of Arab-Israeli relations during the 1980s, yet there is one peace-related episode that deserves attention, given its far-reaching consequences: the aborted 1987 London understanding between Jordan's King Hussein and Israeli foreign minister Shimon Peres. Although formally the 1974 Arab League summit in Rabat gave the PLO the mandate to negotiate the future of the West Bank, it was the failure of the London agreement that led Jordan to relinquish its role as Arab interlocutor. This change was due to the PLO's international ascendency in the early 1970s as a Third World liberation movement, the fact that Jordan sat out the 1973 War, and enmity between PLO chairman Yasser Arafat and King Hussein. The 1970 Black September conflict, in which Palestinians fired on Jordanians and Jordan responded by killing thousands of Palestinians, was not easily forgotten. Hussein saw Arafat's militancy inside Jordan as an effort to create a state within a state, designed to topple him.

Thus, even after the Rabat summit Hussein retained the idea that he would yet regain control of the West Bank, of special significance because of the Al-Aqsa Mosque in East Jerusalem for which his family, the Hashemites, remained custodians. Indeed, Hussein's intention overlay the most important fault line in Israeli politics, with Labor favoring the Jordanian option of yielding most of the West Bank, and Likud firmly convinced that only self-rule suited the Palestinians who lived there. This disagreement came to a head in 1987.

Hussein and Peres met secretly in London on April 11, 1987. Peres alerted secretary of state George Shultz before the meeting and briefed him immediately afterward. The proposal was an international conference that would provide political cover for direct talks between Israel and Jordan about the West Bank. The UN would host the event, which would include the permanent members of the UN Security Council plus Israel and the Arab parties. The basis of participation would be accepting UNSC Resolutions 242 and 338, yet it would be clear that the bilateral committees between the parties, including one between Israel and Jordan, would be responsible for working out solutions.

A number of obstacles prevented realization of the plan. Complicating matters was that Peres was part of a national unity government with rival Likud. After a two-year rotation in 1986, Peres and Yitzchak Shamir switched positions, so now Shamir was prime minister and Peres served under him as foreign minister. This put the United States in a bind, as Peres was hoping Shultz would intervene with Prime Minister

Shamir even before Peres himself had briefed him. In essence, Peres wanted the London agreement recast as a US initiative, believing Shamir would automatically dismiss any idea coming from his Labor rival. As Shultz recalled in his memoirs, "the situation was explosive, especially because Shamir and his Likud party were vociferously denouncing the idea of an international conference of any kind." International parties were crucial to provide political cover to Hussein, as Jordan had not been the official Arab interlocutor since 1974. However, Shamir objected to President Reagan that an international conference would introduce the Soviets back into the Middle East. While Shultz refused to put the conference forward as an American plan, believing it was deceptive, he wanted to explore the substance and achieved Soviet agreement to serving only a ceremonial role. However, Shamir was not convinced the Soviets would confine themselves to a ceremonial role and feared they would align with the Arabs, forcing Jordan to harden its position.

When Shamir and Hussein met directly to discuss their differences in the summer of 1987, Hussein came away convinced that Shamir did not want to yield the West Bank under any circumstances, irrespective of the format of the conference. Meanwhile, Shultz tried to short-circuit Israeli concerns about the possible coercive nature of an international conference by restructuring the conference under the auspices of an existing US-Soviet summit. According to Shultz's memoirs, Shamir was willing to meet in such a setting, but Hussein demurred, and on October 30, 1987, he communicated to Shultz that he distrusted Shamir's intentions.

The failure of the Jordanian option increased public despair in the West Bank, leading to the First Intifada or uprising, which began on December 9. King Hussein announced a Jordanian disengagement from the West Bank on July 1, 1988, leaving the Palestinians to negotiate with Israel for the land. Israeli security officials privately concurred that the failure of London may have been Israel's greatest mistake following 1967. Israel had had a covert relationship with Hussein since the 1960s and viewed the Hashemite Kingdom as a stabilizing force in the region. The aborted London agreement left Arafat and the PLO as Israel's sole interlocutor.

First Intifada, the End of the Cold War/
Gulf War, and the Madrid Peace Conference

Although the First Intifada did not threaten Israel's existence or even its overall control of the territories, it undermined individual Israelis' sense of personal security and drew increasing media attention to the plight of the Palestinians. With the Palestinians garnering international attention and King Hussein having renounced Jordanian claims to the West Bank, the United States embarked upon its first dialogue with the PLO during the twilight days of the Reagan administration. There are clear indications that, relying on the Reagan administration's credibility with the Israeli government, incoming secretary of state James Baker asked Reagan's national security advisor, Colin Powell, to make the move. An administration about to leave office could afford to risk such a controversial move, but the US-PLO dialogue was short-lived. The PLO refused to condemn an abortive seaborne attack on a beach near Tel Aviv or punish its perpetrator, a member of the PLO Executive Committee. The attack, and Washington's response to it, undermined the PLO's bid to participate in the peace process.

However, peace appeared to be a genuine possibility as a result of Iraq's invasion of Kuwait in August 1990 and the subsequent Gulf War that fundamentally altered the Middle East's political landscape. Iraq's defeat by a US-led coalition of European and Arab countries neutralized the greatest potential threat to Israel and temporarily suppressed a major source of Arab radicalism. At the same time, the war sharply eroded the position of the PLO. The Palestinians had enthusiastically embraced Saddam Hussein's call for pan-Arabism and applauded his threat to the rich Gulf kingdoms. They cheered his call to liberate Jerusalem and his use of Scud missiles against Israeli civilians during the war. Saudi Arabia and Kuwait responded to the former by cutting off the aid that provided the bulk of the PLO annual budget and expelled hundreds of thousands of Palestinian workers whose remittances sustained the West Bank economy.

Recognizing the political upheaval in the Middle East as an opportunity to advance the peace process, Washington launched a diplomatic initiative in cooperation with Moscow that resulted in the October 1991

Madrid Peace Conference. Israel conditioned its attendance on Palestinians' participation as part of the Jordanian delegation, excluding members of the PLO, residents of East Jerusalem, and Diaspora Palestinians.
Desperate to regain their footing and confident that they could control
the Palestinian negotiations from PLO headquarters in Tunis, Arafat
and his dominant Fatah faction grudgingly accepted these conditions
and forced the decision on the rest of the organization.

The structure of the Madrid Peace Conference, painstakingly worked
out between Secretary of State Baker and the parties, was a ceremonial
opening that would quickly transition to direct bilateral negotiations
between Israel and the Syrian, Lebanese, and joint Jordan-Palestinian
delegations. But each front was stalled.

Rabin's Road to Oslo

In mid-1992 Yitzhak Rabin was elected Israel's new prime minister.
Rabin was touted as Israel's de Gaulle, the general turned statesman.
He was the IDF chief of staff when Israel won the territories in 1967,
more than tripling the size of Israel. He had served one term as prime
minister between 1974 and 1977 and was defense minister from 1984 to
1990. A centrist, he believed that Begin and Shamir's Likud ideological
focus on settlements and retaining control of the whole of Eretz Yisrael
(i.e., the territories) was misguided, a security liability and not an asset.
As Israel's ambassador to Washington from 1968 to 1973, Rabin valued
close ties with the United States and thought Israel should capitalize on
the strategic opening offered by the collapse of the Soviet Union and
the major blow dealt to Arab radicalism in the Gulf War. Given the
dominant US standing after the Cold and Gulf Wars, now was the time
to move. In his 1992 campaign Rabin advocated a "new order of priorities," giving precedence to domestic concerns such as unemployment
and infrastructure over ideologically motivated spending in the West
Bank. His narrow victory in 1992 was Labor's first return to power since
the Likud's ascent fifteen years earlier and significantly advanced the
peace process.

Rabin and his government were much more flexible, particularly regarding territorial compromise. But while they considered the Palestinian issue the heart of the Arab-Israel conflict, like the Likud they rejected

direct negotiations with the PLO. Yet this position evolved dramatically in 1993 in response to developments. For one thing, nine months after Rabin assumed office, it was apparent that West Bank Palestinians did not accept his leading campaign promise of an autonomy deal. Moreover, they would not act without PLO approval. Rabin deported four hundred members of Hamas to a Lebanese hilltop believing they were intimidating the Palestinians, but to no avail. Finally, it became apparent that the PLO was more flexible tactically than prominent Palestinians from East Jerusalem and the West Bank like Faisal Husseini and Hanan Ashrawi. Possibilities were tested in early 1993 in secret talks in Norway between the PLO and Israeli academics spearheaded by Yossi Beilin, a protégé of then foreign minister Peres. The meetings came on the heels of a new law that rescinded contact between the PLO and Israelis. Beilin alerted Peres, who in turn alerted Rabin. Rabin was skeptical at first, but his views began to change in the spring of 1993. At the time, front-channel negotiations at the State Department were gridlocked, with Palestinians unwilling to take Jerusalem off the table for the period of autonomy. However, the PLO, marginalized in the region following the Gulf War, proved more flexible regarding Jerusalem in the early phase of peace talks. By May 1993, the secret Oslo talks were official and Rabin personally guided them.

The core of Oslo was a declaration of principles that defined what the parties could agree to now, while deferring the toughest issues until confidence could be built over a five-year period. First, the Palestinians would set up a proto-government in Gaza and Jericho. It would spread to all Palestinian West Bank cities shortly thereafter. Arafat, viewed in Israel as an archterrorist, would be setting up a government on Israel's doorstep. Beyond the programmatic specifics about who would have what authority in the West Bank, Israel and the PLO agreed to mutual recognition. This marked the first time after many decades that the two national movements, one Jewish and one Palestinian, recognized that the other existed. On September 13, 1993, at a dramatic White House ceremony, Rabin and Arafat signed a Declaration of Principles and, prompted by President Clinton, also shook hands. Rabin's body language conveyed that he felt conflicted shaking hands with someone he judged to have much blood on his hands. Yet Rabin was never a sentimentalist. He made the move at Oslo fully aware that Israel was embarking on a difficult road. He preferred a path leading to partitioning the land to putting two other values at risk: preserving Israel's character as a nation-state of the Jewish people and as a democracy.

The road was indeed difficult. In mass rallies, Likud members as well as settlers and their sympathizers charged that Rabin had no right to yield Israel's biblical patrimony. Pressure came not only from the Israeli right but also from Hamas, which began blowing up Israeli buses to ensure that the peace process would fail. Yet for Israel Oslo also presented opportunities. The covert Israel-Jordan relationship dating back to the 1960s was no longer encumbered by Palestinian sensibilities. A peace treaty between Israel and Jordan was signed on their southern Arava border, witnessed by President Clinton on October 26, 1994. Israel was suddenly being invited to regional economic conferences with Arabs. The Gulf and North African Arabs participated with Israel in multilateral peace talks dealing with water and arms control issues. Economic growth rose sharply as international investment increased. For Arafat, Oslo represented a reprieve from irrelevance but did not significantly advance PLO standing in the region.

Nevertheless, demonstrations against Rabin's peace efforts intensified, including threats to his life. On November 4, 1995, after speaking at a pro-peace demonstration in Tel Aviv, he was assassinated by a right-wing Orthodox Israeli student, Yigal Amir, who believed Rabin had no authority to yield land divinely promised to the Jews. Leaders around the world mourned Rabin's death while at his funeral President Clinton, King Hussein, and Egypt's Hosni Mubarak gave moving eulogies in memory of their beloved friend and the peace he so courageously pursued.

Netanyahu Inherits Oslo

Shimon Peres, Rabin's longtime rival, succeeded him, pledging to follow Rabin's legacy of peace, an idea that had become associated with both. Peres investigated a possible peace with Syria, but Syrian president Hafez Assad was uninterested. In sympathy with the death of Rabin, polls showed that Peres would handily win the next election; however, after Israel's targeted killing of Hamas's Yihye Ayyash, nicknamed "the engineer" for his involvement in suicide bombings, Hamas struck back with four suicide bombings against Israelis in nine days. The mood in Israel shifted, and polls showed Likud opposition leader Benjamin Netanyahu neck and neck with Peres. Leaders around the world mobilized to stand with Peres, convening a conference against terrorism. Clinton appeared with Peres both at the conference in the Middle East and in Washington. Yet it was not enough. Netanyahu, a vociferous critic of Rabin and Oslo, edged out Peres in the May 1996 election.

Netanyahu promised to uphold Oslo because it was the law of the land, and within his first few months in office, he met with Arafat. But his assurances that he would not overturn Oslo left uncertain whether he would advance it. During his first term, Netanyahu took two key steps that suggested he might do more than expected. In January 1997, he agreed to implement Oslo II in Hebron. This was no small matter given that Hebron, considered the burial site of the Jewish patriarchs and matriarchs—more than any other West Bank city—was imbued with religious significance for Palestinians and Israelis alike. Four hundred settlers inhabited a Jewish neighborhood inside Hebron and seven thousand settlers lived just beyond, in Kiryat Arba. US special Middle East envoy Dennis Ross headed the US effort to broker the Hebron deal. Netanyahu's agreement to cede Hebron might have been seen as the end of the movement spearheaded by the Israeli right seeking to retain control of the whole of Eretz Yisrael and as an unthinkable concession. Yet Netanyahu himself would probably admit it was not exactly a "Nixon goes to China moment" either. In a counterbalancing move to keep the right together and reinforce Israel's hold on East Jerusalem, construction began on Har Homa, a new neighborhood wedged between Bethlehem and Beit Sahur, an Arab neighborhood adjacent to the Old City walls.

Netanyahu's second big move would be agreeing to the Wye River Accord in October 1998, an effort led by President Clinton to ensure that Israel proceeded with further Oslo-mandated interim West Bank pullouts. It was a move from which Netanyahu would not recover. At Wye River, Netanyahu implicitly accepted the idea that if his right-wing coalition fractured as a result of further pullouts, Labor could be Netanyahu's safety net. The Labor party was headed by a Rabin protégé and Israel's most decorated wunderkind soldier, Ehud Barak. Pledges were made not to let Netanyahu fall over the peace issue. But the hard right was furious at Netanyahu's concessions at Wye, and the coalition collapsed. Netanyahu subsequently confided to his closest aides that the lesson he learned from Wye was if you lose "the base," you lose power.

Barak Tries Syrian Breakthrough

Barak's ascent to power in 1999 reawakened hope that peace was possible. His leading campaign promise was that within a year of taking office he would extricate Israel from Lebanon, where the army had been mired since 1982. Israel had minimized its deployment along the Lebanese border, leaving much of the area in the mid-1980s. Technology had made Israel's buffer zone in southern Lebanon irrelevant as Katyusha rockets could be fired over the buffer areas. Given Damascus's control of Lebanon, Barak needed to prioritize the Syrian peace track. And if a peace deal could not be worked out with Syria, Israel would withdraw unilaterally.

Barak attempted to end the entire Israeli-Arab conflict in short order as Clinton, Barak's peace partner, had only a year and a half left in office. If Clinton had misgivings, he did not try to second-guess the Israeli leader, a protégé of Rabin who was willing to advance peace on multiple fronts. Until March 2000, Barak concentrated on the Syrian track, a focus that had both advantages and disadvantages. On the plus side, the Golan Heights was clearly defined and, unlike the West Bank, free from biblical resonances and with few Jewish settlements. Moreover, there was the tantalizing prospect that peace could divide Syria from its backer, Iran.

However, there was no Israeli peace camp supporting a deal with Syria. Israelis saw Assad as an authoritarian leader who routinely facilitated the flow of Iranian weapons to the militant Hezbollah. Since secretary of state Warren Christopher's shuttle diplomacy during Clinton's first term, Assad had studiously avoided any gesture that might enhance Israelis' sense of security. Part of his appeal at home was that, unlike Egypt's Sadat, he would not accommodate Israel. However, by the end of 1999, Assad was getting old and wanted to ensure political succession for his son Bashar after his older son, Basil, was killed in a car accident. The United States initiated a quiet round of intense diplomacy in Shepardstown, West Virginia, in January 2000, but on the eve of Shepardstown there was a massive demonstration in Israel. Barak got cold feet and sent word he could not offer the Golan Heights in return for diplomatic ties with Syria.

A key sticking point dating back to Rabin's period had been Assad's insistence that Syria's sovereignty extend beyond the Golan Heights to the shore of Lake Kinneret. Syrian proximity and sovereignty extending to Israel's major water source was far more complicated than having Assad on the Heights. Syria had hoped a businessman and associate of Netanyahu's named Ronald Lauder could deliver the final concessions. Barak enlisted Clinton to close the deal with Assad in Geneva in March 2000, thinking Clinton might be able to persuade Assad to accept land away from the shore area. Within minutes, Assad demurred, ending the Syria track just three months before he died.

With prospects of peace with Syria now forgone, a chaotic unilateral pullback from Lebanon ensued in May 2000, almost eighteen years after Israel first entered Lebanon. Hezbollah leader Hassan Nasrallah responded by calling on Palestinians to learn that you do not negotiate with Israel, rather you engage in force. Already suspicious, as settlement activity continued during Barak's term, the Palestinians resumed violence on the anniversary of Israel's founding, dubbed al-Nakba ("The Catastrophe"). In retrospect, it was a precursor for the next uprising.

Run-up to Camp David and Beyond

Barak now returned attention to an agreement with the Palestinians. The toughest issues would be addressed at a Camp David summit, but he and top advisors hoped that more minor problems could be resolved in preliminary meetings. However, internecine Palestinian rivalry between Ahmed Querie (Abu Ala) and Mahmoud Abbas (Abu Mazen) derailed the talks in Sweden in the spring of 2000. Abu Ala saw quiet talks in Sweden as a way to narrow the differences between the parties and minimize the number of issues to be discussed in a summit format. Indeed, comparable preparatory talks held in 1978 in Leeds Castle between Egypt and Israel prior to the first Camp David had been pivotal. However, the talks between Abu Ala and the Israeli team involving Israeli foreign minister Shlomo Ben-Ami and top Ehud Barak aide Gilead Sher were immediately leaked, it is widely believed by Abu Mazen, who had been excluded from the talks.

Arafat refused to prepare the Palestinian public for possible compromises. Perhaps the takeaway for the United States should have been:
"If you don't signal compromise, you may not actually be willing to
compromise." Before Clinton would engage in a high-stakes summit,
he dispatched national security advisor Sandy Berger to explore Barak's
bottom lines. Apparently Barak was not forthcoming, fearing that any
concessions would become the floor and not the ceiling in future talks.

Nevertheless, as Barak knew, there was little time left. Clinton did not
want to engage in a messy summit during a general presidential election
when he would soon be leaving office. Moreover, Barak's coalition was
quickly fraying and would soon unravel. To be adequately addressed the
complicated details of the summit require a separate essay, but suffice it
to say that Camp David, which convened in July, failed, and its failure
had long-lasting consequences. Clinton angered Palestinians by blaming
Arafat for the summit's failure. After the summit, Arafat visited Muslim
countries, defending himself for not yielding more to Barak, and report-
edly telling the leader of Indonesia that Israel would not be around in a
hundred years, so major concessions were unnecessary.

While the negotiators agreed to keep talking, their effort was soon
eclipsed by the Second Intifada. It was leaked that during Camp David,
Arafat denied that the Jews ever had a Temple in Jerusalem, angering
President Clinton. Embroiled in a domestic political rivalry with Benjamin Netanyahu, Likud opposition party leader Ariel Sharon declared his
right to walk on the Temple Mount and did so with hundreds of police-
men in tow. The Palestinians rioted in response and the Second Intifada
erupted in September 2000. Was the Intifada a spontaneous uprising
or a prepared and deliberate use of violence to affect negotiations? The
debate is not likely to be resolved. It seems clear, however, that Arafat
made no visible effort to halt the violence. The United States, along with
Egyptian president Mubarak, tried to bring the parties together at Sharm
el-Sheikh to resume talks and contain the violence. Despite their efforts,
the Second Intifada continued unabated.

Clinton persisted, and in December 2000 he proposed the Clinton
Parameters, a range of solutions on contentious issues related to borders, refugees, and Jerusalem. Despite opposition in Israel, Barak was
willing to accept the Clinton Parameters, but Arafat was not. A last-
ditch effort by the parties at Taba—a tiny resort on the Egyptian side of

the border with Israel—timed to begin the day after Clinton left office, fell short. The Barak era began with hopes for completing Rabin's legacy but ended in violence that shattered dreams for peace. Increasingly, Arafat charged that any deal with Israel demanded too many concessions, and he viewed concession as tantamount to betrayal. His attitude is particularly well illustrated by negotiations over the right of return for Palestinian refugees. Arafat, who was part of the post-1948 era, had told refugees of that period to keep their keys to their pre-1948 homes as they would be heading back. Over the course of negotiations it became evident that Israel would not be willing to permit those Palestinians who had left in 1948 to return some fifty years later together with their families. The most realistic solution was that most Palestinians could move to the new State of Palestine in the West Bank. But the gap of expectations inherent in this possibility was too great, and Arafat preferred to have no deal at all than to be charged with having capitulated on this issue.

Gaza Disengagement

The failure of Israelis and Palestinians to end the conflict at the end of the Clinton administration in 2000 preceded four tragic years of the Second Intifada. Over one thousand Israelis and about four thousand Palestinians were killed. New US president George W. Bush would invariably view the intifada through the prism of the 9/11 terror attack of 2001 on the United States Arafat, blamed for Camp David's failure, was now the chief culprit of an uprising that at best he had done nothing to stop. Ariel Sharon emerged as Israel's new leader, as Israel was looking for a fighter since Ehud Barak's peace efforts had failed. The idea of diplomacy now looked hopeless: Sharon was not Barak and Bush was not Clinton; Arafat resumed his former engagement in violence. Yet even in this context there were promising developments, not all of which were directly related to Israelis and Palestinians. In the immediate wake of 9/11, Bush wanted to cement Arab support for a war on terror. Speaking at the United Nations in 2001, Bush was the first American president to announce US support for a Palestinian state. However, his commitment was to a future Palestinian state founded on principles of democratic reform. Moreover, he believed Arafat had lied to him when he denied any connection to the Karine-A incident, when Israel intercepted shipments of Iranian arms intended for Gaza. On June 25, 2002, Bush gave a speech declaring that he did not view Arafat as an interlocutor for peace. This marked the end of nine years of diplomatic investment in Arafat since the White House handshake.

In the period leading up to the Iraq war of 2003, British prime minister Tony Blair was under sharp domestic attack for joining the Bush war effort and for not significantly advancing the cause of Israeli-Palestinian peace. In an effort to help Blair, the White House proposed a Roadmap, a phased approach to solving the Israeli-Palestinian conflict. Unfortunately, the parties had not been consulted on the Roadmap and their commitment to it was limited at best. Moreover, Arafat was still a player. While the Second Intifada raged on, he was hunkered down in his Ramallah compound. Earlier that year, Mahmoud Abbas had been appointed premier to promote the idea of reform. However, Arafat did not support Abbas's control of the security services, and Abbas resigned by the end of the summer of 2003.

The Abbas resignation signaled the doom of Bush's desired institutional reform and left a diplomatic vacuum, one Sharon feared would be filled by far-reaching initiatives. Specifically, he was wary of the Geneva Initiative, which stipulated that Israel should withdraw from approximately 98 percent of the West Bank. Its authors, Yossi Beilin and Yasser Abed Rabbo, were invited to a meeting with secretary of state Colin Powell. Given the enthusiastic reactions in many European capitals, Sharon felt Israel needed to put forward its own idea. He also saw risks in perpetuating the status quo. Once the right-wing's leading icon, Sharon now publicly labeled Israel's control of Palestinians a *kibbush* or occupation, a term that had been studiously avoided by Israeli leaders. In private conversation, Sharon could tick off the demographic ratios between Jews and Arabs from 1917 on. He was convinced Israel needed to act boldly to safeguard its Jewish character.

Sharon turned to Gaza as a place where Israel could take the initiative. The Israeli public readily saw policing Gaza with its 1.5 million Palestinians as a major burden for the Israel Defense Forces. Gaza had none of the strategic advantages of the West Bank, nor did it have its biblical resonance. Yet we should not underestimate the difficulty of the decision. Sharon was the architect of the settlement movement since his role as Gaza commander in the early 1970s. His commitment to settlers and hard-nosed view of Palestinians earned him the nickname "the bulldozer." As part of the Egypt-Israel peace treaty, Menachem Begin had removed 1,400 families from settlements in the northern Sinai. Now, if he gave the order to remove approximately 8,500 Israelis living in seventeen settlements in Gaza, Sharon would be the first Israeli to uproot settlements in the Palestinian context. The move was significant both because it was Sharon's initiative and because it was unilateral and accomplished without a wider final status agreement with the Palestinians.

In a December 2003 speech, Sharon signaled that Israel was prepared to disengage from Gaza. Two months later in a newspaper interview, he made clear that he planned to remove all Gaza settlers. The announcement set off pandemonium on the Israeli right, but Sharon was determined and in August 2005 the IDF evacuated all the Gaza settlers. Angry that the Likud did not rally to support him as one of the architects of the party in the 1970s, Sharon split from the party to launch a more centrist alternative, Kadima or Forward. Tragically, within a month of his move, Sharon suffered a debilitating stroke from which he never recovered.

Challenges of 2006–2016 and Beyond

The Gaza Disengagement led to the bifurcation of the Palestinian Authority (PA). In 2006, Hamas won a plurality in the Palestinian parliamentary election. Some argued that Hamas won the elections by promising to end the corruption of the PA. Others argued that Hamas won because it credited the violence of the Second Intifada with Israel's unilateral disengagement from Gaza. By June 2007, Hamas had pushed the PA and its Fatah backers out of Gaza, confining President Abbas and the PA to the West Bank. Numerous regional and Palestinian efforts have failed to reconcile Abbas and Hamas including Israeli economic restrictions on Gaza, aimed at demonstrating to Palestinians that Hamas could not deliver prosperity.

Repeated cease-fires or de facto cease-fires have punctuated the unbroken hostility between Israel and Hamas. Israel has fought three wars with Hamas since the start of the twenty-first century—2008–2009,

2012, and 2014. Typically, these wars were initiated by rockets fired at Israeli urban areas from within Palestinian urban areas in Gaza, essentially daring Israel to retaliate in the expectation that Israel would hit civilians. Israelis have called the Hamas strategy a "double war crime" that embeds rockets in Palestinian civilian areas and targets Israeli civilian areas. Invariably there are recriminations when Israel directs air power against rocket launchers. Israel responds by citing its "knock on the roof" policy—text messages and leaflet drops in civilian areas warning of an air strike—a high standard not adopted by other armies. Over time the periods between wars have shortened while the wars lengthened, with the summer of 2014 conflict lasting fifty-one days. If many of the rockets in the first campaign came from Iran and other rejectionist elements, by 2014 Hamas was producing and using its own rockets, suggesting that ending the conflict may be even more difficult in the future.

Hamas's strategic environment has worsened with the growing conflict in the region, and in Syria in particular. Its leadership fled Damascus and the Syrian civil war, a move that angered Iran, Hamas's traditional backer. Moreover, beginning in 2014, Arab Sunni governments, with the exception of Qatar, face militant groups at home and have come to view Hamas through the Israeli prism as a destabilizing force. Especially damaging was the Egyptian leadership's crackdown on Hamas and rejection of the Muslim Brotherhood government. With Egypt closing Rafah, Gaza's southern border crossing, and Israel guarding Gaza's other border (with the exception of the Mediterranean Sea), Hamas has been more constrained than ever.

In contrast, Abbas's approach from the West Bank has seemed more like "no peace, no war." During the George W. Bush administration and again during the Obama administration, the United States has made two major attempts to engage Abbas in a peace effort. Bush's secretary of state Condoleezza Rice launched an international conference in Annapolis at the end of 2007, paving the way for close to a year of direct talks between Abbas and Israeli prime minister Ehud Olmert. Forced to resign in 2008 and ultimately imprisoned over allegations of corruption, Olmert used his period as a caretaker leader to extend a far-reaching Israeli offer agreeing to an international consortium over the Temple Mount/Haram al-Sharif. He also agreed to the principle that 100 percent of the West Bank would go to the Palestinians provided they agreed to a territorial exchange of approximately 6 percent of the West Bank to avoid relocation of major settlement centers. Abbas offered 1.9 percent. By September 16, 2008, Olmert explicitly asked Abbas to agree to his offer. Abbas said he would, but at the end of December, Operation Cast Lead was underway in Gaza. Olmert's caretaker term ended in February 2009. Abbas has never explained why he rejected Olmert's offer. Was it because Olmert was a lame duck? Or was it because Olmert could only offer a symbolic return of refugees to Israel, while enabling unlimited Palestinian return to the new Palestinian state? The question is ultimately whether there was any deal that Abbas would have been prepared to accept, especially in view of Olmert's acquiescence to an international consortium surrounding the Temple Mount/Haram al-Sharif that was unprecedented.

This same question would be asked about both Abbas and Olmert's successor, Benjamin Netanyahu, during the last major effort by secretary of state John Kerry in 2013–2014. During President Barack Obama's first term, the media repeatedly reported on differences between Netanyahu and Obama on issues ranging from the Iranian nuclear program to West Bank settlements. These differences notwithstanding, during Obama's second term, newly appointed Secretary of State Kerry devoted nine months to test the possibility of reaching a two-state solution. The idea of a framework was publicly launched to see whether the parties could reach a core conceptual bargain on the issues that divided them such as borders, security arrangements, refugees, Jerusalem, and mutual recognition. While Kerry acknowledged that the parties moved toward each other, ultimately they were unable or unwilling to bridge the gaps.

Both Netanyahu and Abbas can be characterized as risk-averse. Neither sought to shape public opinion but rather reflected the skepticism, if not downright cynicism, that each public felt toward the other side. Almost twenty-five years after the Madrid Peace Conference, polls showed that bare majorities or pluralities in each society still favored a two-state solution. Nevertheless, there was a public disbelief on both sides that this solution would ever occur, given the opposition of the other.

Israel and the PA cooperate on a daily basis to prevent Hamas and other militant groups from infiltrating the West Bank. This apparently successful partnership has not made it possible to seriously address let alone bridge differences over the most contentious issues. One can lament that present leaders fall short of the giants of the previous generation like Sadat and Begin. However, it is also possible that the issues are tougher than those that divided Egypt and Israel, and that it requires more skill, patience, and flexibility to get at the intercommunal core of the conflict than to exchange land for peace. Palestinian denial that Jews are a people entitled to their own nation-state is prolonging the conflict, and it is exacerbated by Palestinian leadership opposition to grassroots people-to-people interaction. Israeli governments may be afraid to address the issue of settlements and the thousands of settlers whose lives must be unsettled if their homes and communities are dismantled. And some responsibility may be shared by Arab regimes, destabilized by the Arab Spring of 2011 and so preoccupied with their own problems that they failed to provide a counterpart to the United States in bringing the parties together.

The peace effort is currently stalled and the actors have changed, but the question of land remains inextricably tied to peace. The conflict has moved beyond one between states and pits Israeli Jews against Palestinian Arabs. The core problem of a century-old conflict once more is how to partition Palestine into independent Jewish and Arab states. The challenge for diplomacy is to maintain the viability of a two-state outcome even if the two-state solution does not seem to be on the horizon. In sum, can diplomacy keep the door open for a two-state approach, even if the parties are reluctant to walk through the door themselves, at least for the present.

RECOMMENDED READINGS

Avineri, Shlomo. *Herzl's Vision: Theodor Herzl and the Foundation of the Jewish State.* Katonah, NY: BlueBridge, 2014.

Makovsky, David. *Making Peace with the PLO: The Rabin Government's Road to the Oslo Accord.* Boulder, CO: Westview Press, 1996.

Rabinovich, Itamar, and Jehuda Reinharz. *Israel in the Middle East: Documents and Readings on Society, Politics, and Foreign Relations, Pre-1948 to the Present.* Hanover, NH: Brandeis University Press, 2008.

Ross, Dennis. *Doomed to Succeed: The U.S.-Israel Relationship from Truman to Obama.* New York: Farrar, Straus and Giroux, 2015.

Ross, Dennis, and David Makovsky. *Myths, Illusions, and Peace: Finding a New Direction for America in the Middle East.* New York: Penguin, 2010.

Shavit, Ari. *My Promised Land: The Triumph and Tragedy of Israel.* New York: Spiegel and Grau, 2013.

GLOSSARY TERMS

Abu Ala (Ahmed Querie)
Abu Mazen (Mahmoud Abbas)
Al-Aqsa Mosque
Arab-Israeli Interstate War
Ashrawi, Hanan
Assad, Hafez al; Hafez Assad
Barak, Ehud
Begin, Menachem
Beilin, Yossi
Camp David Negotiations
Clinton Parameters
Dayan, Moshe
Declaration of Principles (Signed by Arafat and Rabin)
Egypt-Israel Peace Treaty
Fatah
Gaza Disengagement
Gaza Wars, Wars with Hamas
Geneva Conference
Golan Heights, the Golan, the Heights
Hamas
Hezbollah
Hussein, King of Jordan
Husseini al-, Faisal
International Conference at Annapolis
Intifada, First Intifada, Second Intifada
Israel-Egypt disengagement agreement
Kadima (Forward)
Labor
Likud
London understanding (aborted)
Madrid Peace Conference
Meir, Golda
Muslim Brotherhood
Nakba al-
Nasrallah, Hassan
Nasser, Gamal Abdel
Netanyahu, Benjamin
October 1973 War
Olmert, Ehud
Oslo Peace Accords
Palestine Liberation Organization (PLO)
pan-Arabism
Peace treaty between Israel and Jordan

Peres, Shimon
Rabin, Yitzhak
Roadmap
Rogers Plan
Sadat, Anwar
Sadat's historic trip to Jerusalem
Second Sinai disengagement
Sharon, Ariel
United Nations Security Council (UNSC) Resolution 242, 242 (land for peace)
UNSC Resolution 338
War of Attrition
1967 War, Six-Day War
West Bank
Wye River Memorandum

David Makovsky is a senior fellow and director of the Project on the Middle
East Peace Process at The Washington Institute. He is also a lecturer in Middle
Eastern Studies at John Hopkins University's Paul H. Nitze School of Advanced
International Studies and a contributing editor to *U.S. News and World Report.*
His publications include *Engagement through Disengagement: Gaza and the
Potential for Renewed Israeli-Palestinian Peacemaking* and (with Dennis Ross)
Myths, Illusions, and Peace.

SEVEN

Israel in World Opinion

GIL TROY

Introduction

Founded after World War II, the State of Israel matured during the Cold War but has remained embattled—perceived by some as the flashpoint where Islam confronts the West, by others as the keystone to achieving world peace, and by still others as merely a participant in one regional conflict amid many tribal, racial, and religious clashes. No other established country has had its very right to exist challenged by so many, so often, for so long. Yet Israel has also been, in many ways, an upstanding world citizen, absorbing the oppressed, healing the distressed, and inventing miracle technologies while struggling with the challenges entailed in the effort to create a vibrant democracy.

As Israel has both flourished and suffered since 1948, its world image has shifted. In the years following World War II, it was the UN's poster child, the model postcolonial nation state. After the Six-Day War, Israel was cast as the heroic David fighting the Arab Goliath. In today's mix, there are equal parts International Renegade, miraculous Old-New Land, and admired Start-up Nation. This, then, has been Israel's defining dynamic on the world stage. Much like the traditional Jew, this modern Jewish state of only eight million people has been subject to a polarizing, schizophrenic fluctuation between extreme and radically different views, inspiring some, appalling others, but somehow perpetually attracting disproportionate attention.

Israel's Image Post–World War II

These divergent points of view were already present at the inception of
the state, with messianic hopes and utopian visions sitting uncomfort-
ably alongside uncompromising claims and brutal battles. Following
World War II, as the British Empire crumbled, the entire Middle East
quaked. The conflict over Palestine had urgent ramifications in view of
the Nazis' recent murder of six million Jews. Further interest was drawn
by Zionists' bold, attention-getting tactics, such as the protests when the
British turned back 4,500 Jewish refugees who had arrived in Palestine
aboard the *Exodus 1947*, "the ship that launched a nation." Since the
United Nations had been founded in 1945 to help avert future wars, the
fate of the surviving Jews in Palestine could be seen as a test case. A great
deal hinged on whether this new world body could resolve the increasingly violent conflict between Jews and Arabs. An intractable struggle
could reveal the UN to be as impotent as its predecessor, the League of
Nations. Indeed, the Middle East conflict has frequently tested the UN,
exposing the world parliament's greatest weaknesses.

Despite their growing Cold War antagonisms, both the United States
and the Soviet Union supported the General Assembly's Resolution 181.
The Soviet Ambassador to the UN, Andrei Gromyko, endorsed this 1947
partition plan to end the British mandate, declaring: "If these two people
that inhabit Palestine, both of which have deeply rooted historical ties
with the land, cannot live together within the boundaries of a single
State, there is no alternative but to create, in place of one country, two
States—an Arab and a Jewish one."

Broadcast on radio, the vote of 33 to 13 endorsing partition, with 10
abstentions, thrilled Jews worldwide. The international community had
now validated Hatikva, the Jews' millennial hope to return. Moshe Sher-
tok, who headed the political section of the Jewish Agency, the Palestinian Jews' government-in-formation, announced: "This is the first time
that the UN and the civilized world have decided to create a new state."
Today, Israel's critics ignore the Jewish state's special status of actually
having been voted into being by the UN.

Most of the Arab world rejected the compromise. Arab League secretary Azzam Pasha told two Jewish mediators before the resolution
passed: "The Arab world is not in a compromising mood . . . . Nations

never concede; they fight." Six Arab armies attacked when Israel became independent in May 1948—and lost. Israel expanded the territory
granted to it and set more viable boundaries with the 1949 armistice,
demarcated in green ink, the famous, improvised Green Line. While in
1945 it seemed that the twin demons of racism and anti-Semitism had
been buried once and for all by revelations concerning the Holocaust,
Israel's successful establishment and victory over the Arab armies three
years later introduced a new, powerful, redeemed Jew and was met with
a new, powerful unredeemed Jew hatred, sometimes masked as "only"
hostility to Israel.

Time magazine celebrated Israel's founding prime minister David
Ben-Gurion as a prophet with a pistol, gushing: "Out of the concentration camps, ghettoes, banks, courtrooms, theaters and factories of
Europe the Chosen People had assembled and had won their first great
military victory since Judas Maccabeus beat the Syrian Nicanor at Adasa
2,109 years ago." Marveling at this novelty of Jewish might, *Time* declared these new Jews "too tough, too smart and too vigorous for the
divided and debilitated Arab world to conquer."

Israelis felt vindicated yet vulnerable. The fighting killed six thousand
Jews, a catastrophic cost for a country of only six hundred thousand.
Moreover, Israel had achieved an armistice, not peace: It had 639 miles
of hostile borders north, east, and south; Jerusalem was divided and its
Jewish Quarter had been ravaged and lost; the tiny country was a mere
nine miles wide at its narrowest point between Netanya on the Mediterranean coast and Tulkarm. At the outset, the Zionist dream of the Jews
returning to history was realized by a traumatized people, still captive
to historic events and still dependent on the goodwill of others: Czech
pistols, American recognition minutes after the declaration, and albeit
temporarily, Soviet indulgence.

When anti-Semitic riots, along with both popular and governmental
harassment in one neighboring Arab country after another, propelled
some eight hundred thousand Jews toward Israel, the Jewish state absorbed them, making these refugees citizens upon arrival. But the destruction of the ancient North African and Middle Eastern Jewish communities highlighted the ongoing Israeli tragedy. Despite and perhaps
because of the new state's political, cultural, and economic achievements,
peace with its Arab neighbors remained elusive.

Haj Amin al-Husseini, the Grand Mufti of Jerusalem, fused European anti-Semitism with Islamist, anti-Zionist anti-Semitism. Adolf Hitler's friend, the Mufti wrote in his diary that the Jews "spread wickedness and misery throughout the world." They "corrupt morality in every single country, destroy all religions and sympathize with [communist] Russia; they rob people's property, steal money by usury, and distort the prophet's preaching." These classic images and motifs of Jew hatred would live on for decades, especially in the Arab media's cartoons, and in recycled, even televised, adaptations of classic anti-Semitic libels such as "The Protocols of the Elders of Zion."

The blatant hostility of Arab states notwithstanding, Israel's success was acknowledged and appreciated by UN member states. While many young African nations remained beset by postcolonial poverty, dictatorship, and corruption, and the four Asian Tigers—Hong Kong, South Korea, Singapore, and Taiwan—had yet to thrive, Israel, which began in 1948 with few natural resources, a limited industrial base, and mostly untrained immigrant workers, was developing rapidly. Even before the high-tech 1990s miracle, Israeli innovations like drip irrigation and desert agriculture, chemicals, and manufacturing would generate domestic prosperity. Simultaneously, Israel was celebrated for its successful socialist experiment, the kibbutz, and for making the desert bloom, yielding luscious Jaffa oranges.

Diplomatic Outreach to Africa Reflects
Israel's Founding Foreign Policy

From the outset Israel was founded on an amalgam: the Jewish tradition of *tikun 'olam*, or the injunction to repair the world; the Zionist dream to be a model country and "light unto the nations"; its identity as one of the new states after decolonization; and a sense of socialist solidarity, along with an equally powerful Zionist impulse to be safe and "normal." Thus it is perhaps not surprising that Israel's core foreign policy included a redemptive dimension along with its more obvious and pressing concerns with security.

Although he is often thought of as a defensive Zionist fleeing anti-Semitism, Theodor Herzl was a utopian. Like most Zionists and like most Western liberal nationalists, he believed a democratic nation-state could redeem humanity. In *Der Judenstaat* (*The Jewish State*), published in 1896, Herzl wrote: "We shall live at last as free people on our own soil, and in our own homes peacefully die. The world will be liberated by our freedom, enriched by our wealth, magnified by our greatness." This messianic dream included saving African blacks after saving the Jews. Herzl contended that "only a Jew can fathom" African slavery, in all its "horror."

This helps explains why Israelis, and especially Labor Zionists like David Ben-Gurion and Golda Meir, felt what she referred to as a moral obligation to the newly liberated African countries, and a sense of historical mission to help them develop. In 1958, following Golda Meir's first visit to Africa, Israel established Mashav, the Foreign Ministry's Center for International Cooperation. By 2016, Mashav had trained over two hundred thousand international aid workers and assisted people in 140 countries, including some that still refused to recognize the Jewish state. Meir, Israel's foreign minister from 1956 to 1965 and prime minister from 1969 to 1974, would emphasize Israel's commitment: "I am prouder of Israel's International Cooperation Program and of the technical aid we gave to the people of Africa than I am of any other single project we have undertaken." Beyond "enlightened self-interest," she considered this policy "a continuation of our most valued traditions." Dazzled, President Julius Nyerere of Tanzania called Meir "the mother of Africa."

Initially, the Jewish state kept its distance from apartheid South Africa, respecting Israel's African allies and Israel's founding, antiracist ideals. By the early 1970s, Israel had diplomatic ties with thirty-two African countries, and more embassies in Africa than any country except the United States. While fulfilling Theodor Herzl's updating of the traditional vision of being a "light unto the nations" through Mashav, Israelis hoped for a peace payoff too. One popular Israeli saying advised: "The road to Cairo passes through Bamako," Mali's capital.

Israel's budding relationship with Africa was threatened, frequently. Shortly after seizing power in 1952, Egypt's dictator, Gamal Abdel Nasser, had tried to enlist the African nations in his campaign against Israel. Nasser peppered his pan-Arabist vision with anti-Semitic imagery, denounced Zionism as colonialist and imperialist, and claimed that Tel Aviv's generosity was a neocolonialist plot. Vowing to "chase out Israel from Africa," he often annoyed Black African leaders. When the Burmese premier U Nu and his wife visited Israel in 1955, he was the first foreign prime minister to visit the country, and Israelis greeted him like a national hero. U Nu had tried to include Israel in the Bandung Conference of Asian and African countries earlier that spring and had opposed the conference's anti-Israel resolution. When Egypt pressured him to cancel his trip to Israel, Nu canceled his trip to Egypt instead. Premier Nu praised the Israeli government, saying, "It has granted us its aid whenever we requested it." Six years later, Ben-Gurion spent two weeks in Burma, one of Israel's longest official prime ministerial trips ever, studying Buddhism while fulfilling his official duties.

The All-African People's Conference in Accra in December 1958 defeated an Egyptian anti-Israel resolution, replacing it with a milder resolution calling for a fair Middle East settlement. The *Tri-State Defender*, an African American newspaper in Memphis, Tennessee, editorialized a year later: "There is much that Israel can teach Africa and Asia. She is achieving phenomenal success with a soil that is almost barren, and against physical odds that would deter the most hopeful. Today, after only 11 years of existence as an independent and sovereign state Israel is not only capable of maintaining herself but she is able to extend help to others."

Initially, with its abhorrence of racism and outreach to Black Africa, Israel was wary of South Africa, with members of South Africa's large Jewish community frequently caught in the middle. However, as the African countries—and the rest of the Third World—became increasingly hostile, Israel and South Africa became friendlier.

Meanwhile, Arab animosity toward the Jewish state continued unabated among both the masses and elites. Hostility was expressed openly along Israel's southern Negev-Sinai border. Raids by Bedouin smugglers, returning Palestinians, greedy brigands, Egyptian soldiers, and local *fedayeen* "self-sacrificers" became routine, and Israel retaliated against both civilian and military targets.

Relations with Europe in the Shadow of World War II

For all their idealistic affinity for the Third World, Israeli policy makers understood that their young country needed economic, diplomatic, and military support from the major powers. In the Tripartite Declaration of

May 1950, the United States, Great Britain, and France sought to "balance" the supply of weapons to Israel and its Arab enemies in an effort to keep oil flowing from the Middle East to the West. The United States was not yet selling major weaponry to Israel, and France emerged as Israel's main supplier for the next decade and a half as the three-way agreement soon became a dead letter.

Both France and Great Britain supported Israel enthusiastically. Harold Wilson, the British Labor prime minister in the 1960s, explained British sympathy in light of "two thousand years of history and the sufferings of the Jewish people, including the massacres" of World War II. While labeling the Jews "victims" and the Arabs "brutes," many left-leaning Europeans in the 1950s and the 1960s also endorsed Zionism because of the dominance of Israel's socialist Labor party and potent Histadrut labor union. As the rebellion in Algeria, which began in 1954, intensified, the French too edged closer to Israel.

Israel's relations with Germany were understandably touchier. Konrad Adenauer of West Germany understood that in order to move forward, his country needed to provide reparations to Holocaust victims and develop a "special relationship" with the Jewish state. The initial restitution agreement, signed in 1952, triggered riots in Israel and a close Knesset vote. The opposition leader, Menachem Begin, denounced accepting German "blood money." West Germany and Israel only established full diplomatic relations in 1965. During the next half century, Germany would pay over $70 billion to Holocaust victims and Israel, repeatedly trying to normalize relations with Israel yet never fully succeeding.

Relations with Great Britain and France warmed, however, and in late October 1956, the fledgling Israel united with these two major powers against Egypt in the Sinai Campaign. The Israelis sought stability in the Sinai peninsula in the south and joined the French and British military action designed to retake the Suez Canal, which Nasser had nationalized in June. While it demonstrated military competence and conquered the Sinai quickly, Israel stumbled diplomatically. Angry that they had been blindsided, the Americans forced an Israeli retreat. Israel was cast as the French and British imperialists' "stooge," doing their bidding by invading the Sinai that Arabs and Africans considered "African" territory. The Soviet Union, which had hoped that Israel's socialist orientation would propel it into the communist camp, had already soured on Israel and Zionism, and was using its proxy, Czechoslovakia, to supply weapons to Egypt, not Israel.

Following the 1956 Suez-Sinai War, Nasser and other Arab leaders began calling for a "third round" to destroy Israel. As Nasser expressed it in a message to Jordan's King Hussein on March 13, 1961: "The evil introduced into the heart of the Arab world must be uprooted." During the tense buildup to what became known as the Six-Day War, the British maintained their support but the French abandoned Israel. Charles de Gaulle, who was wooing the Third World in an effort to repair the damage caused by the Algerian quagmire, imposed an arms embargo on Israel. By November 1967, de Gaulle's reorientation of French policy to favor the Arabs and France's oil interests smacked of anti-Semitic demagoguery as he famously branded Jews arrogant, "an elite people, sure of themselves and domineering."

The United States, on the other hand, was ready to mobilize in support of Israel. Back in 1948, President Harry Truman keenly felt the popular support for Jewish nationalism, receiving more than 135,000 letters urging him to recognize the Jewish state. During the first decade and a half of Israel's existence, even without strong military ties, the cultural, ideological, political, diplomatic, and sentimental bonds strengthened. President John F. Kennedy praised Israel as "the child of hope and home of the brave." In a long line of presidents who viewed the Jewish state as an ally in upholding democratic values, he said: "It carries the shield of democracy and it honors the sword of freedom."

In August 1962, Kennedy's sale of the Hawk ground-to-ground missile system to defend Israel's airfields marked America's first major arms sale to Israel. Kennedy hoped a reassured Israel would be less likely to plunge into another ill-advised Sinai adventure, would help block Soviet expansion, and might be more open to solving the Palestinian refugee problem. At the same time, deeply concerned about nuclear proliferation, he attempted to inhibit the development of what intelligence reports told him was Israel's nuclear program. With Kennedy's assassination, none of these policy goals were achieved; however, the two countries were propelled closer together culturally, ideologically, politically, diplomatically, and militarily.

Kennedy's successor, Lyndon Johnson, emerged as an even more enthusiastic friend. Capturing the two countries' shared idealism, Johnson
would say: "Our society is illuminated by the spiritual insights of the
Hebrew prophets. America and Israel have a common love of human
freedom and they have a common faith in a democratic way of life." And
when the Soviet premier Aleksei Kosygin asked Johnson why America
supported the three million Israelis against eighty million Arabs, the
president replied: "Because it is right."

The 1967 War: A Turning Point

Americans in particular thrilled to the pioneering, romantic Israel
that had defended civilization against what many then viewed as the
Arab hordes. Over the next decade, some Israeli leaders were almost
as admired and well known as American pop stars. Moshe Dayan, the
one-eyed general who was credited with the lightning-quick Six-Day
War victory in 1967, was the real-life Jewish superman, transforming
the Jews' image from poor bent victims in the dark European ghetto
to suntanned and macho Middle Eastern war heroes. Abba Eban, the
eloquent diplomat, was the Jeffersonian scholar-statesman, articulating
Israel's cause before the United Nations with Oxonian precision brim-
ming with democratic idealism. And Golda Meir, a rare female prime
minister during a prefeminist age, was the Yiddishe mama leading the
nation, combining a reassuring Eastern European maternal image with
an American accent and Israel's cutting-edge pioneering kibbutz spirit.

Despite his affinity for Israel, Lyndon Johnson discouraged Israel from
launching a preemptive strike during the tense spring of 1967. Nasser had
united the military commands of Egypt, Jordan, and Syria. He followed
his bellicose threats to destroy the Jewish state with actions, removing
the UN troops serving as a buffer force in the Sinai, and then blocking
the international waterways toward the southern port of Eilat, the Straits
of Tiran. After a tense May, when Jews in Israel and abroad feared another Holocaust, an Israeli air raid one early June morning destroyed the
Egyptian and Syrian air forces. The ensuing six days of war expanded the
Jewish state by adding the Sinai desert to the south, the Golan Heights to
the north, and Jerusalem as well as the West Bank to the east.

Israel emerged as a winner just as the international community was becoming enamored with losers. In this context, its increasingly close ties with the United States and the surge in the number of Palestinian refugees under Israel's control complicated Israel's relations with Europe and the developing countries. Israel lost its David status and became a Goliath overnight, able to defeat Arab armies with ease—and an occupier responsible for more than one million angry Palestinians. As in 1956, Israel's control of the Sinai—territory they considered part of Africa despite being in Asia—had infuriated many postcolonial Africans. Now the thorough shellacking Israel administered to the Arab armies humiliated and enraged their Soviet patrons.

As Israel's position vis-à-vis the Arab states grew stronger, the conflict shifted: Palestinians took the initiative to advance their rights and launched an independent armed struggle. Various guerrilla movements from the 1950s merged together into the Palestine Liberation Organization (PLO) in 1964. In January 1965 the PLO's main strike force, Fatah, attacked Israel's national water carrier, its first target. The PLO founding covenant called Zionism "a political movement organically associated with international imperialism and antagonistic to all action for liberation and to progressive movements in the world. It is racist and fanatic in its nature, aggressive, expansionist, and colonial in its aims, and fascist in its methods."

The wording of the charter was deliberately chosen. The charismatic and ruthless PLO leader, Yasser Arafat, and his allies understood that beyond terror attacks and diplomatic power plays, they were fighting an ideological war. Rhetoric was important. Targeting world opinion, they played to a Third World, postcolonial solidarity and what would be called a postmodern world glorifying the underdog, especially if the conflict could be cast as people of color opposing Western whites. Exploiting the rise of a global mass media and what the Palestinian intellectual Edward Said referred to as the twentieth century's "generalizing tendency," the Palestinians linked their local story to what Said called "the universal struggle against colonial and imperialism," including "Vietnam, Algeria, Cuba, and black Africa." Well-funded think tanks and publishers publicized this interpretation. Said's 1978 book *Orientalism* built what became the dominant intellectual edifice in the postmodernist academy and among anti-imperialist progressives. It blamed Westerners automatically and took their guilt as a given, even as his postcolonial revolution decried the "Eurocentric" prejudice against Arabs and Islam.

In November 1967, the United Nations Security Council passed Resolution 242, seeking a "just and lasting peace in the Middle East" guided by two principles. First, "withdrawal of Israel armed forces from territories occupied in the recent conflict." For Israelis as well as the American negotiators, omitting *the* before the word *territories* and using the plural meant *some* land, not necessarily *all*. Second was the right for "every State in the area . . . to live in peace within secure and recognized boundaries free from threats or acts of force." This framework, which Security Council Resolution 338 reinforced after the 1973 War, also shaped the road map later adopted by the Quartet—the United States, the European Union, Russia, and the UN—in 2003, with the signing of the Oslo Peace Accords. The notion of "every State" had expanded to include a Palestinian state to be established through gradual negotiations.

Although it annexed East Jerusalem in 1967 and the Golan Heights in 1981, Israel did not annex the West Bank or Gaza Strip, keeping millions in legal limbo. "Israel became an occupying power . . . not simply a Jewish state," Edward Said would claim in 1992, when explaining Israel's growing international predicament post-1967. "The Zionist settler in Palestine was transformed retrospectively and actually from an implacably silent master into an analogue of white settlers in Africa."

Trying to woo the world, Palestinian propagandists wavered. At times they echoed the Arab and Soviet media's crass anti-Semitism. On other occasions, they masked it as "merely" anti-Zionism. Although his goal remained to destroy Israel, Arafat insisted that his call for a "secular democratic state" was "a humanitarian plan which will allow the Jews to live in dignity, as they have always lived, under the aegis of an Arab state." This statement conveniently ignored the Jews' humiliating, second-class *dhimmi* status under Islam and negated Judaism's national dimension. Beneath the intellectual veneer and occasionally cautious language ran an undercurrent of anti-Semitism. Adolf Hitler's manifesto *Mein Kampf* was required reading in some Fatah training camps, where former Nazis trained Palestinian guerrillas to continue Hitler's war against the Jews.

As fighter and propagandist, Arafat mastered the two sides of the terrorist's sword: you could justify violence in an increasingly polarized and relativistic world if the violence came with the right message—and from the right person. The Palestinians terrorized their way onto the world's agenda. Spectacular attacks in Europe, especially the killing of eleven Israeli athletes and coaches during the 1972 Munich Olympics, ultimately compromised Israel's image perversely, with some concluding that such extreme attacks must somehow be deserved. By the fall of 1974, the Arab summit meeting in Rabat recognized the PLO "as the sole legitimate representative of the Palestinian people," while the UN General Assembly cheered Arafat, giving the struggle for a Palestinian state unprecedented primacy.

Paradoxically, the surprise attack that Egypt and Syria launched against Israel on the Jews' holiest day, Yom Kippur, in October 1973 made the Palestinians even more of the focus of the Middle East conflict. This was the last time conventional Arab armies tried to overrun the Jewish state. Ever since 1973 the conflict has been one of asymmetrical warfare and ideological conflict.

The Yom Kippur War—which Israel eventually won—was a sobering turning point for Israel. Domestically, Israelis lost the collective euphoric self-confidence bordering on arrogance that predominated after the 1967 War. The impact went beyond Israel's borders. The oil-rich Arab states led by Saudi Arabia imposed an oil embargo to punish Israel's allies, triggering the great inflation of the 1970s and propelling Middle East matters to the top of the international agenda. Determined that "the Israelis must not be allowed to lose," President Richard Nixon raised the United States' defense readiness condition, Defcon, to level three and approved the dramatic weapons resupply of Israel during the war, deploying waves of airplanes. America's role as Israel's weapons supplier and best friend continued to grow.

In an effort to avoid further economic damage to the West, US secretary of state Henry Kissinger launched his "shuttle diplomacy," first seeking a cease-fire and then initiating the Middle East peace process. Kissinger's success in drawing Egypt from the Soviet into the American orbit culminated with Egyptian president Anwar Sadat's epochal visit to Jerusalem in 1977. Sadat's initiative, which Menachem Begin encouraged and President Jimmy Carter fostered, resulted in the Camp David negotiations and 1979's breakthrough Israeli-Egyptian peace treaty.

The Moves to Delegitimize Israel

During this same period, the Soviet Union exploited Palestinian grievances and Arab anger to outmaneuver the United States in the Cold War.
Smoldering after Israel's swift 1967 victory against Arab forces armed by
the Soviets—and worried about the inspiration this provided to three
million Soviet Jews—the Soviets unleashed their own propaganda campaign against Zionism and Israel. Communist internationalism had always clashed with Jewish nationalism, meaning Zionism. Early Soviet
denunciations of anti-Semitism had morphed into harsh antireligious
and anticapitalist campaigns that scapegoated Jews during Josef Stalin's
era. Still, the Soviets had supported the establishment of Israel, anticipating another socialist ally, and only repudiated Israel after the 1956
Sinai-Suez campaign. Joining the appeal to Third World postcolonial
movements and the Arab world, the Soviets starting denouncing Zionism as imperialist and worse.

On July 5, 1967, one month after the war, Leonid Brezhnev, the Communist party general secretary, charged that "in their atrocities it seems
they [the Israelis] want to copy the crimes of the Hitler invaders." Eventually, the Soviets would mobilize all the media at their disposal. Zionism was "equated with every conceivable evil," Dr. William Korey would
note; "racism, imperialism, capitalist exploitation, colonialism, militarism, crime, murder, espionage, terrorism, prostitution, even Hitlerism."
Commenting on the Soviet's denunciation of Israel in his definitive history of anti-Semitism, Professor Robert Wistrich argues: "Only the Nazis
in their twelve years of power had ever succeeded in producing such a
sustained flow of fabricated libels as an instrument of their domestic
and foreign policy."

This initiative resonated among Third World communities still healing from colonialism, imperialism, and racism, and they were readily
persuaded by the anti-imperialism rhetoric the Soviets used to advance
their own imperialist goals. Characterizing Zionism as racism played
especially well. Equating Zionism with apartheid, and Israel with South
Africa, the Soviet Union discredited Israel while appearing attentive to
African needs. Cajoled by the Soviets and bullied by Arab countries that
wielded petrodollars while enlisting support in the name of Muslim

or postcolonialist solidarity, twenty-one African countries broke diplomatic ties with Israel in the weeks following the 1973 War and gave up a steady flow of Israeli coaching and technology.

This linkage of Israel with South African apartheid outlasted the Soviet Union. Israel's emergence as a regional strongman—and a South African ally—made it easier to cast the Jewish state as the Middle Eastern South Africa, a westernized power flourishing in the Third World. It was too easily overlooked that the apartheid analogy was false, absurd because the conflict between Israelis and Palestinians was national, not racial—there are dark-skinned Israelis and light-skinned Palestinians—and because there had never been legalized discrimination South Africa-style based on race either in Israel or the territories.

Nevertheless, this charge of racism became a convenient battering ram for knocking down the Jewish state. The Soviet strategy built on the new Israeli reality, the growing sympathy for the Palestinian tragedy, the new power of Third World strategy, and the growing backlash against South African racist perversity. The charge of racism, one of the greatest crimes in the international arena, represented Israel as a country unworthy of existing. This modern blood libel thus also excused the Soviets' vulgar anti-Semitism. Amid this great inversion in world opinion, Israel, once considered by many to be above reproach, was increasingly made to appear beneath contempt.

The push to legitimize the PLO—and simultaneously to delegitimize Israel—culminated in 1974: the PLO received observer status in the UN; Arafat addressed the General Assembly; and Soviet satellite nations worked with Arab states to expel Israel from the United Nations. Arafat's speech tailored the Palestinian narrative to suit Third World sensibilities. He envisioned "a new world . . . free of colonialism, imperialism, neo-colonialism and racism in each of its instances, including Zionism."

Arafat rationalized the PLO's murderous methods, insisting: "Whoever stands by a just cause and fights for liberation from invaders and colonialists cannot be called terrorists. Those who wage war to occupy, colonize and oppress other people are the terrorists." Arafat articulated "Che Guevara Rules," glorifying guerrillas, hailing anticolonialist resistance, and relativizing once-universal laws. Rejecting the Western democratic notion that laws and rights should be universal, and anticipating the postmodernism that would shape post-1960s Western intellectual thought, Che Guevara Rules imbued those deemed oppressed with a near-absolute right to use violence and any other tactic.

A year after Arafat's speech, in November 1975, the UN General Assembly validated this Soviet-Palestinian propaganda ploy targeting Israel by condemning one single form of nationalism: Jewish nationalism, meaning Zionism, was equated with racism, including Nazism. The passage of Resolution 3379 transformed Israel's relationship to the UN and the world, souring many Israelis regarding any international structures. It was also the day the UN died for many Americans who had seen their ambitious postwar redemptive instrument devolve into the Third World Dictators' Debating Society, where autocrats cynically exploited democratic prerogatives they denied their own people.

What the American ambassador to the UN Daniel Patrick Moynihan denounced as "the Big Red Lie"—emphasizing its Soviet origins—now had UN approval. Accusations that Zionism was racism, and the comparison between Israel and South Africa, became standard tropes in international discourse. Moynihan's warning that the universal human rights mechanism developed after World War II was being cheapened and politicized proved prescient. Two resolutions accompanying Resolution 3379—including Resolution 3376, which created the Committee on the Inalienable Rights of the Palestinian People—established the UN infrastructure for boosting Palestinians and pillorying Israelis. Two years later, in 1977, the General Assembly created the Division for Palestinian Rights, a well-funded bureaucracy for waging this ongoing war against the Jewish state. The resulting mechanisms have done much to tar Israel's reputation and focus attention so disproportionately on the Palestinian cause. By 1979, the UN's International Convention against the Taking of Hostages made a remarkable exception. It exempted any act committed "against colonial domination and alien occupation and against racist regimes." By providing a rationale that made Palestinian terrorism acceptable and reinforcing the connection between anti-Americanism with anti-Zionism, the UN both excused and facilitated the spread of Islamist terrorism.

Although this carefully crafted demonization strategy was geared to the Arab world and the rest of the Third World, the attack resonated on the American left and in mainstream European circles too. Black radicals took the lead in expressing Third World solidarity. With identity politics ascendant, with the Palestinians cast as the "blacks" of the Middle East, and with the Manichaean, postmodern Che Guevara Rules predominating, left-wing condemnation also grew.

The intensifying US-Israel friendship further alienated European and American radicals from Israel. Bashing Israel became a way for leftists— and especially radical Jews—to prove their radical bona fides. The 1973 War triggered a wave of denunciations from the far left, even as mainstream American public opinion embraced Israel. The antiwar activist Reverend Daniel Berrigan, labeled Israel "a criminal Jewish community" that had committed "crimes against humanity," had "created slaves," and espoused a "racist," Nazi-like "ideology." Professor Alan Dershowitz of Harvard Law School considered this attack the harbinger heralding the left's turn against Israel.

Moynihan had also predicted it. With such an obsession about Israel's alleged crimes, even those who did not want to see the state destroyed would assume it must be guilty of something. Or, as Moynihan put it, "Whether Israel was responsible, Israel surely would be blamed: openly by some, privately by most. Israel would be *regretted*." By 2005, *Die Zeit*'s publisher-editor, Josef Joffee, writing in *Foreign Policy*, would lament that "since World War II, no state has suffered so cruel a reversal of fortunes as Israel," from popularity as that "plucky state" to becoming the "target of creeping delegitimization."

In fact, two forms of delegitimization emerged. "Hard" delegitimization entailed what Joffee called the direct "statocidal" calls from Iranian mullahs, the Hamas charter, the PLO charter, and Hezbollah terrorists to destroy the Jewish state. Arab diplomatic strategy split between fanatics led by the Iranians and realists like the Saudi Arabians and the Egyptians who sometimes secretly cooperated with Israel, even as Israel was frequently demonized in the popular, state-controlled press. The "soft" form, Britain's former prime minister Tony Blair would explain in 2010, "is a conscious or often unconscious resistance, sometimes bordering on refusal, to accept [that] Israel has a legitimate point of view," for example, criticizing Israel for acts of self-defense every other nation would undertake when bombed. Blair called this form "insidious, harder to spot, harder to anticipate and harder to deal with, because many of those engaging in it, will fiercely deny they are doing so." It is this subtler form, often masked in human rights rhetoric, "that is in danger of growing, and whose impact is potentially highly threatening." The UN became the headquarters for this "well-intentioned" "soft" delegiti-mization movement, while proving remarkably hospitable to "harder" delegitimizers too.

It should be noted that Blair, like many critics of delegitimization, also criticized Israeli policy, especially that regarding the Palestinians in the West Bank. He frankly acknowledged that Israeli behavior often exacerbated tensions. Nevertheless, he was convinced that the ongo-ing, obsessive, exaggerated, one-sided demonization of Israel—even by well-meaning human rights activists—inflamed the region and derailed peace efforts.

This "soft" leftist attack on Israel also resonated among some Jews and extended beyond a welcome, vigorous debate about Israel's policies. As one of many movements spawned when traditional Judaism confronted modernity, Zionism was marginal until the trauma of the Holocaust and the drama of Israel's establishment mainstreamed it. Some Jews rejected the Zionist understanding that Jews are a people and not just a faith community, like Christianity. Part of the objection stemmed from a cos-mopolitan critique, the universalist hope that the world would transcend nationalisms, ethnic identities, and religions, and accept all individuals as united by their common humanity.

Such "orthodox" universalist critics had little impact. Ideologically, the UN's 1975 Zionism-is-racism resolution triggered eloquent coun-terattacks defending democracy, decency, and Western values by the American ambassador to the UN, Daniel Patrick Moynihan. His Israeli colleague, Chaim Herzog, would joke that the hateful resolution did more to reinvigorate interest in Zionism than dozens of speeches could have done.

In the 1960s Israel's military victory and its value to the West despite its small size and many enemies were a source of pride. Israel's 1973 counterattack not only taught the American military how to counter Soviet tactics but also provided a bounty of intelligence from captured Soviet weapons. America's Pentagon would continue to benefit from Israel's experience, from the invention of the Uzi submachine gun in the 1950s through twenty-first-century Israeli-American joint projects like armed drones and missile defense systems. Similarly, Israel's stun-ning raid at the Entebbe airport on July 4, 1976, freeing Jewish hostages held by Arab and German hijackers, provided a lesson in how to fight terrorism. The raid, Operation Thunderbolt, seemed more Hollywood fantasy than current-events reality, a drama complete with a martyred hero, Yoni Netanyahu. A year later, Israel cited memories of the Holocaust in supporting its decision to welcome boatloads of Vietnamese refugees—when much of the world spurned them.

Despite these accomplishments, Jewish nationalism remained out of sync with many Diaspora Jews' deepest aspirations. Many Jews were further bonded to the Jewish state by fears of a second Holocaust in the spring of 1967, and they shared the triumphal euphoria in June 1967 when Israeli paratroopers stood for the first time at the Western Wall in newly liberated East Jerusalem. Nevertheless, the great success Jews enjoyed in North America and Great Britain especially, combined with a post-1960s cosmopolitan sensibility, made even many professedly pro-Israel Jews uncomfortable with Zionist ideology. Many ignored the cognitive dissonance—supporting the Jewish state for other Jews in the East while building their homes in the West. But as Palestinian propaganda proliferated and the Middle East conflict festered, more and more Jews distanced themselves from the tarnished image of the Jewish state or became vocal critics of Israel, although the overwhelming majority remained pro-Israel.

Anti-Zionism and Anti-Semitism

Many of Israel's most bitter critics, both Jews and non-Jews, seemed oblivious to the anti-Semitism underlying much of the anti-Zionist movement. At international conferences, demonizing Israel often encouraged demonizing Jews too. After presiding over the World Conference on Women in Copenhagen in 1980, Denmark's culture minister Lise Ostegaard marveled how in this theater of the absurd "a simple majority could turn black into white and white into black," as the conference about women unleashed attacks on America, Israel, Zionism, and Jews. Ann Robinson, of the National Council of Jewish Women, felt doubly oppressed as an American and a Jew. Sonia Johnson, a Mormon, heard delegates pronounce: "The only way to rid the world of Zionism is to kill all the Jews" and "The only good Jew is a dead Jew." Increasingly, especially when Israel's conflict with the Palestinians would flare up in the news, there would be spikes in anti-Semitic rhetoric and violence, particularly in France, with its large community of six hundred thousand Jews.

With the ideological infrastructure intact and specific groups primed to turn on Israel, events in Israel further complicated Israel's image. Menachem Begin's rise to power in the late 1970s was a watershed. Bad enough that his Likud party deposed the romantic, inspirational founding Labor Party of David Ben-Gurion and Golda Meir, of Abba Eban and Moshe Dayan, of the communal kibbutz and the socialist state. But in its stead came a party of capitalists and settlement builders, of passionately religious Jews and too-exotic-by-half Mizrachim, led by the stern, self-righteous, unphotogenic, doctrinaire Begin and his rotund, aggressive, military mastermind, Ariel Sharon. The sense among reporters, diplomats, and even many Jews, including Israelis, was that this is "not my Israel." This feeling grew as the number of settlements in the West Bank and Gaza increased, and despite Begin's leadership and acknowledged achievement in signing the 1979 peace treaty with Anwar Sadat that ended hostilities between Egypt and Israel. The mood turned especially bleak as Israel sank into a debacle, the 1982 Lebanon War.

The Lebanon War was a dramatic—and unwelcome—break with Israel's previous wars. Observers perceived it as a war of choice, not the Ein Breira, do-or-die fights of 1948, 1967, and 1973 (popular memory often overlooked the 1956 anomaly). Unlike 1967's crisp six-day victory, or even 1973's clear, ultimately redemptive if costly three-week reversal, the Lebanon War was a sinkhole. In fact, the Lebanon War would be the new model, a harbinger of quagmire conflicts, unwinnable contests, in areas rife with civilians, with results as cloudy as both the war aims and the moral lines the army tried to draw where combatants hid among innocents.

The massacre of seven hundred to eight hundred Palestinians by Christian Phalangists at the Sabra and Shatila refugee camps, an area of Beirut under Israeli control, traumatized the nation and blackened Israel's reputation. Ariel Sharon, Israel's defense minister, sued *Time* magazine for reporting in February 1983 that on September 15, 1982, he had "discussed" with the Lebanese Christians "the need to take revenge for the assassination" of their commander. A jury found that *Time* had acted negligently and had indeed defamed the Israeli leader but did not have to pay him, because he was a public figure. *Time* proclaimed victory.

Sharon felt vindicated. This stalemate typified many of Israel's propaganda battles. Frequently, the facts vindicated Israel but had little effect on image. The shadow of guilt remained and sullied Israel's reputation.

Israel's reputation was tarnished again in this difficult decade when the Palestinians in the West Bank and Gaza launched their 1987 uprising, called the Intifada. In January 1988, Woody Allen criticized Israel in the *New York Times* for crushing the Palestinian riots so brutally. Critics jumped on the movie comedian's facile, sarcastic bon mot: "Are these the people whose money I used to steal from those little blue-and-white cans after collecting funds for a Jewish homeland?" But Allen's title captured the outrage many Jews and non-Jews were feeling regarding the Jewish state: "Am I reading the papers correctly?" Has David become Goliath, the victim turned victimizer?

Prospects for Peace

Although Israel's growing image problem in the 1980s reflected the changing regional conditions played out in a new ideological context, broader geopolitical shifts generated post-1990s optimism on both sides. The diverse coalition linking Western armies with key Arab states that George H. W. Bush assembled in 1990 to repel Saddam Hussein's invasion of Kuwait, along with the implosion of Soviet communism, advanced the cause of Middle East peace. Israel's restraint during the Gulf War, as it impassively absorbed Iraqi Scud missile attacks to help Bush preserve the global coalition, impressed the president. And somehow, photos of bombed homes in the Tel Aviv area and crying Israelis elicited a positive response. World public opinion seemed to prefer Jews as victims. They were easier to understand than Jews involved in a complicated conflict and in the morally and politically complex task of exercising power in order to defend themselves.

With the first Gulf War successfully concluded, President Bush tried leveraging America's postwar power and prestige to make peace in the Middle East. His pressure prompted the three-day Madrid Peace Conference. Israel demanded reversing the Zionism in Racism Resolution 3379 as a condition for granting the UN observer status at the conference, which, significantly, included Syria, Jordan, Lebanon, and the Palestinians, in Israel's first bilateral talks with neighbors other than Egypt. The resolution offended the then UN secretary-general's sense of fairness and he agreed. Javier Perez de Cuellar explained: "You cannot say that trying and get[ting] a state for your nation is racism, [as] for instance the Kurds or the Basques in Spain are not racist. These are two different things that should not be mixed up."

On December 16, 1991, 111 countries voted to negate the resolution. The repeal provided the former Soviet satellites an occasion to denounce their communist past. Czechoslovakian president Vaclav Havel rejoiced: "We are in a position to decide for ourselves." He explained, "I didn't approve of it then; I don't approve of it now." Once reassured, Israel proved more amenable to compromise. The result was the secret negotiations in Norway, culminating in the Oslo Peace Accords of 1993.

The Oslo Peace Process, for all its misfires, further normalized Israel's relations with the international community. Israel's diplomatic and trade presence spread worldwide. In 1994, Israel and Jordan signed a peace treaty and rumors circulated about a possible Syrian-Israeli peace. That year, Israel's prime minister Yitzhak Rabin and foreign minister Shimon Peres shared a Nobel Peace Prize with Yasser Arafat. Ironically, Rabin's tragic assassination in November 1995, at the hands of an Israeli religious fanatic, demonstrated Israel's new stature. President Bill Clinton made his poignant "*Shalom Chaver*" farewell at Rabin's funeral before leaders representing eighty countries, including Egypt's president Hosni Mubarak, making his first, and ultimately only, trip to Israel—a nonstate visit.

Just as derailing the delegitimization campaign fueled the peace process, the peace process fueled an Israeli boom. The hardscrabble, calloushanded pioneering generation of the kibbutz and the Jaffa orange was now yielding to creative, soft-handed new pioneers of high tech and higher education. As Israel's once-primitive communications and transportation infrastructure developed, brilliant entrepreneurs tapped into Israel's most potent natural resource and renewable source of energy, its people. In agriculture and computers, in mechanics and medicine, Israeli innovation began shaping the world's future. An old tech success like the kibbutz-owned company Netafim was producing smart-drip and micro-irrigation systems in thirteen factories worldwide marketed to 112 countries, while New Age behemoths like Teva started fighting debilitating diseases like multiple sclerosis with Copaxone across the globe. Israel was attracting hardheaded financiers interested in making money by investing in tomorrow's technologies and not relying on softhearted philanthropists.

Unfortunately, the Oslo Peace Process did not end the Palestinians' ideological warfare or disdain for Israel, especially in extreme left and postcolonialist circles. Even during these peace and prosperity years, what the historian Anita Shapira calls this "decade of hope," even as Israelis and Palestinians kept negotiating, Israel bashing increased. The ideological infrastructure articulated in the 1970s, and the rhetorical invective used to explain the 1980s clashes, were accepted without question as givens in the 1990s, ignoring the risks Israel made for peace. This international invective revealed that much of the criticism was existential, not transactional; about what Israel was, not what it did. This bigotry was reinforced by the spread of identity politics in the West, wherein the actor was more important than the act, as well as by the rise of an aggressive Islamist ideology that was hostile to the West and effectively exploited European feelings of white guilt.

This Israel aversion became a tenet of many progressives, as more Europeans simply dismissed Israel owing to a facile conflation of "occupation" with Nazi crimes, and as the red-green alliance, uniting the far left with Islamists, strengthened. Explaining this puzzling, paradoxical alliance, the French philosopher Bernard Henri-Levy suggested that with Marxism's demise, anti-Zionism became the defining prism for the far left, the one given that clarified the world ideologically, even if some facts or alliances proved contradictory.

Thus, the last two acceptable hatreds in the politically correct world, anti-Americanism and anti-Zionism, intertwined. Anti-Semitism, anti-Americanism, Third Worldism, pro-Palestinianism, and antiracism converged with legitimate concerns about Israel's actions in the kaleidoscopic attacks against Israel. The demonization of Israel as the collective Jew questioned whether a Jewish state could possibly also be democratic—even though most European democracies had ethnic and religious dimensions to their national characters. Inherent in this obsession with Israel and the double standards and disproportionate harshness used in judging her were deeply troubling echoes of the West's "longest hatred," anti-Semitism.

Ironically, the collapse of South Africa's apartheid regime in the early 1990s made it easier to cast the Zionist state as the new villain. Radicals now identified Israel as the world's worst racist. Accusations calling Israel an apartheid state spread; it went unnoticed that even as Israel was trying to disentangle from the Palestinians at their insistence, most Palestinians were demanding that their territory be free of Jews.

Yasser Arafat led the Palestinians away from the Camp David negotiations and back to terror in July 2000. As Israel endured waves of suicide bombings during what Palestinians called the Second Intifada beginning in September 2000, the international demonization of Israel and the mainstreaming of anti-Zionism in many circles peaked. An increasingly loud and insistent chorus claimed Zionism was racism, without regard for the UN's repeal; that Israel was an apartheid state, despite the fact that it was enmeshed in a national, not racial conflict with no de jure discrimination; and that Israel was the prime obstacle for peace, even as President Bill Clinton faulted the Palestinians for sabotaging Oslo.

Israel's new position as the world's whipping boy was underscored in late August and early September 2001 when the UN's World Conference against Racism in Durban, South Africa, focused on repudiating Zionism rather than fighting racism. While the Western powers inside the official UN hall blocked the most outrageous attacks, the parallel NGO conference could be characterized without exaggeration as an intellectual pogrom against the Jewish state. A mob atmosphere menaced Israeli and visibly Jewish delegates. Thousands shouted Israel down at mass rallies featuring signs such as "Hitler Should Have Finished the Job." With the parallel NGO declaration endorsing reinstating Resolution 3379, Durban embodied the ideological resurgence of anti-Zionism.

The Israeli Army's reentry into many parts of the West Bank in April 2002 after Palestinian terrorists murdered 130 Israelis in repeated suicide bombings in March focused international attention but little understanding on Israel. The Palestinians' demonstrably false claim that Israeli soldiers had massacred hundreds in Jenin was spread by the media, reflecting that headlines hinged not on evidence but on the Palestinian propagandists' credibility in many circles and Israel's fallen popular standing. Systematic refutation and facts demonstrating the lie had little impact. The effect on world opinion was unchanged by revelations that no massacre had taken place; the damage was done.

University campuses also proved hospitable to the campaign against Israeli injustice. Anti-Israel activists at the University of Toronto initiated the first Israel Apartheid Week in the spring of 2005, helping to ritualize anti-Zionist activities, often in casual disregard of what was happening in the Middle East. Similarly, the BDS movement modeled on the successful isolation of South Africa and calling to boycott, divest from, and apply sanctions against Israel began agitating in universities and in cities with strong progressive pockets. This succeeded more on the far left and in Europe than among centrists and in North America but nevertheless occasioned concern as well as dismay.

Today, both friends and foes of the Jewish state tend to think of Israel's image as negative. Israel's identity is being effectively manipulated and defined by this committed cadre of activists with a clear agenda, a standardized rhetoric, and a ritualized approach. Their work is augmented by the occasional headline-generated outbursts of renewed conflict—and the lethal weaponry surrounding Israel. With Hezbollah missiles and Syrian warheads to the north, and Palestinian rockets to the east and west, and with Iranian nuclear threats just across Jordan, there are enough of these anti-Zionists, and they command enough media attention, to convince many that Israel is not the normal nation the Zionists hoped to establish but the "embattled ally," the "Jew among the nations," yet again feeding, rather than solving, the problem of anti-Semitism.

Strategic, Ideological, Diplomatic, and Economic Standing

These attacks can be considered the international equivalent of a persistent low-grade fever: It could turn more serious at any time but is not crippling or fatal—yet. Despite its enemies' hostility, supporters' worries, and the disproportionate attention this small country commands in the regional conflict, modern Israel has shown itself to be surprisingly robust. Beyond its military might, its standing in the world has grown strategically, ideologically, diplomatically, and economically.

STRATEGIC SUCCESS

The vicious Palestinian terrorist assaults of 2000 to 2005 were stilled by the Israeli army's ultimately effective counterterror tactics and buttressed by the world backlash against terrorism. On September 11, 2001, shortly after the Durban conference, Osama bin Laden's al Qaeda destroyed the World Trade Center in New York and attacked the Pentagon.

For all the complexities that ensued with America's reaction, millions worldwide were shaken by and repudiated terrorism. Palestinian leaders realized that their campaign of suicide bombings was hurting their cause, reinforcing Israel's alliance with the West and marking the Palestinian nationalist movement with the brand of al Qaeda and bin Laden. Prime minister Ariel Sharon's unilateral disengagement from Gaza and parts of the West Bank in 2005 reinforced the pro-Zionist message that Israel was a democracy that had been victimized by terror and was willing to take risks for peace.

IDEOLOGICAL GAINS

Many in the West, especially in the United States, continued to value Israel as a democratic ally. Support for Israel in North America, especially when pollsters offered a choice between Israel and Palestinians, remained extremely strong, with two thirds of Americans polled—and sometimes as many as 80 percent—championing the Jewish state. Support in Europe was spottier, especially when pollsters asked Europeans to single out the countries representing the greatest threat to world peace—with Israel competing with Iran and North Korea for the dubious honor of first position.

In the Jewish community, despite the hand wringing about greater distancing and the claims of political alienation, along Woody Allen's challenge, "Am I reading the papers correctly," support for Israel persisted. Contrary to the oft-articulated fears of losing the youth, the Cohen Center at Brandeis University showed that young Jews between ages twenty and thirty were often more pro-Israel than those in the thirty-to-forty age range. This surge reflected the Jewish community's effective pro-Israel, identity-building initiatives. Birthright Israel-Taglit is the outstanding example. By 2016 this project had given more than five hundred thousand young Diaspora Jews a ten-day trip to Israel—often accompanied by the more than fifty thousand Israeli peers who participated in these *mifgashim*, or encounters.

DIPLOMATIC STANDING

Israel is not the pariah state the headlines might lead readers to believe. By 2016 Israel had diplomatic relations with 159 countries and embassies in 76 countries, frequently characterized by warm ties, thriving trade missions, and mutually beneficial technological exchanges. The Israeli-American alliance remained Israel's bedrock, with European relations a little rockier and more headline-sensitive. Russia and the other former Soviet Union states went from being Israel's implacable ideological foe to wary allies, with a range of diplomatic approaches, as hundreds of thousands of Israelis with ties to that region served as human bridges linking the various countries.

Problems, of course, persisted. Iran rushed toward nuclear power while vowing to end Israel's existence. Turkey turned from an important ally into a fundamentalist foe. The Arab Spring stirred much populist, Islamist anti-Zionism while unleashing dangerous instability. Anti-Semitism metastasized in Europe as Jews in France and elsewhere started living under tightened security and began emigrating to Israel—or other countries. Meanwhile, calls to boycott settlement products gained traction in Europe, as the European Union, alienated by Benjamin Netanyahu's right-wing coalition, became increasingly aggressive.

Israeli diplomats nurtured ties with China, India, and Brazil—acknowledging the size of these countries and particularly enthralled by the old-new dynamic linking Israel, China, and India, three countries rooted in ancient world-defining civilizations and now modernizing rapidly. India became Israel's second-largest market for the country's booming weapons exports.

Among Western diplomats, one can distinguish two separate approaches to Israel, identified by the Israeli-British scholars Jonathan Rynhold and Jonathan Spyer as the "diplomatic" and "strategic" orientations. The "diplomatic" orientation views the Israeli-Palestinian conflict as the keystone to Middle East policy. Reflecting the Arab world's greater size and influence, it usually blames Israel as the root cause of the conflict, the central obstacle to peace and a persistent threat to the smooth flow of oil and diplomatic relations. The "strategic" orientation begins with an ideological affinity toward Israel. It sees Israel as a democratic bulwark for the West against the Islamism, tribalism, and unreason in the region. Even in pro-Israel countries such as the United States, Great Britain, and Canada, the diplomatic corps tends to be "diplomatic" and Arabist, while the legislators and chief executives usually tend toward a more "strategic," Zionist position.

Increasingly this diplomatic approach has become the norm, especially in Europe. Some are openly hostile, like the unnamed British diplomat who in 2001 called Israeli prime minister Ariel Sharon "the cancer at the heart of the Middle East crisis." But this Arabist approach is also a function of institutional considerations, especially the multiple jobs open to diplomats in Arab capitals. As noted earlier, the diplomatic discourse taken up by Western elites is tinctured with anti-Semitism. It is characterized by an obsession with Israel—the collective Jew at the heart of the world's troubles—and by repeated assertions that support for Israel, in an eerie echo of "The Protocols of the Elders of Zion," is artificial "astroturf" imposed by the unnaturally powerful pro-Israel lobby. Nevertheless, the strategic approach predominates, and especially in the United States, popular support for Israel is understood to be authentic, organic, "grassroots," and sprouting from common democratic and liberal values and common interests.

ECONOMIC STANDING

In 2008 as the American economy and so many European economies imploded, Israel's economy held steady. By 2010, the World Bank ranked Israel as one of the thirty countries in the world where it was easiest to do business, with Israel tied for fourth in ease of credit and tied for fifth in protecting investors. One institution alone, the Weizmann Institute of Science in Rehovoth, had researchers who helped develop seven of the world's top twenty-five biotech drugs, including Enbrel against rheumatoid arthritis, Copaxone against multiple sclerosis, and Erbitux against cancer, an astonishing contribution from only one research center in such a small country.

The World Economic Forum's Growth Competitiveness Index ranked Israel 27th out of 133 countries, third in quality of scientific research institutions, fourth in utility patents, fifth in legal rights, seventh in life expectancy, ninth in innovation, and fifteenth in financial market sophistication and availability of the latest technologies. In 2013 *Forbes* toasted Israel as "first in the world in startups per capita, third in Nasdaq-listed companies and the highest R & D expenditure as percentage of GDP."

At times the rhetoric celebrating Israel's technical achievements has seemed cloying, with supporters massing overeager arguments to dem-

onstrate the country's utility. Such efforts betray an uncomfortable inse-
curity, a covert response to a more overt attack, as if Israel's accomplishments could sway those who questioned her very right to exist. Indeed,
like other states, Israel's continued existence is not contingent on good
behavior. For all the strategic, diplomatic, ideological, and economic
achievements listed earlier, Israel's legitimacy is rooted in Jewish history and the Jewish people's identity and was validated by the United
Nations in 1947 in parallel with dozens of other nations, and moreover
by millions of citizens building productive lives since 1948. Yet of all the
countries in the world, Israel alone has been put on probation, as if its
basic rights are open to public scrutiny and debate.

Positive Developments/Positive Image

In 2010 Israel became a member of the Organization for Economic Cooperation and Development (OECD), culminating an acceptance process that began in 1994. It was a triumphal day for the Jewish state. "Acceptance to the OECD was made possible thanks to Israel transforming
into a developed country with a free market, while also strictly adhering to responsible and balanced economic policies in recent decades,"
said Prime Minister Benjamin Netanyahu, himself the former finance
minister responsible for many of these new policies. OECD's acceptance
acknowledged Israel "as a developed economy alongside the most developed economies in the world," Netanyahu said, certifying it "as a
technological and economic force." Condemning the Palestinians for
opposing this move, the prime minister pointed out that despite all the
"lamentations over Israel's international isolation," Israel's international
standing was in fact growing.

America's House of Representatives unanimously passed a resolution
congratulating Israel and the OECD. The resolution celebrated Israel's
"far-reaching economic reforms in recent years with respect to taxes,
labor, competition, capital markets, pension funds, energy, infrastruc-
tures, communications, transport, housing, and other fields, growing its
private sector and streamlining its public sector." The resolution called
Israel "a world leader in science and technology" and "home to the
most high-technology start-up companies, scientific publications, and
research and development spending per capita." Congress predicted that

Israel's membership in the OECD "will strengthen the OECD because of Israel's high living standards, free and stable markets, and commitment to democracy, human rights, and freedom."

While it was developing technologically and economically, Israel had also been developing a reputation for applying its high-tech know-how, military operational brilliance, and humanitarian outreach far beyond its borders. In 1984 and 1991, in Operation Solomon, then Operation Moses, Israel airlifted twenty-two thousand Ethiopian Jews to Israel. The complicated airlifts admittedly caused many complicated absorption challenges. Still, both vindicated Israel's original mission to serve as a refuge to Jews at risk while marking the first time an overwhelmingly white country rescued thousands of blacks on the grounds that they were brethren and declared them fellow citizens. Similarly, the wave of over a million immigrants from the former Soviet Union ended decades of oppressive Soviet restrictions on Jewish emigration while marking the largest per capita influx of refugees from communist oppression to freedom. And the IDF, the Israeli army, for all its image challenges, became known for deploying its medical tents, search-and-rescue teams, and other lifesavers globally, be it responding to the bombing of the American embassy in Kenya in 1998, the Indian Ocean tsunami in 2004, the Pakistani earthquake in 2005, the Haitian earthquake in 2010, or the Japanese and Turkish earthquakes in 2011. Long before Westerners even noticed the problem of Syrian refugees, some casualties from the Syrian civil war received lifesaving treatment in Israeli hospitals—although they were compelled, once home, to deny who saved them. More broadly, Israel's elaborate, sophisticated civil society has many NGOs linking the Israeli people to those suffering around the world, including IsraAID, the Israel Forum for International Humanitarian Aid, the First Israeli Rescue and Search Team, Israeli Flying Aid, or Save a Child's Heart.

In the Middle East's rocky and often inhospitable soil, in a region where ancient cultures have been subject to benighted dictatorships and societies to poverty and limited development, Zionists are realizing their commitment to building a thriving, productive, safe, and free modern democracy. Theodor Herzl's *Altneuland*, set in the biblical land of milk and honey, has become an old-new land modeled on Zionist and Jewish values and effectively engaged in the global economy. Like virtually every other state, Israel is not perfect. Still growing and stretching, it deserves to be recognized for what it is—a near miracle, a tiny but thriving Jewish state and a struggling and worthy democratic, albeit imperfect jewel in the Middle East.

RECOMMENDED READINGS

Oren, Michael. *Power, Faith, and Fantasy: America in the Middle East, 1776 to the Present.* New York: Norton, 2008.

Spiegel, Steven L. *The Other Arab-Israeli Conflict: Making America's Middle East Policy, from Truman to Reagan.* Chicago: University of Chicago Press, 1985.

Troy, Gil. *Moynihan's Moment: America's Fight against Zionism as Racism.* New York: Oxford University Press, 2013.

Wistrich, Robert. *A Lethal Obsession: Anti-Semitism from Antiquity to the Global Jihad.* New York: Random House, 2010.

Wittstock, Alfred, ed. *The World Facing Israel, Israel Facing the World: Images and Politics.* Berlin: Franck and Timme, 2011.

GLOSSARY TERMS

Adenauer, Konrad
Arafat, Yasser
Bandung Conference
Begin, Menachem
Ben-Gurion, David
Camp David Negotiations
Eban, Abba
Exodus 1947
Fatah
fedayeen
Green Line
Herzl, Theodor
Herzog, Chaim
Hezbollah
Histadrut
Husseini, Haj Amin al
Intifada
Israeli-Egyptian Peace Treaty
King Hussein
Labor Zionism
Madrid Peace Conference
Meir, Golda

Gil Troy is Professor of History at McGill University and a Shalom Hartman Engaging Israel Research Fellow in Jerusalem. He is the author of *The Age of Clinton: America in the 1990s*; *Moynihan's Moment: America's Fight Against Zionism as Racism*; and *Why I Am a Zionist: Israel, Jewish Identity and the Challenges of Today*. He is a regular columnist for the *Jerusalem Post* and the *Daily Beast*.

EIGHT

Israel: A Jewish Democracy[1]

YEDIDIA STERN

Introduction: Jewish Identity and Commitment to Democracy

The Jewish people lived outside their historic homeland, Eretz Yisrael, for nearly two thousand years. Their exile to the Diaspora was a lengthy process. The two main landmarks are the destruction of the Second Temple in 70 CE and the suppression of the great revolt against Rome in 135 CE, after which the Jews lost control of their fate as a nation. During their exile the Jews lived as individuals, as families, and as communities, but not more than that. They gathered in communities isolated from each other across vast regions of the globe; they spoke the idiom of their country of residence, setting aside their own tongue (preserved as an esoteric language of prayer and study); they lacked centralized leadership; they were persecuted in many locations and over different periods, and in important ways they lived outside history. For most of the period they had a collective consciousness based on religious faith and historical memory, which preserved them as a unique group, but they did not hold a territory and did not have the responsibility for managing a pub-

---

[1] The statistics in this chapter are based on several surveys conducted by the Guttman Center in the Israel Democracy Institute—some of them in cooperation with the Avi Chai Foundation—in recent years. See http://en.idi.org.il/tools-and-data /guttman-center-for-surveys/about-the-guttman-center. For the most detailed information, see *A Portrait of Israeli Jews: Beliefs, Observance and Values of Israeli Jews, 2009,* http://en.idi.org.il/events/conferences-and-seminars/findings-of-the -third-guttman-avi-chai-report.

lic domain, with all that this entails. In the absence of a Jewish public sphere, the Jews were not required to decide together, as a group, issues that national groups in charge of a public space must address.

Political Zionism and its realization with the creation of the State of Israel changed this situation. In a dramatic move, culminating in the middle of the twentieth century, millions of Jews immigrated from Yemen, Poland, Russia, Iraq, and dozens of other countries to Eretz Yisrael. Today Israel is home for the largest concentration of Jews in the world, who make up more than three quarters of the citizens of the State of Israel. Having achieved control over their lives, Jews in Israel must address questions that are new for them, including the two that lie at the center of this chapter: What is the shared vision of the Jews that the State of Israel was intended to fulfill? And now that they have rejoined history, what is the manner in which the Jewish people intend to organize the public space?

In the first part I address the question of the identity of the State of Israel. Israel is defined as a "Jewish state," but the meaning of this definition is controversial among Israelis. In the second part I address the question of regime and the form of political organization of the State of Israel. On this issue there is no controversy: the Israelis have long chosen democracy not only as a regime but also as a system of moral and cultural values. The reality of life in Israel, however, raises challenges about the seriousness of the Israeli public's commitment to democracy. The two issues of Jewish identity and commitment to democracy are interrelated. Indeed, the main challenge of Israeli society today is to find the desirable balance between the Jewish (particular) characteristic of the nation-state and its democratic (universal) characteristics.

The State of Israel and Jewish Identity

Until a few generations ago, most of the Jewish people relied on a common cultural base: religion. They studied the same texts, perceived as formative of identity (Torah—the Written Law, the Oral Law, and the other scriptures); they maintained a certain lifestyle that was rather similar in the various Diasporas (observance of the commandments according to Halakha, the body of Jewish law, especially the legal part of the Talmud, that supplements the scriptural law); and they shared their symbols and historical memory. But in modern times, when religion lost its dominance as an attribute of identity for a significant portion of the Jewish people, the collective self-definition of the Jews was undermined, and this has become a major bone of contention between large groups of Jews. Jewish lifestyle is no longer uniform, as it used to be. The common denominator of the Jews, once self-evident, has become elusive.

In light of these developments, Zionism proposed to form the Jewish people into a group by establishing a common concrete country, the state of the Jewish nation. In this sense, one can regard Jewish nationalism of the nineteenth and twentieth centuries as a heroic effort to create a new center, a political one, capable of sustaining the Jewish collective under conditions of cultural and religious polarization. Professor Avi Ravitzky and I have argued elsewhere that the dispute over Jewish identity was a formative factor of the Zionist revival. Zionism was intended not only to allow Jews to defend themselves physically and to establish a territorial homeland but also to consolidate their collective consciousness once more, after religion ceased to be a significant factor in this respect.

The leaders of the State had hoped that its establishment would decide the question of national identity of the Jews. The ingathering of the Jews from the Diaspora in a single territory under one flag, clear dominance of one language and the development of local culture, the establishment of organized government and social institutions to regulate the life of all citizens, partnership in protecting national security and promoting collective interests—all these and other factors were expected to result in the formulation of a common national identity for Jews living in Israel.

In practice, however, the present-day State of Israel has failed to bring into being one solid national Jewish identity. On the contrary, it was precisely the changeover from life organized around community to national life that brought to the surface pressing questions on which there was no broad consensus among modern-day Jews. Ideological and ethical controversies, which in the Diaspora were only minor or hypothetical, have become practical questions that touch upon the very foundations of Israeli life, and the parties to the controversy are required to reach a decision about them in order to sustain the nation-state.

At the root of the controversy is a fundamental question: what is the role and purpose of Zionism and of the State of Israel? Some suggest that it is to conserve the evolutionary continuity of the previous Jewish existence in the Diaspora, but in the Land of Israel. Others believe that the return to history, to accountability for sovereignty, was designed to enable a new, revolutionary start for Judaism, dominated by the "new Jew." The following is an outline of the dispute.

Mainstream Political Zionism in the first half of the twentieth century, led by David Ben-Gurion, the architect of the State, rebelled against the traditional Jewish identity and sought to divorce itself from it. Ben-Gurion and his colleagues attempted to shape a new Jewish identity that would be statelike in character—that is, it would replace the community-based identity of the Diaspora with a national identity that would shape various aspects of Israeli life—secular in worldview, and modern and forward-looking in orientation. They proposed to break away from what they perceived as the atrophy of exile and aimed to create a new image of the Jew as audacious, pioneering, independent, and sovereign. They rejected the world of Jewish creativity in exile—Talmud, Halakha, philosophy, poetry—and instead proposed to found the new Jewish Israeli identity on the historical narrative of the Bible, which took place in the Land of Israel. Ben-Gurion envisioned a romantic leap from the ancient world in the Land of Israel (Eretz Yisrael) to the present in the State of Israel. Everything that occurred in between, the formative Jewish experience of two thousand years, seemed to him irrelevant and even a hindrance in the path of Political Zionism.

At the other extreme is the Haredi (Ultra-Orthodox) community, a small portion of which is anti-Zionist and the majority a-Zionist. The *haredim* are not interested in renewal but in continuity. They are opposed to the "new Jew" and regard the "old Jew," the Diaspora Jew from Eastern Europe, as an ideal, sacred figure. For them the State of Israel is not a goal but rather a means designed to enable the reconstruction of the flourishing religious Torah world that was destroyed in the Holocaust in Europe. The State lacks any value, except to the extent that it can help rebuild the glorious Jewish past. Therefore, the *haredim* do not share the vision of Zionist revival and do not attach any importance to the State from the point of view of Jewish identity and culture.

Between these two extremes is a third group, of Religious Zionists. On one hand, this group regards itself as a full partner in the Zionist project and has contributed to and fully supported the realization of the Zionist revolution. Like Ben-Gurion, it sought a new beginning, a nation-state of the Jewish people. Some of its prominent leaders even cast this pursuit in religious terms, translating the Zionist vision into messianic language. On the other hand, the group is completely and fully committed religiously, to the tenets of Judaism and the traditions developed over many generations. Its commitment to the observance of Jewish law is absolute, and its primary language is religious, guided by theological thinking. The two characteristics of this identity group, based on which it is referred to as Religious Zionism, led to the expectation that it would serve as an important bridge between the two camps. The common Zionist denominator binds it to Ben-Gurion and to the secular camp: together they left the ghetto and established an exemplary independent Jewish state in the Land of Israel; together they have explored the myriad possibilities that modernity has to offer; together they will be a light unto the nations; together they are motivated by a national activism and grasp the imperative of the historical moment. At the same time, the common religious denominator ties the Religious Zionists to the Haredi camp. Like the *haredim* they also adhere to the supreme value of ensuring continuity between the previous and present generations; they firmly believe that the present cannot exist detached from the sources of spiritual life provided by the past and without actively maintaining ancestral traditions; and they too reject the aim of Secular Zionism for normalization. In short, they do not want the Jews to be "like all the other nations."

All three groups have been relatively successful in realizing their goals and the three positions are well represented in Israel in the twenty-first century. The Political Zionism of Ben-Gurion created a strong, independent, modern, and technological State. In spirit, the State of Israel is close to the liberal Western countries, and by means of the State the Jews have become a "normal" group. The *haredim*, for their part, function as a closed community that knows how to take advantage of the State to promote its own interests, without renouncing its special character. The State of Israel funds and nurtures the Orthodox Torah world, so that today the number of Torah scholars who devote their life to learning in Israel is larger than it has ever been in the history of the Jewish people. The middle group of Religious Zionists has also evolved over the years into a significant movement in the Israeli landscape, far beyond their quantitative representation in the population. Its members are planted in the center of Israeli life in all its facets and are perceived as leaders in society as a whole. This is a particularly activist group, and their involvement in national life makes them a driving ideological, revolutionary, and trail-blazing force. It is fascinating to see how the Religious Zionist community has transformed itself in recent decades from a relaxed, self-effacing, and consensus-seeking group to being the catalyst of Israeli society.

The fact that each of the three groups is successful and has prospered in the last generation raises a question as to how they manage to live side by side given that none is prepared to settle for protecting its own lifestyle and interests but seeks to impose its preferences on all Jews living in Israel. The vision of each embraces the State and society as a whole, and therefore they twist each other's arms whenever national questions concerning the common space arise. This is because a common feature of each of these three Jewish identity groups is complete confidence in the correctness of their way. Each one operates from a position of "truth." Each is grounded in a sense of certainty, indeed "knowledge" that history is on their side.

Secular Zionism assumed that the religious version of Judaism was likely to wane, wither, and eventually disappear. It took pride in the fact that only when the national leadership was placed in secular hands did Jewish existence become secure, and the Jewish people finally succeed in advancing to statehood. It looked around and found ample evidence that science, progress, enlightenment, and education were crowding out religion and diminishing its role worldwide. Therefore, in the first four decades of statehood, Secular Zionism was the backbone of Israeli society, and it marginalized the religious and Haredi worldviews. The revolt against tradition and the assumption that it should be relegated to the past resulted in open divorce from the treasures of Jewish culture—the Jewish bookshelf—a literary heritage created mainly by religious Jews. Thus, in practice, Israeli discourse and classical Jewish culture were alienated from each other; the Jewish character of the State and of its key institutions, such as academia, law, politics, and culture, was increasingly attenuated.

The *haredim*, on their part, believe that secular Judaism suffers from an internal contradiction. As they see it, the existence of secular Judaism was possible only because tens of earlier generations of Jews had clung to their religious traditions; it was learning Torah and strict observance of ritual requirements in practice that enabled them to maintain their unique identity against all odds. Religion is the bridge over which the Jewish people marched on this journey from the glorious past, through the dark millennia of exile, to the current period. According to their interpretation, Jewish existence today is the fulfillment of the divine promise whose realization is contingent upon scrupulous observance of the old way of life, now and in the future. The Jewish nation does not exist in, of, and for itself; its very existence hinges on religious commitment. Therefore the idea of a secular Jewish state is a contradiction in terms and by definition cannot survive over time. It follows that there is no room for any substantive dialogue about lifestyle or the appropriate vision for the State of Israel. The State itself is a new phenomenon, to be regarded with suspicion. One can make use of it, but only by maintaining a proper distance from it and by firm and uncompromising action to bring it onto the main Jewish Haredi path, the trajectory of which is known only to them.

The middle camp of Religious Zionists finds it difficult to bridge the polar worlds of the Secular Zionists and the *haredim*. This is primarily because a central portion of the Religious Zionist leadership holds a theological position that places Zionism and the State of Israel in a messianic context. In their opinion, Secular Zionism and its astonishing success in establishing the State are a ploy adopted by God to make good on His promise to redeem the Jewish people. The full cooperation of portions of the Religious Zionist movement with Secular Zionism is not because it accepts the latter as a "legitimate" worldview, important in itself, but because it recognizes Secular Zionism as a necessary tool for achieving the religious objective of national salvation. According to this view, one should read hidden theological meanings into the secular agenda for the State. Jewish history is not set in motion by man; it is directed by God, who uses the State and its secular leadership as pawns in order to achieve His goals. Religious Zionism ascribes a mythical dimension to Zionism and regards the State as the "beginning of our redemption" (from the "Prayer for the Well-Being of the State of Israel" recited in synagogues on the Sabbath). The national revival is only the first stage, to be followed by a religious revival as part of the redemption plan that draws nearer the coming of the Messiah. This is an instructive and deep dialectical process, which, like its predecessors, wants to apply the particular vision of the group to the entire Israeli public space.

Thus, none of the three main Jewish visions offers a program for a shared life or the option of a shared, unifying identity that accepts the others as they are. The partnership is practical and operational, but it is not about understanding the Zionist act and shaping its vision. Rather, three parallel identities exist side by side, with each camp developing its own distinct narrative with regard to the reality of shared living in the State of Israel. In other words, in the shared Israeli space three monologues are buzzing vigorously, but there is no real dialogue. Occasionally, the parties are willing to be tolerant toward each other's differences, but they have not been willing to conduct an inclusive discourse. Nevertheless, since the first decade of the twenty-first century there has been a considerable move toward a correction—at least on the ground. The three main identity camps are beginning to show signs of sobriety and of recognizing the need to make the real coexistence richer.

The culmination of the secular uprising against tradition is behind us. Recent studies indicate that about 80 percent of the Jewish population in Israel is sympathetic to the Jewish tradition and toward the traditional Jewish lifestyle. Traditional Jewish practices are accepted by a very large part of the public. In many cases there is no religious intent behind this, but an acknowledgment that the rituals and the Jewish calendar are significant from the perspective of Jewish identity. It would be difficult to find a moving vehicle on the roads in Israel on Yom Kippur. On the eve of Passover almost all Jews hold a traditional Passover ceremony, the Seder. In 96 percent of the homes of Jews in Israel a mezuzah—a parchment inscribed with a quotation from Deuteronomy—is affixed to the door frame. The last survey conducted by the Israel Democracy Institute in 2012 found that about 80 percent of Israeli Jews said they believe in God. Interestingly, when Israeli Jews were asked to define their relationship to tradition, contrary to common belief, the largest group identified themselves not as secular but as traditional (a group distinct from both Religious Zionists and the *haredim*). There was a striking illustration of the numbers of Israelis who comprise this group when about one seventh of the Jewish population attended the funeral of a popular rabbi, Ovadia Yosef. They are not atheists and are not rebelling against tradition. Rather they are at home in the ritual and emotional world of traditional

Judaism but are not committed to the religious way of life and do not see themselves as bound by the authority of the religious legal system. For example, they will attend synagogue on Friday nights and will conduct the religious ceremony following it at home, but will drive to a soccer game on Shabbat itself. They will keep their home kosher but will eat out in a nonkosher place, as long as it does not serve a very explicit, symbolic, nonkosher food like pork. Therefore they are not "religious" in the sense commonly accepted in Israel.

Another indicator of a changing attitude to tradition among Secular Zionists is a growing phenomenon of "Jewish renewal" in Israel, whereby secular people establish a connection with the classical texts of the Jewish bookshelf, study them for their enjoyment, and find personal and national significance in them. Israeli culture increasingly echoes a particular Jewish voice drawing on precisely the texts that Ben-Gurion sought to exclude. This is an ongoing process of reshaping the nonreligious Jewish identity based on terminology, values, symbols, and collective memory originating in Jewish religion. While traditionalism is common among the general Israeli public, the Jewish renewal is more prevalent among the intellectual elites, cultural and media figures, and opinion leaders in Israel. These no longer rebel against the Jewish past but seek to integrate and continue it, in their fashion.

The *haredim* are also at a crossroads. Admittedly, the separatist Haredi rhetoric has not changed, and their great masses still live "behind sacred walls." In other words, Haredi men have traditionally spent their entire lives studying Torah. They did not acquire a general education, serve in the army, or join the labor force. As a result, most of the community lives in abject poverty. But it is possible to detect tectonic changes that suggest a maturation toward forging a life of cooperation with the rest of the population: in the last decade, thousands of *haredim* have begun seeking higher education—studying law, computer science, engineering, and social work in special programs and institutions designed for their needs as a first step toward integration into the Israeli labor market; increasing numbers of *haredim* enlist in the IDF, despite the objection of their rabbis; and although the Haredi community has a principled objection to the internet, the information highway, with all its positive and negative effects, is penetrating into many Haredi homes; and a Haredi middle class is taking shape, joining the consumer culture and seeking to improve the future of its children. Even the grip of the rabbis on the Haredi population is loosening, and the community is undergoing a process of democratization, albeit a limited one. These beginnings have a great potential for creating a continuing change that would allow the Haredi voice to integrate more harmoniously into the concert of Israeli identities and soften the separatist Haredi position that has isolated this population from the public domain and from the State.

Finally, with regard to Religious Zionism, in my estimation it is being disabused of the messianic approach to the Zionist idea. The Six-Day War, which restored Jewish government to areas that were part of the kingdom of David, ignited the messianic spark. But the hope that a linear redemptive process, without setbacks, had been set in motion was shattered. Contrary to the wishful thinking and the omniscient predictions of some of the spiritual leaders of this community, the State of Israel began a painful process of surrendering parts of the homeland, whether in the effort to reach peace agreements or unilaterally. The project of settling Judea and Samaria continues to this day, but it appears that the main force driving this movement is mostly national, security-oriented, and economic, but not necessarily messianic. Most of the Religious Zionist camp wants to integrate into the state and into its leadership on a basis other than sectarian identity. Many religious Members of Knesset (MKs) today were elected on the rosters of general political parties and not of sectarian religious ones. As Religious Zionism abandons the redemptive interpretation of the State, a dialogue with the secular public, without condescension, becomes more possible.

I have outlined here the intra-Jewish controversy regarding the identity of the State of Israel. But this is not enough. Israel is home to a national minority group, Palestinian Arabs, representing about 20 percent of the citizens of the State of Israel (within the internationally recognized borders of the State, that is, the Green Line). What is their position with regard to the question of the identity of the State? The Zionist ethos—a school curriculum based on Jewish culture, Hebrew as the language of the State, the Jewish anthem and state symbols, the Law of Return guaranteeing precedence in immigration to members of one people—already marks the public space. To the extent that the Israeli public space goes on to acquire an ever-richer Jewish character (and lately some of the political parties in Israel are pushing in this direction), the sense of exclusion and alienation of Israeli Arabs from the Israeli public domain is likely to increase. How do they respond to this?

According to the Democracy Index 2013 (published by the Israel Democracy Institute), about 40 percent of Israeli Arabs are very proud or proud of being Israelis (as opposed to 83 percent of Israeli Jews). More than a third of Israeli Arabs are willing to recognize the right of the Jewish people to a nation-state, similar to many nation-states in Europe, for example. They endeavor to establish a Palestinian nation-state alongside Israel, and when it is established, their demands for the division of the public space between the Jordan River and the Mediterranean will be satisfied, so that both peoples have a public space in which to build and nurture their collective identity. These citizens focus their claims on a demand for full civil equality and not on the Israeli identity discourse. If the constitutional definition of the state included not only the current two components—Jewish and Democratic—but also a third one, an egalitarian state, more than half of Israeli Arabs would support it.

Others, including most of the intellectual, religious, and political leadership of Israeli Arabs, are not satisfied with equal rights and demand to cancel the Jewish character of the State. They contend that true equality cannot be achieved as long as one national identity takes precedence over the other. They require that all components of the Israeli space—sovereignty, territory, norms, and symbols—be neutralized and freed from any particular identity. They are unwilling to settle for rights granted to a national and cultural minority and claim that the Jewish majority must erase its identity and implement it only at the substate level. According to them, the State should be a neutral field, transparent and hollow, with a universal character. A few radicals even condemn Israel as "the result of a colonialist action," part of a conspiracy of elites aimed at a takeover of the Middle East by Westerners. Whatever their internal divisions and lack of consensus about identity, most Israeli Jews are unwilling to consider erasing their collective identity from the public space. In effect, they understand this as a demand that Jews renounce the realization of their right to self-determination in the geographic space of the Land of Israel. The call reveals a bias against the Jewish national identity alone vis-à-vis many and varied other national identities that have established nation-states worldwide, and whose right to do so is unquestioned. Jews in Israel cannot agree to that.

As I have tried to show, we are facing a complex controversy between Jewish citizens and some Arab citizens as to the legitimacy of the definition of the State as Jewish, and among Jewish citizens themselves about the meaning of the Jewishness of the State. The ongoing debate about the identity of the public space makes life in Israel exciting, challenging, and at times painful. The Israeli agenda is jam-packed with conflicts and struggles relating to all components of the collective identity: nationality (relations between the majority and the minority), religion (relations between religion and state), and culture (relations between Western and Jewish culture). Given this turbulent background, the importance of decision-making processes in society and the State is clear. The next section addresses this issue.

The State of Israel and the Democratic Regime

The Declaration of Independence of the State of Israel, the constitutive document drafted with the establishment of the State and signed by its founders, defines the State of Israel as a "Jewish state." It does not explicitly state that it is also a "democratic state." But the content of the declaration makes it clear that the intention of the founders was to create a political sovereignty committed to a democratic form of government and worldview. Thus, the declaration makes explicit that the State "will ensure complete equality of social and political rights to all its inhabitants irrespective of religion, race or sex; will guarantee freedom of religion, conscience, language, education and culture."

Four and a half decades after the establishment of the State, the Knesset decided to enshrine the promise inherent in the Declaration of Independence regarding the identity of the State in a binding legal document. In 1992, the Knesset enacted the most important Israeli law: "Basic Law: Human Dignity and Liberty," which affirms that the State of Israel is a "Jewish and democratic state." The common interpretation of the term *Jewish state* is not merely demographic, a state in which most of the citizens are Jews, but also and mainly substantive: a state in which the public space is characterized by Jewish identity. Thus, the double definition, Jewish and democratic, raises an internal tension between the unique Jewish identity characteristics of the State and its universal democratic ones.

Let us review the facts. To what extent is Israel a democracy? What do Israelis think about the degree of democracy of their country, and how is it ranked from an external perspective, compared with other democracies?

In general, an overwhelming majority of Israelis, about 85 percent, share the view that the democratic system is the appropriate system of government for Israel. The minority that opposes democracy generally reports theological preferences, the rule of God rather than the rule of the people, not a preference for any other civilian regime. The prevailing view is that Israel should strive to be a democracy both in the formal sense (system of government) and substantively (democratic values and culture). There is not a single significant political figure in Israel who tries to be elected on a platform seeking to undermine any aspect of the democratic nature of the state. But if we consider actual responses to these general statements more closely, the picture becomes more complex.

For example, when Israelis are asked whether they agree with the statement that Israel needs "a strong leader who doesn't have to acquiesce in the Knesset or abide by the result of elections," most disagree, but nearly a third express their support. When Israelis are asked to what extent Israel is a democracy, three quarters believe that it is sufficiently democratic or not democratic enough, but one quarter believe that Israel is too democratic.

A similar division appears when Jews in Israel are asked which part of the dual definition of Israel as "Jewish and democratic" they prefer: two thirds prefer the dual definition or its democratic part, and one third indicate that the Jewish part of the definition is more important to them than the democratic part. In other words, if members of this group identify a contradiction between democratic and Jewish values (according to their interpretation), they are likely to abandon their commitment to democracy. Naturally, the *haredim* and the religious form a great part of this group.

When asked about their level of trust in state institutions, Israelis express exceptional confidence in the IDF (95 percent). The Supreme Court, which has been under ongoing attack in the last decade, still commands a respectable level of confidence of around 70 percent (far greater than the level of trust of the American public in the US Supreme

Court). The government (60 percent) and the Parliament (53 percent) score relatively low, and the political parties receive an embarrassingly low vote of confidence (33 percent). Reviewing these data, you can probably appreciate the complexity of evaluating the democratic robustness of Israel.

What is the quality of the democracy in Israel compared with other democracies? Israel is positioned in the middle of the scale on some key issues (democratic political culture, economic freedom, freedom of the press, functioning of the government, and corruption); relatively high on specific issues (gender equality, political participation); and relatively low on some important issues (civil rights, freedom of religion, national tensions, etc.). The low ranking extends to issues affected by the controversy surrounding the identity of the State, as described earlier. The general factual picture that emerges is of a country whose democratic self-image is clear; whose commitment to the principles of democracy, at the symbolic and normative level, is unquestioned; but which faces complex challenges in applying this commitment in practice.

How did Israel reach this situation? Considering the historical background of the establishment of the State and the reality since then, the current commitment of Israelis to the democratic system is remarkable. To understand this, the following facts must be taken into account.

First, there is the *absence of a tradition of sovereignty.* In ancient times, when the Jews enjoyed self-rule in the Land of Israel, the country was a monarchy, as was common in the ancient world. Admittedly, the Jews developed important mechanisms to limit the executive power of the king (for example, the king was subject to the rule of law, contrary to what was customary in the ancient world), but it is clear that the overall political experience was not democratic. Subsequently, the Jewish historical experience developed under conditions of exile, without responsibility for a geographic territory. Therefore, the framework of Jewish existence was based on families and communities, which greatly limited the possibility of developing a significant democratic tradition at the national level. Indeed, if we relied on the intellectual and practical Jewish tradition in order to deal with the main issues that democratic regimes confront today—system of government, structure of the state, separation of powers, and so on—we would find it difficult to come up with answers.

Second, there are *competing sources of authority*. The *haredim*, the religious, and many traditionalists perceive God as the source of authority for Jews as individuals and as a collective. This has not only abstract implications in the world of ideas but also practical ones: Judaism is a legalistic religion based on the religious legal code or Halakha. Rabbis, who are widely accepted as interpreters of Halakha, use their authority to make religiously binding rulings on a wide range of topics relating to all aspects of life. In other words, confronting the authority of the elected democratic institutions in Israeli society are undemocratic power centers that derive their authority from religion, which, as already noted, is an important component in the Israeli experience. Numerous points of friction between the Halakha and state law include a wide variety of issues: purely religious matters such as the demand to enshrine in state law several commandments of the Jewish religion, such as halakhic rules concerning marriage and divorce; political matters, such as the view that the Halakha prohibits relinquishing any areas of the historic territory of the Land of Israel as part of peace agreements with the Palestinians; and the struggle for jurisdiction between institutions, that is, civil versus rabbinic courts.

Third, there is the *composition of the population*. Before Israel's establishment and in its early years, most citizens were Jewish refugees. They came from dozens of countries in Europe, Africa, and Asia, almost all of which were not democratic. Moreover, during the 1990s and the first decade of the twenty-first century, Israel absorbed a million immigrants from the former Soviet Union. This means that nearly 20 percent of the population was raised under a communist regime. Thus, many Israelis are first- or second-generation citizens in a democracy and lack a living democratic tradition, unlike, say, Americans, in whom the democratic ethos has been inculcated over many generations.

Fourth is *the existential threat*. The State of Israel was established after the Jewish people were devastated by German fascism, which destroyed six million of them. Already on the day the State was established, May 15, 1948, it was thrust into a military campaign, the War of Independence, against seven Arab armies that attacked it from all sides. Since then the country has been permanently engaged in defending its citizens and its very existence. To this day, Israel is exposed to constant assault from domestic and international terrorism and from other countries, Iran in particular, whose ultimate and declared goal is to destroy the Jewish state. It is difficult to find even one example of a country whose legitimacy is the subject of debate by other states. It is not surprising, then, that this existential challenge has impelled Israel to function as a modern Sparta, a muscular, military state that cannot afford the "luxury" of fully democratic conduct.

Against the background of these baseline characteristics—the absence of a deeply rooted tradition of sovereignty, competition between the theological and the political, the personal experience of Jews who immigrated to Israel from the undemocratic countries, and the existential security threats—Israel's commitment to a democratic regime and culture from the moment of its establishment and throughout its existence is a unique phenomenon, and its significance should not be overlooked. The effects of some of these characteristics have been mitigated. The composition of the population has changed and the proportion of native Israelis born into a democracy has increased. Moreover, the absence of a sovereign tradition during two thousand years in exile is gradually being replaced by a tradition of Jewish sovereignty. Nevertheless, the other baseline characteristics, the competing sources of authority and the existential threat, still significantly influence the Israeli public space.

Furthermore, over the years new challenges have been added. The central development is Israel's gradual transition from operating in a mode of consensual democracy to one of democracy in crisis. In the first thirty years, Israelis conducted their lives with the objective of reaching agreements despite profound identity disputes. The Jews worked on the "common" and the three groups discussed earlier were willing to make far-reaching concessions, each on matters of great importance to them, in order to preserve the cooperative fabric. The status quo agreement on questions of religion and state is an excellent example. This accord, signed in 1947 before the establishment of the State, guarantees the position of religion in the public sphere with respect to several important issues such as the laws regulating marriage and divorce and the nature of the Israeli Sabbath. In those early decades, Israeli Arabs had not yet developed their independent national identity, or at least had not turned it into a political program. But since the 1970s, sociological processes have diminished the level of consensus between the parts of Israeli society. The shift in dominance in society; political changes such as the decline of the Labor movement and the rise of the right; security developments including repeated victories in regional wars that brought a certain relief, albeit temporary, of the security threat; the ongoing controversy surrounding the future of the territories in Judea and Samaria and the peace agreements; and not least, the strengthening of Palestinian national identity—all of these changes and more have sharpened the adversarial character of Israeli existence to current levels, which can be characterized as frantic and almost neurotic.

Controversies that smolder beneath the surface periodically break out into the open and threaten crisis. There are many notable examples: the assassination of Prime Minister Yitzhak Rabin in 1995, as a result of hostility of the religious and political extreme right to his foreign policy that supported the peace agreements; the demonstration by hundreds of thousands of *haredim* before the Supreme Court in 1999, in defiance of its authority to decide on matters of religion and state; the events of October 2000, when thirteen Israeli Arabs were killed by security forces during riots fueled by nationalist sentiments; the trauma surrounding the evacuation of close to ten thousand Jewish settlers from the Gaza Strip as part of the unilateral disengagement carried out by Prime Minister Ariel Sharon in 2005; and many more.

Other democracies have similarly experienced acute crises: the murder of US presidents and the evacuation of millions of French settlers from Algeria are but two examples. But the Israeli case is probably unique because of the cumulative burden of stressors—religious, national, and security. Moreover, unlike almost all Western democracies, Israel does not have a full constitution. For historical reasons, Israel did not enact a constitution at the time of its establishment, and to this day efforts to fill this lacuna have failed because of the continuing lack of consensus over the identity of the State. The practical significance of this reality is that the basic principles of democracy—for example, the separation of powers, including the division of powers between the courts and Parliament, and crucial democratic values such as human rights (political, social, or other)—are not constitutionally protected. The Israeli Supreme Court has taken it upon itself to defend the values of democracy, which it does with considerable success. But in the absence of a formal constitution, Israeli democracy is exposed to future dangers.

The State of Israel is a unique political organization. On one hand, it is the first democratic state in the history of Jewish civilization; on the other hand, it is the first Jewish state in the history of democratic tradition.

For most Jews in Israel, the uniqueness of the double commitment to democracy and Judaism is not a constraint but an existential necessity. The Jewish identity of the State is its raison d'être. The democratic commitment of the State is crucial for ensuring its existence. The Israeli challenge is to maintain both focal points of identity and way of life, the Jewish and democratic, through a continual dialogue between the two. The points of contact and inclusion between democratic and Jewish existence are many. For example, the values of human rights, which are at the core of liberal democratic culture, are deeply rooted in Jewish culture, and Jews have always been, and continue to be to this day, at the head of the human rights camp. But, as noted earlier, there is an inherent tension between the "Jewish," which is particular, and the "democratic," which is universal. The status of Arab citizens in the Jewish state is a challenge coming from one direction; the status of the Jewish religion in a democratic, nonreligious state is a challenge from the other direction.

The State of Israel and its young and vital society have achieved unquestionable and impressive successes. Among the important ones are the robustness of the democratic regime in Israel and the broad commitment of Israelis to democratic values and culture. But we should not assume that democracy in Israel is guaranteed for the future. Continual efforts are required to consolidate and protect it. At the same time, the State of Israel cannot be satisfied with a "normal" democratic existence and should not divest itself of its Jewish uniqueness. The strength and resilience of the country depend on the ability of the Israelis to fill the State of Israel with the rich content of the Jewish nation, culture, and religion. The State of Israel exists under the brilliant light pouring in through two large civilizing windows: the traditional Jewish and the Western democratic. This wealth is entrusted to its citizens and must be maintained and safeguarded for their benefit.

RECOMMENDED READINGS

Avineri, Shlomo. *The Making of Modern Zionism: Intellectual Origins of the Jewish State*. New York: Basic Books, 1981.
Oz-Salzberger, Fania, and Yedidia Z. Stern, eds. *The Israeli Nation-State: Political, Constitutional and Cultural Challenges*. Brighton, MA: Academic Studies Press, 2014.
Ravitzky, Aviezer. *Messianism, Zionism, and Jewish Religion Radicalism*. Chicago: University of Chicago Press, 1996.
Rubinstein, Amnon. *The Zionist Dream Revisited: From Herzl to Gush Emunim and Back*. New York: Schocken Books, 1984.
Yakobson, Alexander, and Amnon Rubinstein. *Israel and the Family of Nations: The Jewish Nation-State and Human Rights*. London: Routledge, 2009.

GLOSSARY TERMS

Basic Law: Human Dignity and Liberty
Declaration of Independence of the State of Israel
Green Line
haredim
Law of Return
Status Quo Agreement
Wars: War of Independence; Six-Day War
Zionism: Political Zionism; Religious Zionism; Secular Zionism

Yedidia Stern is Vice President of Research at the Israel Democracy Institute and Professor at Bar-Ilan University Law School. He is co-editor of the scholarly journal *Democratic Culture* and of the series *Israeli Judaism*.

NINE

Citizenship and Democracy in Israel

DONNA ROBINSON DIVINE

"THE STATE OF ISRAEL will be open for Jewish immigration and for the Ingathering of the Exiles; it will foster the development of the country for the benefit of all its inhabitants; it will be based on freedom, justice and peace as envisaged by the prophets of Israel; it will ensure complete equality of social and political rights to all its inhabitants irrespective of religion, race or sex; it will guarantee freedom of religion, conscience, language, education and culture; it will safeguard the Holy Places of all religions; and it will be faithful to the principles of the Charter of the United Nations."

—FROM ISRAEL'S DECLARATION OF INDEPENDENCE, MAY 14, 1948

Introduction

From the moment Israel declared its independence as a Jewish and democratic state, it draped itself in both *ambiguity* about the meaning of its core principles and a *challenge* to make public policies match the ideals enshrined in its foundational document. There was ambiguity because no single definition of a Jewish state had been adopted by the World Zionist Organization (WZO) and because there has never been a consensus in political theory on the conditions necessary for a democratic regime. There was also an implicit challenge in the proclamation: the standards used to measure the quality of the country's democracy would have to be adjusted as its Jewish identity evolved. For when ordinary citizens confront novel situations, they are likely to reach different understandings of their ideals and also of the political realities they are willing or able to accept. And while the proclamation is a description of Israel's identity and not a fully formed doctrine of government, it has, nevertheless, generated a dynamic notion of citizenship that allows for and even encourages future generations to apply and/or redefine it in ways appropriate for their needs and demands. This has also been the case in the American experience, where the citizens' practice of democracy continually develops and expands it. In response to changing needs and demands, Israel has become more democratic and more Jewish in ways its founders could not have imagined. How this came about is the story I wish to tell, partly because it is so important and partly because it has never fully been told.

The Ambiguities of the Term *Jewish*

It was primarily secular, not religious, nationalists who led the Zionist movement from its establishment in the last decades of the nineteenth century, and this secular leadership was largely responsible for Israel's founding as a Jewish state in 1948. Because they were seeking a political solution to real problems of nationalism and dictatorship, some of these Zionists generated ambitions not simply for a state and society but also for redemption. They were motivated by their belief that a Jewish state and society could provide a new kind of social order without hierarchy, without exploitation, and with justice and equality for all.

From the outset, however, there were more debates and controversies than consensus over how to achieve independence and about what it would mean for the kind of society to be created in a truly Jewish state. Many Zionists argued that work, as opposed to textual study and religious law, was the vehicle for creating community and homeland. They wanted to transform the discursive language that connected a people to its sacred canon and ancient stories so it could express the utilitarian and commonplace. In a revived Hebrew language, a new vocabulary would be invented to reflect the ideals of labor believed essential to building the new society and the new Jew. The new "religion of labor" required rituals and a liturgy, and the verb *to build* was central to both. The land, the family would be reconfigured, and the individual would be transformed as Jews pressed their claims for self-determination and were inspired to commit to a national renewal to be carried out, literally, with their own hands.

The open-ended disposition to change was inscribed into Zionism's DNA at its beginnings, and not surprisingly, these early Zionists embraced many disparate visions of a transformed Jewish society. And although the demands of establishing a sovereign state may have tempered some of their zeal for utopia, it did not entirely eliminate the ambition. But figuring out how to create utopia had to come after political leaders dealt with the pressing tasks that confronted the new state. First and foremost, a government had to be structured to meet demands for food and shelter, security, jobs, and education. To discharge these responsibilities required that power be transferred from an array of pre-state organizations whose leaders were convinced of their institution's primacy, not only because of its national goals—to redeem the land and transform the people—but also because up to that point, several of them had been operating with quasi-sovereign authority.

No wonder, then, that at the time of Israel's founding, the issue of concern was less to secure the rights of citizens than to unify the decentralized configuration of Jewish authority that had developed between 1918 and 1948, the years of British rule over Mandate Palestine. The Jewish residents who had come to Palestine committed to transforming the land and the Jewish people typically formed Zionism's most energetic and iconic political movements and parties. They held fast to diverse ideologies and/or represented particular economic and social interests. But alongside these staunchly Zionist activists were many who had emigrated chiefly to escape persecution. They did not aim to remake themselves or their nation and had no intention to shed the customs and traditions of their ancestors. To further complicate matters, there were also the Ultra-Orthodox, intensely religious groups who considered the idea of Jewish sovereignty profane.

This heterogeneity may help explain why Zionists were compelled to cast their claims as arguments. Another reason may be that Zionism won international legitimacy before it was fully embraced by Jews across the globe—or even by all Jews resident in the Land of Israel. In 1922, the League of Nations awarded Great Britain the Palestine Mandate in order to facilitate the development of a Jewish National Home. That too conditioned how they understood the exercise of state power. During the Mandate period, there were heated debates between Zionists and others in Palestine's Jewish community: Why were they living in the land of Israel?

What were their goals for the future and how were they to be achieved? Palestine's Jewish residents regarded themselves as part of a single people, yet some disputed the authority to establish an independent state run by elected officials when sovereignty rightfully belonged to God, whose precepts could be interpreted only by properly ordained (Orthodox) rabbis. Indeed, some argued that Jews could survive and adhere to the strictures of their religious code without Jewish sovereignty. Zionists responded by extending aid to the Ultra-Orthodox precisely to show them the tangible benefits they might gain from a Jewish state. Cooperation between Zionist agencies and rabbis representing the Ultra-Orthodox population were forged even before the state was established, and intensified as conditions in Europe deteriorated and immigration certificates to Palestine became precious tickets to survival. In other words, religious doctrine and ideological principles alone did not determine political behavior, and the principled hostility between Zionists and anti-Zionists did not necessarily preclude cooperation on joint ventures.

Israel's first generation of leaders viewed accommodating the demands of the Ultra-Orthodox as a small gesture to a community that had been decimated in the Holocaust and seemed to be in the last throes of life. They expected these last remnants to wither and fade, overtaken by more robust secular Jews who with boundless energy were determined to build a new Jewish society. Yet the diversity of views of Jewish sovereignty represented by a wide variety of institutions convinced Israeli political leaders to create an inclusive electoral system. Already at the beginning of statehood, powerful incentives were forged to ensure that even the most marginal groups could compete for parliamentary seats. It seems obvious with hindsight that incorporating so many disparate positions in the political process would inevitably have profound cultural ripple effects. And indeed public discourse was marked by contention, argument, and a heavy reliance on a language oriented to the future that became one of the many resources deployed in the struggle for political power.

Ambiguities of Democracy

Israel's founders saw the establishment of the state as a central and decisive phenomenon in the national life of the Jewish people and touched with universal significance. Yet they were unable to write a constitution to mark its break with Palestine's colonial past. In fact, as we will see, Israel preserved mandatory laws, stipulating that they would be carried over unless specifically repealed or replaced by new legislation. Without a constitution to delineate the distribution of power and the fundamental rights of individuals, the parliament had the task of proposing and passing on Basic Laws. These laws were to acquire special designation because they would be issued by the parliament deliberating not simply as an ordinary legislature but rather as if it were a constituent assembly. The Basic Laws would embody the principles and values guiding the state, interpreted by some politicians as the core elements of a process to enact a constitution.

The hopes of fulfilling Zionism's grand visions were encouraged by Israel's founding. Yet there were doubts and concerns that the new state lacked sufficient resources for the many urgent tasks confronting it. Consider the issue of immigration. Israel clearly desired and needed new citizens, and the right of Jewish immigrants to citizenship was enshrined in its first Basic Law of Return. Yet most newcomers arrived with few possessions and unprepared for the conditions in which they found themselves. The new state's efforts to provide immigrants with food, shelter, and supplies were hardly adequate. The sheer number of people—over seven hundred thousand in the first four years after independence—called for a response on a much larger scale than the sovereign institutions of the newly created state could handle.

The cost of immigration and absorption convinced Israel's Provisional Government to try to limit the numbers entering in any month. But Israeli officials could control only the gates to immigration; they exercised no influence over the exit passages. European immigration turned out to be larger than expected and to exceed, by enormous amounts, the anticipated costs. When governments in Iraq and Yemen announced that Jews who wished to live in the new Jewish state had to leave immediately or risk losing the right to leave at all, Israel's government complied. However, the country was unprepared and ill equipped to accommodate the needs of such large numbers. For the immigrants, conditions were arduous and the process of absorption painful; for politicians and administrators, absorption always verged on the edge of disaster.

The disruption and disorder that accompanied the rapid influx of immigrants were on such an unprecedented scale that Israel quickly relinquished total control of the process. The Provisional Government turned to the Jewish Agency and even non-Zionist Jewish immigration rescue services such as the Hebrew Immigrant Aid Society (HIAS) or the American Joint Distribution Committee to share tasks, financial burdens, and power. The complexity of negotiating this apparently commonsense solution should not be overlooked. The representatives of the Provisional Government derived authority for their diplomatic duties from a sovereign Zionist nation-state whose borders could be plotted on a map. The work of the Jewish Agency and other rescue organizations cut across many geographic boundaries and was predicated on sovereignty tied to the Jewish people, who lived in many lands. As one would expect where institutions are thrust together in a significantly changed and unprecedented political context, there was both confusion and disagreement: What was the exact design of the country's distribution of governmental powers? How did the idea of a Jewish sovereign state that claimed to represent the interests of all Jews across the globe comport with the actual national state with real citizens and definable—though contested—borders? Particularly critical for Israel in these early years of statehood was another question: how would this emerging conception of nationhood affect the country's Arab residents? The country's foundational document declared that they would share equal political rights as citizens. Yet their antagonism to the growing Jewish majority was bound to be augmented by the dislocations and violence of war.

At issue, then, was a clash between a concept of national identity that took membership in "the tribe" as the basis of solidarity and a notion of citizenship that reflected the corporate interests of the Jewish people but emphasized the individual, political, and civil rights of all citizens. The former proclaimed the Jewish identity of the state, and perhaps reflected the conflict that had divided Jews and Arabs in Palestine even before Israel's founding. The latter highlighted democracy and projected the image of an undifferentiated and sovereign people dedicated to principles of common rights and the common good. But the proclamation simultaneously asked for peace with the Arab countries waging war against the Jewish state even as it extended rights to its Arab citizens. In other words, it implied both a condition for citizenship and a standard for measuring deviance—namely, peace agreements with the Arab states— that was clearly beyond the control of the Arabs who found themselves living within Israel's borders. This meant that the principles that shaped Israeli citizenship were grounded in a willingness to acknowledge the legitimacy of the Jewish state.

Even after Israel won its independence and armistice agreements had been signed, there were still deep cleavages within its Jewish population. There were disputes over borders and security and unanswerable questions about how this newly established nation would create a political framework for making ordinary life possible. An array of associations, movements, institutions, and political parties had been functioning for many decades and proposing a variety of strategies to address these issues. Often organizations that championed the same ideal fought hard to ensure that their particular approach would prevail. When Israel was established, the remaining old problems were supplemented by a host of new ones. The state did not resolve many of the old ones nor did it shed its strategies for handling these kinds of challenges. Perhaps because Israeli democracy originated in the context of both British colonial rule and a national struggle, independence did not automatically erase the divergent ways Israelis had previously imagined their Jewish state. Those who had formerly pressed for national transformation still had their voices in certain ministries controlled by the Labor parties and in organizations such as the Histadrut. They were determined to protect what they viewed as labor's economic interests. Those committed to Religious Zionism's vision worked to instill their values through the distinctive publicly funded educational system, by asserting religious control over marriage and divorce, and by ensuring that the country would follow the Jewish calendar.

The country's most serious domestic problems, immigration and economic development, however, could not be addressed adequately by either utopian or religious commitments. These pressing needs provided the impetus for developing a new language of citizenship built around the newly created governmental structure. This ideology—dubbed *mamlakhtiyut*—argued that many of the tasks previously performed by the leading nation-building institutions, such as the Jewish Agency and Histadrut, must now be performed by the state. Its advocates saw *mamlakhtiyut* as the triumph of general over partisan interests. Opponents, mostly on the left, dismissed this ideology because of its association with the state. They charged that it would deprive the country of its idealism and weaken the organizations responsible for building the workers' economy.

It is not surprising, then, that no rigorous and precise description of citizenship was formulated by the new Jewish state. Nevertheless, there seemed to be widespread agreement on certain general concepts. First, judging by the lively uncensored debates that have characterized Zionist and Israeli politics, the political culture entailed a strong if largely implicit commitment to individual rights such as those pertaining to free speech and press. Second and perhaps most distinctively, sovereignty generated a series of obligations rather than a "bill" of individual rights. The language of obligations rather than of rights characterized discourse at the state's founding, largely owing to the dominant labor movement. Security needs topped the list, which is understandable given the circumstances. The list of government obligations then focused on developing the labor economy, a major category that included educating the next generation and providing services to absorb the newly arriving immigrants.

The obligations of citizenship, however, were not placed upon the entire population, nor were they expected to devolve upon residents equitably. Israel's democracy recognized that the Ultra-Orthodox denied the legitimacy of a Jewish state and that the Arabs were assumed hostile to its existence. It therefore exempted both groups from many of the most onerous nation-building burdens and granted each a great deal of cultural and religious autonomy. The groups were not subjected to enormous pressure to assimilate to the dominant culture, nor were they pressed to accept its warrant for public service. Obeying laws and paying taxes would suffice. The outcome was that Israel's citizens did not have identical obligations. This can be read as a sign of the law's respect for the country's diversity and the integrity of the communities that it encompassed. At the same time, these differences fostered weakness and dependence. The negative consequences in these communities gave rise to more serious problems later and help explain why the country's discourse on citizenship has continued to provoke dissent.

The state's founders took for granted that democracy should permit voters to hold those in power accountable. Leaders were responsible for the policies they pursued as well as the problems they failed to resolve. This assumption was drawn from their own experiences in Zionist politics when they had managed institutions that represented their interests under British rule. Believing that all adult citizens should have the right to cast equally weighted votes for their representatives and, through them, to participate in making decisions, Israel's founders established a parliamentary system of government. Elections were required to be held no later than every four years, with voters casting their ballots for political parties rather than for individuals. The country would serve as one electoral district with a very low threshold needed to win a seat, and with paper ballots counted to determine the political parties winning parliamentary seats on election day. This, then, is how the system operates in Israel today. Voters basically go to the polls and cast a single vote for one of the various national lists that are running. Seats are allocated to the various lists in proportion to the votes won. The specific candidates chosen from the winning lists are determined by the list's own ranking of these candidates—sometimes but not always through primaries. No single political party has ever received a majority of votes or parliamentary seats in any general election, so the leadership has always been forced to broker agreements and govern through a coalition. The self-governing framework the Jewish community in Palestine adopted under the British also incorporated principles critical to sustaining a democracy. In addition to free speech and a free press, they gave ample latitude for organizing political movements that could compete in elections. The latter was the decisive mechanism for resolving conflicts and constituting governments. Thus, many of the social norms that supported democracy took hold even before the state was founded, and while some have been revised, none has been reversed.

From the start, however, the language of obligation almost entirely obscured a language of common political rights. These two discourses and the relationship between them developed in response to the country's changing society and politics. The most far-reaching influence on this discourse of citizenship came from the intersection of economic development and electoral politics. Over time these embedded the language of individual rights deeply in the culture, destabilizing but not replacing the language of obligation. How and why this occurred tells a great deal about the nature of Israeli democracy. It also illuminates the kinds of bonds the state forged with its minorities and vulnerable communities.

This discourse on citizenship has been one of the most striking and least understood aspects of Israeli democracy. As in many democracies, citizenship in Israel is a complex phenomenon: it provides rights, imposes burdens, offers a sense of attachment, and makes available a set of opportunities. If we wish to understand not only how the country operates but also how a Jewish state can be a viable democracy, we must examine how this multilayered idea of citizenship applies to four sectors of Israeli society: Arabs, Mizrachim, Ultra-Orthodox, and women.

First Encounters

It is important to repeat, at the outset, that the languages of democracy and citizenship evolved within the contours of a society and polity that were themselves developing. Israel's founding in the midst of war produced severe dislocations for Jews and almost total chaos for the Arabs who remained within its borders. Independence for the Jews was named al-Nakba, or "The Catastrophe," by the Arabs. Once part of Mandate Palestine's majority population, Arabs found themselves a distinct minority when the guns were silenced and the truces declared. War had reduced their numbers to one tenth of the Jewish population. Almost strangers in a strange land, Arabs were unsure of how they would be treated and what would happen to their lands and homes. They and the Arab States that had deployed their armies to stop the establishment of a Jewish state had suffered a monumental and unfathomable defeat.

Arabs saw loss wherever they turned. Their villages either were abandoned or were becoming sites for new Jewish communities. The so-called mixed cities of Tel Aviv-Jaffa, Haifa, Tiberius, and Safed were transformed into Jewish centers. The country's most contested site—Jerusalem—was bisected by the war and ruled by the then enemy states of Jordan and Israel whose citizens waited uneasily for what was commonly expected to be the conflict's next round of battles. Families were now often spread across enemy lines with loyalties strained by distance and conflicting demands for survival. Their most prominent urban leaders were residing in other Arab countries. Bereft and abandoned, Palestinians were forced to acknowledge both their dashed hopes for ejecting the Jews from the region and the precariousness of their new situation.

Citizenship

Notwithstanding declarations of equality and freedom for all, Arab citizens of Israel soon encountered numerous differences between declared principles and actual policies. Not all government advisors assumed it was necessary to establish a special security regime for the Arab population caught within Israel's new and fragile borders. Some advocated extending benefits and aid to this demoralized, frightened and impoverished community. They maintained that despite the enormous challenges facing the Jewish state, including the refusal of Arab leaders to accept a formal end to hostilities, Israel could win the Arabs' loyalty with generosity and sensitivity. But their arguments did not persuade those responsible for shaping Israel's initial relationships with its Arab citizens.

In areas densely populated by Arabs, a military administration was installed that marked the community as hostile, presumably supportive of Israel's enemies, and therefore a danger to the newly founded Jewish state. While state policy encouraged Jewish immigration, when Palestinians tried to return to their homes and villages from their refugee camps in other lands, this was labeled as infiltration, as jeopardizing lives, and as undermining the safety of the state. The ministry charged with addressing minority issues was also responsible for the police force. Until 1966, that military administration governed most Arab towns and villages, supervising movement and activities and reinforcing the distinction between Arab and Jewish citizens.

Of course, there were good reasons for Israel's policy makers to worry about security. Some Palestinians did make their way back to harvest crops or reclaim their homes. However, others crossed the armistice lines to continue their war against the Jewish state and its population. The Arab wars against Israel did not end in 1949, when truce agreements were signed and armies were ordered to return to their home bases. Hostilities continued, although they were less organized. And for Israel's Jews, the war with the declared intention to eradicate the state was impossible to forget. Reminders were everywhere: on gravestones, at battle sites, in the wounds on people's bodies, in the shortages of food and shelter. Jews memorialized the war and its costs as a reminder of their determination to reclaim their homeland and construct a modern state. It made sense to

Israel's leaders, in this context, that the rights and obligations of citizenship could not be equal for groups whose avowed hostility to the Jewish state was rooted in nationalist or religious ideologies. In practice this meant grouping Arab citizens according to religious, ethnic, and tribal categories. It was on this basis that the law determined both access to resources and obligations. For example, Druze and Bedouin were drafted into the army, but Muslim and Christian Arabs were not.

To enhance security, the Israeli military began to wrap a tight security network around areas inhabited by Arab citizens and to watch for signs of discontent. Village leaders were instructed to gather weapons from residents and to provide lists of people who had left their homes during the war and might want to return. Some tens of thousands eventually did come back although primarily to reunite with their families. Few recovered any land. Israel seized lands deemed abandoned and placed them with the Custodian of Abandoned Properties even if owners had moved from one village to another within the state borders and not to enemy territory. A distinction was made between Arabs deprived of their land because they fled or were driven across the borders that defined the Jewish state until June 1967 and those who fled their homes and villages but remained within the so-called Green Line. But ultimately this made little difference, and several regulations passed in Israel's first years after independence made it almost impossible to honor most property claims. By 1958, according to one estimate, only 209 people of the tens of thousands of Israeli Arabs classified as absentees received certificates returning their property to them.

Interestingly, not all lands were seized by Israel. Arab villages in the so-called Little Triangle—an area in the center of the country running along the former Israeli-Jordanian border—were occupied by Iraqi troops during the hostilities. The area's inhabitants had been subjected to rape and robbery by the poorly trained soldiers. The territory was eventually handed over to Israel by Transjordan's King Abdullah, who had earlier declared it a duty to wage war against the Jewish state. The transfer brought a sense of relief to the residents but also a feeling of profound betrayal.

Being dispossessed of land sometimes meant starvation. Many Arabs were now deprived of their traditional livelihoods and could not seek alternatives since the regulations of the military administration restricted their movements. Moreover the condition of postwar Israel was itself dire. The combination of limited opportunities and want drove many of the remaining Arab leaders to forge cooperative relations with members of the military administration and with leaders of Mapai, the dominant political party in these early years. Such personal and political alliances brought goods and services to Arab towns and villages as well as favors to individuals. While these leaders were sometimes denounced as traitors, it was eventually acknowledged that their approach served their community well. The changes in perspective are an implicit acknowledgment not only of the particular challenges that confronted Israeli Arabs but also of the vast improvements brought to individuals by widening their access to education and jobs.

Accommodating the new reality seemed the only way to recover from the devastating consequences of 1948 and the war Arabs waged against partitioning Palestine. Too exhausted to continue their opposition, and too few to mount serious protests, many, though by no means most, Arabs who opposed Israel's policies did so by voting for the Communist party during general elections. The communists were steadfast in calling for an end to Israel's military administration and in promoting equal rights for all Israelis. They helped devise a new language for understanding citizenship that entailed at least some of the reasons the government offered when it finally dismantled the military administration in 1966. Political party leaders noted the contribution of Arab labor to economic growth and the relative peace enjoyed by Israelis after the 1956 war. Many politicians also believed that the military administration kept a majority of Arab votes tethered to the dominant Mapai party, which controlled the security apparatus. Market forces and greater security converged to expand Israel's definition of citizenship. Still, Arab citizens were not free from scrutiny even after the military administration came to an end. Emergency regulations from the mandatory period that had been incorporated into Israeli law could be applied when deemed necessary.

Since it affirmed Israel as the site of the Jewish homeland, the Declaration of Independence accorded Jews membership and a stronger claim than citizens whose rights were predicated on residence. But because the nation was promulgated as a democracy, the rights the declaration guaranteed had significance. While the primacy of Hebrew was an explicit sign of Jewish sovereignty, Israel recognized Arabic as one of its official languages, a significant mark of respect for the culture of the country's largest and most troubling minority. Language is an instrument of identity formation, and the capacity to use it in public life is critical to defining a community and safeguarding its traditions. Support for the Arabic language helped sustain the national identity of Israel's Arab citizens, although fluency in Hebrew was necessary for integration into the country's labor force and advancement through its mainstream institutions. Israel has rejected proposals to include Arab citizens in the defining characteristics of the state, yet at the same time it adopted policies that strengthened the attachment of this population to its national identity.

For all these inequalities, citizenship did include individual rights that entitled Arabs to demand services and access to resources. These, of course, helped improve the standard of living of Israel's Arab citizens across a number of dimensions. Levels of education, employment, health, housing, and income have risen for Israeli Arabs since 1948. Life expectancy for both Arab men and women has increased, while infant mortality has declined dramatically. In 1948, 80 percent of Arabs were illiterate; by 1988, only 15 percent. The number of Arabs attending universities has grown by a remarkable 700 percent, even though their numbers are still below the percentage of Jewish university students and do not represent an equal share based on the Arab population. These statistics measure progress and also reveal inequality. Rates of poverty and levels of crime are higher for Arabs than for Jews, and average incomes for the two communities are distinctly unequal.

When Arabs make their sense of grievance public, the country's political leadership typically draws as thick a verbal veil as possible across national differences, emphasizing that Arabs have always had rights consistent with citizenship in a democracy: they enjoy ever-expanding freedoms of speech, press, and assembly; they can vote and form political parties to run for Parliament even on platforms that deny legitimacy to the very electoral mechanisms that brought them to power. And while these assertions do not obscure the reality of the inequities, they have also proved to be a powerful reason to avoid channeling sufficient resources to address the inequities and the feelings of alienation.

So central has the Jewish state become to the collective consciousness of Arabs that this is now a very different community than the one conquered in 1948. And even when the same people dominated local affairs, political behavior changed. For the most part, the political class is less socially homogeneous. Politics is no longer the domain of only the landowners or the elderly. Professionals and merchants are more dominant in cities and in towns.

Demographic changes, prompted by Israeli policies, have emboldened village leaders to demand more resources in order to meet the expectations and needs of the residents who voted them into power. Mayors of Arab towns have engaged in strikes that caught the attention of national ministers who provided more funds for schools and for upgrading the local infrastructure, perhaps also hoping to serve their own electoral interests. Even politicians from the most hard-line parties whose platforms virtually ignore the demands of Israeli Arabs have forged alliances with local Arab leaders. After all, once they achieve office, their ministries might dispense services wanted by this community. Conscious of the critical importance of Israel's administrative hierarchy, Arab mayors have increasingly sought to raise their village to town status so as to gain better access to resources and to tighten their relationship with the national government.

Life in the Jewish state has required Arab citizens to make many uncomfortable adjustments. Nevertheless, it has had profound implications for how Arabs understand citizenship as comprising a calculation and pursuit of their interests, a definition of their identity, and an assessment of their political rights. Particularly for those born and raised in Israel and able to acquire university degrees and professional status, engaging in political activity has come naturally. A number of Arab professional associations have undertaken aggressive action to protest against inequities in the delivery of goods and services to their communities by invoking the country's proclaimed ideals. A number of human rights organizations also fund direct challenges to practices that have historically privileged Israel's Jewish citizens. One important judicial case disputed the Jewish National Fund's refusal to sell a home to an Arab in a community that was being developed on land owned by the state. In a landmark decision, named after the family initiating the complaint—Qa'adan—Israel's Supreme Court ruled that the state cannot discriminate on the basis of religion or nationality when it leases (which in Israel means effectively selling) its lands to its citizens.

Some Arab professionals have proposed an even more radical thesis of citizenship in a series of documents known as "The Future Vision." They call on Israel to recognize the Palestinian right of return and to divest itself of its Jewish identity. Israeli Jewish intellectuals and politicians tend to see these documents as a reflection of deep-seated Arab alienation and as yet another attempt to deny Jews their right to self-determination. For that reason, these documents have not elicited popular support. The idea that citizenship comprises individual rights rather than differently distributed obligations has burned rather than built bridges to fellow Jewish citizens who serve the state and risk their lives to defend the nation. In fact, even most Israeli Arabs, who declare their Palestinian identity, describe their positions in Israeli society in a language rooted in forms of action—education, work, ambition—that suggest solid attachment to the country if not to all government policies.

Israel's electoral system has drawn both favorable attention and criticism. The system allows the state's ethnic and religious communities as well as its many ideological movements to gain seats in Parliament and a public platform for their views and policy preferences. Opinion is divided about whether parliamentary representation has compromised Israel's governing capacity and stability. But questions of efficacy aside, from the beginning the system has given Arabs the opportunity to find seats and a voice in Israel's Parliament even if they didn't gain access to policy-making positions. Israeli Arabs who have served as government ministers have come through the ranks of Jewish, not Arab, political parties, and no Arab political party has been invited to join any government coalition.

Today, Israeli Arabs are not only fragmented politically but divided over whether engaging in political action is useful or important. The northern branch of the Islamic movement in the country, for example, argues against political participation since this kind of activity amounts to a tacit acknowledgment of Israel's legitimacy. Several Arab political parties, including Balad and United Arab List, seem to focus more on resolving the country's dispute with the Palestinians or on how it responds to terror actions launched from neighboring countries than on local issues that are of immediate concern to Israel's Arab citizens. Arab voting rates in general elections have declined over the years. This is less a result of injunctions from Islamists or indifference to regional politics than a consequence of apathy that seems to be a general characteristic of populations plagued by higher-than-average crime and unemployment.

While Israeli rule has not heralded the dawn of a new age for the Arab population, it has disrupted old traditions. Israeli Arab women have the right to an education, the vote, and the possibility of working outside the home, but these policies also cast Arabs into the throes of modernization. That they are now earning higher wages and have a higher standard of living does not change the fact that Arabs are paid less than their Jewish counterparts. Inequality in the workplace is a reminder of their subservient status and parallels inequality in education, with a school system that does not provide all the skills and amenities offered in the best Israeli schools. Moreover, many Israelis acquire advanced technological skill through the army, an experience that excludes most Arabs. One might say that the Arab community in Israel is struggling to keep up with the rapid changes in the "Start-up Nation" to which it is attached but to which it is not yet fully hooked up.

Land Expropriation

As we have seen, the 1948 War affected Israeli Arabs not only geographically but economically. Before 1948, Arabs owned about 4.2 million to 5.8 million dunams of land (roughly 1 to 1.5 million acres) while Jews held about 2 million dunams privately. Today, Israeli Arab lands comprise only about 0.7 million dunams. This is all they retained of the 4 million dunams that belonged to people who became refugees or was controlled by the Muslim endowment system or *waqf.* The Israeli government seized lands to develop Jewish towns in the Galilee: Upper Nazareth, Ma'alot, Carmiel, and modern Tsfat. Lands claimed by the Bedouin in the Negev have also been transferred to the state. To appreciate the tremendous impact of this loss we must consider that it is magnified by the growth rate of the Arab population. Since they became citizens of the Jewish state, Israel's Arab population has grown sixfold while its land holdings have been reduced. For many Arabs, then, 1948 did not look like a war over national rights so much as one fought for access to land. The effects of Israel's land policies were felt immediately as this population relied heavily on agriculture to meet its daily needs. One reason for the dispossession was the Zionist commitment to nation-building. In the early years the state handed over significant amounts of land to the Jewish National Fund, the agency in charge of redeeming land during the Zionist struggle to establish Jewish sovereignty. The ideal of settling Jews on the land had shaped Zionist policies during the period of the British Mandate, and no one thought that goal had been reached when the state was declared in 1948.

In instituting its land policies, as in other matters, Israel consulted laws Great Britain used to govern property rights during the Mandate. These laws, some of which reflected earlier Ottoman practice, gave the state latitude to expropriate land that was not harvested or occupied by owners. Given the turmoil of the 1948 War, there were many such Arab lands, and the laws enabled Israel to transfer vast areas to the Guardian of Absentee Property, leaving Arab towns and villages with no more than 2.5 percent of state land at their disposal. Eventually most of this land was designated for use as a means of imprinting the new Jewish national identity throughout the country.

In considering why the Supreme Court has generally upheld this state practice, it is important to observe that Israel's political culture, un-like the foundational principles forming constitutional doctrine in the United States, does not hold private property as a fundamental natural right and as essential to safeguarding freedom. It is widely believed that there is a bias inherent even in Israel's judiciary and revealed by the Court's interpretation of a 1943 mandatory law that allows land to be transferred from private to state ownership for public use. Critics claim this was done precisely because the law serves as a legal instrument for stamping a Jewish national identity on the land. But this view presumes that Israel's Supreme Court possessed a clearly defined authority from its founding, when its judicial power was actually untested and uncertain.

Examining the Supreme Court's position on land expropriation dis-closes the dilemmas confronting the Jewish state. It had to establish policies that would address a significant number of critical issues such as providing immigrants with food and shelter and securing the lives of citizens while simultaneously fulfilling its utopian redemptive ideals. And all this had to be accomplished in a transitional period when the government itself was not certain what powers it actually possessed. The Supreme Court justices were gradually emboldened to grant hear-ings to people whose property was expropriated by the state. Yet only after a 1986 ruling from Israel's Attorney General did they embrace the notion that the Court could offer protection against such state-initiated expropriation.

What were the reasons for this judicial deference to the state? The answer is complex. First, although the Jewish state won its War of Independence in 1948, it neither fully secured its borders nor was granted full recognition. The land continued to be contested by divergent national claims and competing holy writs. Second, the Supreme Court had not yet established its own latitude for interpreting and tempering executive orders, let alone parliamentary mandates. Justices adopted a cautious judicial philosophy generally known as formalism. This type of legal reasoning indicates that nothing should be done beyond applying and enforcing the literal commands of the law. Third, at Israel's founding, Supreme Court justices were effectively limited in the exercise of their authority by the uncertainty of their tenure and the difficulty of enforcing their judgments against the will of the executive or of the legislature, since the latter holds ultimate authority in a parliamentary system of government.

Perhaps these problems also stemmed from the fact that, as we have noted, the country had no written constitution and thus could not provide the Supreme Court with a textual reference. Israel's justices not only were divided on how and when to exercise the authority of judicial review; they also questioned whether they possessed the prerogatives of that authority. The 1992 Basic Law on Human Dignity and Liberty provided the conceptual framework for the Court to broaden its protection of individual rights—including the right to private property—and to withdraw some issues from the realm of Jewish nation-building to the context of a universal principle accorded to all citizens. But even when the Supreme Court moved beyond the strictures of formalism with regard to the civil rights of Israel's citizens, it still ruled largely in favor of the expropriation of privately owned land.

The culture of Zionist nation-building had, by definition, a deep animus to private property, and this left traces not so much on the form of Israel's economic policies as on assumptions underlying the country's public discourse. Without deeming the idea of private interest illegitimate, Israelis are inclined to regard it as compromising the public good. In light of this, the notion that Israel expropriated lands to advance its political interests against Palestinian Arabs must be tempered. Although this claim has been continuously raised, it ignores the fact that Court rulings have sustained the expropriation of privately owned Jewish property as well. Whatever one thinks of these decisions, they are impossible to understand without reference to the country's deeply ingrained cultural values. Israel is a country whose norms and values run decidedly against the idea that the right to private property is a natural and unalienable right. Instead it privileges the rights of the community.

As noted earlier, the Zionist ambition to remake Jewish identity was deeply infused with the idea that physical labor on national land was redemptive. During Israel's first years, the intense pressure to accommodate the urgent needs of a large flow of Jewish immigrants evolved as a cultural and moral mission. Necessity encouraged the transfer of land from private to public and national use. To establish its legal authority and earn the respect of Israel's citizens, the Supreme Court had to reflect the country's core convictions and beliefs. Just as it writes and conveys its opinions in the Hebrew language, it conceives and frames its judgments within the web of cultural understandings that it shares with the people it serves. Because expropriation of land is a concrete manifestation of sovereignty, for as long as Israel is besieged, the Supreme Court is likely to commit its rulings to what is widely understood as a defense of Jewish statehood.

The many-sided conflicts over Israeli democracy came to focus with hurtling force on March 30, 1976, with demonstrations against land confiscations. Until protests erupted against a purported Jewish plot to seize the Haram al-Sharif and destroy the Al-Aqsa Mosque in October 2000, the 1976 disruptions were the most successful or, depending on ethnicity and perspective, the most frightening call to action issued by Israeli Arab citizens. Both clashes seemed like timely indictments of Israel's security policies and even its military dominance. Israeli Arabs have continued to mark March 30, dubbed Land Day, with demonstrations to remind the country's citizens that Israel's public policies have failed to match its purported democratic values.

Why the major protests started in 1976 and not earlier is complicated but not mysterious. Arab leaders called for strikes and demonstrations not simply to document what had been long-standing Israeli legal practice and hence common knowledge but rather to change the dynamic and shift the burdens of proof. By 1976, they had sufficient numbers, sufficiently documented grievances, and sufficient confidence in their own political capacity to strike a new tone and embark on a new direction to make their voices heard. For Arabs, the land confiscations are elemental evidence of their subordination that is so fixed as to be unimpeachable. Land Day is thus a term with powerful resonance.

Citizenship for Israel's Arabs has produced tensions and contradictions since the country's policies have been forged to heed imperatives that often conflict with one another. Policies must expand opportunities and help shore up the economic well-being of the Arab population, but they must also ensure security. Almost all policies have been unequal to the demands placed on them and have achieved far less for Israel's Arab citizens than expected or desired. But Israeli citizenship has brought the benefits of freedom and expanded opportunity even while it has triggered feelings of unease in those who have thought most deeply about what it means for a Palestinian to live in a Jewish state.

Mizrachim and Identity Issues

The tension between the two vocabularies, citizenship as obligation and citizenship as rights, had very different consequences for Israel's immigrants from the Middle East and North Africa. Coming in large numbers and tripling Israel's population in the decade following the establishment of the state, they were not a numerical minority. Nevertheless, they were often caught in some of the same snares as the Arab population because they were perceived by the largely European-born ruling establishment as inferior, in need of civilizing and of identity transformation. Arriving without resources, they were typically shunted into poorer border regions and left to make do under conditions of extreme hardship and with little support.

Those responsible for these policies, Israel's first generation of leaders, labeled themselves *chalutzim*—pioneers. As the name suggests, they had not simply moved to a new land but believed they had reclaimed and re-created it. The culture they celebrated and the infrastructure they were building were not only real and tangible; they were also mental and emotional. The new national culture was uniformly imposed. Its refusal of ethnic and religious variety exacted a heavy price from new immigrants whose lifestyle did not match the authorized culture. The profile of the Mizrachim was taken as confirmation of negative stereotypes, and they were often blamed for delaying the forces and benefits of progress. Thus, the policies directed at absorption derived from a fear that people coming from societies presumed to be premodern were tied to religious traditions incompatible with the work ethic necessary for empowering the new state.

The Zionist ambition to create a new Jew, shorn of the customs of family and country of origin, was repudiated when the Labor party lost the 1977 election. The kibbutz and *moshav*, Zionism's storied achievements, had been held up as testimonials to the capacity of the state's political system and its committed citizens to translate egalitarian ideals into reality. Once shining examples of Zionist success, these famously utopian egalitarian communities were burdened with ideological doubts, heavy debts, and high operating costs. However tightly they gripped the imagination, by 1977, these venerable Zionist institutions were clearly losing ground and could not operate without generous subsidies from the nation's treasury. Even they would have to engage in profitable enterprises if they wanted to survive.

The new political movements that rose to power in the 1977 election were located at the center and right of Zionist politics and were more concerned with settling Jews in the territories conquered in 1967 than with sustaining the productivity of the agricultural collectives, regardless of their status. The electoral power that brought the Likud into the prime minister's office nurtured a self-confidence that radiated to other domains as well. It strengthened an ambition to reform or reconfigure the hierarchies that until that time had structured society and dominated culture. *Judaism* began to take over part of the niche in public discourse once occupied almost exclusively by the word *Zionism*. Today, several Israeli political parties comfortably assume the mantle of Jewishness. Their intent is not so much to disavow Zionism—though some, like the Shas party, do so in name if not in practice—as to dismantle the hegemony and elitism inscribed into the country's public discourse. No serious politician misses the North African Maimuna festival marking the end of the spring Passover holiday. Once denigrated as central bus station music, Mizrachi songs composed and performed in the style of

Jews from Arab countries dominate Israel airwaves. Instead of transforming "class into nation," one is tempted to say that in 1977, the country began to move away from a celebration of workers and agriculture to
a publicly acknowledged respect for rabbis and Jewish traditions, and in
the process inevitably changed Israel's discourse on citizenship.

Arabs who embraced a notion of citizenship that privileged individual rights and denied the state an official national Jewish identity cast
themselves into a *kulturkampf* they could not win. By contrast, Middle
Eastern immigrants and their descendants invoked Judaism to make
their case for inclusion with access to power and resources. Judaism has
its own imperatives. It is a potent force for revealing and correcting im-
balances in the power structure precisely because it can bring different
sectors of the population together in shared alliances. The Mizrachim
did not pledge allegiance to an ideology of individualism that they knew
to possess too little resonance in Israel's political discourse. As a result,
their demand to be recognized as different and included equally in the
culture has proved less threatening and has reinvigorated the Israeli tradition of citizenship as obligation.

We have already noted that Zionists initially encouraged immigrants
to divorce themselves from the Jewish culture in the lands of their birth
and to embrace the new secular culture that was developing in the Land
of Israel. But curiously enough, the narrative of negating the Diaspora
could not be sustained. As the "Start-up Nation" displayed its innovative
enterprises in the global market and competed to have its companies
listed on the US stock exchange, it was forced to reconsider identity.
The new Israeli identity that devalued the older Jewish identity of the
Diaspora compromised the ability of Israelis to engage with people, including Jews, across the globe for economic ties and political support.
In negotiating the global village, culture and identity are assets. Today
Israel is more disposed to acknowledge a common Jewish identity than
to negate the history and deny the attributes of the Diaspora. Examples
abound from the 2013 general election campaign where videos promoting the so-called secular political parties featured Jewish artifacts and
religious garb. Perhaps the most striking example is the way the newly
formed party—Yesh 'Atid or "There is a Future" embraced the religious.
The party's leader is former journalist Yair Lapid, the son of MK Yossi
Lapid, the latter associated in earlier elections with attacking the role of

religion in Israel's public sphere and directing his animus against the Ultra-Orthodox. His son, Yair, incorporated rabbis into prominent positions in his newly created political party, including one self-described as Ultra-Orthodox. Some of the people elected to Israel's Parliament on this party list are immigrants from the United States, and one is from Ethiopia. Geography no longer delineates a dividing line between the values of the old, rejected Diaspora Jew and the *sabra*, the new Jew created in Israel. No longer pressured or motivated to negate the Diaspora, Israelis seem eager to open up their culture and society to the lands their ancestors left and rejected.

Although they devalued what they regarded as a culture made moribund by its rigid piety and political passivity, Zionists preserved connections to the lands of their birth. But integration into the global economy, even if it arose from the narrowest of economic motivations, has profoundly affected that relationship. No longer propagating an indictment against Diaspora culture, Israel now brings together a vocabulary of national attachment with a language of religious identity. The story about settling the land in Judea and Samaria is not simply about redeeming it; the narrative is also about sanctifying it. Political leaders routinely seek the blessings of leading rabbis before elections, while many in the country invoke rabbinic authority to legitimize their policy preferences. Israel enthusiastically supports programs like Birthright (Taglit) that bring young Diaspora Jews to Israel to enable them to feel that they are stepping not only on holy ground but also and more importantly on common ground as well.

Paradoxically, Jews committed to strengthening Jewish identity and defending Jewish interests have presumed that nationalism and religion were disjunctive and, for that reason, a wedge issue driving Israeli and Diaspora Jews apart. Indeed, long before the recent controversies over military service for the Ultra-Orthodox or over the attempt to create separate and unequal space for men and women in buses and on sidewalks in Ultra-Orthodox neighborhoods, Judaism and Zionism were cast as adversaries. Zionism aimed to transform the structure of Jewish life, though without totally detaching it from its history and from many of its traditions. It preached rebellion as much against the shackling of Jews by the agents of Jewish religion as by alien rulers; independence meant Jews would be liberated from the rule of rabbis no less than from that of the czars. Drawing the line sharply led to the misapprehension that all Jews in Israel fell clearly on one or another side of the cultural divide, a fallacy that should have been exposed by the vitality of the Religious Zionist movement.

The 1967 War may have shifted the boundaries between religiosity and secularism, but the notion of two distinct realms never resonated with the population in Israel coming from the countries of the Middle East. Nor did classical Zionism's ambition to redefine what it was to be a Jew lodge itself in the imagination of Middle Eastern Jews who adhered to traditions and religious rulings from past generations and who considered the country's holy status the reason for their attachment to it. Today, Judaism has refashioned what it means to be a Zionist. Cloaking nationalism in a religious framework has inserted traditional ideas, values, and even discussions of the classic texts from which these notions are drawn into the general public discourse in new and interesting ways.

Zionism thus serves the rhetorical needs of political parties that are competing for votes in a highly charged system. As long as Israel's right to exist as a Jewish state is contested, Zionism is an emblem of Jewish national rights and a defense against yet another attempt to destroy the Jewish people. Economic and social issues are often viewed as consequences of how well the outgoing government has handled security and stood its ground against international diplomatic assaults.

Today's increasing references to Zionism in Israeli political discourse say less about Israel's past than about how one or another particular political party intends to navigate the country through its current difficulties. While in theory Zionism always aspired to inclusiveness and solidarity, in practice, as we have seen, it often marginalized those whose lifestyles did not measure up to the ideals it advanced. Nevertheless, its ideological commitments still serve as reference points for Israelis in the margins.

In Israel today a public avowal of Zionism may be read as a sign of integration into Israeli society and as an appeal to the country's national identity for authenticity. In contemporary Israeli politics, Zionism signals absorption and a demand for inclusion into the national culture.

But Zionism still does not readily include Israeli Jews who hold strong religious commitments. For them, a language of identity must include Judaism. And even as Judaism is invoked to modify the classical Zionist aim to transform Jewish identity, references to Zionism are used to buttress arguments for separating the religious and public spheres.

Zionism reminds some Israelis of their alienation, of their own dispossession and the sense that the country still belongs to the descendants of the European pioneers who built the state. At the same time the language filled with references to Jewish values and the deference displayed to clergy and to religious demands makes others feel like strangers in their homeland. Fortunately, this evolving public discourse allows more of Israel's Jewish citizens to recognize themselves as part of the country's national narrative.

Women

The idea that citizenship entails obligations has always imposed gender-specific burdens on Israel's Jewish women. Jewish national consciousness flowed as much from numbers as from territory. It was generally recognized that the success of the struggle to establish a Jewish state during the period of British rule depended significantly on population growth and size, though the demographic issue was seldom fully and publicly addressed. The mandatory regime itself insisted that the number of Jewish immigrants (without capital) be fixed in accordance with the country's estimated economic absorptive capacity. In its first years, Israel encouraged large-scale Jewish immigration even though, as we have seen, state resources and capacities were inadequate to support their absorption and adjustment. Israel's first prime minister, David Ben-Gurion, was certain of military victory in the country's war for independence but unsure there was a large enough population to hold the Jewish state. Families were encouraged to procreate and stipends were awarded to large families until the government realized that too many such prizes were going to Israel's Arab citizens.

The dilemma for women becomes apparent when we recall that Zionism, particularly in one of its many socialist variations, was expected to serve as an avenue to their own liberation. The work of collective redemption always took precedence over individual interests and personal desires, however, for men as well as for women, but this ethic affected the latter with special force. Like men, women believed that redemption came through work, particularly agricultural labor, but it was far more difficult for women to find the kind of jobs they had been taught to respect so they too could contribute to realizing the national project. Even in agricultural collectives and cooperatives, women were typically assigned traditional chores. Cooking, laundry, and childcare were deemed appropriate in accordance with the patriarchal values many subconsciously continued to uphold. And above all, there was the sacred commandment to produce children.

Thus the story of Israel's female population since 1948 can be read as a striking example of the conflict between two values: the cultural pressure to discharge what are widely believed to be women's duties, and the effort to reconceive Jewish society and transform both men and women from passive objects to active subjects who take charge of their own history. Assigned the primary role for raising children, Israel's women were presumably understood to be bringing up a nation. But the cultural message for Jewish women was clear. The vaunted experiments with community-based child-rearing on the kibbutz did not entirely replace the family or liberate women from their presumed obligation to bear children. To appreciate the crucial role of procreation in Israeli culture, note how it shapes the public policy priorities of the gay community: their demand for government funding to support subventions for surrogacy is stronger than demands for same-sex marriage. Regardless of economic conditions, funding for the latest fertility treatments has always been ample and readily available to all who want them. Moreover, there is no required link between procreation and marriage. Even unmarried orthodox women are supported in their desire to bear a child. People who have chosen not to have and/or raise children are reluctant to speak or write publicly about what is still a relatively rare decision.

The pressure to bear children did not erase the need for most married women to work both before and after the founding of the state. The imperative was economic. No feminine mystique operated in Israel, but neither were women treated the same as men in salaries or job opportunities. While both men and women worked and productive labor was celebrated, women typically filled subordinate roles whether in the military, civil service, agriculture, or the private sector. There was a gender-based division of labor. Particularly since the growth and expansion of Israel's economy in the past two decades, women have been empowered by new opportunities, particularly when these careers are viewed as fulfilling obligations of citizenship rather than as a means to individual self-fulfillment. Perhaps the relatively small labor market contributes to the fact that the culture does not emphasize the value of a personal career. As with so many activities, work was understood as serving a national value and purpose and was not seen primarily as a means to personal satisfaction.

As the country's economy expanded and more employment opportunities opened up for men and women, gender gaps in salaries and rates of promotion increased. Seeking an explanation for the gaps and occasionally invoking the feminist discourse developed in the United States and in Europe, some Israeli women, especially those with university degrees, began pushing for policy changes to help women make their way to new careers and to high-level positions in them. Not unexpectedly, their campaign was more effective when women used the language of obligation to insist on equality in sharing the burdens of Israeli citizenship than when they used the language of equal rights developed in other countries. Recently, Israeli women have become eligible for combat positions in the military and in the highest ranks of the officer corps. Women are also finding opportunities in high-tech companies.

In areas subject to personal status laws and governed by clerics—marriage, divorce, and adoption—inequities for females, of whatever ethnicity, still abound. Religious laws almost always restrict the rights of women to initiate divorce and secure custodial rights over children after the dissolution of a marriage. Honor killings, when a female is murdered by male relatives if she is suspected of sullying the family honor, are all too common in Arab communities, and Arab women who work often have to hand over their salaries to their husbands.

Many secular Israelis have stated that they see themselves ensnared by the same web of religious restrictions that confined the Jewish people in exile. Some ask why a Zionism that gave Orthodox rabbis the power to preside over marriage and divorce should not be held accountable for failing to liberate the Jewish people from the rule of rabbis. Israel's founders thought of themselves as involved in decisions that would affect the destiny of the country and of the Jewish people for generations to come. That assumption, it is posited, should have called forth the most resolute exercise of rational behavior. An agreement to vest power in clerics seemed, at the very least, incongruous with classical Zionist goals. But if one shifts perspective, the agreement to connect rather than separate religion and state looks like something altogether different. Zionism's aim to transform Judaism made it sensible to preserve the starting point and the alternative to what was believed the new dynamic and attractive meaning of being Jewish. The ranks of those bound to tradition was expected to be naturally and quickly depleted when people had another Jewish model before them. They would surely choose the new Jewish life created in and by secular Zionist Israel. There were also practical reasons to allow religious traditions to control life transitions. If the Jewish state served the interests of all Jews, the state had to acknowledge the sizable pool, in Israel and abroad, that felt comfortable with these rituals and rules.

That the rules regarding marriage, divorce, adoption, and conversion are hotly debated is not a new development. It does seem significant that these debates have gained considerable traction among activists who call on the government to dismantle the religious monopoly over personal status issues and complain that these stringent rules are imposed by a community that does not even share the fundamental obligations of citizenship. Herein lies a cautionary tale for all Israelis who wish to influence the future direction of the country. Not by rights alone will they be able to ensure their freedoms regardless of religion, ethnicity, and gender but only through an expansion of their duties as citizens in a state that gives expression to the historic rights of the Jewish people.

Israelis pay a high cost for their independence and are naturally disposed to calculate their citizenship in terms of its burdens: excessive taxes, onerous ongoing military service, religious strictures that appear stifling to some and insufficient to others. But citizenship in Israel is not understood as an end in itself. It is still expected to uphold substantive purposes: to give rise to the idea of Jewish sovereignty and to nurture a deep attachment to the country as the historic homeland of the Jewish people. If not all of Israel's citizens can enjoy the benefits of that attachment, at the very least, they must have a place in the Jewish state that accords them protection and meaningful freedom and opportunities. That is the story of the national challenge issued by the proclamation for the Jewish state, a hope and a promise yet to be fulfilled.

RECOMMENDED READINGS

Chowers, Eyal. *The Political Philosophy of Zionism.* New York: Cambridge University Press, 2011.
Divine, Donna Robinson. *Exiled in the Homeland: Zionism and the Return to Mandate Palestine.* Austin: University of Texas Press, 2009
Gavison, Ruth. "Constitutions and Political Reconstruction? Israel's Quest for a Constitution." *International Sociology* 18:1 (March 2003), 53–70.
Kaplana, Misra, and Melanie S. Rich, eds. *Jewish Feminism in Israel: Some Contemporary Perspectives.* Waltham, MA: Brandeis University Press, 2003.
Migdal, Joel S. *Through the Lens of Israel: Explorations in State and Society.* Albany: SUNY Press, 2001.
Peleg, Ilan, and Dov Waxman. *Israel's Palestinians: The Conflict Within.* New York: Cambridge University Press, 2011.
Sasley, Brent E., and Harold M. Waller. *Politics in Israel: Governing a Complex Society.* New York: Oxford University Press, 2016.
Shapira, Anita. *Israel: A History.* Waltham, MA: Brandeis University Press, 2012.
Smooha, Sammy. *Still Playing by the Rules: Index of Arab-Jewish Relations in Israel, 2012.* Jerusalem: Haifa University Press, 2013.

GLOSSARY TERMS

Al-Aqsa Mosque
American Joint Distribution Committee
Basic Law on Human Dignity and Liberty
Green Line
Haram al-Sharif
HIAS (Hebrew Immigrant Aid Society)
Histadrut
Jewish Agency
Jewish National Fund (JNF)
Land Day
Law of Return
mamlakhtiyut (statism)

Mapai
Nakba, al-
Religious Zionism
Shas
World Zionist Organization (WZO)
Yesh 'Atid

Donna Robinson Divine is the Morningstar Family Professor of Jewish Studies and Professor of Government, Emerita at Smith College. Her most recent book is *Exiled in the Homeland: Zionism and the Return to Mandate Palestine.*

TEN

Israel, American Jews, and Jewish Peoplehood[1]

STEVEN BAYME

Introduction: The Question of Jewish Peoplehood

The concept of Jewish peoplehood provokes serious questions about Jewish experience and identity. Are Jews members of a particular faith or an ethnic grouping? Does Judaism promise individual self-fulfillment or does it focus on national redemption? The either-or formulation of the questions is misleading; the answers go well beyond a simple assent to one or the other choice. Historically to be a Jew connoted a quest for personal meaning, common ties with fellow Jews, and pursuit of the distinctive national agenda of the Jewish people. Moreover, the concept of Jewish peoplehood is embedded in a narrative with a religious base. The exodus from Egypt is a story of divine redemption; God, not Moses, led the Jews as a people from bondage. It remains a critical motif and is a central historical memory. That act of divine redemption became generally expressed in the idea of a "Chosen People."

Yet after the Enlightenment, and especially with the rise of Zionism and the establishment of the State of Israel, questions that had been more theoretical and philosophical became political, controversial, and even uncomfortable. "What do Israel and peoplehood have to do with me?"

[1]I wish to thank Drs. Erica Brown and Steven M. Cohen for reading earlier drafts of this paper and offering many valuable comments, Dr. Theodore Sasson for sharing with me some important data, Drs. Ilan Troen and Rachel Fish for their overall guidance and comments, and Dr. Carol Troen for her expert editing. They all, of course, are in no way responsible for any errors of fact or interpretation.

Bonds with other Jews approximate tropes of tribalism. They may be too shallow to provide a real sense of unity beyond occasional anxiety concerning a common Jewish fate. Moreover, tribalism has connotations of racism, insiders and outsiders, and of privileging one people over another. These ring negatively for individuals brought up to appreciate and seek out diversity in friends and colleagues. Theologically, too, Jewish peoplehood raises questions: Why would God choose a particular people when all of humanity comprises God's creation? Most significant for our purposes, if the Jewish State of Israel is the fulfillment of Jewish peoplehood, what is its relationship to Diaspora Jews? And furthermore, what are our responsibilities to support Israel? How can American Jews respond when Israeli actions seemingly run counter to universalistic ethics that we as Americans value?

Thus, my task is complex. I want to address peoplehood for a twenty-first-century audience at a time when the concept of a Jewish people may be dissonant with American values of individualism and equality for all. Moreover, the State of Israel sharpens the issues. Discord in Zion contravenes the hope and perhaps an unreasonable expectation for a harmonious and unified people in the homeland. First, Israel represents the success narrative of the Jewish people. Yet that success coincided with a tragedy for Palestinians resident in the Jewish homeland. Second, Israel infuses Jewish peoplehood with great pride as an example of what Jews may do once returned to sovereignty and statehood—construct a state upon the twin principles of Judaism and democracy. Yet Israel poses a concern for Jews everywhere when others perceive her as a pariah state. Last, Israel represents the Jewish collective ethos, of which the kibbutz comprised a singularly successful and unique institution. Yet today, the values of individualism and personalism rejected by Israel's founders have penetrated virtually every corner of Israeli society including the kibbutz. What has been and what is now our relationship as American Jews to this vibrant, complex, evolving, and imperfect society?

The goal of this chapter, then, is to explore how the Zionist project has caused us to reexamine our ideas of peoplehood and how American Jews have maintained and also wrestled with their relationship to the new Jewish state since the establishment of Israel in 1948 and through the first decade of the twenty-first century.

Zionism, Anti-Zionism, and Non-Zionism

The concept of an international Jewish people bound together by ties of homeland, heritage, aspirations, and mutual responsibility for communal welfare has deep roots in Jewish historical experience. The biblical prophets addressed Jews both in their homeland and in the Diaspora. In a message recorded by Josephus, two Jewish generals in Egypt warned Queen Cleopatra (c. 105 BCE) not to invade Palestine lest she incur the wrath of the Jews of Alexandria. The renowned second-century Talmudic sage Rabbi Akiba undertook a trip to Babylonia, ostensibly to raise funds for Palestinian academies, but also, historians speculate, to appeal for support for the Bar-Kochba rebellion against Rome. During the medieval period, rabbinic leadership conducted an ongoing correspondence with Jewish communities throughout Europe and North Africa (now referred to as Responsa literature) regulating daily Jewish life and adjudicating questions of Jewish law. Moreover, as the need arose, Jewish communities undertook rescue missions to ransom co-religionists captured and sold into slavery irrespective of where these people were from—a remarkable illustration of the rabbinic adage "All Jews are responsible for one another." These exemplify that the Jews considered themselves a people not simply by virtue of inhabiting the same land in an increasingly remote past.

The concept of an international Jewish people assumed new significance in the modern period. Western Jews undertook diplomatic missions to mitigate the effects of the 1840 Damascus blood libel and to secure the release of Edgar Mortara, a Jewish child in Italy baptized by his nurse in 1855 and held in the custody of the Catholic Church. The campaign failed to secure the child's release, but the concept that assertive Jewry would assist endangered Jews elsewhere assumed new significance. Similarly, Jews from different lands philanthropically supported the Old Yishuv—the settlement of Jews in Palestine prior to modern Zionism. Although subsistence on international Jewish dole constituted an embarrassment for world Jewry, few denied responsibility for indigent Jews. Thus, for example, in the latter half of the nineteenth century, Jewish historian Heinrich Graetz, together with B'nai B'rith International, undertook a fund-raising campaign to build a Jewish orphanage in Jerusalem. These initiatives both derived from and manifested Jewish peoplehood in premodern and modern times, and significantly it was often secular and westernized Jews who assumed responsibility for fellow Jews, including Orthodox and even Ultra-Orthodox brethren and for the Jewish homeland.

With emancipation, it seemed initially that the restrictions and limitations on Jewish life in the Diaspora would be lifted and that Jews would be at liberty either to assimilate or to maintain their traditional way of life. However, modern Zionism denied that emancipation could solve the Jewish Question. Leon Pinsker had earlier advocated cultural assimilation for Russian Jewry, but the pogroms of 1881 convinced him that Jews must practice "autoemancipation": They could emancipate themselves and attain normalcy as a people only by acquiring a land and language of their own. For Pinsker, Zionism constituted Jewish self-reliance. The Jews would free themselves by acting as a people.

In 1895 Theodor Herzl wrote *The Jewish State*, a pamphlet that echoed much of Pinsker's *Autoemancipation*. Yet whereas Pinsker was pessimistic about securing Gentile cooperation, Herzl optimistically anticipated their assistance in creating a Jewish commonwealth. Convinced that emancipation could succeed in Western Europe only if Eastern European immigration ceased to hinder the process of assimilation, he transformed Zionism from a theoretical formulation to an actual movement. Anti-Semitism, Herzl argued, coerced the Jew into left-wing revolutionary movements. Gentile governments would facilitate the Zionist project because they too desired a solution to the Jewish Question, and the result would be a united front of Jews.

Yet the efforts of the Zionist project to unite world Jewry met with resistance. Some, particularly within Liberal Judaism, adopted the banner of anti-Zionism because they saw Judaism as a faith but not as a historically binding commitment that united the Jews as a people. British Jews, for example, identified as "Englishmen of the Mosaic Persuasion"; their homeland was Britain, not Palestine. A striking proponent of this anti-Zionism was Edwin Montagu, the head of the British India Office. Montagu entered the British cabinet during World War I just as Britain debated whether to issue the Balfour Declaration in support of a Jewish national home in Palestine. As a Jew in the cabinet he exerted far more influence on the issue than normally would have been accorded the head of the India Office, and Montagu mounted a last-gasp struggle against promulgation of the Balfour Declaration. His argument is instructive. He charged the government with abetting the anti-Semitic forces of England, who desired to rid England of her Jewry. Moreover, he drew a distinction between Zionist Jew and British Jew. Zionists in England, he argued, descended from foreign stock. In contrast, the British Jew looked to England as his only homeland. On the night the Balfour Declaration became public, Montagu confided to his diary that Balfour had struck an irreparable blow to "Jewish Britons."

Although today it is largely discredited within Jewish communal debate, anti-Zionism once occupied a respectable position. Orthodox anti-Zionists, exemplified by Agudat Yisrael, argued that Zionism represented an ill-advised and theologically forbidden attempt to "force the end," that is, hasten the redemption, the end of exile, and the coming of the Messiah, which had to be left to God's will and not "forced" by the acts of man. But by the 1930s Agudat Yisrael had shifted to a position of non-Zionism, supporting the activities of Jews in Palestine although still rejecting the idea of a Jewish state.

Vastly more significant and more creditable in America was the anti-Zionism of Reform Judaism. Reform rabbis, with some notable exceptions, argued that emancipation was the sole solution to the Jewish question, and not Jewish statehood. With the growing threat to European Jewry, by the 1930s Reform Judaism too had abandoned anti-Zionism; its 1937 Columbus Platform articulated support for Jewish peoplehood and the building of Palestine while remaining silent on the question of Jewish statehood. Yet when in 1943 the Reform movement officially endorsed statehood and the Biltmore Program of the American Jewish Conference, approximately one third of the rabbinate withdrew to form the American Council for Judaism, which remained adamantly opposed to Jewish statehood.

This divide between Zionists and anti-Zionists led to a public rupture within world Jewry and ultimately weakened Jewish political responses to the crisis of the 1930s and 1940s. Naturally, there were efforts to repair the rift. Non-Zionists opposed Jewish nationalism yet supported Jewish settlement and development in Palestine. The Jewish Agency was created in 1930 to provide opportunities for Zionists and non-Zionists to work together on projects benefiting Jewish life in Palestine. Hadassah Women's Zionist Organization of America undertook a program of medical relief culminating in the building of Hadassah Hospital as an illustration of nation-building, while it was non-Zionist fund-raisers and philanthropists who greatly assisted in the development of the Hebrew University. Notably, in the postwar years when American Jewry debated the partition of Palestine, the non-Zionist American Jewish Committee belatedly opted to support partition, although the anti-Zionist American Council for Judaism clung to the definition of the Jews as members of a faith rather than a people and rejected a Jewish state.

Since 1948 distinctions between Zionists, non-Zionists, and anti-Zionists have largely waned. The Jews' return to sovereignty and statehood constituted the success story of the modern Jewish experience. The undeniable change in the status quo was an opportunity that challenged the Jewish people to shape its own destiny. Of course, even then there was dissent. On the religious right, Satmar Hasidim described the Jewish state as a satanic creation—a trope echoed by Iran and al Qaeda in the twenty-first century. Conversely, on the religious left, while the overwhelming majority of Reform Jews adopted Zionism after 1948, a tiny minority of rabbis and laymen sustained the American Council for Judaism into the twenty-first century. Finally, beginning in the 1950s, a small group of Israeli writers and intellectuals known as Canaanites sought to clearly demarcate Israel from the Jewish people. Their intellectual heirs, post-Zionist thinkers in the 1990s, decried Israel's links with world Jewry as retarding her integration into the Middle East. But effectively, Zionism "conquered the communities"; whatever their ideological differences over the meaning of Jewish identity, the notions of peoplehood and state sovereignty became facts of life for Jews in all the lands of their dispersion.

Ingathering the Exiles

Following the establishment of the State, the practical challenges inherent in the notion of peoplehood became increasingly apparent. It was necessary to unify large numbers of Jews from a wide variety of backgrounds, cultures, and languages. Not only was the state responsible for their physical well-being, but it also had to provide the means for them to learn about each other and to establish common ground for living and working together. In addition, the new state had to develop

working relationships with Jewish communities in the Diaspora, and in
particular, the Jews of the United States, the largest and most important
Jewish community in the world at that time.

HOLOCAUST SURVIVORS

From its inception, Israel acted both in concert and at times in tension
with Diaspora Jewish communities to rescue and absorb Jews under
threat. Holocaust survivors saw little future in Europe and by 1951, some
360,000 had settled in Israel. Absorbing these refugees into the new
society was complicated. Zionists had been striving to re-create themselves as "new Jews." They saw themselves as strong, self-sufficient, fully
committed to overcoming hardships as they rebuilt themselves and their
new homeland, and as having shed the Diaspora mentality of accommodation to Gentile expectations. The influx of Holocaust survivors
who had been so brutally victimized echoed the stereotype of Diaspora
helplessness this Zionist narrative rejected.

As quickly became evident, the facts belied the stereotype. In the
1948 War, survivors comprised 25 percent of the combatants and absorbed 15 percent of the casualties. Surviving the horrors of Europe
usually entailed uncommon strength and fortitude and a willingness
to take risks. Their overall integration into Israeli society within a relatively brief span of time constituted one of Israel's earliest if not greatest
successes.

Nevertheless, survivors initially encountered considerable ambiva-
lence. They were the remnants of the Diaspora that had been rejected
and left behind. Perhaps, too, their presence reminded the Zionists that
even they had been unable to rescue Hitler's victims. Yet the public trial
in Israel of Rezso Kasztner in the mid-1950s and later of Adolph Eichmann in 1961 opened up a conversation. Survivors who had hesitated to
speak about wartime experiences that were dissonant with the dominant
Zionist narrative began to tell their stories and assert their rightful place
within Israeli society. The very fact that testimony about crimes perpetrated in the 1940s was elicited and the voices of the victims were heard
in a public trial affirmed Israel's identity as state of the Jewish people. In
turn, Israeli leaders, notably Prime Minister Menachem Begin, invoked
Holocaust memory as a unifying identity for Jews everywhere.

MIZRACHIM

No less challenging was the process of absorbing eight hundred thousand refugees from Arab or Muslim lands. Initially neglected in academic discourse and overlooked by the establishment whether in Israel or abroad, these individuals transformed Israeli demographics and ethnic identities in profound and lasting ways.

By the end of Israel's first decade, 125,000 Jews had emigrated from Morocco, and 123,000 from Iraq. Libyan Jewry sold its property at bargain-basement prices and quickly left following pogroms in 1945 and 1948. Syria, following a 1948 pogrom in Aleppo, blocked the assets of her Jews, many of whom escaped to Israel via Lebanon. Approximately half of the 100,000 Jews residing in Iran left for Israel while the more affluent remained under the shah—only to find their security and self-confidence shattered by the 1979 ascendancy of the Ayatollah Khomeini. Operation Magic Carpet brought in 49,000 Jews from Yemen, most of whom had little in common with Israel's more western norms and culture.

Israel's Law of Return, a bedrock principle of the Jewish state and rooted in the conception of Jewish peoplehood, promised any Jew an immediate right to Israeli citizenship upon relocation to Israel. Nonetheless a host of social, economic, and cultural challenges militated against quick absorption.

A major question pertained to education. The state aspired to imbue new immigrants as expeditiously as possible with Israel's Western culture. Religious leaders protested that Israeli authorities were defying parental wishes by placing children in secular schools. Ways to assign schools so the education accorded with parents' values had to be worked out. Yemenite Jews in particular struggled against absorption officials, generally Labor party bureaucrats, determined to undermine their traditional culture and values.

All immigrants, whether from Europe or the Middle East, endured hardship and primitive conditions in the hastily built *ma'abarot* (transit camps), intended as temporary absorption camps where immigrants were sometimes stranded for years. A housing shortage mandated delays in providing the new immigrants with suitable shelter, a situation satirized in Ephraim Kishon's acclaimed film *Sallah Shabati* (1964). The harsh conditions within the refugee camps abetted the feelings of Mizrachim that they were being discriminated against. Iraqi Jews in particular, who regarded themselves as the best-educated elements within Iraqi society, found their reduced status degrading and mounted demonstrations against Israeli racism. There are also disturbing stories of the vanished children in the 1950s. Yemenites have charged that hospitals kidnapped newborn babies and young children, informed their parents that the children had died, and then gave them over for adoption to Ashkenazi families. Although never completely verified nor refuted, the allegations reinforced the impression that Mizrachim were treated as outsiders to Israeli society and augmented their resentment of "insider" Ashkenazim.

At the core of the divide lay the demand that the Mizrachim assimilate and relinquish their heritage and traditions, as if these were merely vestiges of a primitive culture and had no value. By the late 1950s sporadic outbreaks of violence occurred because of frustration at the lack of opportunities in employment and housing. By the early 1970s the Israeli Black Panthers coalesced to advocate forcefully for the rights of Mizrachim.

The privations and degradation experienced by the immigrants is one part of a complex story. The massive immigration from Arab lands imposed heavy burdens upon the new state, and the state persevered in what it defined as the "holy work" of immigration. A comparison of the numbers of Arab/Palestinian refugees to the influx of Jewish refugees from Arab lands defuses the myth of Israel as a "settler" or "colonial" state and demonstrates that an exchange of populations had in fact occurred in the region. The election of Menachem Begin in 1977 symbolized the triumph of the outsiders, notwithstanding Begin's own roots in Ashkenazi Poland, and marked significant progress in integrating Mizrachim in the latter part of the twentieth century. By the 1990s, Ehud Barak had persuaded the Labor party to apologize for its mistreatment of Mizrachim. By the twenty-first century, even covert expressions of bias against Mizrachim are unacceptable, and Mizrachi figures have entered virtually all portals of Israeli society. Increased intermarriage between Ashkenazim and Mizrachim also suggests that the ethnic divide is narrowing. Although resentments persist, as evidenced by the electoral success of the Shas party, most would agree that integration of the Mizrachim today is far more advanced than at any earlier point in Israel's history.

The difficulties encountered by the state and the people notwithstanding, entire Jewish communities were rescued from chronic persecution and enabled to begin new lives in Israel. The Mizrachim were one of many immigrant groups, whether from the former USSR, Ethiopia, or the United States, that effectively challenged Israel to realize its vision of being the state of the entire Jewish people in all its many hues. The variety of customs, heritage, and folklore make Israel a culturally diverse society. It is a singular achievement of the state and its people that this ingathering of the "tribes" enriched the totality and simultaneously maintained social cohesion.

ETHIOPIAN JEWRY

Few events illustrate Jewish peoplehood better than the rescue and absorption of Ethiopian Jews, who differ in practices, heritage, and skin color. Initially Israel had ignored Ethiopian Jewry, partly out of deference to Ethiopian dictator Haile Selassie, who did not wish to see the Jews leave. Menachem Begin's election signaled a new Israeli attitude, and Israel began looking for ways to come to the aid of Ethiopian Jewry.

While Jews the world over united to rescue this tribe and support its resettlement, only Israel could effect the rescue. Thus the success of the mission depended on cooperation between Diaspora Jewry and Israel. American Jewish organizations, particularly the American Association of Ethiopian Jews (AAEJ) and the North American Conference on Ethiopian Jewry (NACOEJ), advocated bringing the plight of Ethiopian Jews to public attention and urged the Jewish establishment to broadcast their full engagement in rescue. Israeli officials objected, fearing that such consciousness-raising would undermine covert rescue activity. The outcome was that Israel partnered with American Jewish philanthropists and the Joint Distribution Committee (JDC), who called for a massive infusion of funds, amounting to $300,000,000, for a rescue and resettlement mission. This assistance of Diaspora-based philanthropy enabled Israel to take responsibility for the rescue and absorption of thousands of Ethiopian Jews who thereby realized their hope of one day returning to Zion.

In 1984 Israel began spiriting Ethiopian Jews out of Sudanese camps where they had been told to gather and flying them to Israel. In May

1991, some 14,310 Ethiopian Jews were brought out within a mere day and a half. Over 100,000 Ethiopian Jews live in Israel today, counting those who came via Operation Moses in 1984 and Operation Solomon in 1992 and their families. These numbers include approximately 20,000 Falash Mura, descendants of converts to Christianity who expressed the wish to return to Judaism and who today occupy a somewhat anomalous position between Judaism and Christianity.

The community has faced serious problems, and the long and complicated process of its absorption and acculturation continues. The trek from their villages to Sudan had to be undertaken in secret and on foot. Miles of desert and difficult terrain had to be traversed by families, including infants, young children, and the aged. The journey was arduous and dangerous, and between five thousand and six thousand people died en route. Added to the trauma of the journey has been the destabilization of community and family life and the encounter with the unanticipated modernity and secularism of Israel. It is encouraging that 95 percent of all Ethiopian eighteen-year-old males serve in the army, compared to an overall rate of 80 percent for Israeli Jews, but over 60 percent are on the welfare rolls. Ethiopian leaders claim that Jewish schools, supervised by the rabbinate, were teaching students that their Judaism was incorrect, while the authority of Kessim, or Ethiopian rabbis, was not recognized and they were barred from officiating at life-cycle ceremonies. Moreover, the Chief Rabbinate mandated a modified conversion procedure on the grounds that Ethiopian Jews were not fully Jewish, notwithstanding the 1973 ruling of the Sephardi Halakhic decisor Ovadia Yosef that Ethiopian Jews were descendants of the long-lost tribe of Dan.

Racism has also been an issue. Symbolically, the major crisis in absorption occurred during the 1996 Blood Affair, when it was revealed that blood donated by Ethiopians had been discarded by hospitals for fear of contamination with the HIV virus. In the 1980s Ethiopian Jews had mounted only a silent protest at the office of the Chief Rabbinate against the mandated symbolic conversion.

Over the last two decades, as it has gained experience and confidence, the Ethiopian community has been more forceful in voicing its grievances. The trauma suffered by an entire community that had for centuries lived separate from Jewish communities around the world, and differences of color and culture—including the shock to the Ethiopian newcomers that their fellow Israeli Jews were white—have made the process of absorption extremely complicated. Yet the prognosis is good. Like other non-Western immigrants Ethiopian Jews are making their way into Israeli life, including the Knesset, at a pace that may be inadequate but is steady.

SOVIET JEWISH IMMIGRATION

"Let my people go" became the slogan for the movement to secure freedom of immigration for Soviet Jews. Victims of communist repression, Soviet Jews became a cause célèbre for world Jewry following Israel's victory in the 1967 war. Elie Wiesel, Moshe Decter, Jacob Birnbaum, and the Student Struggle for Soviet Jewry (SSSJ) had already begun calling attention to the plight of Soviet Jews in the early 1960s. Yet only at the end of the decade could one speak of a full-blown Soviet Jewry movement. Persisting over two decades, this movement attained its greatest success in securing freedom of immigration in the late 1980s.

The question of Soviet Jewish immigration tested the limits and definition of Jewish peoplehood. The first Soviet Jewish immigrants designated themselves Prisoners of Zion and headed for Israel when they were granted permission to leave the USSR. Surprisingly, Soviet authorities acquiesced, despite the objections of Arab states. The Soviets explained that Jews immigrating to Israel were cosmopolitans who wished to return to their homeland and reunite with their families. By contrast, immigration to the United States was denied because it implied that the Soviet Union was not the "workers' paradise" Lenin and Stalin had proclaimed it to be.

By the late 1970s, however, more Jews were immigrating to the United States than to Israel. Generally these were individuals persecuted for having been born Jewish who were seeking personal freedom. Leaving the USSR on visas to Israel, many "dropped out" in Vienna and Rome to secure resettlement in the United States with the assistance of Jewish organizations. Israel claimed that its passports were being abused and urged action to divert immigration to Israel. The immigrants themselves at this point were less likely to be Zionists and more likely to be highly educated Jews from the major urban areas in Russia, hoping for greater opportunities in the West.

Tensions erupted over these "dropouts" or *noshrim*. The Carter administration had generously offered matching grants to benefit refugee resettlement in the United States. Israel claimed that Soviet Jews were not refugees inasmuch as they already had a homeland in Israel. Moreover, Israel needed the population increase and felt it could hardly compete with living conditions in the United States. Prime Minister Yitzchak Shamir stated explicitly that Israel required greater numbers of immigrants from the Soviet Union because of Israel's own demographic challenge of maintaining a Jewish majority.

Although American Jews clearly preferred that Soviet Jews immigrate to Israel, which needed to increase her Jewish population and was established precisely to provide a refuge for Jews, they upheld the principle of freedom of choice. They recalled a time when their own grandparents had opted to live in the United States upon leaving Russia. They also remembered an era when America's doors were closed to Jewish immigration in pronounced contrast to the liberal policies of the Carter administration. The American Jewish community could hardly mandate destination, even in the face of Israeli demands. Yet by 1989 American Jewish leaders acquiesced to Israel's arguments. Financial considerations were paramount, as America was no longer so willing to allocate generous financial assistance to resettlement. Rather than having Russian émigrés settle in the United States, America extended "loan guarantees" allowing Israel to borrow funds from American banks at reduced rates to support resettlement.

The ensuing Soviet Jewish immigration transformed Israel demographically. Israel now received close to two thirds of Soviet immigrants. During the 1990s, some 1.1 million Soviet Jews settled in Israel and now comprise about 18 percent of the total Jewish population. In 1990–1991 alone Israel absorbed over twice the number of Soviet Jews as it had in the entire decade of the 1970s.

Once again, the new wave of immigration posed challenges of absorption into Israeli society. Many immigrants were overeducated and underemployed. They needed to acquire Hebrew language skills, retraining, and licensing—whether in medicine, engineering, or other professions—before they could work in their fields. The unemployment rate for Soviet immigrants reached 40 percent in the 1990s. A further complication for both the state and individuals was that a significant number could not claim halakhic status as Jews because their mothers were Gentiles. They were admitted under the Law of Return, a secular law of the state that awards immediate citizenship to any Jew who wishes to settle in Israel. The law provides a liberal and inclusive definition of eligibility extended to all Jews and their non-Jewish family members. But the authority vested in the Chief Rabbinate on questions of identity and religion meant that matters of personal status—such as marriage and burial—would be administered entirely through Orthodox religious *batei din* (courts) that adhered to halakhic definitions of who qualified as a Jew. Put simply, the question of Jewish peoplehood in the Jewish state and the definition of Jewish personal status crossed a boundary line between religion and society. Moreover, some 20 percent of new immigrants made no claim at all to be Jews. The presence of some three hundred thousand Russian immigrants whose halakhic status as Jews was problematic hindered their integration into Israeli society and has further complicated the meaning of peoplehood.

Israel and American Jewry

THE BEN-GURION-BLAUSTEIN AGREEMENT

A unique aspect of Jewish peoplehood that had to be addressed following the establishment of the state of Israel is a simple demographic fact: for over two thousand years a majority of world Jewry has resided outside the borders of the Jewish homeland. This fact mandated that the new Jewish state needed to define its relationship with the Diaspora, and particularly with American Jewry, the world's largest Jewish community.

Virtually from the moment the state was declared, tensions with American Jewry were evident. At least four questions of principle divided Israel and American Jewry:

1. Who may speak on behalf of the Jewish people?
2. Does Israel's Law of Return inflict a problem of dual loyalty upon American Jewry?
3. Should Israel call for American *aliya*?
4. May Israel and American Jewry intervene in the internal matters of one another's societies?

David Ben-Gurion, Israel's founding prime minister, sought to answer these questions through agreement with the most important of the "non-Zionist" American Jewish organizations, the American Jewish Committee (AJC), whose leaders were greatly discomfited by calls for *aliya*. After an exchange of correspondence over many months, Ben-Gurion and AJC president Jacob Blaustein reached an accord in August 1950. Its key provisions included the following:

1. Israel gave up the dogma of exile. The language of *aliya* must stress the virtues of helping to build a new society—the distinctively American trope of pioneering and building democracy—rather than underscore the dangers of anti-Semitism.
2. AJC joined the pro-Israel consensus, a major boost for pro-Israel supporters. Blaustein promised continued American Jewish political and philanthropic support.
3. Leaders of both Israeli and American Jewry affirmed the principle of mutual Jewish responsibility. At the same time they pledged to avoid interfering in the internal affairs of the other.

The Ben-Gurion-Blaustein agreement was formally drawn up between Israel and AJC, but in practice it defined the relationship between American Jewry and Israel for several decades, notwithstanding occasional breaches of the principle of noninterference. The Conference of Presidents of Major Jewish Organizations was established in 1955 on the principle that whatever differences existed among American Jews, they stood steadfast and united in support of Israel and the policies of its legally elected democratic government. Similarly, the American Israel Public Affairs Committee (AIPAC), which registered officially as a pro-Israel lobby in 1954, grew exponentially over the succeeding decades. Jewish organizations were particularly outspoken in advocating strong and continued US support for Israel. As will be noted, the pro-Israel consensus remained largely intact until the 1990s. Their efforts were crucial during the wars of 1967 and 1973, when American Jewry rallied in support of diplomatic and military aid to Israel during her most dire moments of need.

American Jewish economic support for Israel also persisted over the ensuing few decades. Although UJA (formerly United Jewish Appeal) contributions to Israel declined from $224 million in 1994 to below

$170 million per year in 2010, the total funds raised including by diverse "friends of" Israeli institutions (NGOs) have approximated $1.5 billion per year. Aside from the important contributions these monies have made toward building Israeli society and alleviating poverty, the philanthropy also validated continued US economic support for Israel (totaling $3 billion in economic and military aid by the 1990s) by demonstrating that American Jewry truly cared about Israel's future. UJA Project Renewal was especially successful. It strengthened bonds of peoplehood by providing direct contact between donors and Israelis, explicitly twinning American communities with counterparts in impoverished Israeli neighborhoods.

American *aliya*, by contrast, was less successful. The number of *olim* rarely exceeded two thousand per year, and of these perhaps as many as a third returned to the United States for economic, family, or social reasons. During Israel's initial two decades, close to 70 percent of *olim* were non-Orthodox. After the 1967 war, the Orthodox share doubled and by 2000 had increased to 80 percent of American *olim*. In recent years the Nefesh B'Nefesh program, offering grants to new *olim*, has increased the numbers of mostly but by no means exclusively Orthodox immigrants to over three thousand per year.

Although they never emigrated in large numbers, American Jews have contributed significantly to Israeli academic, intellectual, and religious life. Very few have entered Israeli politics. On the West Bank, Americans formed some 10 to 15 percent of the Jewish settler population. There have been several infamous extremists such as Meir Kahane and Baruch Goldstein, but the majority has had a liberal American university education and they are often among the more moderate voices of West Bank settlers. More generally, while few American Jews entered politics directly, many more have been hyperactive politically—in Peace Now, Gush Emunim (Bloc of the Faithful, the West Bank settlers' movement) civil rights, environmental issues, and in the sphere of Israel-Diaspora relations.

To be sure, American Jewry has experienced considerable tension with Israel over the question of religious pluralism. Over 75 percent of religiously identified American Jews define themselves as non-Orthodox. The total number of Conservative and Reform congregations in Israel has increased considerably in recent years, yet Israel grants a monopoly over issues of personal status to the Chief Rabbinate, an entirely Orthodox, and more recently an Ultra-Orthodox, institution. As a result, Israel's message to non-Orthodox American Jews often becomes translated as "your Judaism is not true Judaism and your rabbis are not rabbis." Given the absence of civil marriage in Israel, all weddings are religious and only Orthodox rabbis may officiate at them. Liberal rabbis may not officiate at life-cycle ceremonies. Women of the Wall, a coalition of American and Israeli women, has sought the right to hold prayer services at the Western Wall but has encountered stiff resistance from Orthodox authorities.

Tensions erupt periodically, most notably controversies over conversion. Israel's Law of Return extended its benefits to family members of Jews, even if they are practicing Christians. However, the "who is a Jew" clause within the Law of Return is far more restrictive. This clause specified that one qualified as a Jew only if born to a Jewish mother or a convert to Judaism. Periodically the religious parties demand that converts be defined as Jews only if converted under Orthodox auspices. This problem has been particularly acute for Soviet immigrants, since as many as a third of them are of questionable Jewish status. Although they reside in Israel and received immediate Israeli citizenship, their right to marry Jews, as well as other matters of personal status, has been sharply restricted by the Chief Rabbinate, which does not recognize them as Jews given that often their mothers were Gentile. Thus far, efforts to amend the Law of Return so as to impose a halakhic definition of who is a Jew have been defeated, in part because of Diaspora opposition. The ambiguities and tensions, however, remain unresolved. The issue is similar to the problem with the Kessim of the Ethiopian community and the lack of respect for traditions and culture of the Yemenite Jews, or Conservative and Reform rabbinates for that matter.

In 1994 Deputy Foreign Minister Yossi Beilin challenged the very underpinnings of the Israel-Diaspora relationship. In public lectures and subsequently in a widely cited volume, he called for them to be reconsidered and adjusted to fit changed circumstances. Beilin argued that Israel had become a prosperous country and no longer needed external, especially American Jewish, assistance. He advised American Jewry to devote its resources to Jewish education inside the United States rather than treat Israel as a dependent family member. This part of his thesis emanated from Oslo-era optimism during which he and others assumed that Israel could tend to her own social welfare needs and could attain peace and stability without massive infusion of American assistance. His critics argued that whatever the chances for peace, tensions between Israel and her neighbors would persist, to say nothing of the threats of Islamic fundamentalism and the specter of nuclear proliferation in the region.

Beilin apparently underestimated how American Jewish support for Israel enhanced ties of peoplehood between the world's two largest Jewish communities, and his remarks evoked a firestorm. In the furor over Beilin's remarks, several of his more compelling themes were overlooked. Beilin argued that Jewish peoplehood was too often tied to perceptions of Jewish vulnerabilities, and Jewish unity too often evoked by external threats. The paramount factors of common heritage and aspirations seemed to be disregarded, especially since the Holocaust. He charged that the curriculum of Israeli education neglected both Judaic heritage and the continuing relevance of Diaspora Jewry. At the same time, he advocated an end to the Orthodox monopoly and called on the state to accept non-Orthodox or even secular conversion. Unfortunately, most of Beilin's innovative proposals to address the spiritual and educational dimensions of Jewish peoplehood were ignored. With the notable exception of Birthright Israel, the program he conceptualized and advocated to introduce young Jews to Israel, his call to expand the basis of peoplehood fell largely on deaf ears.

THE QUESTION OF DISSENT

The "pro-Israel consensus" among American Jews remained largely intact until the 1990s. American Jewish leaders had defined their role politically as advocating American support of Israel and the policies of its democratically elected government. In the early 1950s Hadassah was possibly the first Jewish organization to so define its appropriate role. Both AIPAC and the Conference of Presidents quickly followed Hadassah's lead.

Several factors account for the pro-Israel consensus. US officials, notably Assistant Secretary of State Henry Byroade, argued persuasively in 1954 that no president could be expected to receive multiple Jewish delegations. He urged Jewish leadership to coordinate their position and only then approach the president. In effect Byroade was counseling Jews to maximize their political influence by speaking with one voice.

Byroade's analysis resonated with the experience of the 1930s and 1940s, when the absence of Jewish unity had badly weakened rescue initiatives. The Roosevelt administration, reluctant in any case, had found it convenient to ignore requests of American Jewry given their internal disagreements about rescue proposals. Whether a more unified approach would have been more effective is debatable. What is not debatable is that American Jewish leaders believed they failed at least partially because of the absence of unity. The slogan "never again" came to mean: "Never again should Jewish leadership be so fragmented."

Surprisingly, the pro-Israel consensus lasted for several decades. Groups outside the consensus—such as the American Council for Judaism—were marginalized. Non-Zionist groups like AJC, still affirming that Israel was not the center of the Jewish people, became mainstays of the consensus. Most American Jews saw Israel as a David threatened by Goliath, wanting peace yet confronted by neighbors bent on her destruction.

Dissenting voices were heard more frequently after the 1967 War. American Jews challenged the policy of building Jewish settlements on the West Bank and joined Israelis calling for a Palestinian state. At the time, both positions were at odds with the policies of Labor prime ministers Levi Eshkol, Golda Meir, and Yitzhak Rabin, although Ben-Gurion himself had warned that continued occupation of the West Bank would threaten Israel's future as a Jewish state if only for demographic reasons.

The 1973 Yom Kippur War convinced many that settlements and continued occupation bred only further conflict. Breira (A Choice), a left-of-center grouping founded in 1973 outside the Jewish establishment, advocated alternatives: a cessation of warfare with the Arab world and Palestinian rights to statehood. Its leaders charged that American Jewry stifled candid debate and criticism of Israeli policies. These incipient voices of dissent, notably Americans for Peace Now and New Jewish Agenda, began crystallizing in the 1970s and became particularly outspoken following the 1982 Lebanon war.

Among Israelis, open opposition to Israel's policies vis-à-vis the Palestinians grew following the 1977 election of Prime Minister Menachem

Begin and his Likud party. Begin and his followers argued that the territories were liberated, not occupied, and regularly referenced Israel's historical claims to Judea, Samaria, and the Gaza Strip. This public debate in Israel legitimated differences of opinion among American Jews who now felt free to question Israel's policy on settlements and the future of the territories. Leonard Fein, a leading American Jewish public intellectual, called on distinguished American Jews to sign open letters of protest urging the prime minister to adopt a more dovish policy. New Jewish Agenda, organized in 1979, partially as a successor to Breira but with a broader set of issues to pursue, urged a halt to settlement activities, establishment of a Palestinian state, and negotiations between Israel and the Palestine Liberation Organization (PLO), whose covenant called for the destruction of Israel. New Jewish Agenda persisted until 1992 and actually won entry to several Jewish communal bodies and forums. It was more successful in doing so than its predecessor, Breira, partially because it used a far more Jewishly identified vocabulary and because it worked cooperatively with more established Jewish organizations, for example, with local Jewish community relations councils.

The Jewish establishment largely stood steadfast in its support for Israel. AIPAC in the 1980s became the "darling" Jewish organization because of its effectiveness as a pro-Israel lobby. The 1982 Lebanon War evoked considerable protest in Israel and the United States, as happened during the Vietnam War. Jewish leadership, however, supported the war, although several prominent figures in the establishment subsequently regretted that support. Rabbi Alexander Schindler, leader of Reform Judaism, embraced the prime minister and in many ways legitimated him for an otherwise skeptical American public. Whatever Schindler's misgivings about settlements and the Lebanon War, he maintained that his responsibilities as a Jewish leader mandated that he support Israel's government. Similarly, other prominent American Jews, witnessing what Yeshiva University president Norman Lamm termed a "media pogrom," hurried to defend Israel in the court of public opinion. Nonetheless, the Lebanon war was the first war in Israel's history that did not see an increase in UJA donations.

The pro-Israel consensus continued to fray. In 1991, President George H. W. Bush sought to condition loan guarantees to help resettle Soviet

Jewish immigrants on Israeli promises not to settle the immigrants on the West Bank. Prime Minister Shamir resisted, claiming that resettlement was a humanitarian rather than political issue, and American Jewish leaders largely agreed. Americans for Peace Now, however, broke the taboo against Jewish organizations lobbying in opposition to Israeli governmental policies and supported the president on loan guarantees. In turn, conservative groupings, notably the Zionist Organization of America (ZOA) and the National Council of Young Israel, followed and began to lobby in opposition to American financial support for the Oslo peace process and aid for the Palestinian Authority, again in direct contrast to the policies of the Israeli government. For the first time in Israel's history, domestic American Jewish groupings were asking the US government to oppose officially sanctioned Israeli public policies. In doing so, they were subverting Israeli democratic processes that had resulted in legally elected governments whose policies were not to their liking.

If Oslo exacerbated the fraying of the American Jewish pro-Israel consensus, the post-Oslo period signaled its coming apart. American Jews were increasingly skeptical about Palestinian intentions to make peace with Israel. But it also appeared that by continuing to build West Bank settlements, Israel too was hindering proposals for peace.

In 2008 J Street—a "pro-peace, pro-Israel" lobby—proposed itself as an alternative to AIPAC. Its name signaled that J Street was different. It stood apart from most lobbies housed on K Street in Washington, DC, which has no J Street. And it undertook to represent the "Jews" in the street who supported Israeli critics of its government's policies and were not represented by AIPAC and the Jewish establishment. In practice J Street lobbied for increased US pressure to bring the parties to a peace agreement. While the Jewish establishment argued that peace had to be negotiated directly between the parties, J Street believed that only Washington could bring about a peace treaty. It contended that Jewish efforts to align Washington with Jerusalem actually prevented the United States from exercising a strong leadership role in peacemaking. Absent from J Street's argument was whether the Palestinians would accept the legitimacy of a Jewish state, set aside a Palestinian right of return, and abandon Palestinian rejection of Israel.

THE DISTANCING HYPOTHESIS

The question arises as to whether such public dissent and criticism of Israel express or even encourage a distancing between American Jews and the Jewish state. Writing in the *New York Review of Books* in the summer of 2010, Peter Beinart, a well-known Jewish intellectual and former editor of the *New Republic*, charged that the Jewish establishment had alienated young American Jews through its steadfast support for Israel. Beinart argued that younger American Jews are becoming distanced—less attached to and less supportive of Israel. They have been alienated by Israeli policies and criticize American Jewish leaders for giving them unstinting support. In some measure, the Birthright Israel program was a response to this perception of distance and was designed to deepen ties between younger American Jews and Israel.

Beinart claims that younger Jews question the wisdom, even the morality, of Israeli policies. But how is their criticism to be read? A recent study of Jewish Theological Seminary rabbinical students and practicing rabbis found that younger rabbis and rabbinical students preferred J Street to AIPAC. Their critique entailed strong feelings for Israel accompanied by dismay at Israel's continuing occupation of the West Bank. Similarly, many younger Reform Jews define social justice as a core Jewish value and prefer J Street as more in sync with that value.

Are younger American Jews distancing from Israel, then? The answer depends on the sample. The responses of younger Jews as a whole, for example, differ from those of children of mixed marriages, who do tend to be more distant from Israel. So the answer depends on whether one is looking for casual ties to Israel (no decline) or for more intense attachments. Moreover, the concept of peoplehood itself has come increasingly under attack. Many young Jews today associate it with tribalism, if not outright racism, an attitude that reflects both the realities of assimilation and the blurring of boundaries that inevitably follows as well as the ascendancy of globalist and cosmopolitan values among millennials (those born after 1980). Researchers Steven M. Cohen and Ari Kelman report that over 50 percent of non-Orthodox Jews under age thirty-five say they would not perceive the destruction of Israel as a "personal tragedy." Similarly, in an online exchange, the editor of Jewcy.

com pronounced peoplehood an obsolete concept for young Jews. This tendency is buttressed by post-Zionists, such as the radical Israeli professor Shalom Sand, who has gone so far as to argue that the very idea of Jewish peoplehood is an invented myth without historical basis.

Distancing and increased criticism may also be a function of assimilation; that is, Jews who distance themselves from Jewish matters generally also are more distant from Israel. Whatever the variables, dissent is not equivalent to distance. Those openly critical of Israeli policy may be less distant; a vocal critique reflects both engagement and attachment. They would be indifferent if Israel did not matter deeply.

Israel and Jewish Identity

The Zionist philosopher Ahad Ha'am envisioned Zionism as the creation of a cultural center in the Jewish homeland that would strengthen Jewish identity worldwide. In this respect he parted company with Zionists who denied the value and viability of the Diaspora. Rather, according to Ahad Ha'am, a spiritual center in Palestine would serve as a beacon of pride and resource for world Jewry, even though only a minority would actually settle in the Jewish homeland.

The narrative of Israel represents partial fulfillment of Ahad Ha'am's vision. The rejuvenation of the Hebrew language, the creation of a modern state and society, the achievements of Israel as a Jewish state, and, last but hardly least, her sheer survival in the face of implacable enemies bent on her destruction have all proved enormous sources of pride for world Jewry.

Israel's successes as a nation-state have enhanced the pride Jews have taken in themselves as a people. No democracy in history has been perfect, but by comparison with other liberal democracies, Israel scores favorably on most democratic criteria. Diaspora Jews, particularly those living in Western democracies, justly take pride in an Israel committed to values shared by their own societies.

Yet on issues of identity, Israeli society and Diaspora Jewry often appear to be operating on parallel rather than intersecting tracks. Jewish identity in Israel suggests participation in the collectivity of the Jewish people. Diaspora Jewish identity, especially among those renewing their sense of Jewishness, is often deeply personal and existential, reflecting more a quest for individual meaning than membership in the collective Jewish enterprise. Moreover, Jewish identity in the United States generally is expressed through religious frameworks—approximately 80 percent of American Jews identify with one or another of the major religious streams. By contrast, in Israel there is a divide between the ultra-Orthodox minority and some national religious groupings that identify religiously and wish to impose their will, and a secular majority for whom the Jewish people and its culture matter far more than religious faith.

BIRTHRIGHT ISRAEL

American Jews have wondered if there was anything they could do to ensure their grandchildren would continue to identify as Jews. Birthright is the signature program adopted by Jewish leaders in 1999 to ensure future Jewish continuity. Explicitly linking Jewish peoplehood and identity with Israel, Birthright awards a free trip to Israel for every American Jew aged eighteen to twenty-six who has not been there previously on an organized program.

Birthright's sponsors aim to provide a direct encounter with the Jewish state and Israeli Jews that will strengthen Jewish identification by demonstrating what the Jewish people have accomplished through sovereignty and statehood. The program took into account that American Jewish travel to Israel was exceptional rather than normative. As of 2000, fewer than 40 percent of American Jews had ever visited Israel, compared to 66 percent of Canadian Jews and 75 percent of Australian Jewry. To be sure, Orthodox Jews visited Israel far more frequently. Thus the primary purpose was to ensure that non-Orthodox young people would have a firsthand encounter with Israel.

The Birthright program enjoys widespread support. Jewish groups across the spectrum—from Chabad to Reform—administer the ten-day trips. The pollster James Zogby opined to his Lebanese American colleagues that they needed to emulate the model of American Jews and launch a Birthright Lebanon project for their own people.

In numbers alone, Birthright far exceeded expectations. In 1987, fewer than 13,000 American Jews visited Israel through organized programs. By 2012, some 330,000 participants had joined Birthright trips, an average of 26,000 per year with a peak of 45,000 in 2008.

Philosophically, Birthright makes a profound statement about Jewish peoplehood and Israel-Diaspora relations. First, the program signals that as of 1948, being a Jew entails a relationship to Israel and the inborn right, fully supported by the American Jewish community, to visit the Jewish state. Second, as a partnership between megaphilanthropists, Jewish federations, and the government of Israel, Birthright articulates the value of mutual Jewish responsibility—not only to counter external threats but also to strengthen Jewish identity and peoplehood. Geared to adolescents and postadolescents, Birthright communicates the critical significance of continuing to become educated Jewishly, not stopping after Bar or Bat Mitzvah. Finally, Birthright constitutes a powerful emotional experience that links one's personal and individual story to the collective narrative of the Jewish people. At a minimum, it provides participants an experience in Jewish peoplehood and collectivity.

The early data on Birthright's first decade are encouraging. Seventy-eight percent of participants considered it important to raise children as Jews, compared to 71 percent who had not been on the trip. Although the data on marriage patterns among alumni are necessarily more limited, 72 percent of married alumni had chosen Jewish spouses, in contrast to 46 percent among married nonparticipants.

Whether such transformative experiences can sustain long-term Jewish identity, of course, is an empirical question and warrants longitudinal study. Only a small number of alumni, for example, have joined Jewish organizational activities. Birthright's backers agree that whether participants make a second trip to Israel at their own expense is a critical measure of long-term attachment.

Conclusion: The Meaning of Jewish Peoplehood Today

In the twentieth century, peoplehood was central to Jewish life. The two dominant events of the century, the Holocaust and the birth of Israel, delivered an unequivocal message about common Jewish fate and destiny. By century's close, however, the basis of peoplehood had been attenuated. Trends of mixed marriage and assimilation blur formerly held definitions of membership in the Jewish people, while currents of Jewish renewal, often expressed through spirituality and individual identity, reject peoplehood as tribalism. The broader currents of pluralistic America encourage fluidity of ethnic and religious identities and encourage further blurring of boundaries.

Issues of identity and belonging are far from being resolved. In 1983 the Reform movement adopted a radically changed definition of who is a Jew to include children of Jewish fathers and non-Jewish mothers. In doing so it shattered a two-thousand-year-old consensus that limited membership in the Jewish people to children of Jewish mothers and converts to Judaism. And when Orthodox parties pressed for Knesset legislation to ensure that only halakhic criteria would define a Jew for purposes of the Law of Return, the liberal religious movements of North American Jewry were deeply affronted. Finally, the assassination of Prime Minister Rabin by an Orthodox Jewish nationalist exposed mutually exclusive conceptions of Jewish identity, peoplehood, and statehood.

Thus, today, Jews are divided over questions of religion, culture, and politics. Hebrew, once the common language of Jews everywhere, no longer serves as a vehicle for international Jewish discourse. Those for whom Jewishness is the core of their way of life and system of beliefs are divided from those for whom it is peripheral or irrelevant.

For all these differences, there are substantial commonalities that enabled Jews to work together as a people to attain freedom of emigration for Soviet Jewry and effect the rescue of Ethiopian Jews in 1984 and 1992. These efforts were made not for individuals but on behalf of the Jewish people. The successful ingathering of the exiles to the Jewish state entails a commitment to a society in which Judaic and democratic principles coexist and reinforce one another. In effect, Israel is redefining the meaning of Jewish peoplehood. It is the latest and possibly the most exciting chapter in the annals of Jewish experience, and, as such, difficult to ignore.

Politically, Israel serves as a statement of permanent Jewish refuge. Less than a century ago, there was no such refuge. Chaim Weizmann testified before the British Peel Commission in 1938 that the world was then divided between places that did not allow Jews to live and places which did not permit them to enter.

Today, demographically, Israel is in ascendancy over the Diaspora. For millennia, more Jews lived in the Diaspora than in the Jewish homeland. That demographic pattern is being reversed. Israel's positive birthrate, coinciding with attrition in the Diaspora, increasingly makes Israel the primary, although by no means exclusive, expression of Jewish peoplehood in the contemporary world.

Last, Israel has transformed the meaning of Jewish identity in the modern world. A Jew in the twenty-first century has a connection with Israel, the Jewish state, by right of birth.

The ongoing agenda for Israelis remains daunting. Israel confronts its own demographic dilemma of preserving a Jewish majority as key to remaining both a democratic and a Jewish state. The secular-religious divide within Israeli society warrants a new social contract between Jews in which different ideologies of Jewish expression may compete harmoniously rather than intensify polarization between Jews.

American Jewry, too, has much to address in its relationship with Israel. While academic study of the Holocaust is widespread, the study of Israel is mostly absent from the curriculum of Jewish schools. As a result, knowledge and understanding of Israeli history, politics, and culture are limited even among well-educated American Jews. Barely a third of American Jews have ever visited Israel, notwithstanding their relative affluence and propensity to travel.

Among young American Jews today, distancing from Israel appears to be part of a larger distancing from Jewish matters generally, especially where children of mixed marriage are concerned. This suggests that the primary challenges that face the American Jewish community are how to counter assimilation and ensure future Jewish continuity. A serious relationship to Israel remains part of that greater dynamic and overall challenge.

Is Jewish peoplehood a salient concept for twenty-first-century Jews? Clearly the concept has been attenuated by polarization among the Jewish religious movements, currents of extremism within the Jewish body politic, an American ethos of personalism and self-gratification, our failure to acquire Hebrew as a common Jewish language, and levels of assimilation that profoundly threaten future Jewish continuity. Still, as we have seen, the concept of Jewish peoplehood retains considerable power in the twenty-first century. But it is Israel that has effected a sea change in the very idea of Jewish peoplehood. In our lifetime a sovereign and democratic Jewish state embodies the complicated and conflicting values of tradition and modernity, the collective and the individual;

it is a living laboratory experiment in identity formation. Jews everywhere have a stake in the creation and success of this still-new Jewish democracy that, notwithstanding significant shortcomings, promises to revitalize Jewish peoplehood with the historical homeland of the Jews at its center.

RECOMMENDED READINGS

Beinart, Peter. *The Crisis of Zionism.* New York: Times Books, 2012.
Eisen, Arnold. *Galut.* Bloomington: Indiana University Press, 1986.
Elazar, Dan. *The Other Jews: The Sephardim Today.* New York: Basic Books, 1989.
Gitelman, Zvi. *Becoming Israelis: Political Resocialization of Soviet and American Immigrants.* New York: Praeger, 1982.
Kelner, Shaul. *Tours That Bind: Diaspora, Pilgrimage, and Israeli Birthright Tours.* New York: New York University Press, 2010.
Kolsky, Thomas. *Jews against Zionism: The American Council for Judaism, 1942–1948.* Philadelphia: Temple University Press, 1990.
Lazin, Fred. *The Struggle for Soviet Jewry in American Politics: Israel versus the American Jewish Establishment.* Lanham, MD: Lexington Books, 2005.
Rynhold, Jonathan. *The Arab-Israeli Conflict in American Political Culture.* Cambridge: Cambridge University Press, 2015.
Sasson, Ted. *The New American Zionism.* New York: New York University Press, 2015.
Seeman, Don. *One People, One Blood: Ethiopian Israelis and the Return to Judaism.* New Brunswick, NJ: Rutgers University Press, 2010.
Segev, Tom. *The Seventh Million.* New York: Farrar, Straus and Giroux, 1993.
Troen, Ilan, ed. *Jewish Centers and Peripheries.* New Brunswick: Transactions, 1999.
Waxman, Dov. *Trouble in the Tribe: The American Jewish Conflict over Israel.* Princeton, NJ: Princeton University Press, 2016.

GLOSSARY TERMS

Agudat Yisrael
Ahad Ha'am
AIPAC (American Israel Public Affairs Committee)
American Council for Judaism
American Jewish Committee
American Jewish Conference
Americans for Peace Now
Balfour Declaration

Barak, Ehud
Begin, Menachem
Ben-Gurion, David
Biltmore Program
Birthright Israel
B'nai B'rith International
Canaanite movement
Chabad
Chief Rabbinate
Columbus Platform
Conference of Presidents of Major Jewish Organizations
Eichmann, Adolph
Emancipation
Gush Emunim
Hadassah Women's Zionist Organization of America
Herzl, Theodor
J Street
Jewish Agency
Jewish Question
Joint Distribution Committee (JDC)
Judea and Samaria
Kasztner, Rezso
Labor party
Law of Return
Lebanon War (1982)
Liberal Judaism
ma'abarot
National Council of Young Israel
New Jewish Agenda
Old Yishuv
Operation Magic Carpet
Operation Moses
Operation Solomon
Oslo Peace Accords
Palestine Authority (PA)
Palestine Liberation Organization (PLO)
Prisoners of Zion
Reform Judaism
Shas
UJA (United Jewish Appeal)
West Bank
Yom Kippur War
Yosef, Ovadia
Zionist Organization of America (ZOA)

Steven Bayme is Director of the Contemporary Jewish Life Department of the American Jewish Committee and of the Koppelman Institute on American Jewish-Israeli Relations. His recent publications include *American Jewry's Comfort Level* (with Manfred Gerstenfeld) and *Continuity and Change: A Festschrift in Honor of Irving Greenberg* (with Steven Katz).

ELEVEN

"Jewishness" in Israel:
Israel as a Jewish State

DAVID ELLENSON

Introduction: Political/Public
and Personal/Private Dimensions

This chapter addresses "'Jewishness' in Israel: Israel as a Jewish State," on two distinct though closely interrelated planes. One dimension can be identified as political or public, while the other concerns issues more properly labeled personal or private.

Regarding the political or public dimension, we ask: how is the State of Israel to define what it means to be a "Jewish state"? The return of the Jewish people to power in their ancestral homeland brought with it a responsibility that Jews in the Diaspora had never had to confront during eighteen centuries of political exile. How would a nation-state where Jews had sovereignty and constituted the majority define and express Jewishness in the public square? Together with this, we also require an analysis on the personal plane. How have individual Jews comprehended and configured their personal approach to the question of Jewishness in a setting where they do not live as a minority among a Gentile majority?

The chapter examines the continuing efforts of the State of Israel to resolve this question of Jewishness in public life by focusing on three areas of major importance: personal status and governmental support for Jewish institutions; the Law of Return and the frequently contentious and related issues of "who is a Jew?" and Jewish conversion within Israel; and the challenge of ensuring pluralistic religious and cultural expression for Israeli Jews.

Religion and State: America and Israel

The American reader needs to understand that the United States approaches the relationship between religion and state very differently from Israel and most other nations in the West. This difference has significant implications for how Jewishness is expressed in Israel in both public and private arenas. The Israeli Declaration of Independence, adopted on May 14, 1948, proudly proclaimed, "The State of Israel . . . will foster the development of the country for the benefit of all inhabitants; it will ensure complete equality of social and political rights to all its inhabitants irrespective of religion, race, or sex; it will guarantee freedom of religion, conscience, language, education, and culture." On December 15, 1791, the Bill of Rights, first proposed on September 25, 1789, was ratified and the amendments contained therein were appended to the Constitution of the United States. The First Amendment begins with the words, "Congress shall make no law respecting an establishment of religion, or prohibiting the free exercise thereof."

Each text enshrines a liberal democratic Western ethos that upholds the principle of religious freedom. Individual religious beliefs are seen as matters of private choice, not subject to governmental policy or coercion. This principle of religious liberty is so vital that each government pledges to protect this freedom through law.

However, unlike the Israeli Declaration of Independence, the American Constitution has an Establishment Clause that extends the principle of "free exercise" to include a prohibition against governmental advancement of religion. Thus, a fundamental difference characterizes Israeli and American approaches to this liberty. American affirmation of this principle of free exercise evokes a Jeffersonian image of a wall of separation between religion and state. *In the American model, complete disestablishment of religion is required.*

This American notion of religious disestablishment is totally foreign to Israeli society. With respect to our topic of Judaism in Israel and what Jewishness entails, this has two important consequences: the State of Israel funds religious institutions and schools, Jewish, Muslim, and Christian ones as well; and the state allows for Judaism to find expression in public life and control areas of private life in ways that would be unthinkable in an America that possesses a different tradition of religion-state relations.

Along with the promise of "complete equality of social and political rights to all its inhabitants irrespective of religion, race, or sex," the Israeli Declaration of Independence declares "the establishment of a Jewish State in Eretz Yisrael, to be known as the State of Israel." Even as the State guarantees freedom to all its inhabitants, it unapologetically defines itself as a "Jewish State" and identifies the State of Israel as the homeland of the Jewish people. The quality of Jewishness is thus built into the very fabric of the foundational document of Medinat Yisrael.

In addition, American readers must bear in mind that the demographic, cultural, and religious backgrounds of the overwhelming majority of the Israeli Jews are distinct from the backgrounds of most North American Jews, and this distinction has real consequences for the way Jewishness is understood and manifest in Israel. The 2009 Guttman Report on the identity and beliefs of Jewish Israelis indicates that the overwhelming majority of Israeli Jews feel that Israel ought to be a Jewish state; almost three quarters of that population asserts that "there ought to be some relation between religion and state in Israel" so that the Jewish character of the State can be maintained. These attitudes must be understood and appreciated as an ingrained part of the heritage of contemporary Israelis and—notwithstanding changes in recent years— they continue to impact how Israeli Jews view Judaism and Jewishness.

In their insightful 1983 study of attitudinal differences between Israeli and American Jews, *Two Worlds of Judaism*, Steven Cohen and Charles Liebman note that the American affirmation of individualism is "foreign to Israeli political culture." Israelis "are less sensitive to private rights of the individual" and less tolerant of minority groups than Americans. American Jews, as members of a minority informed and protected by the Bill of Rights, "support the most extreme form of separation of religion and state." Israeli Jews see society as "a community or extended family." In sum, Israel's "collectivist heritage" allows Israeli Jews to support an establishment of Judaism that is unknown in America. And, as I will explain, this "collectivist heritage" and approach to Judaism is a natural outgrowth of the cultural-demographic-religious backgrounds of most Israeli Jews.

Israel is a highly pluralistic society, with Jews coming from all parts of the world and its citizenry inclined to define itself as secularist. However, unlike Jews in virtually every other part of the Western world and cer-

tainly in the United States, most Israeli Jews are not familiar with the religious pluralism of denominations, nor do they identify themselves—as
most American Jews certainly have—in primarily religious terms. After
all, as Will Herberg pointed out in his classic 1954 *Protestant-Catholic-
Jew*, the United States viewed Jews as part of a religion, and "Jewish
distinctiveness" in America was justified in religious terms.

In contrast, the majority of Jewish immigrants to Palestine between
1918 and 1948 came from Central and Eastern Europe and from communities where Jewish religious pluralism was virtually nonexistent and
in which Judaism was viewed as much in political-cultural as in religious
terms. Moreover, after the establishment of the State, most Jewish immigrants to Israel hailed from North Africa, the Middle East, and Asia,
where liberal varieties of Judaism were similarly unknown. These Sephardi *olim* from Eidot Hamizarch (Middle Eastern Jews) who form the
numerical majority in contemporary Israel were, as Janet Aviad, then a
professor at the Hebrew University in the late 1970s, observed, "highly
traditional and religious." Thus the overwhelming majority of Israeli
Jews come from communities that did not regard Judaism principally
as a religion, were unfamiliar with denominational Jewish differences,
and did not regard state support of religion as improper.

Approximately one million immigrants from the former Soviet Union
who surged into Israel between 1989 and 2006 have been added to this
mix. These Jews emerged from a communist background and knew
virtually nothing of religious Judaism. Like earlier waves of *olim* from
Northern Africa and the Middle East, these immigrants are unfamiliar
with the modes of religious identity that characterize most American
Jews, but in contrast to them, most are also fiercely secular.

In short, the lived experience of most Israeli Jews does not include
the modes of religious identification and commitment that mark North
American Jews, their institutions, and their attitudes toward religion
and state. While they have had little or no experience of Jewish religious
denominations, they are comfortable with the notion that the state supports religious institutions and their clergy. Their stances and views toward Jewishness in the private and public spheres are thus distinct from
the positions and outlooks of American Jews. An understanding of these
fundamental differences must be borne in mind as we now consider how
Israeli Jews appropriate Jewishness in public and private life.

Judaism in the Public Square: Israel as a Jewish State

Defining what it would mean for Israel to be a Jewish state and how Judaism would find expression in the public life was a challenge from the
outset. A deep divide between secular and religious sectors of the Jewish
population prevented an Israeli constitution from being written. Traditional religious elements in the Yishuv insisted that a Jewish state must
be in complete keeping with the laws of Torah, while secularists such as
Prime Minister David Ben-Gurion could not countenance a constitution
that accorded only with Jewish law while omitting essential elements
drawn from the Western political tradition.

Rather than engaging in what would have undoubtedly been a bitter
and contentious *kulturkampf* over these areas of principled disagreement
between secular and religious factions, Ben-Gurion forged a compromise
with representatives of the Orthodox Agudat Yisrael prior to the creation
of the State. On June 19, 1947, in anticipation of the establishment of a
state, Ben-Gurion sent a letter to the leaders of Agudat Yisrael. Cosigned
by Rabbi Judah Leib Fishman (Maimon) and Yitzhak Gruenbaum of the
Jewish Agency, the letter asserted that in the about-to-be-born State of
Israel there would be religious freedom in the private sphere. However,
the authors also agreed that traditional Jewish observance and authority
would be maintained in many aspects of Israeli public life.

There was so much historical precedent for the position affirmed by
Ben Gurion and his co-signators at the Jewish Agency that the arrange-
ment is referred to as the Status Quo Agreement. The agreement basically retained the status of the religious establishment as it was during
both the pre-1917 era under Ottoman rule and in the post-1917 Mandate
period when Palestine was controlled by the British.

The agreement stipulated that Saturday (Shabbat, the Jewish Sabbath)
would be the national day of rest. Most businesses would be closed and
the Israeli state-supported airline, El Al, would not fly on the Sabbath.
There would also be no public transportation on the Jewish Sabbath.
An exception to this ban on public transportation was made for Haifa
in consideration of its large Arab population and the influence of labor
unions so powerful that the city was called Red Haifa.

Continuing the tradition established by the British in 1921 when Rav
Kook was appointed first Chief Ashkenazi Rabbi to administer Jewish

religious affairs in the Yishuv, the agreement was to operate within the framework of a dual-office Chief Rabbinate in which there would be an Ashkenazi and Sephardi Chief Rabbi to be financed by the state. Subsequent legislation passed during the first five years after independence spelled out precisely what obligations the state was undertaking: to assist in building and maintaining synagogues and other religious institutions and structures and to finance the salaries of rabbis and religious officials of other religions in the state. As noted earlier, this state-assumed responsibility for the religious needs of its inhabitants is in keeping with notions of religious establishment commonly practiced throughout Europe and the Middle East.

With regard to Jews and Judaism, the Status Quo Agreement provided for rabbinical authority over kashrut. All kitchens in government-run agencies would be kosher, and restaurants that wished to advertise themselves as kosher would have to be certified under the supervision of the Chief Rabbinate. In addition, it was officially forbidden to raise pigs, a provision never fully enforced.

Ben-Gurion also agreed that there would be three educational streams —national religious, secular, and independent Ultra-Orthodox (Hinukh Atzma'i under the supervision of Agudat Yisrael)—and that the Hinukh Atzma'i stream would have complete autonomy in determining its educational curriculum unfettered by the supervision of the State. Finally, the Chief Rabbinate was given control over Jewish burial, and it was agreed that matters of personal status—Jewish marriage, divorce, and conversion—would be conducted by rabbinical courts staffed by rabbinical judges approved by the Chief Rabbinate in every Israeli city and town. In sum, what had been operative during the pre-state period of the British Mandate in regard to religion in general and Jews and Judaism in particular—including a state-subsidized rabbinate (exclusively Orthodox)—would continue to be operative in the nascent State of Israel.

Before concluding this discussion of Judaism in the public square, I want to emphasize that the political compromise that Ben-Gurion and the leaders of Agudat Yisrael negotiated at the birth of the State was possible because virtually all Israeli Jews—secular and religious—felt that public expressions of Jewish religious tradition were fundamental to the new society. Israel aimed to include Jews from every part of the world, and removing Judaism completely from the public sphere would have led to the "dejudaization" of Israeli society. This possibility is rejected by a broad consensus of Israelis even today. Even among secular Israelis, the ascendancy of national modes of identification, language, culture, and political aspiration, including some public modes of Jewish religious expression that support and sustain Jewish national identity, are regarded as indispensable in the Jewish state. Symbols, ideas, and values that are the products of Jewish historical religious culture remain central. Moreover, the Jewish religious and cultural elements of Israeli identity have political implications. This helps explain the presence of the chief rabbis at many important civil functions, including state funerals that are conducted in accord with religious law. It also underlies the fact that while the victories achieved in the 1967 Six-Day War and conquests of the Western Wall and Judea and Samaria could have been viewed in totally secular nationalistic terms, they were actually seen by many in light of historical Jewish religious consciousness.

Still, there is a significant divide that marks Israeli life concerning religion and the role Orthodox Judaism is permitted to occupy in the public square. Most Israeli Jews understand the Western Wall as a traditional religious shrine, and the activity deemed most proper at the Wall itself remains prayer. The ongoing public struggle of Women of the Wall insists that women have a right to pray out loud and wear a *talit* (prayer shawl) there, yet the religious authority in charge of the Wall is an Orthodox rabbi and the decorum established there—even as it is severely challenged—remains consonant with Haredi religious sensibilities. Many though hardly all Israeli Jews remain indifferent to this dispute. Many North American Jews are seriously roiled by this struggle. The divide that separates American Jewish attitudes on this matter from the sensibilities of Israeli Jews clarifies the nature of Israeli Judaism and the way it is expressed in public life. Religious symbols provide important sources of legitimization and identity for Israel's Jewish citizens. The details of the 1947 Status Quo Agreement continue essentially in force in Israeli public and educational life, and the Chief Rabbinate remains a potent political institution with wide-ranging powers as a result of this history and on account of such attitudes.

There have been changes in elements of the Status Quo Agreement. For example, with the arrival of large numbers of immigrants from the former Soviet Union during the 1990s, a demand for pork led to a Supreme Court ruling in 2004 that local governments could not ban the sale of pork. Suburban malls and numbers of businesses and restaurants are increasingly open on the Sabbath in areas of secular Jewish population. Most significantly, more and more Israeli Jews—secular, Reform, Conservative, and Orthodox—now regularly challenge the monopoly of the Chief Rabbinate over matters of personal status. Indeed, these challenges stand at the center of contemporary Israeli and diasporic Jewish concerns and promise to create significant shifts in how Israel defines "Jewish belonging" in both the private and public arenas. We will now turn to a description of the multilayered complexity of this issue.

"Who Is a Jew?"—The Law of Return and
Personal Status in the Jewish State

In 1950, the State of Israel passed the Law of Return, a law that grants every Jew the right to acquire immediate citizenship. The Law of Return defined a Jew as a person born to a Jewish mother, or who has become converted to Judaism and is not a member of another religion. The Law was intended to express the raison d'être of the Jewish State as proclaimed in the Israeli Declaration of Independence—the Ingathering of the Exiles. It is based on the principle that every Jew is a potential citizen of Israel.

In addition, through an amendment to the Law enacted in 1970, non-Jewish spouses of Jews are eligible for immediate Israeli citizenship under the Law of Return, as are persons with even one Jewish parent or grandparent and their spouses. In this way, no one defined as a Jew—even under the racist Nuremburg Laws in Nazi Germany—will be denied citizenship in a nation-state and suffer the fate of millions of Jews during the Holocaust who died because no state would allow them entry. Thus, the Law of Return not only expresses the Zionist-Jewish national ideal of Israel as the homeland of all Jews but also affirms that Israel is a refuge for every individual identified as part of the Jewish people and who shares in Jewish destiny.

There were attempts to amend the Law of Return in 1972 and later in 1988 to stipulate that only people converted to Judaism in accordance with Halakha under Orthodox auspices could be considered Jews, and these were defeated in the Knesset. In no small measure, successful rebuttal of these amendments was due to unified protests of diasporic Jewish communities who saw them as constituting a disenfranchisement of the Conservative and Reform movements by the Jewish state. In the aftermath of the 1988 controversy over this proposed amendment, the Israeli Supreme Court ruled explicitly in 1989 that people converted to Judaism by non-Orthodox rabbis in the Diaspora were to be included as Jews under the Law of Return. The Israeli Supreme Court expanded this position in 2002 and 2005, ruling that Israeli citizens who were converted by Reform and Conservative rabbis in Israel as well as abroad must be registered by the Interior Ministry in the Population Registry as Jews.

Nevertheless, the Law of Return is a civil law that defines who is eligible for immediate citizenship in the Jewish State, whereas matters of personal status for Israeli citizens that involve marriage, divorce, and burial remain firmly and exclusively under the control of the institutions of the Chief Rabbinate. An example will help clarify the significance of this division of power. A notable incident involved Galia Ben-Gurion, granddaughter of David Ben-Gurion. During World War II, her father, Amos, served in the British Jewish Brigade and married a woman in London who was converted to Judaism by a Progressive rabbi. The couple and their child, Galia, subsequently returned to Israel. Her citizenship as an Israeli Jew under the Law of Return was never in question. However, when twenty-two-year-old Galia applied to the Haifa rabbinate for her forthcoming wedding, she was refused permission to marry because the rabbinate considered her mother's conversion halakhically invalid. They viewed her mother and therefore Galia as non-Jews, and Galia had to undergo an Orthodox conversion before the rabbinate granted her a license to marry.

The kind of dilemma that faced Galia Ben-Gurion and the two-tiered system that separates citizenship from matters of personal status have been a central concern for decades. A person who qualifies as a Jew under the Law of Return can be granted citizenship, registered as a Jew in the Population Registry, and for all practical purposes participate fully as a Jew in Israeli society, serving in the army, paying taxes, and attending schools as a Jew. However, recognition as a Jew in Israeli civil law and life does not require the Chief Rabbinate to acknowledge such a person as a Jew for purposes of personal status so that same individual may be unable to be married, divorced, or buried as a Jew in Israel.

However, recent events have focused attention on these concerns and caused North American and Israeli Jews to address the practical implications of the debate around this issue. A major impetus has been demographic pressure resulting from the huge Russian *aliya*. Many of the more than one million people from the former Soviet Union who entered Israel in the 1990s and the early years of the twenty-first century under the Law of Return are either intermarried or the children of intermarriage. Hundreds of thousands whose mothers are not Jews are considered non-Jews by the Chief Rabbinate. Although they may live as Jews in a manner that is indistinguishable from millions of other secular Israeli Jews, they are not able to marry as Jews in Israel because—as we have seen—matters of personal status are under the control of the state-sanctioned Ultra-Orthodox Chief Rabbinate. Although these Russian immigrants and their children now identify with the Jewish people and live as Jews in the Jewish state, they cannot be married in a state-sanctioned Jewish wedding nor can they be buried in a Jewish cemetery.

Conversion would seem to be an option, and many would like to convert to Judaism so as to be able to marry other Jews and be eligible for burial as Jews within Israel. However, the Israeli High Rabbinical Court has held that would-be converts have to affirm an obligation to observe every single commandment in the Torah (which few would likely do), and that their conversions can be retroactively annulled if they subsequently fail to do so.

This latter position was publicized in a notorious decision that High Rabbinical Court Judge Rabbi Avraham Sherman issued in 2007. In that decision, the Haredi Rabbi Sherman retroactively annulled conversions to Judaism conducted under the authority of religious Zionist Orthodox Rabbi Haim Druckman and his previously government-sanctioned Conversion Authority. This decision called into question the Jewish status of more than ten thousand Israelis converted under the supervision of Rabbi Druckman. From the time of the Talmud through Rabbi Abraham Isaac Kook in the twentieth century, the dominant tradition in Jewish law has always held that once a conversion is performed, it is irreversible. Nonetheless, Sherman's ruling reverses this stance and has the potential impact of disenfranchising countless converts and their families. Moreover, Rabbi Sherman goes even further. In a 2011 interview, he questioned the validity of "all modern-era conversions in Israel and in the world since the start of the Jewish Enlightenment period." He further stated that all Israeli converts must "undergo examination by an authorized rabbinic court before they can enter the community of the Jewish people. They are not Jews for certain."

Given his legal authority, the decision and attitudes evidenced by Rabbi Sherman led to a plethora of protests. The Israeli Supreme Court officially reversed the specific Sherman decision, though the Court did not rule in principle that conversions could not be retroactively annulled. Knesset member David Rotem subsequently introduced a conversion bill into the Knesset to resolve the many dilemmas tens of thousands of people in Israel—particularly those of Russian origin—confront as they seek to affirm the rights of marriage and burial as Jews that they feel ought to be theirs. Rotem and his supporters noted that these people—often born of non-Jewish mothers and Jewish fathers—live as Jews, they speak Hebrew, and they and their children serve in the Israel Defense Forces. He pointed out that they have cast their lot with the State of Israel, and that they advance and share the collective fate of the Jewish people. Rotem proposed empowering city rabbis—a number of whom, though Orthodox, are lenient on matters of conversion—to perform conversions. He further stipulated that the conversions these rabbis performed would be deemed irreversible by the state. In these ways, Rotem intended to resolve the legal-religious Jewish status of these people in the State of Israel.

The Rotem bill was not passed. Critics claimed this was because Rotem had acceded to Haredi demands that all conversions to Judaism in Israel would now be subject to confirmation and approval by an increasingly Haredi rabbinic establishment. If this was a precondition for passage of his bill, the proposed solution could hardly resolve the predicament. The opponents of the Rotem bill claimed that few city rabbis would act on the basis of lenient and inclusive halakhic precedents to formally convert people of nonhalakhic Jewish status. Moreover, they argued that conversions conducted by Modern Orthodox rabbis would by and large be defined as illegitimate by the Haredi rabbis, in whom authority would now be completely vested. They charged that the Rotem bill would only exacerbate the legal limbo these people confront as they seek to lead normal lives as Israeli Jews.

Furthermore, the Rotem bill would have rescinded Israeli Supreme Court rulings that currently grant legal recognition to conversion by Reform and Conservative rabbinic courts in Israel for purposes of Israeli citizenship. This raises the specter that the Law of Return itself—which includes Jews converted to Judaism under non-Orthodox auspices outside Israel—would one day be redefined so as to exclude non-Orthodox converts from being considered Jewish in Israel. Inasmuch as most Jews outside Israel identify as Reform, Conservative, or Reconstructionist, many saw the Rotem bill as tantamount to a declaration of war by people in governmentally sanctioned positions of power against liberal religious Jews in particular and Diaspora Jewry in general. This is why the leaders of all branches of non-Orthodox Judaism as well as Jerry Silverman of the Jewish Federations of North America were vehement in their united opposition to the passage of this proposed bill. They argued that the impact on the unity of the Jewish people worldwide would be disastrous should the Knesset pass this bill.

The issue of "who is a Jew" is far from resolved, and the State has not yet come up with a satisfactory compromise on matters of personal status among the diverse religious and secular elements that comprise the Jewish people. The problem is unlikely to disappear from the Israeli and Jewish public scene in the near future. On the contrary, it is likely to remain a scorching issue on the Israeli and Jewish public agendas. Diverse proposals—ranging from the institution of civil marriage in Israel to extending legal recognition in determining matters of personal status to lenient-ruling Orthodox and perhaps even non-Orthodox rabbis—will continue to be put forth and debated. Indeed, in a recent contretemps, Israel's Chief Rabbinate refused to accept the testimony of the well-known American Orthodox rabbi Avi Weiss as to the Jewish status of an American who wished to be married under the auspices of the rabbinate in Israel. While the Chief Rabbinate ultimately reversed itself and arrived at an agreement with the Orthodox Rabbinical Council of America to avoid future confrontations between the American Orthodox rabbinate and the Chief Rabbinate, the incident illustrates the dimensions of this problem and how far removed the state is from a solution. In the interim, 'Itim, an Israeli organization headed by American-born Orthodox rabbi Seth Farber, fills a vital function by assisting Israeli Jews who have problems with the Chief Rabbinate over personal status surrounding conversion, marriage, and burial.

In light of this state of affairs, it is hardly surprising that the government-sponsored Central Bureau of Statistics (CBS) found that between 2004 and 2006, 9.6 percent to 12 percent of Israeli couples married outside Israel. More than sixty thousand Jewish couples during those same years chose to cohabit without benefit of marriage. Known as *reputed spouses (yedu'im ba-tzibur)*, they "enjoy a wide array of rights, very close in scope to those enjoyed by married couples," although the Israeli Supreme Court has explicitly rejected their status as common-law marriages. *Haaretz* reported in 2011 that for a variety of reasons, twenty thousand Israeli Jews marry abroad annually, suggesting that these trends continue. It is widely assumed that some of these couples married this way because they were banned from religious marriages. Others choose to avoid the religious establishment altogether as a form of protest against the religious monopoly enjoyed by the Chief Rabbinate and the religious coercion it represents. An option for the latter is provided by a group of Orthodox rabbis with more moderate views known as Rabbanei Tzohar. Led by Rabbi David Stav, they offer an Orthodox rabbinical alternative to the Chief Rabbinate. While this group of rabbis has enjoyed significant success and popularity among secular Israelis, the Chief Rabbinate has attempted to prevent them from conducting marriages, and conflicts between Rabbanei Tzohar and the Chief Rabbinate remain unresolved.

The Evolution and Renewal of Personal Jewish Religious-Cultural Expression

As we have seen in reviewing the complex issues of Judaism and Jewish status in the public square, Israeli society has traditionally viewed Jewish religious identity as defined by halakhic observance. The divide this has occasioned in the religious-cultural identification of Israeli Jews has been marked by the terms *hiloni* (secular) and *dati* (religious), a distinction many still use to describe themselves and their self-understanding of themselves as Jews. The use of these terms loses something in translation across cultures, however. American readers may be surprised that even today, surveys indicate that a significant majority of Israeli Jews who consider themselves secular mark the Sabbath in some way, observe Passover with a Seder and by avoiding bread, fast on Yom Kippur, light Hanukah candles, and observe traditional Jewish rites surrounding life-cycle ceremonies, including marriage.

The classical *hiloni-dati* dichotomy for understanding how Israeli Jews express their religious and cultural identity as Jews remains intact even as it is clearly no longer adequate. Efforts by secular Israelis to reconstruct Jewish identity in new and innovative ways and to gain public recognition for these new personal expressions of Jewishness are still labeled *hiloni* even as they are challenging the fundamental codes and conventions and redefining the Jewish component in Israeli Jewish society.

The vigor and fluidity of the innovative and dynamic movement of hundreds of thousands of Israeli Jews in search of Jewishness is captured in an Israeli television documentary, *The Transparent Kippa*, that aired in 2006. This program illuminates the mosaic of novel ways contemporary Israeli Jews choose to manifest their personal Jewish religious and cultural identities and demonstrates how increasingly porous and changing the boundaries are. The program highlights four types of religious and secular Jews and their nontraditional paths to spiritual renewal and Jewish identification: a doctor who grew up *dati* now, in his own words, "wears a transparent kippa" and "practices the religion of a single Jew"; a couple whose education was aggressively secular and anti-religious send their children to a mixed religious-secular school where the secular and the religious meet and mutually influence and interact with one another to form a novel form of Israeli Jewish expression; a man from a Haredi Hasidic background now defines himself in "secular-Hasidic" categories; and an individual raised as a completely secular Israeli has established a popular secular yeshiva in Tel Aviv where secular Israelis can immerse themselves in classical Jewish texts.

The Transparent Kippa opens a window to the previously dominant system as it is being actively transformed by Israeli Jews seeking Jewish cultural and religious personal forms of identification and self-understanding. These changes are further evidenced in a Jewish renewal movement that has been taking root during the past two decades. A range of secular alternatives dedicated to intensive Jewish learning and Jewish ritual practices like Tel Aviv's secular yeshiva depicted in *The Transparent Kippa* have sprung up. One, Panim, serves as an umbrella organization for forty such renewal groups—and there are many more such bodies—that accommodate more than 380,000 Israeli Jews currently studying annually in these institutions and organizations. The Hakhel Festival held during Sukkot and the study programs on the eve of Shavuot throughout the country draw hundreds of thousands of nominally secular Israeli Jews anxious to garner Jewish wisdom and Jewish identity from studying the classical texts and learning about religious traditions. Such developments indicate that the modes of Jewish expression developed by the socialist Zionist pioneers of Israel in the early years of the State are no longer sufficient to capture the diversity of Jewish understandings that even so-called secular Israeli Jews now manifest. Of course, this current generation of Israelis is not as steeped in classical Jewish sources nor as familiar with traditional Jewish praxis as their forebears were. Their return to the texts and explorations with the practices of Jewish tradition undoubtedly reflect a search for roots and authenticity that earlier generations were eager to abandon.

A sampling of several of these programs and institutions will give the reader a more concrete sense of the extent of this renewal. HaMidrasha (Educational Center for the Renewal of Jewish Life in Israel) is located on Kibbutz Oranim and headed by well-known Israeli educator Moti Zeira. Founded in 1989, it aims to "facilitate the transmission of Jewish culture in a way that inspires and informs the Israeli Jew's quest for meaning, dialogue and voluntarism . . . [and] . . . to help secular Israelis address issues of personal and collective Jewish identity and to create a more pluralistic cultural and spiritual landscape in Israel." HaMidrasha reaches more than forty thousand Israelis, and it has now begun to undertake the establishment of a seminary for the education of "Secular Rabbis."

Alma, founded in 1996 by Ruth Calderon, a secular Israeli who received her doctorate in Talmud from the Hebrew University, is a response to "Bialik's call to reawaken Hebrew culture." This institution intends "to reclaim and revive learning classical Jewish texts," so that Hebrew culture can become an "essential element of pluralistic Jewish identity in Israel." Calderon was elected to the Knesset as a member of the Yesh ʿAtid party. In her first speech on February 17, 2013, she electrified the Knesset and a large part of the Jewish world in both Israel and the Diaspora by using the occasion to teach a lesson from the Talmud. Her act was an assertion that this foundational text of the Jewish people is the property of all Jews. The declaration by an ostensibly secular Israeli—and a woman!—was unprecedented in the annals of the Knesset and Israeli history.

Another model is provided by Elul. Founded in 1989, this study center "uses traditional and modern Jewish texts to create pluralistic dialogues in a beit midrash style that are relevant and current." Elul addresses both the public and individual aspects of Jewish expression: "Our goal is to return to our roots in order to find a pluralistic definition of who we—as individuals and as a nation—are today. On an individual level, this strengthens the Jewish identities. On a national level, this restores to Israeli society the dignity and respect for pluralism and social justice that were born from our rich Jewish tradition. Jewish culture and religion are rich in ideas and values to be proud of. Elul makes this possible."

The development of novel modes of Jewish identity and learning is not confined to the world of secular Israeli Jews. In the Orthodox world, Nishmat, founded in Jerusalem in 1990 by Rabbanit Chana Henkin, aims "to open the gates of higher Torah learning to women." Nishmat has flourished and thousands of women have taken advantage of the educational opportunity to enter the realm of traditional Jewish texts and law. Moreover, Nishmat has developed a Yoetzet Halakha (female halakhic consultant) program to train women in Jewish law. More than eighty women have graduated from the program so far with the expertise and knowledge in areas of Jewish law formerly limited to men.

These organizations represent only a small portion of the vital developments in a Jewish cultural and religious renaissance that is engaging many Israeli Jews who seek to invest their lives with meaningful expressions of their Jewishness. The status quo that juxtaposed socialist Zionist understandings of Judaism and secular identity with Haredi adherence to seemingly unchanging and rigid Jewish tradition is changing. Instead, exciting, evolving and conflicting modes of Jewish commitment and identity can be seen in Israel every day. Even while it remains in the Israeli mind-set, the dichotomous distinction between *hiloni* and *dati* is being insistently challenged. It has proved an inadequate framework that cannot comprehend the diverse expressions of Jewish identity and life in Israel today.

Jewish renewal, together with opposition to the control exercised by the Chief Rabbinate and its bureaucracy over Jewish personal status, have also changed the perception of Reform and Masorti (Conservative) Judaism in Israel. A study undertaken in 2011 under the aegis of the Avi Chai Foundation found that 8 percent of Israeli Jews identified themselves as Reform or Conservative. In addition, 60 percent of all Israeli Jews now believe that the Reform and Conservative movements should be recognized by the state and that the rabbis of these movements ought to be able to conduct legally sanctioned weddings. Moreover, 34 percent of Israeli Jews surveyed stated that they had attended a ceremony or service where a non-Orthodox rabbi officiated. The Israeli Reform and Masorti movements report that they conduct approximately 3,500 Bar or Bat Mitzvah ceremonies as well as about 1,200 weddings each year. These liberal Jewish religious movements do not have the large formal memberships that they enjoy in North America. Nevertheless, Tali schools under their aegis are providing an enriched Jewish curriculum for secular Israeli Jewish students throughout Israel. It is also significant that during the first decade of the twenty-first century, more than a hundred Israelis were ordained as Conservative and Reform rabbis by Machon Schechter and Hebrew Union College in Jerusalem, and now serve the rising numbers of their congregations. These figures suggest that the liberal movements are having a substantial even if indirect impact on Israeli society and are catalysts for reconstructing the relationship between religion and state as well as supplying new options for Jewish religious and cultural belonging.

As I have tried to show, the identity of Israel as a Jewish state and the expressions of Jewishness in the state are multilayered and complex as well as dynamic and evolving. Judaism is surely essential to the public life of the state and vital to the construction of an Israeli Jewish community and identity. It is clear that as issues of Judaism and Jewishness in public and private spheres of life continue to evolve in Israel over the next decades, these matters of grave import must necessarily engage both the Jewish state and the Jewish people.

RECOMMENDED READINGS

Blecher-Prigat, Ayelet. "A Basic Right to Marry: Israeli Style." *Israel Law Review* 47:3 (November 2014), 433–460.

Bystrov, Evgenia. "Religion, Democracy, and Attitudes towards Civil Marriage in Israel." *Current Sociology* 60:6 (2012), 751–770.

Ellenson, David. "'The Rock from which They Were Cleft': A Review-Essay of Haim Amsalem's '*Zera Yisrael*' and '*Makor Yisrael.*'" *Jewish Review of Books* (Winter 2012), 41–43.

Goldberg, Harvey. "How Do We Know When a Society Is Changing? Reflections on Liberal Judaism in Israel." In Fran Moskowitz, Steve Sharot, and Moshe Shokeid, *Toward an Anthropology of Nation Building and Unbuilding in Israel*, pp. 215–228. Lincoln: University of Nebraska Press, 2015.

Hartman, Donniel, Ruth Calderon, and Naamah Kelman, "Jewish Renewal in Israel," *Journal of Jewish Communal Service*, 85:1 (2010), 73–83.

Levy, Shlomit. "The Many Faces of Jewishness in Israel." In Uzi Rebhun and Chaim Israel Waxman, eds., *Jews in Israel: Contemporary Social and Cultural Patterns*, pp. 265–284. Hanover, NH: University Press of New England, 2004.

Triger, Zvi. "Freedom from Religion: Civil Marriage and Cohabitation of Jews Enter the Rabbinical Courts." *Israel Studies Review* 27:2 (Winter 2012), 1–17.

Zakheim, Dov. "Transforming Israel's Chief Rabbinate." *Conversions* 17 (2013), 81–114.

GLOSSARY TERMS

Agudat Yisrael
Aliya
Judea and Samaria
Law of Return
Six-Day War
Status Quo Agreement
Yesh 'Atid
Yishuv

David Ellenson is the Director of the Schusterman Center for Israel Studies and Visiting Professor at Brandeis University. His most recent book is *Jewish Meaning in a World of Choice*.

TWELVE

Contemporary Christianity and Israel

YAAKOV ARIEL

Introduction: Changing Attitudes toward Jews and Israel

In December 1993, the Holy See signed an agreement with the State of Israel that entailed mutual recognition and a full diplomatic relationship. In June 2004, the Presbyterian Church USA adopted a resolution "to initiate a process of phased, selective divestment in multinational corporations operating in Israel." The Vatican's recognition and the Presbyterian divestment can be seen as watershed events. Yet these are only two dramatic moments from a range of opinions and attitudes within these two important groups, and from the multifaceted history of Christian interactions with the state of Israel more generally.

Israel has stirred strong, complex, and diverse reactions among contemporary Christian groups. For most Christians, Israel has not been just an ordinary state, one among the many. It was a Jewish state, a novelty in modern history, and a controversial entity to boot. Even before 1948, Christian leaders voiced strong opinions on the Zionist movement and the building of a Jewish commonwealth in Palestine. Christians have both supported and militated against the Zionist movement, showing interest and sympathy along with suspicion, antagonism, and rejection.

There are no easy generalizations to simplify the subject. The Christian world is particularly diverse and even within the same traditions, different groups and members have voiced varied opinions or changed their views throughout the years. In order to assess the spectrum of Christian attitudes toward and interactions with Israel, we will need to examine different Christian groups and movements. In addition, one should note that theological tracts and official declarations do not reflect the entire spectrum of Christian opinions. We will look beyond the declarations and decisions of theological and ecclesiastical elites, and pay attention to attitudes and actions of rank-and-file Christians as well. There are noticeable gaps even between the opinions of leaders and spokespersons of various Christian groups and the laity of their communities. Finally, Christian opinions on and interactions with Israel have been dynamic and evolving so that groups shift their positions in response to both external pressures and internal changes within the groups.

Christian attitudes toward Israel cannot be separated from the tenets of faith or from the social and cultural atmosphere and political standings of the different Christian groups. Since the founding of the State, there have been important developments in the way Christian groups and churches relate to Jews and Judaism and how they understand the role that the Jewish people play in God's plans for humanity. While Middle Eastern churches have largely maintained traditional Christian theological understandings of Judaism and Jews, and for the most part were not motivated to change their positions, a movement of interfaith dialogue and reconciliation has occasioned more cordial and approving attitudes on the part of Protestant and Catholic thinkers and groups.

To appreciate the significance of these changes, bear in mind that historically, Christian thinkers considered the Jews a misguided, even accursed people. Having rejected their Messiah, the Jews lost their position as the covenant people, and God's promises to Israel were transferred to the Christian Church. Judaism, as a separate faith from Christianity, had no intrinsic value or purpose except as a group bearing witness to the triumph of Christianity. The Jews' dispersion among the nations, according to that view, was a prophesized punishment for their wickedness and blindness, and the curse plaguing the Jews had also left its mark on the country. Consequently, when Zionism appeared on the scene, while the movement enjoyed support among pietist and evangelical Christians, many mainline church leaders opposed it with apprehension.

Christian opinions have also been influenced by the Arab-Israeli conflict and the commitments of different segments of Christianity to Arabs in the Middle East, to protecting postcolonial nations, and to establishing cordial relations with Muslim communities worldwide. Moreover, they have been affected by Israeli actions and policies relating to the Christian world and its expectations and reactions, as well as the voices of non-Israeli Jews, such as leaders of Jewish American organizations who have attempted to foster better relations between Christian churches and the State of Israel. In other words, the relationship between contemporary Christianity and Israel has not been unilateral.

Thus, this chapter will survey the changing attitudes toward Jews and policies toward Israel among mainline Protestants, conservative evangelicals, dissenting Protestant churches, the Catholic Church, and Orthodox and Middle Eastern churches, which have been of vital importance for both Christians and Jews. Israel has depended, from its inception, on Christian acceptance and support, and has suffered, at times, when such support was withheld. For Christian groups and thinkers, relating to Israel sometimes touches a sensitive nerve, highlighting and problematizing the way Christians define their own role and place in history. In addition to theological principles and social policies, relations are also driven by practical considerations. For example, churches that have not recognized Judaism as a legitimate religious community have nonetheless built a good working relationship with Israel's government and people.

With this brief overview, we are ready to examine how these complex and varied considerations have differentially affected virtually all Christian groups in their relations toward Israel.

The Complex Views of Mainline Protestants

Mainline Protestants are members of veteran and national Protestant churches who have not chosen the conservative evangelical path. Such groups tend to be more progressive in their social and political outlooks and have joined the ecumenical road of Christian unity and the interfaith approach to other religions. Liberal and mainline Protestants have largely transformed their opinions on Jews and Judaism, but their views on Jews and Israel in the last half century have been marked by dual tendencies. Along with greater recognition and tolerance, their attitudes toward Israel and its policies have become increasingly critical. Once again, we must keep in mind that Protestants have not spoken in one voice.

While "Christian Zionists," for the most part conservative Protestants with pietist or evangelical leanings, gave moral and political support to the Jewish Zionist movement in its early stages, many Protestant thinkers, leaders, and laypeople were skeptical about the movement and its goals. Like their Catholic and Orthodox counterparts, many Protestants objected theologically to the notion of Jewish existence outside the confines of the Church and could not accept the legitimacy of a Jewish commonwealth in the Holy Land. Since the early nineteenth century, Protestant groups had labored in Palestine and the Middle East, establishing a large number of mission stations, churches, hospitals, and other enterprises. They were afraid that a Jewish commonwealth might have negative repercussions for Christian freedom of worship and the propagation of the Gospel. Protestant activists who identified with the Arab cause saw Zionism as a threat to Arab nationalism, and at times, to British, American, or other Western interests.

The British Mandate government encouraged and protected the Christian communities, and Protestants in particular thrived under its rule. A number of Protestant churches established or enlarged their presence in the country, opening numerous congregations and schools, and several thousand Arab Christians abandoned Orthodox, Catholic, or Monophysite affiliations for Protestant churches, especially the Anglican Church. Such a move often improved career and economic opportunities. Anticipating the end of the Mandate, Protestant leaders worried that Arab or Jewish governments that would replace the British would not offer the same securities, let alone privileges to Christian communities and missions.

Presbyterian positions on Zionism offer an excellent example of the variety of Protestant opinions. In the 1920s–1930s, the denomination turned into a battleground between progressive modernists and the more conservative evangelical elements, which at the time were known as *fundamentalists*. The Presbyterian Church continued to include a minority of conservative pro-Zionists, but in the post–World War II era the denomination emerged as one of the most progressive religious groups in contemporary Christianity, and its commitments and preferences on social and global issues influenced the group's position toward Israel and the Arab-Israeli conflict.

Attitudes of liberal Protestants toward Jews and Judaism changed significantly during the 1950s–1970s, partly under the influence of Reinhold Niebuhr, a leading Protestant theologian in the 1930s–1960s. Niebuhr's groundbreaking outlook recognized and accepted Judaism as a religious tradition standing on its own outside the confines of Christianity. Turning his back on traditional supercessionist Christian opinions, as well as on the triumphalist liberal Protestant attitude prevalent before World War I, Niebuhr argued that Jews possessed high moral standards and social consciousness. Consequently, he militated for respect and recognition for Judaism as a sustaining religious tradition, alongside the Christian Church.

In the early 1940s Niebuhr and other Protestant thinkers and activists founded the Christian Council for Palestine, a mainline Christian Protestant group that advocated the establishment of a Jewish state in what was then British Palestine. The group influenced American Christian opinions in the immediate period before the establishment of the State of Israel. In view of later developments, it is remarkable that mainline and liberal Protestants organized such a group, joined by thousands of American Protestant ministers. From the late 1940s and until the late 1960s, many progressive Protestants and leaders in Europe and America supported Israel and sympathized with its struggles. They viewed the Arabs as the main aggressors in the 1948 war and gave Jewish and Israeli needs and concerns priority over Arab complaints. Among the Protestant leaders who supported Israel was Martin Luther King Jr., the charismatic African American theologian and civil rights leader, who was assassinated in 1968 before he could follow through on his plans to visit Israel. From John Steinbeck to Gore Vidal and from Pete Seeger to Ella Fitzgerald, prominent American writers, performers, and social activists identified with Israel, as did many American Jews.

The attitudes of liberal Protestants toward Jews were already changing significantly in the 1950s. Their new outlook was further boosted by Vatican II, a Catholic Ecumenical Council convened intermittently between 1962 and 1965 that led to a historic breakthrough in interfaith relations. A number of Protestant churches and interdenominational groups, in the spirit of Vatican II, issued statements, including a retraction of the deicide charge, designed to clear the air in relation to the Jews. Some of these statements exceeded Vatican II in their attempt to change attitudes. Most Protestants engaged in the dialogue during that golden era of Christian-Jewish reconciliation supported Israel, even if they were critical of some of its policies. There were also liberal or mainline Protestant thinkers and groups who were antagonistic to Israel and blamed it for the 1948 War and the Palestinian plight. But activists of the interfaith movement generally expressed good will toward Israel, as part of a larger atmosphere of understanding toward Judaism and Jews. This would change gradually in the wake of the 1967 War, and by the 1980s, a more critical judgment of Israel would come to dominate liberal Protestant attitudes.

Throughout the 1980s–2010s, liberal and left-wing Christians established contacts with Palestinian activists and spokespeople as well as with Israelis and Jewish activists, who are openly critical of Israeli policies if not of the Zionist project at large. International Protestant bodies changed along similar lines. In 1948, representatives of mainline Protestant churches established the World Council of Churches, which initially promoted a moderately friendly attitude toward Israel. But during the 1960s–1970s, its membership grew to include Greek Orthodox and Middle Eastern and Third World churches as well, transforming the organization's attitude toward Israel profoundly.

In changing their attitudes and building new appreciation for Jews, Protestants, like their Catholic counterparts, were motivated, at least in part, by a sense of guilt over the historical role of Christian supersessionist outlooks and anti-Jewish accusations in bringing about the mass murder of Jews during World War II. A number of Protestant thinkers acknowledged that Nazi hatred of Jews had been fed by ages of anti-Semitic incitement stemming from Christianity's open hostility. In response to strong Jewish objections voiced continuously in the midst of the evolving dialogue, Protestant churches decided to end their missionary enterprises among Jews. This affected Christian presence and activity in Israel, where the remaining missions have been chiefly under the auspices of conservative Protestants. The liberal segments of Western Christianity gave up on their former exclusivist approach and accepted the idea that other churches and even non-Christian religions could offer moral guidelines and spiritual meaning to their adherents, Judaism not excluded. In contrast, conservative Christians have continued to insist that Christianity is the only viable path to salvation. Most Orthodox,

Middle Eastern, and Third World churches share this belief, although they typically have not engaged in evangelizing the Jews.

Recognition was accompanied by efforts to eradicate longstanding prejudices. Having acquitted Jews of the killing of Jesus, Western liberal Protestants and Catholics went a step further to clear the atmosphere of hatred. In the late 1960s, they examined textbooks used in their religious schools and removed passages with anti-Jewish overtones. Not only liberal churches but conservative ones as well have become more sensitive to the manner in which they present Jews in their publications or sermons. Moreover, Liberal Protestant and Catholic theologians have undertaken to examine the corpus of Christian writings in order to revise defamatory ideas and claims that produced the negative images of the Jews. This does not mean that the old accusations against Jews were eradicated from Christian popular culture. For example, negative depictions of Jews in stage and film productions of the Passion play continue despite the spirit and aims of the movement of Christian Jewish reconciliation.

A number of Protestant and Catholic liberal theologians turned reconciliation with the Jewish people into their vocation. Franklin Littell and Alice and Roy Eckardt are among those who carried Niebuhr's views into the 1970s–1980s and remained ardent supporters of Israel. Yet while their opinions were influential, they were countered by pro-Palestinian voices within their own churches and traditions.

In this connection we should note the growing interest among Christian thinkers, scholars, clergymen, and students in Jewish thought, history, and texts. Indeed, Jewish Studies in different forms have become part of the curriculum at Protestant and Catholic universities, seminaries, and divinity schools. "Old Testament Theology" may now be labeled "Hebrew Bible," and Christian students increasingly read biblical Hebrew in the pronunciation prevalent in modern-day Israel. Christian seminaries organize study tours to Israel to acquaint their students with the historical geography of the place as well as with contemporary history and politics. Their itineraries, recommended literature, and speakers reflect the groups' attitudes toward Israel. It is not uncommon for Protestant activists to arrive in the Holy Land for the first time with strong preconceived notions of the realities of the place. Protestant pilgrims, or for that matter members of other Christian groups, often focus either on the Israeli or the Palestinian side of the country.

As attitudes of mainstream Christian activists toward Israel became more critical, Jewish representatives often tried to persuade Christian participants in the dialogue of the importance of the Land and State of Israel for the Jewish people and their faith. In this they were not always successful. Both Jewish and Christian observers have complained that while overt anti-Semitism has become much less acceptable in Western societies, covert forms of anti-Jewish sentiment underlie disproportionately harsh judgment of Israel. The same churches that now recognize Judaism as a legitimate faith are also harbingers of anti-Israeli lines. The Presbyterian Church USA provides an excellent example. In June 1987, the General Assembly of the Presbyterian Church adopted "A Theological Understanding of the Relationship between Christians and Jews," which brought to fruition more than a quarter century of liberal Protestant and Jewish reconciliation. At about that time the Presbyterian Church also adopted a pro-Palestinian stance, passing resolutions in favor of a Palestinian state and supporting the Palestine Liberation Organization, with Presbyterian churches inviting PLO representatives to present their case.

Since the late 1960s, liberal Christian groups and organizations, including the World Council of Churches, have sided with national liberation movements against colonial regimes and actions. Israel's victory in the 1967 War and occupation of populated Arab territories recast it as a colonial outpost. During the 1960s–1980s, Western churches in the Holy Land, including Anglicans, Lutherans, and Catholics, underwent a process of "indigenization," instating Palestinians as their leaders and giving Palestinians greater standing and voice. It is not surprising that this process of indigenization of local churches has also affected the negative turn of the discourse. Some of Israel's most outspoken Christian critics in the 1980s–2010s have been Palestinian clergymen, such as Canon Naim Ateek, who found willing audiences for the Palestinian versions of Liberation Theology, a school of Christian thought influenced by Marxist ideas, which emphasizes social and political justice. A symbolic development has been the sharp change in the depiction of Israel in the progressive Protestant publication *Christianity and Crisis*, which Reinhold Niebuhr founded, and where he published a number of pro Zionist essays. The periodical took such an anti-Israel twist in the 1970s that Niebuhr's widow requested that her late husband's name be removed from the publication.

As I have tried to demonstrate, mainline Christian denominations speak with different voices, although the general trend today is critical of Israel and its policies. Within the same Western churches, both American and European, there are theologians committed to goodwill toward Judaism who, for the most part, show support for Israel and appreciate and emphasize its positive characteristics. Many of them have lived in Israel, at least for a while, and studied or worked there, becoming acquainted with the country, its issues, and its culture. That was the agenda of activists and theologians such as the Dutch Reformed ministers Jacobus Schoneveld and G. H. Cohen Stuart, and the German Lutheran pastors Petra Heldt and Michael Krupp, who have published articles and books on Judaism and Israel and voiced supportive opinions both in intra-Christian gatherings and in interfaith forums. They do not represent their churches as a whole, however. Their churches include activists and theologians who promote justice for Third World nations and who, since the events of September 2001, are less concerned with Christian-Jewish relations than promoting dialogue with Arabs and Muslims. While the liberal and mainline attitudes to Israel have become more critical, evangelical attitudes have, for the most part, remained supportive and appreciative.

Conservative Evangelical Christians and Israel

Like their liberal counterparts, conservatives are not cut from one cloth. There are hundreds of denominations that are mostly or fully evangelical, with minority enclaves of conservative evangelicals in a series of mainline or liberal denominations, such as the Presbyterian Church USA. Moreover, there are thousands of independent evangelical congregations. This huge movement encompasses a variety of liturgies, cultures, languages, ecclesiastical structures, and theological differences, as over the idea of predestination. Nevertheless, almost all evangelicals share some creeds and cultural attitudes: the Christian Bible is held to be God's message to humanity; they read the sacred Christian scriptures more literally than their liberal counterparts do. Their understanding of the Bible has strongly influenced attitudes toward the idea of a Jewish return to the Holy Land and the creation of the State of Israel.

A major component of evangelical theology is the belief that only those who accept Jesus as their savior will be guaranteed salvation and eternal life. This means it would be irresponsible to grant legitimacy to the religious beliefs of others, and of questionable benefit to dialogue with representatives of other faiths. However, evangelicals have established channels of communication with Jews and Israel. While they insist on Christian evangelical moral and spiritual exclusiveness, most evangelicals view the Jews as historical Israel, the object of biblical prophecies about the Davidic kingdom that will be reestablished when the Messiah arrives and Israel is restored to its land.

In contrast to liberal Christian notions of progressive millennialism, the messianic faith to which many evangelicals adhere depicts the arrival of the Messiah as a dramatic event following a harsh period of apocalypse. Israel looms large in this catastrophic vision. The country will serve as an End Times ground zero, the focal point of the apocalyptic era. It will be in Jerusalem that Antichrist will reign and reestablish the Temple and the Temple sacrifices, and it will be in the Valley of Megiddo, in northern Israel, that the battle of Gog and Magog will take place. Accompanied by the true Christian believers, Jesus will arrive on earth on the Mount of Olives, overlooking the Temple Mount. He will reign over a global millennial kingdom from Jerusalem, David's eternal capital, with Jews serving as his assistants. This is a unique case in which members of one religious community believe members of another religious tradition have an essential and constructive role to play in God's plans for global redemption. According to the evangelical eschatological scheme, the Jews will return to their ancient homeland, "in unbelief," before accepting Jesus as their Savior, and they will establish a political commonwealth there that will serve as a stepping-stone on the road to the messianic kingdom. For the Jews, the interim years of the Great Tribulation that stand between the current era and messianic times will be known as the Time of Jacob's Trouble. Living in spiritual blindness, the Jews will let themselves be ruled by the Antichrist, an impostor posing as the true Messiah, who will inflict a reign of terror including on the growing number of Jews who accept Jesus during this period. The arrival of Jesus with the truly converted will end the Antichrist's rule and bring about the kingdom of Christ on Earth. All Jews who survive the turmoil and terror of the Great Tribulation will accept Jesus as their Savior.

The Jews' role in this millennial scenario can well explain the interest of evangelical groups and individuals in the Jews and their national
restoration. Beginning in the nineteenth century, evangelicals have advanced initiatives intended to bring about the national restoration of
the Jews in Palestine. Predating the rise of Political Zionism, most such
efforts were designed to persuade the British, German, or American
governments to intercede with the international community and the
Ottoman Empire with a view to creating a Jewish commonwealth in
that land. It is not surprising, then, that in 1896 when Theodor Herzl
began seeking international recognition for the idea of a Jewish commonwealth in Palestine, evangelicals offered support. William Hechler,
a German-British pietist-evangelical and ardent premillennialist, became an advisor to Herzl and served as his liaison to Protestant rulers
of Germany. Zionist leaders had little understanding of premillennialist
Christian theology; they viewed it as a somewhat eccentric conviction
but appreciated the support it provided their cause. Evangelical Christians had mixed feelings about the Zionist movement. Reactions to the
rise of the movement and its endeavors were favorable, and their reports
on developments in Palestine are reminiscent of those of Jewish Zionists, but they were disappointed by the secular character of Zionism and
complained that the Jews were unaware of the real significance of their
own national movement. These misgivings notwithstanding, Christian
supporters began to coordinate their efforts with Jewish Zionists who
valued the Christian engagement on behalf of the Zionist cause—for
example, their efforts to persuade President Woodrow Wilson to allow
his British allies to issue the Balfour Declaration in 1917.

Evangelicals welcomed the Balfour Declaration as well as the British
takeover of Palestine, developments that indicated the ground was being
prepared for the coming of the Messiah. Many interpreted the turmoil
and hardships that beset the Jews between the two world wars in light
of their eschatological beliefs. They protested restrictions on Jewish immigration and settlement that the British periodically imposed. They
also criticized the Arabs' hostility toward the Zionist endeavor and their
violence against the Jews. Attempts to thwart a Jewish commonwealth
in Palestine were equivalent to blocking God's plans for the End Times.

Evangelical Christian protests over British policy in Palestine only
succeeded in modifying it somewhat. During that period, conservative

evangelical political power and influence in Britain and America were on the wane. The movement in Britain declined sharply, and in America after the Scopes trial in 1925, conservative evangelical leaders no longer saw themselves as influential national figures capable of advancing an international political agenda. Evangelical political involvement resurfaced only after World War II and the establishment of Israel, when it again played an important role in molding policies toward the Jewish state, especially in America,. Evangelicals welcomed Israel in 1948, and evangelical writers published sympathetic books and articles on the young Jewish state. They were unhappy with the secular character of Israeli society and culture and critical of the failure to separate church and state in a country they considered a democracy. However, witnessing such developments as the mass immigration of Jews to Israel from Asian, African, and Eastern European countries enhanced their messianic hopes.

Contrary to a common perception, evangelical Christian supporters of Israel did acknowledge the plight of Palestinian Arabs who lost their homes in 1948 and became refugees in Arab lands. They asserted that the Land of Israel could maintain an Arab population alongside its Jewish inhabitants and that Israel had an obligation to respect human rights and treat the Arabs justly. However, only a minority of evangelical Arabs adopted a pro-Zionist stance.

Israel's dramatic victory in the June War of 1967 as well as its gains in territory strengthened the evangelical belief in Israel's role in bringing the coming of the Messiah. From the 1970s to the 2010s, conservative evangelicals have been Israel's most ardent supporters in the American public arena. Likewise, the growth of evangelical populations in Latin America and other parts of the world encouraged favorable positions toward Israel and Jewish causes—for example, facilitating Jewish immigration from the Soviet Union in the 1970s–1980s. Growing in numbers and self-confidence during these years, evangelicals have become one of the most influential political and cultural camps in the United States and beyond. Their premillennialist-motivated pro-Israeli stand meshed with what they considered to be the importance of Israel for the Cold War struggles of America against the Soviets, and later with the fight against Muslim terror. A friendly attitude toward Israel has thus been compatible with the evangelical position on America's global policy.

A review of the way evangelical support for Israel has affected US presidents since the mid 1970s is instructive. Conservative evangelicals were disappointed with Jimmy Carter, a progressive evangelical who became president in January 1977. Representing Progressive Evangelicalism, a minority trend within the larger evangelical movement, this evangelical president took great interest in the Middle East and brought Egypt and Israel to sign a peace treaty, but he played the role of an American statesman with progressive agendas. The messianic hope of paving the way for the Davidic kingdom was not his concern. Ronald Reagan, who succeeded Carter four years later, often followed Christian evangelical agendas and hinted at his own premillennialist understanding of the course of history. His policy toward Israel was adopted by his successor, George H. W. Bush, who was also close to Christian evangelicals and relied on their support. While other considerations, too, account for Reagan's and Bush's policy toward Israel, the favorable evangelical attitude and insistence that America protect the Jewish state played a part.

In contrast to Reagan and Bush, Bill Clinton, an evangelical Christian, received little support from evangelicals, who have seen him as representing liberal values they have mostly opposed. Yet Clinton, who showed genuine concern toward Israel and tried to bring the Palestinians and Israelis to sign a peace treaty, grew up in the Bible belt and attended a Southern Baptist church in his hometown in Arkansas. George W. Bush's administration, on the other hand, was strongly influenced by evangelical, pro-Israeli sentiments. A committed conservative Christian himself, Bush relied heavily on evangelical support, and in addition to extending political backing and financial assistance to the Jewish state, he avoided initiating diplomatic moves that might upset evangelicals with millennial convictions.

Finally, before his election, Barack Obama and his wife, Michelle, were members of a charismatic African American church in Chicago. While African American churches typically share evangelical theological convictions and morality, their political messages are often different from those of white evangelical churches. They tend to be closer to liberal Christians on social and global issues and often take postcolonial views and identify with Third World nations. Some African American ministers hold to a premillennialist faith, and while many African American churches and congregants show sympathy to Israel, others have adopted a more skeptical view of the country and its place in the Middle East. Obama's even policy toward the Middle East, on the whole friendly toward Israel, seems to reflect neither evangelical premises nor anti-Israel liberation theologies.

Pro-Israel Organizations

Since the 1970s, dozens of pro-Israeli evangelical organizations have operated in the United States and in other nations with evangelical presence. Their leaders have lectured, distributed printed and electronic material, convened pro-Israel conferences, and organized tours to the Holy Land. A number of such groups have also been engaged in evangelization efforts among the Jews. The last decades also saw an increase in the actual presence and activity of conservative Christians in Israel. Tours of evangelical groups increased, as did the numbers of field-study seminars and of volunteers coming to kibbutzim or archaeological digs. Evangelical Christians have even established institutions of higher education in the country. Set up by Douglas Young, the Institute of Holy Land Studies, which changed its name to Jerusalem University College, offers courses on the Middle East, the Bible, and archaeology to evangelical students from Christian colleges in America and other countries who spend a semester or two in Jerusalem.

The most visible evangelical organization in Israel has been the International Christian Embassy in Jerusalem (ICEJ). In the 1970s, premillennialist Christian activists in Jerusalem of different nationalities founded a local fellowship to muster support for Israel and counterbalance anti-Israel sentiments in the Christian world. In 1979 the group launched its first yearly Tabernacles festival, a weeklong assembly of Christian supporters of Israel, highlighted by a march through the streets of Jerusalem. In 1980 the activists founded ICEJ as an act of sympathy and support for Israel on the part of Christians. The embassy chose as its logo two olive branches hovering over a globe with Jerusalem at its center and announced: "This symbolizes the great day when Zechariah's prophecy will be fulfilled, and all nations will come up to Jerusalem to keep the Feast of Tabernacles during Messiah's reign on earth." Israeli officials welcomed the new organization. It made the point, they believed, that although many countries had removed their embassies and consulates from Jerusalem because of Arab pressure, the Christian world backed Israel.

The embassy has wished to represent Christianity worldwide, and has made an effort to open branches and gain supporters in as many countries as possible. Embassies around the globe distribute ICEJ printed and electronic materials, recruit pilgrims for the annual Tabernacles gatherings, and collect money for the embassy's philanthropic enterprises in Israel. The embassy provides welfare services, distributing money and goods to needy Israelis. Orthodox rabbi Yehiel Eckstein established the International Fellowship of Christians and Jews, which emphasizes the importance of Israel for Jews and evangelicals alike and promotes support for Israel as a common basis for cooperation and understanding between the two groups. The International Fellowship has collected hundreds of millions of dollars, which helped in the immigration and absorption of Jews and financed social programs.

Liberal Christians and supporters of the Palestinian cause argue that the political support of conservative evangelicals for Israel is unjust. Together with members of Middle Eastern churches they have signed petitions condemning Christian Zionism. The negative responses of liberal and Middle Eastern churches help explain the Israeli leadership's welcome of its unexpected evangelical allies. Yet while some American Jewish activists appreciate the support of conservative Christians, others like Reform rabbi Eric Joffee see evangelicals as a threat to an open pluralistic society. Moreover, while evangelical opinions on Jews have improved considerably in the last decades, they deny that Judaism can grant salvation and that secular-induced policies can offer the desired peace and security that the Jews are hoping for. Until the Jews accept Jesus as their personal Messiah they will remain in a state of spiritual and moral deprivation.

Evangelical Missions

Missions to the Jews have been high on the evangelical agenda since the rise of the evangelical movement at the turn of the nineteenth century. Propagating Christianity among the Jews meant teaching God's first nation about its role and purpose in history, as well as saving some of them from the turmoil of the Great Tribulation. Often, the same people are active on two fronts: promoting support for Israel and evangelism of Jews. The largest and best-known mission of our time, Jews for Jesus, works to promote pro-Jewish and pro-Israeli sentiments, calling its music band the Liberated Wailing Wall. Simultaneously, another evangelical messianic group associated with the future of the Jews came into being. A movement of Jewish converts to evangelical Christianity, Messianic Judaism amalgamates evangelical theology and personal morality with Jewish customs, symbols, and identity. The new movement has carved a niche for itself within the larger evangelical community and, among other activities, promotes support for Israel in evangelical circles. Especially since the 1970s, thousands of Messianic Jews have immigrated to Israel and established a growing number of communities there.

The goals of Messianic Jewish groups and missions to the Jews are to increase support in the Christian community for the idea that the Jews are central to God's plans for humanity, and that they must be evangelized and Israel supported. For groups such as Jews for Jesus, the Chosen People Ministries, or the Friends of Israel, the two aims are inseparable. As a rule, Israeli leaders overlook the connection between support for Israel and evangelism. In their effort to build good relations with Christian nations and groups, Israeli governments have pledged not to interfere with missionary operations in Israel. Orthodox Jewish activists have protested against the missions, and have occasionally harassed missionaries, but a series of governments refused to change the policy, and the Israeli police were assigned to protect missionary centers.

Responding to the growing pro-Israeli influence of premillennialist evangelical groups on American political life since the late 1970s, the Israeli government has cultivated the support of conservative evangelicals. Israeli officials speak at evangelical conferences and meet with evangelical leaders and groups as part of the latter's touring schedules in Israel. Occasionally, this policy has met with internal Israeli opposition. In 1978 Orthodox members of Begin's government initiated legislation intended to restrict missionary activity. The legislation forbade offering economic incentives in exchange for conversion and was inherently ineffective, since contrary to myth, missionaries were not "buying" converts, and at any rate, the Israeli government was reluctant to enforce the law. In the 1990s, antimissionary sentiments were again running high, and a number of Orthodox and non-Orthodox members of the Knesset came out with initiatives to outlaw missionary activity. In 1996, an initial first-round proposal to curtail missionary activity passed the Knesset vote. Evangelical missionaries operating in Israel called upon their supporters around the globe to protest the impending law. Israeli embassies were virtually flooded with letters. Many directly addressed the prime minister's office in Jerusalem. Benjamin Netanyahu, the prime minister at the time, who had offhandedly supported the bill, changed his mind and opposed it. This turn of events highlights the nature of Israeli real-politik: Israel accepts extensive support from Christians whose values and agendas do not always agree with its own.

A number of evangelical Christians and Israelis have also cooperated, in surprising ways, outside the confines of governments. One such enterprise has been the mutual attempt at rebuilding the Temple following the 1967 war, when evangelical Christians saw this as the one event standing between this era and the next. A striking demonstration of the growing prominence of the Temple in evangelical messianic thought can be found in Hal Lindsey's *The Late Great Planet Earth*, an evangelical best-seller that appeared in 1970. However, while many Israelis understood the outcome of what they have come to call the Six-Day War in messianic terms, most did not wish to rebuild the temple. Moreover, the Temple Mount was a holy Muslim site with historical mosques and other shrines, and the Israeli government chose to maintain the status quo on the Mount. A number of rabbis even declared that Jews were forbidden to enter the Temple Mount since Jews are required to purify themselves with the ashes of the Red Heifer before entering the Mount, and there was the danger they might step on restricted sacred ground, such as the Holy of Holies, which even ordinary priests (*kohanim*) were not allowed to enter.

Nevertheless, since the 1970s a number of evangelical groups and individuals have promoted rebuilding the Temple through a variety of activities intended to facilitate Jewish preparation for this undertaking. In addition to searching for the exact site of the Temple, Christian proponents have sought the lost ark, a quest that inspired a number of novels and a movie based in part on a real-life figure. Evangelicals have also searched for the ashes of the Red Heifer and have even attempted to breed red heifers. The rebuilt Temple features in novels and fictions, most prominently the series *Left Behind*, published in the late 1990s and early

2000s, which sold tens of millions of copies. These books demonstrate that evangelical Christians have modified their End Times scenarios, wishing to reassure their Jewish friends they are considered positive players in the evangelical vision of Messianic Times.

As I have tried to show, the Jewish state offers many evangelicals a validation of their faith and hope for the future. Yet because they expect Israel to play a role in the events that precede the second coming of Jesus to Earth, the peace negotiations between Israelis and Palestinians and the Oslo Accords have caused apprehension. Some evangelical Christians have even warned Israelis and others against what they considered unwise and unwelcomed political developments. However, at this stage, most Christians expecting the Second Coming of Jesus maintain their interest in and devotion to Israel.

Dissenting Protestant Churches

Some mention should be made of dissenting denominations within Protestantism—among them, Jehovah's Witnesses, the Seventh-Day Adventists, and the Mormons—all of which evolved in the course of the nineteenth century. These groups hold to the centrality of the sacred scriptures, at times adding corpuses of writings, other than the Old and New Testaments, to their canons. During the twentieth century, these groups became increasingly global, drawing most of their converts from outside the United States, and are among the fastest growing contemporary religious groups.

The roots of the Seventh-Day Adventists go back to the early 1840s, when, stirred by predictions made by William Miller, a preacher from upstate New York, a large movement of Protestants awaited the second coming of Jesus. In October 1844, the last of the dates Miller set for Jesus's return came and went, without any apparent difference in the order of the world and human routine. However, some of Miller's followers became convinced that the messianic age had begun—not on Earth, but in heaven. Under the leadership of Ellen White, during the 1860s–1870s Adventists established a nonmainstream denomination. They celebrated Saturday rather than Sunday as their Sabbath and promoted healthy life based on exercise and vegetarianism. The attitude of the Seventh-Day Adventists toward Judaism and Jews has for the most part been cold. Neither Miller nor White assigned Jews a positive role in their eschatology, maintaining the traditional Christian belief that the Jewish role in history ended with Jesus's death on the cross, nor did Adventists consider Palestine to have special messianic or other significance. Still, a number of Adventists settled in the country. By the turn of the twenty-first century, a number of Adventist thinkers joined the movement of Jewish-Christian reconciliation. Jacques Doukhan, a professor of Hebrew and Jewish studies at the Adventist-affiliated Andrews University in Michigan, established an institute for Jewish-Christian relations and reconciliation as well as a journal, *Shabbat Shalom*, dedicated to Christian-Jewish rapprochement. Doukhan's book, *Israel and the Church: Two Voices for the Same God*, reads much like other books of Protestant and Catholic theologians who validate Jewish existence outside the Church. Such Adventists take a friendly view and in general have not been among Christian groups that promote adversarial attitudes toward Israel.

Jehovah's Witnesses is the current name of a group founded in the 1870s by Charles Taze Russell. While Russell believed the Jews had a central role in the heavenly plan of redemption and often preached on Jewish restoration to Zion, his successor, Joseph Franklin Rutherford, instigated a theological turnabout. The change in name, in 1931, from Bible Students to Jehovah's Witnesses expressed a new exclusivist outlook. Jehovah's Witnesses believe they alone are fulfilling God's will and reject all other religious expressions. Likewise they anticipate the kingdom of God as the only legitimate political entity; they take no part in politics and refrain from serving in the armed forces; they also refuse to take part in civil religious celebrations, such as Thanksgiving and Christmas. They have no use for Israel, the state or the land, and, considering the Jews to be a legitimate object of missionary activity, have made hundreds of converts in Israel.

Mormon interest in the prospect of the Jewish return to Palestine goes back to Joseph Smith, the Book of Mormon, and the Mormon elder Orson Hyde's tour of Palestine in 1841, in which he "dedicated" the land for its Jewish inhabitants. Smith and his followers have viewed themselves as members of the tribe of Joseph and understood America to be the Promised Land. Mormon sacred scriptures speak about Judean refugees making their way from Jerusalem to America at the end of the

First Temple period and of Jesus blessing America. Likewise, they speak about America in messianic terms and cast their experiences in their first generation in biblical terms, as the sons of Israel crossing the desert toward the Land of Zion-Deseret.

While identifying America with Zion and themselves as Israelites, Mormons have not made supersessionist claims in relation to Jews and Judea. They recognize the Jews as the Children of Judah and the Land of Israel as a second Zion, the gathering place of the Jews at the end of the era, when they accept Christianity in its rightful Mormon version. Mormon prophets and elders have looked favorably upon the Jewish return to Palestine. LeGrand Richards, a member of the council of twelve elders, published a book about Israel in 1954, which resembles books written by evangelical Christians at the time. In the 1970s Brigham Young University established an academic center near Jerusalem, in Kibbutz Ramat Rachel, where hundreds of Mormon students came to take courses, mostly about Israel, the Bible, and the Middle East. Wishing to encourage Mormon involvement with Israel, Teddy Kollek facilitated the allocation of a large piece of land on the Mount of Olives for building a permanent compound. Brigham Young University raised tens of millions of dollars and built a magnificent center, designed by the Israeli architect David Reznik, overlooking the old city of Jerusalem. The Jerusalem center has opened its doors to Israelis, conducting series of concerts. Likewise, the Mormon Tabernacle Choir has visited Israel and included "Hatikva" and "Jerusalem of Gold" in its repertoire.

The project caused a controversy in Israel, with Orthodox Jews protesting the allocation of land to a religious group known for its extensive evangelism. Consequently, the Mormon Church and the Israeli government signed an agreement, according to which Mormon students who come to study at the Brigham Young campus in Jerusalem would not evangelize during their stay in Israel. Both the building of the campus, the only one outside Utah and Hawaii, and the agreement not to evangelize have been outstanding in Mormon global policies. While Mormon attitudes toward Israel have, on the whole, been supportive, since the 1980s, the Mormon Church has forged a balanced policy in relation to the Israeli-Arab conflict. The Brigham Young center in Jerusalem has played a role in implementing this policy. Among other ventures, it asks its students to study and spend time in the Palestinian community as well as among Israelis. Attitudes toward the Middle East are not a matter of dogma, and while many Mormons are overtly supportive, there are other voices too. Ironically, the move of the Mormon campus to the Mount of Olives, near the Arab neighborhood of A-Tur, has contributed, at least in part, to the shift in policies. The Mormon University had to consider its Arab neighbors, and became aware, more than before, of the possibility that borders may shift and neighborhoods in East Jerusalem may find themselves under new jurisdictions.

The Catholic Church and Israel

Catholic attitudes toward Israel have changed dramatically, becoming more accepting and friendly. While the Catholic Church is, in principle, a global, united, and hierarchical religious body, it is more diverse than is often assumed. Catholics in the West were generally impressed by the new theological constructions of the 1960s–1980s as well as by papal declarations and gestures regarding the relationship between the Church and the Jewish people. However, this was hardly the case in the Middle East.

Until the 1960s, the attitudes of the Catholic Church toward the Zionist movement and the State of Israel could be summarized as apprehensive. This does not mean that there were not Catholic dignitaries, such as James, Cardinal Gibbons, who supported the idea of the Jewish return to Palestine. Likewise, there were Catholic laypeople who showed sympathy for Israel. Most of the countries that voted in favor of the partition of Palestine and the establishment of a Jewish state on November 29, 1947, were Catholic, as were some of the diplomats most sympathetic to the Jewish cause. Church leaders, however, were typically suspicious of a Jewish state and how it might affect sacred Christian sites and the extensive infrastructure of Catholic institutions in the Holy Land, including hundreds of churches, monasteries, convents, schools, hospitals, and hospices for pilgrims. Dozens of Catholic orders labored in the country. The Franciscan order has been "the Custodian of the Holy Land" since the fourteenth century, representing Catholic interests and providing services to pilgrims and residents. There were also tens of thousands of Catholics among the Arab population, many of them Greek Catholics, Syrian Catholics, and other Uniate groups, who recognized Rome and the pope but maintained independent liturgies and church structures. Wishing to protect Christian interests in the country, Catholic and other Christian leaders proposed the internationalization of Jerusalem, Bethlehem, and Nazareth, a plan the UN endorsed.

Zionist and later on Israeli leaders have recognized the importance of Catholic opinions to the country's international standing and have made concerted efforts to obtain Vatican approval. Theodor Herzl met with Pope Pius X in January 1904, in an attempt to convince the Holy Father to endorse the Zionist plan, but the pope refused to offer his approval. Catholic theology was clearly supersessionist, and Pius expressed the Christians' long-standing frustration that the Jewish people failed to accept the Christian faith. Catholics gave voice to this bitter notion in a Good Friday prayer that decried Jewish blindness to the truth of the Gospel. It was also no coincidence that the pope asked Herzl why "it must be Jerusalem." He might not have minded Zionism so much if it had not reclaimed the Holy Land. His concerns were shared by other Catholic prelates, including Francis, Cardinal Spellman, who in the late 1940s and early 1950s continued to advocate the internationalization of Jerusalem, even after Israel and its Arab neighbors signed a cease-fire agreement in January 1949.

Following the establishment of the state, a reserved yet operating relationship developed between Catholic institutions and the State of Israel. The war and the redrawing of borders changed some of the priorities of Catholic groups. Many Catholic institutions on the Israeli side of the border found themselves without their Arab pupils and patients and, like similar Protestant enterprises, began to take an interest in the growing Jewish population in the country. Giving a high priority to the relationship with the Catholic Church, Israeli officials made attempts to establish diplomatic relations with the Holy See, but the Vatican was in no hurry to recognize Israel. This was evident when Pope Paul VI went on a pilgrimage to the Holy Land in January 1964. On crossing the border from Jordan in Megiddo, he was greeted by Israel's president, Zalman Shazar, who welcomed him to Israel. In his response, Paul VI thanked "the authorities" but pointedly omitted mentioning "Israel." From a Catholic perspective, Israel was a new entity and there was no proof that it was there to stay.

Ultimately, the movement of interfaith dialogue and rapprochement, in which the Catholic Church became a major player, helped ease some of the Catholic skepticism toward Israel. Such a breakthrough on a global scale occurred during and following Vatican II, the Catholic general council that convened intermittently between 1962 and 1965. Initiated by Pope John XXIII, the council aimed at reforming the liturgy, changing the relationship between the hierarchy and the laity and between the Church and contemporary culture. The council also attempted to put to rest some of the old hostilities between itself and other Christian churches, as well as with non-Christian religions. The potential for improving Christian relations with Jews and Israel was not lost on Jewish leaders, and a number of Jewish organizations lobbied for the inclusion of Judaism in the council's agenda for reconciliation. Toward its conclusion, Vatican II came out with a groundbreaking resolution on the relationship between Christianity and Judaism. Among other things, the document warned against the accusation of deicide, the claim that the Jews collectively and in all generations were responsible for the crucifixion. The resolution facilitated further dialogue and additional declarations on the part of mainline Christian churches in relation to the Jews.

Following the 1967 War, as the scope of Catholic property and interests under Israeli control grew considerably, the Vatican was satisfied that the Israeli government was committed to protecting Christian sites. Among other gestures, the Israeli government paid reparations and subsidized repairs of Catholic buildings that were damaged during the war. The Catholic Church has tried to display a friendly and sympathetic attitude toward both Israelis and Palestinians. Since the 1960s some Catholic orders, such as the Brothers and Sisters of Zion, have been committed to improving Christian-Jewish relations, but the Church does not always speak in one voice. Even members of the same order have voiced different opinions. Within the Dominican order, for example, there were clear pro-Israeli (albeit not uncritical) voices, such as those of Marcel DuBois and other founders of Bet Isaiah in West Jerusalem who came to Israel in the early 1960s to get close to the Jews in their own land. Members of the Dominican scholarly institute École Biblique, in the eastern part of the city, have been less interested in Israeli society and culture and less sympathetic to Israeli agendas. The 1970s were also the years of the indigenization of the Catholic Church in Israel and the West Bank and the appearance of Arab Catholic leaders openly antagonistic toward Israel.

However, in spite of a complicated political divide and an active pro-Arab lobby, Vatican-Israeli relations improved and the level of representation and interaction between Israeli and Vatican officials was on the rise even before the official signing of mutual recognition agreements. The peace negotiations in the late 1970s between Israel and Egypt and later on between Israel and the PLO played a part in the Vatican's willingness to establish full diplomatic relations with Israel. The completion of the agreement took place at the same time that Israel and the PLO signed the Oslo Accord, and Israel signed a peace agreement with Jordan. Pope John Paul II's visit to Israel in 2000 was very different from his predecessor's, Paul VI's, thirty-six years earlier. John Paul II made a point of relating to both the State of Israel and the Palestinian Authority as fully legitimate. The head of the Catholic Church demonstrated unprecedented friendliness and sympathy toward Jewish religious and national symbols. Among other gestures, John Paul II placed a note in the Wailing Wall, stating his hope for world peace.

Sensing an imbalance of sentiments and power in the local Church, the Vatican has recently created an alternative autonomous bishopric, the St. James vicariate, for Hebrew-speaking Israeli parishioners. Headed by David Neuhaus, the vicariate promotes Hebrew liturgy and a Jewish-friendly environment. Another development that has shaped Catholic life in the country is the growing number of guestworkers from Catholic nations, such as the Philippines. For many of them, their churches serve as centers of their home cultures and meeting grounds with compatriots. Ironically, while the indigenization of the church meant recognition of the Arab culture and sentiments of the local Catholic population, the amalgam of Catholic parishioners has become more global and diverse with the influx of new ethnic elements. Similar developments have taken place in the Orthodox churches, as a result of dramatic demographic change.

Orthodox and Middle Eastern Christianity and Israel

Most of the focus of both statespeople and scholars has been on Western Christianity and its attitude toward Israel. However, most Christians in the Middle East, including in Israel, have been affiliated with Orthodox, Monophysite, or Uniate churches. The different political and cultural realities in which they have operated have led to very different theologies and liturgies, as well as worldviews from their Western co-religionists. Not surprisingly, this includes their opinions on Jews and Israel and their interaction with that country. By and large, Orthodox and Middle Eastern churches have not undergone the same theological transformations that affected the Catholic and Protestant churches in the second part of the twentieth century, and they continue to hold supersessionist views. Their interactions with Israel tend to be guided by pragmatic rather than theological considerations.

These churches own extensive property in Israel, operate multiple institutions, and minister to tens of thousands of lay members in numerous congregations, especially in Jerusalem, Jaffa, Haifa, and the Galilee. They also operate vast properties consisting of lands, buildings, churches, monasteries, and educational and welfare institutions. The Greek Orthodox Church is the largest owner of real estate in Jerusalem, and Jewish neighborhoods as well as central government buildings occupy its property. Its leaders routinely negotiate with Israeli officials over real estate transactions, although the Church does not sell its property but rather offers long terms leases. The vast property of the Greek Orthodox Church and its potential for lucrative deals has occasioned fraud on the part of Israeli businessmen. Other veteran Christian churches, such as the Armenian Orthodox Church, also own considerable property and negotiate with Israeli authorities and private citizens over their material interests.

Local churches must accommodate conflicting Arab and Israeli pressures to cooperate and conform. They are aware that borders and powers can shift, and their first priority is to protect their own interests. Many built pragmatic relationships with Israeli authorities after the 1948 War and following the June 1967 War in Israel's newly occupied territories. Especially since the Oslo Accord, even when they are situated on the Israeli side of the fence, these Christian churches are careful to comply with Palestinian officials, whether for pragmatic or ideological reasons. Such diverse and complicated relationships require Israeli officials who are knowledgeable, solid, subtle, and tactful to set agendas and interact with Christian leaders, communities, and institutions. According to Israeli journalist Arnon Regular, this is not always the case.

In the early years of the state, Israel established a special department for Christian churches in the Ministry of Religious Affairs. Its first director, Yaakov Herzog, was one of the young state's star officials and later became director general of the prime minister's office. As this department weakened, other agencies including the Department for Christian Churches and Institutions in the Ministry of Foreign Affairs contributed to determining the country's policy toward Christian churches and agencies. From 1965 to 1994, Teddy Kollek was mayor of Jerusalem and served as a liaison between Israeli interests and Christian churches, communities, dignitaries, and visitors. At other times, military and district officers handled Christian affairs.

Although not by design, much of Israel's policy toward Christian communities has been determined by state relations to religion. Churches enjoy autonomy, and within their own traditions a monopoly, not only in theological and liturgical matters but also in personal realms, including marriage, divorce, burial, and legacies. The state's educational system is also arranged according to confessional affiliations, as is the Israeli Scouts. The State subsidizes the church hierarchies, pays salaries, repairs buildings, and reimburses church dignitaries for taxes they have to pay when buying or importing cars. According to Daniel Rossing, who directed the department of Christian communities in the Ministry of Religious Affairs in the 1980s, it would have been in the country's interest to have offered more generous financial assistance.

Even if local church leaders were not always enthusiastic about Israel, they often chose, for pragmatic reasons, to establish a working relationship. A case in point was Archbishop George Hakim, head of the Greek Catholic Church in Israel between 1948 and 1967. Hakim was no Zionist but called upon his community to integrate themselves into Israeli society and institutions. He joined the Histadrut, the Israeli workers' union, which provided members with medical coverage, and had clinics built in Arab towns and villages. Hakim appeared as a dignitary at state receptions and showed initiative and leadership in various Israeli civic projects. However, when he was elected the Metropolis, head of the Greek Malakite Catholic Church in the entire Middle East, he moved to Damascus and changed his messages. In Syria he represented himself as an Arab patriot and distanced himself from Israel. When Bishop Hilarion Capucci, head of the Greek Catholic Church in East Jerusalem and the West Bank, was arrested in 1974 on charges of smuggling arms from Lebanon to Israel, Hakim defended his colleague's actions.

Especially after June 1967, Israeli officials became involved in intra-Christian battles over privileges in sacred sites and found themselves arbitrating and maintaining peace between feuding Christian churches. In addition to perennial skirmishes between Orthodox and Catholic priests over rights and territories in the Holy Sepulcher, in Jerusalem, and the Church of the Nativity, in Bethlehem, there have also been competing claims over territory and privileges between Armenian-Orthodox and Syrian-Orthodox, and between Ethiopians and Copts over a disputed wing attached to the Church of the Holy Sepulcher.

Negotiating the competing claims of these churches is not easy. Israeli leaders have not shied away from taking sides as in the elections for the Greek patriarch, whose church is particularly important because of its size, political connections, and extensive real estate holdings. The Jordanian government and the Palestinian Authority have also exercised their influence, as have different factions within the Greek Orthodox Church and community. The Israelis sided in 2001 with Bishop Timothy, a Greek-speaking member of the Order of the Holy Sepulcher, over and against Arab-speaking Palestinian-backed candidates. The struggle of Palestinian Greek Orthodox to gain control of the Greek Patriarchate of Jerusalem began already in the late nineteenth century, but Israeli officials were not in a hurry to aid Palestinians in this battle. While they have often been able to build good working relationships with most Christian groups, the experience of the last century demonstrates that an even and impartial attitude would engender greater trust on the part of the local Christian communities.

Many Palestinian Christians, especially members of the Greek Orthodox and Greek Catholic churches, supported the Palestinian national movement. As early as the British Mandate period, Palestinian Greek Orthodox activists disillusioned with the Greek-speaking leadership of their church joined the Communist party or Palestinian national causes. Palestinian Christians, including priests and ministers who grew up in the Anglican, Greek Orthodox, and Greek Catholic communities, notably Mitri Rehab and Naim Ateek, have become spokespeople for Palestinian causes in the Christian world and have published books on the Palestinian plight that feature Liberation Theology. They are welcomed voices in the international Christian discourse on Israel and Palestine, invited to give talks and participate in conferences all around the globe. However prominent, their voices are not the only ones within their communities. A surprising development among rank-and-file Christians in Israel and the Palestinian Authority is that the spread of Islamic movements among Palestinian Arabs has led many Christians to feel uneasy and vulnerable. While some have responded by immigrating to Western nations, others have reconsidered their attitudes toward Israel and its role in the Holy Land. In the first decade and a half of the twenty-first century, hundreds of Arab Christians volunteered to serve in the IDF, something they had not done before. Christian Zionism, previously very rare among Arabs, has become more popular, even among Copts in Egypt. Nevertheless, the Christian-Arab diaspora persists in voicing criticism of Israel and its policies. Likewise, the Arab-Christian religious leadership has avoided expressing opinions that might jeopardize their position with the Palestinian national movement. Between 2010 and 2015 clashes erupted when priests either blessed or condemned Christians from the Israeli Arab community who enlisted in the IDF.

Another unexpected development has been the demographical and ethnic changes within the Israeli Christian scene. In the 1990s–2000s, tens of thousands of Provoslav Russian Orthodox settled in Israel as part of the larger Russian Jewish immigration. Most of these Russian Christians have some Jewish ancestry or have been married to people of Jewish ancestry. Most have built their lives within the Jewish Israeli society and identify with the country. Their sons and daughters serve in the IDF. The number of Russian churches being limited, many attend Greek Orthodox churches, often operated by Arab priests, and this changes the amalgam of such churches and their atmosphere. Many communities that were previously almost exclusively Arab have become Israeli-Jewish-friendly-Arab. Such changes are bound to have long-term effects on the cultural characteristics and political agenda of local Christian communities.

Conclusion

The large spectrum of attitudes all around the Christian world reflects the different Christian traditions, faiths, ideas, social thoughts, ethnic loyalties, and cultural biases. Knowing where churches, thinkers, and communities stand on current Christian theological, moral, and social issues, as well as their national affiliations and international networks, can illuminate their positions toward Israel.

Perhaps the most important observation is that the positions Christian churches, laypeople, and thinkers adopt toward Israel are dynamic and have shifted over the past six and a half decades. Some changes stemmed from reconfigurations of opinions and priorities within the particular Christian groups, while views have also shifted in response to developments within Israel or in reaction to its military and political standing. Consider these examples: liberal Protestants, who, during the 1940s–1960s, largely supported Israel, have come to criticize her since the 1970s; the Catholic Church, which until the 1960s was mostly apprehensive, has changed its position toward Judaism and Jews, and later on toward Israel. It came gradually to recognize Israel and in 1994 established full diplomatic relations with it, while at the same time attempting to do justice to the Palestinians and reassure them of the Vatican's goodwill. Although evangelical positions have been more consistent, they too have been influenced by developments in Israel as well as by increased interaction between evangelical Christians and Israeli Jews. Liberal Western Christians have differentiated, at least in part, between their new understanding of the Jews and their position on Israel and Middle East politics. In Middle Eastern churches, political views, pragmatic considerations, and ethnic loyalties have shifted, while theological views have generally remained constant.

Christian attitudes toward Israel have often affected Jewish and Israeli interactions with Christian groups. Jewish representatives in official interfaith dialogue meetings have tried to convince liberal Christians that if they respect Judaism and Jews, they should also support Israel. These efforts have not always been successful. By the 1990s, most liberal Christians were more concerned about relations with the Muslim world than with amending their historical relationship with the Jews, and Israel's relations with liberal Christians soured. The Israeli leadership has been more proactive since the late 1970s in encouraging the efforts of pro-Israel Christian evangelical groups to muster support for Israeli causes. Israeli officials also established friendly ties with numerous Catholic dignitaries and orders and built a working relationship with the Vatican.

But only in the 1990s, during the papacy of John Paul II and with a breakthrough in Palestinian-Israeli peace negotiations, did the Vatican fully and openly recognize Israel and establish diplomatic relations with it.

Finally, we should note that Israeli policies affect Christian opinions, at least partially. Some Christian groups and thinkers might not be impressed by Israeli policies and overtures, and would make up their minds based on theological principles, political stands, and global images and affiliations. However, especially Christian residents of the country are impressed by Israel policies, attitudes, and actions, as well as day-to-day interactions with local Jewish and Muslim populations. The more fair, impartial, inclusive, and solid Israeli policies are, the more secure, protected, and welcome Christians feel; the more integrated they become, the more supportive their attitudes toward Israel are bound to be.

RECOMMENDED READINGS

Ariel, Yaakov. *An Unusual Relationship: Evangelical Christians and Jews*. New York: New York University Press, 2013.

Colbi, Saul. *A History of Christian Presence in the Holy Land*. Lanham, MD: Lexington Books, 1988.

Eckardt, Alice, and A. Roy Eckardt. *Encounter with Israel: A Challenge to Conscience*. New York: Association Press, 1970.

Feldman, Egal. "Reinhold Niebuhr and the Jews." *Jewish Social Studies* 46:3/4 (Summer-Autumn 1984), 293–302.

Guter, Yael, and Jackie Feldman. "Holy Land Pilgrimage as a Site of Inter-Religious Encounter." *Studia Hebraica* 6 (2006), 87–94.

Leighton, Christopher M. "The Presbyterian Jewish Impasse." In Jonathan Frankel and Ezra Mendelsohn (eds.), *The Protestant-Jewish Conundrum: Studies in Contemporary Jewry*, vol. 24, pp. 106–125. New York: Oxford University Press, 2010.

May, Melanie A. *Jerusalem Testament: Palestinian Christians Speak, 1988–2008*. Grand Rapids, MI: Eerdmans, 2010.

Madsen, Truman. *The Mormon Attitude toward Zionism*. Haifa: Haifa University Press, 1980.

Merkley, Paul C. *Christian Attitudes towards the State of Israel*. Montreal: McGill-Queen's University Press, 2001.

Spector, Stephen. *Evangelicals and Israel: the Story of American Christian Zionism*. New York: Oxford University Press, 2009.

Sundquist, Eric J. *Strangers in the Land: Blacks, Jews, Post-Holocaust America*. Cambridge, MA: Harvard University Press, 2005.

Walvoord, John. *Israel in Prophecy*. Grand Rapids, MI: Zondervan, 1962.

GLOSSARY TERMS

Balfour Declaration
British Mandate
deicide charge
Histadrut
Liberation Theology
Oslo Peace Accords
Political Zionism
Supersessionism
Wars: 1948 War; 1967 War; The June War of 1967; The Six-Day War

Yaakov Ariel is Professor of Religious Studies at the University of North Carolina at Chapel Hill. He is the author of *Evangelizing the Chosen People: Missions to the Jews in America, 1880–2000* and *An Unusual Relationship: Evangelical Christians and Jews.*

THIRTEEN

Perceptions and Understandings of Israel within Islam

NORMAN A. STILLMAN

Introduction

Israel is situated not only in the center of the Arab Middle East but within the heart of the even greater Islamic world, which extends from Morocco on the Atlantic to the west, to Turkey in the north, and to Iran, Pakistan and Central and South Asia to the east. Like Judaism, Islam is far more than a religion. It is a religious civilization with regional and national variations, to be sure, but it also has a political dimension: it regards its members as being part of a polity, the Umma, the Community of the Believers, or the Community of the Muslims (Ar. Ummat al-Mu'minīn or Ummat al-Muslimīn). This concept has its parallel in the Jewish conception of 'Am Yisrael, the People of Israel. Hence the Palestinian-Israeli conflict, which in its wider manifestation becomes the Arab-Israeli conflict, has ramifications throughout the much larger contemporary Islamic world whose perceptions and understandings of Israel, of Zionism, and of Jews are influenced by the ongoing conflict between Israel and the Palestinians.

However, another important factor plays a role in Muslims' perceptions and understandings of Israel, Zionism, and Jews—namely, the religion of Islam itself. Before the advent of the modern Zionist movement, the subject of Jews, Judaism, and the Land of Israel as the home of the biblical Israelites was by no means a tabula rasa for Muslims. Until the mass exodus of Jews from the Islamic lands following the establishment of the State of Israel, over a million Jews lived in Muslim countries. In fact, for a millennium, from the midseventh century until the beginning of the seventeenth century, most of the world's Jewry lived in the Dār al-Islām (the Domain of Islam). On the whole, Jews welcomed the Muslim Arab conquerors of the Middle East and the Iberian peninsula. Islamic rule was considerably more tolerant than that of the Christian Byzantines in the Levant and North Africa and the Visigoths in Spain. For Muslims, Jews, Christians, and Zoroastrians were People of the Book (Ar. *ahl al-kitāb*), recipients of a genuine divinely revealed scripture. As long as they surrendered, paid taxes, and acknowledged the suzerainty of the Islamic state, they were considered protected people (Ar. *ahl al-dhimma* or *dhimmīs*) under the aegis of the Muslims. In exchange for their submission, they were entitled to freedom of religion, freedom of economic endeavor, and a high degree of internal communal autonomy, which in premodern times was no small concession and is the source of the Islamic world's well-justified historical reputation for tolerance. During the Middle Ages, Jews took part in the economic and intellectual life of the Muslim world on a scale unprecedented until the modern era, and outright oppression and persecution were rare and never on a scale comparable to the sufferings of Jews in Christendom. The premodern Muslim world had its share of negative perceptions of Jews and Judaism, but these were nowhere as virulent as European, Christian theological, and popular animus. Indeed, they were most often offset by positive perceptions and by the generally tolerant social system that provided a place for non-Muslims, including large numbers of Christians, Jews, and Zoroastrians in the public space. This overall tolerance, however, would change markedly in modern times for several reasons—only one of which was the establishment of the Jewish state and the unresolved conflict between Israel and the Palestinians.

The Contemporary Scene

With few exceptions, the present-day Islamic world exhibits a marked general hostility toward Israel and Jews. This hostility is found among most mainstream Muslims, both secular and religious, irrespective of whether they are the majoritarian Sunnis, who constitute approximately 90 percent of the world's billion Muslims, or the minority Shiʿites. It is found as well as among the militant Islamists, who hold both a political and religious vision of Islam. Although in discourse aimed at Western consumption, a distinction has often been made between Jews and Zionists, claiming that it is only the latter who are enemies, not Jews per se, this distinction is almost never maintained in speech or writing aimed at the Muslim public. What is even more disturbing is that contemporary Islamic anti-Israel and anti-Jewish animus is replete with the tropes and themes of both European medieval and modern post-Enlightenment anti-Semitism. These notions are found among the principal tenets of virtually every contemporary Islamist group, whether dubbed "militant" or "moderate" by Western governments and pundits. These include the various Sunni groups such as the Muslim Brotherhood, Dāʿish (also known as ISIS and ISIL), al-Qāʿida, al-Jamāʿa al-Islāmiyya, and Ḥamas in the Middle East, or Jamīʿat al-ʿAdl waʾl-Iḥsān and al-Nahda in the Maghreb, or Ḥizb al-Taḥrīr in Europe, or the Shiʿite ones such as the Khomeinists in Iran and Ḥizbollāh in Lebanon. These groups hold a wide variety of theological views and doctrines. However, they all share a rejection of Western secularism and the utopian goal of establishing a society that is completely Islamic in culture and governed by Islamic law, first in their own countries and eventually throughout the entire world. They also tend to see the world as a Manichaean dichotomy between good and evil and maintain the traditional vision of the world as divided into the Dār al-Islām and the Dār al-Ḥarb (the Domain of War), which is that part of the world that has yet to be subjugated to Islam and with which there is perpetual conflict under the obligation of jihād, or holy war. Although a temporary cease-fire (Ar. *hudna*) may be negotiated between the two domains, there can be no permanent peace between them. No less significant as far as Jews and Israel are concerned, virtually all contemporary Islamists share a number of anti-Semitic beliefs among their principal tenets.

The most common anti-Semitic notion among the broad spectrum of Islamist groups is that of a universal Jewish conspiracy as depicted in the enduring classic of modern European anti-Semitism, "The Protocols of the Elders of Zion." Ayatollah Khomeini writes in his *The Trusteeship of the Jurisconsult* (Pers. Vilāyat-i Faqīh: Ḥukūmat-i Islāmī) that the true aim of the Jews "is to establish a world Jewish government." Khomeini, like other Islamists, also adopts other classical tropes of European anti-

Semitism. He describes Jews as predatory exploiters who had spread throughout Iran and had gained control of its markets. In Khomeini's eyes, the Arab-Israeli conflict is "a war of all Muslims together against the Jews and their leaders." In another of book of collected excerpts from his writings, titled *Confronting Israel* (Ar. Tujah Isrā'īl), Khomeini makes no distinction between Jews and Israelis. They are part of the same international conspiracy.

The Palestinian Ḥamas movement, founded in Gaza in 1987 as a local branch of the Egyptian Muslim Brotherhood and voted into power in the Gaza Strip in 2007, draws upon the libels of the "Protocols of the Elders of Zion" in its Islamic Covenant (1988) and other publications, accusing Jews of a universal conspiracy for world domination. It accuses them of instigating the French and Communist Revolutions and having their fingerprints on every war that has ever broken out anywhere. It claims that the Zionists control the imperialist states, were behind the establishment of the United Nations, and that the Freemasons, Rotary and Lions Clubs, and B'nai B'rith are all Zionist fronts.

Even a relatively moderate Islamist such as Rached Ghannouchi, the leader of the Tunisian Nahda (Renaissance) party, the senior partner in the coalition government in power in Tunisia from October 2011 to January 2014, argues that there are among Jews "good people" (namely those opposed to Zionism), and not all are "polytheists." Nevertheless, he goes on to claim that Zionists want to inherit both the Umma and the West and lead the entire world. They want to replace Washington with Jerusalem as the center of power and destroy all humanist principles underlying civilization—again, a fallback to "The Protocols."

For Sheikh Abdessalam Yassine, leader of the Moroccan Jamī'at al-'Adl wa'l-Iḥsān (Justice and Charity Group), who is also considered a relative moderate, Jews are the embodiment of evil and all that plagues the modern world. Zionism and Jewry are synonymous. Jewish Hollywood is an accomplice in the Zionist world conspiracy. Yassine's book *Winning the World for Islam* contains a lengthy anti-Semitic diatribe and has been translated into several languages including English and French. For the Muslim Brotherhood, which came to power through free elections in post-Mubarak Egypt in 2012 but was overthrown by a military coup in July 2013 and still commands the support of large numbers of the population, Jewry is the first and most pernicious of the four great evils to be combated. The others are "the Crusade" or Christian imperialism, communism, and secularism. An article from the October 1980 children's supplement of the Brotherhood's magazine *al-Da'wa (The Call)* quotes a supposed Jewish book (again "The Protocols") in which it is written, "We Jews are the masters of the world, its corrupters, the fomenters of sedition, its executioners!" The article calls upon young Muslims to "annihilate their existence." The founding leader of al-Qā'ida, Osama bin Laden, in his 1998 Declaration of the World Islamic Front for Jihad against the Jews and Crusaders always places Jewry at the top of the list of enemies to be confronted by holy war, referring to a "Crusader-Zionist alliance" that inflicted devastation on Iraq and claiming that "the Americans' aims behind these wars [in Iraq and Afghanistan] are religious and economic, the aim is also to serve the Jews' petty state and divert attention from its occupation of Jerusalem and murder of Muslims there."

One of the principal elements that sets most Islamists apart from traditional Islam is their adoption of an anti-Semitic worldview in which the fantasies of "The Protocols" are justified by proof texts from the Qur'an and Ḥadīth (the traditions of the Prophet Muḥammad). This view, its theological justification, and indeed a great deal of the overall social and geopolitical analysis of Islamists owe much to the thought of the Egyptian Ḥasan al-Bannā' (assassinated 1949), founder of the Muslim Brotherhood, and to the widely disseminated writings of the philosopher of the movement, Sayyid Quṭb, who was hanged by Gamal Abdel Nasser in 1966.

Although initially a phenomenon of Muslim countries, Islamism has spread to the Islamic diaspora communities of Europe and the Americas. The radical Islamist Hizb ut-Tahrir (Party of Liberation), which is particularly active in the United Kingdom, maintains its web pages in several European languages. It brands Jews as "a slanderous people" and incites Muslims to "kill them wherever you find them." In North America, Islamist preachers, often with a Wahhabi (a strict, fundamentalist branch of Ḥanafī Sunnism and the official rite of the Kingdom of Saudi Arabia) or Muslim Brotherhood background propagate anti-Semitic ideas in sermons and addresses. Groups such as the Muslim Arab Youth Association distribute pamphlets with such titles as "America's Greatest Enemy: The Jew!" and books such as *The Struggle for Existence between the Quran and the Talmud.* However, because of the overwhelming popular outrage in the United States toward Islamist militants in the wake of the September 11 attacks on New York and Washington, such groups and organizations have tended to mute their anti-Semitic rhetoric in public except on university campuses where they have considerable leftist and Third World activist allies.

But it is not only among the Islamists, who after all, represent a small, albeit activist minority among Muslims, that such anti-Semitic ideas have currency. These views are held by many members of the broader Muslim population as well, and this is a worrisome trend and has no long-term roots in Islamic history. For example, when the Malaysian prime minister Mahathir Mohamad, said in a speech before the Organization of the Islamic Conference in October 2004 that "today the Jews rule the world by proxy" (an allusion to the topos of "The Protocols of the Elders of Zion"), he not only received unanimous applause from the kings, presidents, emirs, and ministers in attendance but was praised by a number of well-known figures, among them the Afghan president, Hamid Karzai.

The ubiquity of anti-Semitic notions throughout the Islamic world and among a broad spectrum of Muslims living in Western Europe and other diasporas is a concomitant of Muslim emotional and political engagement in the Palestine issue. But it is important to note that such widespread fantasies as the Blood Libel (the accusation that Jews use the blood of non-Jewish children in their unleavened bread for Passover) featured in print and popular television dramas (e.g., the twenty-nine-part Ramadan special *al-Shatāt* [*The Diaspora*] produced in Syria in 2003) or the almost universal conviction that there is a Jewish conspiracy to dominate the world have no precedence in traditional Islamic thought. Like so many aspects of modernity in the developing world, these ideas are patent Western imports, historically un-Islamic, and have been branded as such by a few bold and enlightened Muslims, such as Soheib Bencheikh, the former Grand Mufti of Marseilles, the Pakistani-Canadian writer and intellectual Tahir Aslam Gora, and the groups Muslims against Anti-Semitism, which was established in the United Kingdom in 2007, and the Muslim Committee against Anti-Semitism in Canada.

Traditional Islamic Perceptions of Jews
and the Land of Israel

Muslim attitudes toward Jews and the land which is now the State of Israel are also shaped by the religion of Islam, which includes Jews and the Holy Land within its sacred history and worldview. Like Judaism, Christianity and other great religions, Islam includes many things in its scripture and theological literature that can give rise to contradictory ideas. This is the case with regard to Jews, Judaism, and the Land of Israel. Furthermore, it must be kept in mind that Islam i(1) is a religion with a corpus of doctrines, beliefs, and practices that have evolved over 1,400 years and have been subject to widely varying manifestations and interpretations; (2) originally was a body politic, united at first but becoming more divided over time; and (3) remains a civilization that despite local and regional differences has nevertheless significant elements of unity amid the variety.

As in the case of Christianity, the relationship between Judaism and Islam goes back to the very founding of the new faith: Jews figure into Islam's theological worldview, and Jews lived as a subject population under Muslim rule, sometimes under better, sometimes under worse conditions. In general, Jewish life under Muslim rule was best during times of political, economic, and social stability, notably the eighth to the twelfth centuries in the Middle East under the Abbasid and Fatimid caliphates, the tenth and eleventh centuries under the Umayyads and Taifa rulers in Iberia, and the fifteenth to the seventeenth centuries under the Ottomans in the Balkans, Anatolia, and the Middle East. Jewish culture developed and flourished during these periods, when, up until the beginning of the seventeenth century, the majority of world Jewry actually lived in the Islamic world.

A number of fundamental notions in Islam about Jews and Judaism have their origins in the Qur'an, which according to Muslim belief is the verbatim word of God vouchsafed to the Prophet Muḥammad by the Angel Gabriel, just as in Christianity certain basic attitudes are grounded in the New Testament. However, because Islam, unlike Christianity, did not begin as a sect within Judaism or claim to be *verus Israel* (true Israel), Muslim scripture and later theological writings (with the exception of the Sīra, or canonical biography of the Prophet Muḥammad) do not exhibit anything comparable to the overwhelming preoccupation with Jews that one finds in the New Testament, the writings of the Church Fathers, and later Christian theological literature. Jews are mentioned frequently in the Muslim scripture and canonical literature. In the earlier parts of the Qur'an, which date from the time that Muḥammad preached in his hometown of Mecca (ca. 610–622), there is frequent reference to the Children of Israel (Ar. Banū Isrā'īl). Most of these references are to the biblical Israelites, although a few are clearly referring to contemporary Jews (e.g. Suras 26:197 and 17:101). The Children of Israel are described as having a genuine divine revelation and like the Christians are a "people of the book" (*ahl al-kitāb*), i.e. a people of scripture. The stories of the Israelites echo the Bible and Midrash (Jewish homiletic lore) and are both positive and negative. In later verses of the Qur'an that were revealed to the Prophet in Medina between 622 and 632, the term *Yahūd*, the usual word for "Jews" in Arabic today, appears along with Banū Isrā'īl and is overwhelmingly pejorative. This is primarily due to Muḥammad's inimical encounter with the Jewish scholars in Medina who contradicted him, mocked what to them were his mistaken versions of biblical lore, and rejected his prophetic mission. Jews in the Medinese suras are associated with strife. They (along with the Christians) are accused of believing that they alone are beloved of God and have salvation (Suras 5:18 and 2:111). They pervert words and blaspheme (Sura 4:44). They are usurers and corrupters. They have slain prophets (Sura 2:261). They have tampered with the texts of the Scriptures (Suras 3:78, 4:46, and 5:13). Along with the pagans, they are the Muslims' worst enemies, are untrustworthy, and ought not to be taken as friends by the Believers (Sura 5:51 and 82). And according to the Qur'an, Jews are fated for a painful doom (Sura 4:161).

These highly negative depictions of Jews were expanded and amplified in the early Islamic hagiographic literature on the life of the Prophet and his companions (the Sīra, the Kitāb al-Maghāzī, and the Tabaqāt Ahl al-Ṣaḥāba) and in works of Qur'anic exegesis (*tafsīr*). In these texts, the conflict with the Jews of Medina takes on epic proportions, and the Jews appear as caricatures—villainous, malicious, deceitful, but totally lacking in resolve. Though wicked and treacherous, they never seem terribly effectual or possess any of the demonic qualities attributed to them in medieval Christian literature. Their ignominy stands in stark contrast to Arab Muslim heroism and conforms to the Qur'anic image of "wretchedness and baseness stamped upon them" (Sura 2:61).

In the canonical traditions of Muḥammad's words and deeds known as the Sunna, in the small proportion of narratives where Jews are mentioned in a positive or neutral light, they are usually termed Banū Isrā'īl, and in negative passages as Jews. Thus up to modern times, *Israelites* and *Children of Israel* were often the polite way of referring to Jews in Arabic (a semantic parallel to the early modern French usage of *israélite* as a more polite term than *juif*). However, since the establishment of the Jewish State, the word *Isrā'īlī* has taken on a new resonance that is in fact far more negative than *Yahūdī* (the singular of *Yahūd*).

These generally negative images of Jews, enshrined in scripture and religious lore, would be given new emphasis in modern times both as a result of the diametrically opposed reception of Western modernity by Jews and Muslims during the period of European colonial domination and as a result of the Israeli-Palestinian conflict. However, for long periods of history, a number of significant legal and social factors mitigated their potentially baneful force. First and foremost among these mitigating factors was the fact that despite his evolving hostility to Jews and Christians, Muḥammad never questioned the basic validity of their religions. They were only to be fought against until they submitted to Muslim rule as humble tribute bearers in accordance with the clear Qur'anic injunction of Sura 9:29. As long as they accepted their subordinate status and paid the prescribed poll tax (Ar. *jizya*), they were not only to be tolerated, but were entitled to be protégés (*dhimmīs*) of the Muslim commonwealth.

A second factor that mitigated the harmful effects of anti-Jewish prejudice was that the Sharī'a, or Islamic sacred law, prescribed one and the same legal role of *dhimmīs* for Jews, Christians, and Zoroastrians in the Muslim state. The Jews shared their inferior status with these far more numerous and, hence, conspicuous religious communities, and this diffused some of the anti-Jewish sentiment within the broadly anti-*dhimmī* context. Furthermore, Jews were spared the onus of suspicion increasingly harbored toward some Christian communities from the period of the Crusades onward, that they were friendly to the European Christian enemy and a potential fifth column. This perception changed radically in modern times when large numbers of Jews of the Islamic world began to seek a modern education. This was often accomplished with the help of their Western brethren and such international Jewish organizations as the Alliance Israélite Universelle (founded in 1860) as Jews saw a better future for themselves either under European colonialism or in a revived Jewish homeland. A frequent claim by some in both the Islamic and Western world is that it was only the advent of Zionism and the ensuing Palestine conflict that drove a wedge between the Jews who had lived in the Islamic world for centuries and the Muslim majority. But the parting of the ways had begun more than a century earlier. In Europe, the Jews greeted emancipation and modernization as an opportunity for greater assimilation into the surrounding culture. But the response of the Islamic world was quite the opposite. The Muslim majority perceived the West's growing economic, political, and cultural intrusion during the course of the nineteenth and well into the twentieth century as a serious threat; the Jews and most native Christians viewed it as an opportunity to liberate themselves from their traditional humble and subordinate status as *dhimmīs*.

Throughout the Middle Ages and well into the nineteenth century, rather than seeing Jews as having powerful friends and allies abroad or as potential traitors, Arab, Turkish, and Persian Muslims generally perceived them more condescendingly than they did native Christians. Medieval Muslim theologians, irrespective of whether they were Sunni or Shi'ite, devoted only a very small part of their polemics against other religions to Judaism. There is simply nothing comparable in traditional Islam in quantity and rarely in sheer vitriol to the Adversus Judaeos literature of the Church Fathers and their medieval successors. Occasional anti-Jewish propaganda appeared, usually when a prominent Jew or group of Jews were perceived to have egregiously transgressed the boundaries of propriety as stipulated in the theoretical pact of protection governing *dhimmīs* by rising too high in government service and behaving arrogantly. Such anti-Jewish propaganda and polemics were in fact no different from anti-Christian tracts, and frequently the two were combined. The kind of virulent anti-Jewish railing that has become a staple of television preachers in many Middle Eastern countries today would have been exceptional in earlier eras, although they draw upon an existing well of traditional material.

Just as traditional Islam had a place for Jews and Judaism within its sacred history and worldview, so too it had a place in its religious thought for Jerusalem and the Land of Israel. In the Qur'an (Sura 5:21), Moses tells the Israelites, "O my people, go into the Holy Land (Ar. *al-arḍ al-muqaddasa*) which God has ordained for you." The appellation of "the Holy Land" was common in early Muslim usage, but was later dropped and replaced by al-Sha'm (also al-Shām), the designation for Greater Syria and including the Land of Israel, Lebanon, and Syria proper. This term is also found in the Ḥadīth and in statements by prominent early Muslims quoted by the Arab historians. The land was holy because it was the birthplace of prophecy and divine revelation. It was the home of biblical figures revered in Islam as prophets—Abraham, Isaac, Jacob, David, Solomon, and Jesus. In one tradition, attributed to a companion of the Prophet, it is said "that nowhere was a messenger sent by God except in al-Sha'm," and when he was not from al-Sha'm, he was at least transported there in a nocturnal apparition [like Muḥammad or Ezekiel]. The mystical night journey of the Prophet from Mecca to the furthest mosque (*al-masjid al-aqṣā*) related in the Qur'an (Sura 17:1) was understood by later Muslims as the Prophet's having been transported either in body or spirit to Jerusalem [which, however, is never mentioned in the Qur'an by name], from whence he ascended into heaven.

In medieval Arabic, Jerusalem comes to be called al-Bayt al-Muqaddas, or "The Holy House" (cf. the Hebrew name for the Temple itself—Beit Hamikdash), and al-Quds in modern Arabic usage. At first it is revered as the site of the foundation stone of the world, revealed to the conquering Caliph 'Umar in 638 by the famous Jewish convert to Islam, Kaʿb al-Aḥbār, a major source of many Jewish traditions on the sanctity of Jerusalem and the Holy Land. During the first century of Islam, the tradition gained currency that Jerusalem was the third holiest sanctuary in Islam after Mecca and Medina. In Islamic eschatology, Jerusalem would be the site of the Last Judgment and the holy Kaʿba would be miraculously transported to the Temple Mount. Prior to the loss of the city to the Franks, Jerusalem did not play a central role in Islamic thought, but in response to the Crusades, Muslim theologians began to emphasize a much more exclusivist Islamic heritage for the city and a body of literature was built up on the merits (Ar. *faḍā'il*) of Jerusalem. However, some Islamic scholars opposed excessive veneration and popular pilgrimage

(Ar. *ziyāra*) rituals practiced by Muslims in Jerusalem, Palestine, and the surrounding countries. One of these scholars, Aḥmad ibn Taymiyya, is the intellectual forefather of the present-day Wahhābīs of Saudi Arabia and of many Islamist groups.

The Modern Era and the Clash of Nationalisms

The heightened emphasis on the sanctity of Jerusalem and the Holy Land in reaction to the Crusades made the loss of the land to Israel and especially Jewish sovereignty over Jerusalem a theological problem for many Muslims in modern times. Already in the late nineteenth and early twentieth century, some theologians like the reformer and revivalist Rashīd Riḍā in Egypt expressed their deep concern that the nascent Zionist movement was seeking not merely a refuge for Jews, but sovereignty in the Holy Land, and he warned his co-religionists that for this reason Zionism posed an existential danger to the Islamic world.

On the other hand, some political figures in the Arab world did not at first view the Zionist endeavor as inimical. The governor of Alexandria and later prime minister of Egypt, Aḥmad Zīwar Pasha, exhibited an early friendly attitude toward Zionism and attended two mass Zionist rallies in his city in November 1917. More significantly, the emir Faisal, later first king of Iraq, who led the Arab Revolt against the Turks together with T. E. Lawrence, met with the Zionist leader Chaim Weizmann on two occasions in 1918 and on January 3, 1919, two weeks prior to the opening of the Paris Peace Conference. The two men signed the agreement bearing their names in which they committed to work cordially together and with goodwill; to encourage immigration of Jews into Palestine on a large scale while protecting the rights of the Arab peasants and tenant farmers; and to safeguard the free practice of religious observances. The early nonideological pragmatism of these political figures would be echoed for a brief interlude in the late twentieth century by a few leaders such as President Anwar Sadat of Egypt, King Hussein of Jordan, and King Hassan II of Morocco. However, any positive or even neutral attitudes toward Zionism in the earlier period quickly vanished as the Arab world was increasingly disappointed at the failure of rising national aspirations in the aftermath of World War I and the almost total domination of their lands by European powers.

The Balfour Declaration, the collapse of the Ottoman Empire, and the awakening of national aspirations stirred up considerable enthusiasm for the Zionist idea among Jews living in Islamic countries, particularly in the Arab world. However, this initial enthusiasm was quickly dampened with the rise of militant pan-Arab nationalism in Syria and Iraq and pan-Islamic movements in Egypt and elsewhere. It was also tempered by the French authorities in the Maghrebi states, where many Jews were also attracted to the French *mission civilisatrice*, which was fostered by the colonial authorities and by the Alliance Israélite Universelle network of schools, which provided many North African Jews as well as Jews in other Islamic countries with a Western education and an entry ticket into the modern economy. And lastly, open expression of pro-Zionist sentiment became increasingly muted in many Islamic countries (Tunisia being a notable exception) as Arab-Jewish relations in Palestine deteriorated from 1929 on and a climate of fear began to descend upon many Jewish communities in the Arab world.

The events in Palestine had evoked little attention in much of the Arab and wider Islamic world until 1929, when in August of that year widespread rioting broke out among the local population in the wake of a perennial dispute over Jewish prayer at the Western (Wailing) Wall at the base of the Temple Mount. The rioters killed 129 Jews and injured over 300 more. The police and British troops in turn killed more than 100 Arabs in putting down the riots. The Muslim religious and political leader in Palestine, the Mufti Ḥājj Amīn al-Ḥusaynī depicted the incident as a case of Jews attempting to usurp Muslim sacred precincts and British bias in favor of the Jews, and in the Arab world the riots elicited an outpouring of sympathy for Palestinians and anti-Zionist anger. In an effort to foster these sentiments, the Mufti called for universal Muslim solidarity in defense of Arab Palestine and its Islamic holy places. To this end he convened a World Islamic Conference in Jerusalem in December 1931, which was attended by delegates from every Muslim country except secularist Turkey, which declared its opposition to the "use of religion as a political instrument." The conference marked an important turning point in the wider Muslim world's perception of Zionism and Jews. One of the resolutions adopted by the delegates specifically called for defending the Holy Land against the Jews. Following the conference, the Mufti pursued his ties with Islamic organizations throughout the world such as the Young Men's Muslim Association and with nationalists in various Arab countries. These groups actively disseminated Palestinian anti-imperialist and anti-Zionist—and not infrequently, anti-Jewish—propaganda materials in their own countries.

World War II put a temporary halt to open pan-Arab and pan-Islamist activities; the two major imperial powers in the Arab world, England and France, clamped down with censorship controls, aware that widespread sympathy among Arab nationalists lay with the Axis. However, throughout the war, the Mufti Ḥājj Amīn al-Ḥusaynī, who had fled to Berlin in 1941, broadcast incendiary messages in Arabic against the Allies, the Zionists, and the Jews.

The end of the war witnessed a renewed surge of Arab and Jewish nationalism. It set in motion a concatenation of forces that in short order would lead to the termination of the Palestine Mandate, the Arab-Israeli War, the creation of the State of Israel, the flight of Palestinians from the new Jewish State, the mass exodus of Jews from the Arab countries (mostly to Israel, but also to France and other destinations), and the end of imperial domination in that part of the world.

Perceptions of Israel since 1948

The defeat of the Arab armies that tried to put an end to the nascent State of Israel in the 1948–1949 War, the ensuing Palestinian refugee problem, and the subsequent defeats in 1956 and 1967, exacerbated the anti-Zionist and anti-Jewish sentiments in the Arab and wider Muslim world. Israel's stunning six-day victory in the 1967 War, even more than the earlier victories, lent credence to the anti-Semitic myths of a worldwide Jewish conspiracy which, as noted previously, had been imported into the Arab and Islamic world earlier, but only now gained widespread, general acceptance. Furthermore, many of the most negative notions about Jews and Judaism, which were but a part of the diverse corpus of Islamic theological and legal literature and had in earlier times been counterbalanced by more positive perceptions, now took on a new centrality.

After Egypt successfully crossed the Suez Canal and fought the Israelis in the Sinai to a stalemate in the 1973 War, Egyptian president Anwar Sadat, a pragmatic and visionary politician, was emboldened to make his peace initiative with Israel in 1977. As a practicing Muslim,

Sadat was able to justify his peace with Israel citing Islam even as he had made war with it citing Islam. His lead was followed by the kings of Jordan and Morocco, both descendants of the Prophet Muhammad and thus of impeccable Islamic lineage. But the prevailing mood within the Islamic world and even within the three leaders' own countries was one of strong opposition. Sadat was assassinated on October 6, 1981, and his successor, Hosni Mubarak, maintained a cold peace with Israel while at the same time allowing for anti-Israeli and anti-Semitic rhetoric and imagery in the media and the mosque. The success of Islamist political parties across the Islamic heartlands has made even the most pragmatic and modern of politicians wary of following Sadat's path. Thus, for the time being, it is only in Islamic Diasporas in Europe and North America that a very small number of Muslim religious leaders and secular Muslims feel secure enough to voice more liberal perceptions of Israel and Jews. The present turmoil throughout the Islamic world is not conducive to more nuanced attitudes toward the Jewish state and the Jewish people; however, that does not mean that such attitudes might not be voiced and even prevail in the future, should the present malaise within so many Islamic societies be alleviated.

RECOMMENDED READINGS

Encyclopaedia of Islām, 2nd ed. Leiden: Brill, 1960–2009, 12 vols. plus index.

Encyclopedia of Jews in the Islamic World. Leiden: Brill, 2010, 5 vols.

Laskier, Michael M., and Yaacov Lev, eds. *The Divergence of Judaism and Islam*. Gainesville: University of Florida Press, 2011.

Mandel, Neville J. *The Arabs and Zionism before World War I*. Berkeley: University of California Press, 1976.

Mayer, Tamar, and Suleiman A. Mourad, eds. *Jerusalem: Idea and Reality*. London: Routledge, 2008.

Stein, Kenneth W. *Heroic Diplomacy: Sadat, Kissinger, Begin, and the Quest for Arab-Israeli Peace*. New York: Routledge, 1999.

Stillman, Norman A. "Antisemitism in the Contemporary Arab World." In Michael Curtis (ed.), *Antisemitism in the Contemporary World*, pp. 70–85. Boulder, CO: Westview Press, 1986.

———. "Islamic Fundamentalism." In Richard S. Levy, Dean Phillip Bell, William Collins Donahue, Kevin Madigan, Jonathan Morse, Amy Hill Shevitz, and Norman A. Stillman (eds.), *Antisemitism: A Historical Encyclopedia of Prejudice and Persecution*. Vol. 1, pp. 360–361. Santa Barbara, CA: ABC-CLIO, 2005.

———. *The Jews of Arab Lands: A History and Source Book*. Philadelphia: Jewish Publication Society, 1979.
———. *The Jews of Arab Lands in Modern Times*. Philadelphia: Jewish Publication Society, 1991.

GLOSSARY TERMS

al-Qaeda (al-Qāʿida)
Balfour Declaration
Emancipation
Ḥamas
Hezbollah (Ḥizbollāh)
Husseini, Haj Amin al- (Mufti Ḥājj Amīn al-Ḥusaynī)
Muslim Brotherhood
Ottoman Empire
"Protocols of the Elders of Zion"
War: Arab-Israeli War, 1948–1949 War; 1967 War; 1973 War

Norman (Noam) A. Stillman is the Schusterman/Josey Professor of Judaic History Emeritus at the University of Oklahoma and Founding Director of its Center for Judaic and Israel Studies. He is the executive editor of the five-volume *Encyclopedia of Jews in the Islamic World*.

FOURTEEN

"Hebrewism" and Israeli Culture

RACHEL S. HARRIS

Introduction

Asher Ginsberg (1856–1927), better known to his readers as Ahad Ha'am (One of the People), believed that Theodor Herzl's plan for a politically independent Jewish home in Palestine was doomed to fail. It was not anti-Semitism that was leading to the destruction of Jewish life, but Jewish assimilation that led to a loss of identity. He thought uniting Jews under a cultural umbrella—irrespective of where they might live—would secure the future of the Zionist movement. Palestine could then serve as a "spiritual homeland" for the Jews. There, the best and brightest individuals would form an intellectual and cultural nucleus and serve as a model for others in the Diaspora to emulate. He believed most Jews should immigrate instead to the United States.

After more than two thousand years of being dispersed across the globe, Ahad Ha'am feared there was not enough in common to unite the Jewish people under a banner of nationalism. Rather, he promoted cultural Zionism, the unification of Jews by means of language, literature, music, and the arts, a Hebrew Renaissance focused on a collective history. Through creating this common experience the Jews would eventually have a strong enough sense of identity, including shared values, to enable them to establish a new national homeland. Only in this way could the home that would be built become a Jewish state rather than just a State of the Jews. At the heart of this ideology was the belief that Jews should reject the Diasporic way of life, with its stigma of poverty, religious observance, and oppression, and tainted by the languages of peoples among whom they lived. Instead the Jews must re-create themselves in the image of a new, secular Hebrew.

Among the earliest disciples of these notions was Eliezer Yizhak Perelman (1858–1922), who changed his name to Eliezer Ben-Yehuda when he arrived in Palestine. Believing that the only way to enhance the Jewish struggle for national revival would be through the transformation of Hebrew from a literary language to a spoken vernacular, Ben-Yehuda went about reviving the sacred language to make it suitable for modern usage. After settling in Jerusalem in 1881, he devoted himself to this project. His children were the first to be raised with Hebrew as their mother tongue. He initiated classroom instruction in Hebrew, founded the Hebrew Language Council (the forerunner of today's Academy of the Hebrew Language), edited newspapers, and for forty years worked on a great dictionary that included many of the neologisms he had invented. This resurrected language was taken up particularly by the immigrants of the Second Aliya (1904–1914), for whom using the unfamiliar Hebrew in daily life became a badge of honor. They adopted the Sephardi (Yemenite) pronunciation, which they believed was closer to the speech of biblical times and so distanced them from the religious Ashkenazi (Eastern European) Hebrew of their childhood and the Diasporic world they were trying to escape.

By the time the British came to rule over Palestine after World War I, the Hebrew language had become sufficiently widespread that a generation of Hebrew speakers were able to advocate for it to become one of the national languages of the Mandate, alongside Arabic and English. Though many of the early immigrants continued to speak Yiddish, as well as the many other European languages with which they were familiar including Russian, German, English, and French, the promotion of Hebrew was such a central tenet of Zionist ideology that gangs of youths roamed the streets of the newly built Tel Aviv, accosting those who clung to their immigrant languages and failed to use it. In the 1920s the center of Hebrew letters and the Hebrew publishing industry moved from Europe to Tel Aviv, and Ahad Ha'am was among the members of the relocated literary circle. At the same time an educational war took place in Israel over the language of instruction in schools. Many of the Zionists had imagined that German, which represented high European culture, would be the primary language of advanced education, but students and teachers alike protested, and Hebrew became the language of instruction throughout the Jewish community's many schools in Palestine, even before the State was established.

In the late nineteenth and early twentieth centuries, the idealistic pioneering youths wishing to immigrate to Palestine through the Chibat Zion (Lovers of Zion) organizations, which included Bilu and the Odessa Committee in their ranks, quickly learned that speaking Hebrew proficiently could significantly strengthen their application. Zionist youth movements in Europe became an important way to disseminate Hebrew and cultural Zionism, often known as Hebrewism. Along with language classes, instruction in agriculture, and the imparting of socialist ideals, these groups promoted singing, dancing, and literature. In both high and low culture, an ideology that secularized the Jewish religious traditions while linking the present landscape to a biblical history imbued the young generation with Hebrewism whose symbols and meaning would persist long after the State of Israel was created.

The move of Hebrew letters and culture to Tel Aviv in the 1920s assured Hebrew's hegemony as the essence of *Hebrewness*, and later *Israeliness*. Yet the creators of the new culture were drawing on two distinct traditions: European notions of art, literature, theater, and music (through both high and low culture), and the aesthetics and exoticism of the Levant. From the beginning Hebrew culture was a hybrid. It reflected the impact of the alien Middle Eastern landscape, ideas about a Jewish homeland, and merged them with the aspirations of individuals educated with the values of European culture. In the early years, the division between high and low culture in music, dance, and art emerged as a debate. At least in the pioneers' imagination, Hebrew culture, abetted by a labor Zionist philosophy that lauded the collective, labor, and agriculture and idealized folk traditions and crafts, opposed the foreign polyglot European bourgeois culture as seen in opera and ballet along with the individualism of a decadent urban society. In reality, the contrast was less clearly demarcated, and even the bourgeois culture that developed in Tel Aviv during the 1920s and 1930s had a great deal in common with the locale and the Zionist project, including the use of Hebrew. Moreover, both high and low culture were imported from abroad (whether it be cowboy films or opera productions), while the local variant of Hebrew culture crossed the social divide. It was clear that the influence of Hebrewism was everywhere, and culture was used to institute Hebrew and Zionist values.

During the 1950s the waves of migration of Jews from Arab lands, the Near East, and India changed the country's demographics. Bringing their own unfamiliar languages and cultures, the newcomers often experienced discrimination from European Jews who viewed them as "black." This tension ultimately erupted during the 1970s and 1980s when the Mizrachi Black Panther movement created a Mizrachi consciousness that came to be incorporated in mainstream Israeli culture. But even toward the end of the 1960s and 1970s, Hebrewism in its traditional form had lost its dominant position in Israeli society and was being slowly supplanted as Israelis increasingly engaged with foreign cultures and found new ways to modernize. The tension between these often contradictory drives was to shape and reshape Zionist culture over the twentieth century.

Music

During the late nineteenth century in Eastern Europe, young men and women composed songs that described the beauty of the land of Israel and glorified its landscape, the endeavors of the pioneers, and the spiritual redemption that labor offered. These idyllic tunes became the basis for a secular folk culture within the framework of the kibbutz and youth movements in the Yishuv (the Jewish settlement in Palestine). They embodied social codes that were a contrast to the traditional Jewish hymns and Sabbath songs that represented the old Jewish ways with which many of the first generation of Zionists had grown up. The new music was sung in communal gatherings, and under the influence of European socialist movements the feeling of togetherness infiltrated every aspect of this cultural experience. Known as Shirei Eretz Yisrael, these "Songs of the Land of Israel" became a vital part of the social codes in Israeli society constituting a repertoire that evokes national sentiment, even into the present.

The sing-alongs, and the group dancing that often accompanied these encounters, were a vibrant part of pioneer life. Though thousands of these songs were composed, a smaller number were canonized, regularly performed at national events and on public occasions, and collected in

shironim (songbooks) by national institutions and other central organizations within the Yishuv. What characterized this music was that the
songs were in Hebrew, and though musically it varied widely, drawing
on styles as diverse as Slavic folk tunes and martial music, it was meant
to be sung by a wide swath of the population through *shira be tzibur*
(public singing). These songs were composed for acoustic instruments,
usually guitar, piano, violin, or accordion; the lyrics often addressed
the landscape or nationalist themes and introduced oriental elements in
otherwise European styles. At times music was composed to accompany
poems of distinguished writers that had struck the imagination of the
public, and unlike with the anonymous folk music of other cultures,
here the composers and lyricists were generally known. Material written between the 1920s and 1960s forms the substance of the golden age
of Zionist music.

The influence of this collective singing lasted long after this early period, with radio and television programs creating sing-along shows that
revived the old music. Classic pop and folk singers such as Arik Einstein,
Yehoram Gaon, and Ofra Haza did popular covers or wrote new songs
in the same mode, and for many this material served as a secular form
of prayer. The regular use of the Shirei Eretz Yisrael on memorial days
and public holidays maintained their role in creating national identity
and a clear sense of belonging. The rise of Mizrachi music in the 1970s
and its increasing public presence over the next thirty years, along with
an attendant financial influence on the music industry, affected the attitude toward traditional Israeli music with its nostalgia for the early
state-building years. Rather than diluting its importance, for veterans
these old songs evoked the heroic past and the Ashkenazi Zionist ideals
that had once shaped the nation. In encouraging their ongoing public
performance they were reaffirming their position and ideology within
the increasingly diverse Israeli society.

Alongside ideologically driven music, there were two other major
influences during the early period of communal singing: cabaret in Tel
Aviv that offered comic skits and musical interludes, and the IDF military troupes that emerged in the late 1940s and significantly impacted
the Israeli cultural scene until the 1970s. These two areas would go on
to inform the development of modern Israeli culture in the later part of
the twentieth century.

If the Songs of the Land of Israel were Israeli folk music, disseminated through youth movements and the kibbutzim with the aim of inculcating the Zionist ethos among its participants, then cabaret music was popular culture. Associated with Tel Aviv's urbanity and petit-bourgeois lifestyle, this music served no ideological agenda and was created purely for entertainment. The popularity of cinema in Tel Aviv during the 1930s, which brought international films, particularly musicals, to the city, created a vibrant social life and local cosmopolitanism that called out for the rhythm and styles of American jazz, Argentinian tango, ballroom dances, and popular swing. The antithesis of traditional folk music, popular music celebrated the individual. This light music catered to both a local population (Jewish, and a growing Arab middle class) and to the British personnel stationed in Palestine during the Mandate. It was separated from the forms found in other Western countries by a commitment to Hebrew lyrics that recognized the importance of a Jewish national culture.

Many of the musicians who played in cafés, nightclubs, ballrooms, and casinos and on the stage were recent immigrants from Europe, where they had trained. They were well acquainted with European and American popular music, though their repertoire also included the homegrown variety mainly developed through the theatrical revue. A number of satirical theatrical companies developed in the new Zionist city, and while they often attacked the British, local public figures, and the politics of the day, their harshest criticisms were reserved for the Zionist workers' parties and the Jewish establishment. This cultural conflict often led to companies being closed down while others rose in their place. But there were also extremely successful groups. Hamatateh lasted from 1929 into the early 1950s, and its ranks included giants of Hebrew poetry, including Leah Goldberg and Nathan Alterman. Among the company's singers was Yossef Goland, whose crooning style signaled a break with the operatically trained (or cantorial) singers that preceded him. Unlike the communal singing, here it was the individual and the soloist whose position mattered. Hamatateh and another revue company, Li-La-Lo, served as incubators for many of the artists, writers, composers, producers, and directors who were to shape Israeli culture with the advent of radio, television, and a local film industry later in the century. At the same time theater also began to flourish in Palestine. In

1928, Margot Klausner helped bring Habima, a Hebrew-language company that had been operating in Moscow over the previous decade, to Tel Aviv, where Habima went on to become Israel's national theater. Given the demand for full theatrical culture, and inspired by the success of Habima, several other theaters were founded during the pre-state period, including the Eretz Yisrael Theater and the Ohel Theater, and in 1944 the Cameri was established as Tel Aviv's municipal theater.

Significantly, through the 1930s and 1940s the members of both light and serious theater companies were mostly European immigrants who brought their sensibilities from lands far from the Mediterranean climate, but by the 1960s what remained of these companies had been mostly taken over by a new generation, born in Israel and raised within its ideological and cultural values. This generation of *sabras* influenced a change in the style, satire, and music in Tel Aviv, and in time the huge differences between culture in the city and the works being produced within the youth movements, kibbutzim, and army disappeared.

While these Tel Aviv performances belonged to private enterprise, there were also nationally known entertainment troupes that belonged to the Israeli Defense Forces (IDF). The Chizbatron performed comedy and music for the Palmach (the pre-State Jewish militia), and with the establishment of the IDF, many units developed their own individual groups. These prestigious performance companies led to professional careers for innumerable actors, singers, writers, and directors following their military service. The *lehaqot tzeva'iot* or military troupes (sing. *lahaqah tzva'it*) became household names dominating the popular music scene between the 1950s and the 1970s, and a select group of albums, particularly *Songs of the Six-Day War*, had huge international followings. The rise of the popularity of this music within the civilian market coincided with the development of Israeli radio from its origins as PBC (the Palestine Broadcasting Company) to the newly renamed Kol Yisrael (the Voice of Israel). Of its four original stations, one was specifically dedicated to playing Israeli popular music. But it was the army radio station Galai Tzahal (Galatz), which broadcast music, plays, poetry, and news in the spirit of Israeli *sabra* identity, together with its offshoot Galgalatz in 1993, which may have had the greatest impact on the dissemination of Israeli music, especially since for a long time these were the only stations to broadcast through the night.

The military ensembles functioned as a form of repertory theater whose purpose was to entertain the troops and raise morale. Like the youth movements before them, these groups also had an ideological role. They educated the recruits, often first- or second-generation immigrants, in the values of Hebrewism and the essence of Israeliness. Paradoxically, though they were army companies, they often sang about peace or performed satirical skits mocking military life. The men and women who participated in the ranks of these artistic companies could only do so for the duration of their army service (two to three years), and the turnover of these groups was frequent with new and veteran members overlapping, together creating and performing materials specifically tailored for their unit. In the early years of the *lehaqot*, sets were simple, musical instruments were minimal and mobile as with the Shirei Eretz Yisrael, and performers were often shipped out to bases in the field. But after the Six-Day War, a change in the military ethos and influences from American pop music and large-scale musicals such as *Hair* led to more sophisticated performances. The large sets and casts meant that these shows were no longer mobile, and instead troops were bussed in to these venues for the performance. *The Troupe* (1978), an Israeli movie whose fictional troupe captures the halcyon days of the *lehaqot tzeva'iot*, is also an example of the significant cultural influence these groups had on Israeli culture. Several of the leading actors in the film had served in Lehaqat Hanahal (the Nahal Troupe) and other military troupes where they had learned their craft. By the 1980s these groups had lost their status and their music had been superseded by new musical styles. The troupes that remained rarely composed new material, instead teaching and performing the Shirei Eretz Yisrael or the old military repertoire that had crossed over and become Israeli popular standards.

While the troupes were undoubtedly affected by the spirit of antiwar music and the resurgence of the folk scene, the influence of international musical tastes and trends is evident in the direction they took from the 1960s onward. New underground bands, Lehaqot Haketzev, markedly influenced by Anglo-American music, were reshaping the future of Israeli popular music. Choosing to sing in English, often with little formal musical training, their groups were dominated by electric guitars, keyboards, and drum kits, signaling a radically different musical style in Israel. Little known outside Tel Aviv nightclubs, few could get any kind of recording contracts, and radio steered away from their music, which was in many respects considered un-Israeli. Young people seemed divided: those who participated in the youth movements and stayed true to *sabra* ideology allied with the *lehaqot tzeva'iot* and those who were corrupted by following this decadent music. As with rock and roll elsewhere, the music was seen as deleterious to moral well-being. This concern was aggravated by the poverty and Mizrachi origins of many of the practitioners (and followers) who were labeled hooligans (*chah-chahim, pushtakim*). As this music moved out of the periphery, it became the forerunner for Israeli rock that began to develop during the 1970s to much greater acclaim.

By teaming up with artists who had received their training in the *lehaqot tzeva'iot*, and composing songs in Hebrew, the rockers were able to move closer to the mainstream. Arik Einstein, a graduate of Lehaqat Hanahal known for his renditions of Shirei Eretz Yisrael, was attracted to this new sound, and after several unsuccessful attempts he made the album *Shablool*, often considered the beginning of Israeli rock. The musicians embraced bass guitar, drums, and electric guitars, but the lyrics and style lacked the angry, aggressive stance of its foreign origins. Israeli rock did not need to assert its difference in the ways other cultures had. It was rebellious precisely because it had moved away from Hebrewism. Using what he had learned from his experience making rock music, Arik Einstein returned to Shirei Eretz Yisrael, making three albums of these classic songs, but now with a revised tempo and style more appropriate for contemporary Israeli audiences. The effect was to realign rock music, making it a part of the Israeli fold. By the 1980s, bands like Mashina, imitating the two-tone, reggae styles of the British band Madness, introduced a new alternative rock scene to Israel. Similarly, Aviv Geffen's successful use of glam rock styles in his performance (something Zvika Pick had tried much earlier, but failed at) moved alternative rock into the mainstream and made it some of the best-selling music in Israeli history.

At the same time, fearing the disappearance of authentic Hebrewism, the Israeli establishment began to hold song competitions. Though they were many and varied, including the Competition for Children's Music, the Israeli Song Competition, and the Oriental Music competition, the different names were a pretense, and for most entries the musical arrangements, orchestration, and choice of singers were similar and often flattened differences. Many of the featured songs became immensely popular, and not always the competitions' winners. They were covered by nascent Israeli television and played widely on the radio. For example, Naomi Shemer's composition "Jerusalem of Gold" was played at the Israeli Song Competition (though it was not competing) and became an instant success. Two weeks later, the Six-Day War and its attendant reunification of Jerusalem immortalized what was already a popular song about the city, transforming it into an unofficial Israeli anthem. In time, the Israeli song competition was succeeded by the competition to choose an Israeli song for the Eurovision Song Contest, which Israel won three times (1978, 1979, 1998).

Though rock had become mainstream by the 1980s, *muziqa Mizrachit* still remained on the fringes of the commercial Israeli establishment. Ethnic music and Oriental sounds had been sanitized in popular music, appearing since the 1960s in films and in the public airing of the Oriental song competition. Where it appeared, Mizrachi music was often heavily branded as Greek music, thereby creating the impression that it was Mediterranean rather than Arab. The *muziqa Mizrachit* movement started in the 1950s, with Jewish immigrants from Arab lands. Restricted to family celebrations and local events within Mizrachi communities, it was often played by homegrown performers, many of whom had been musicians before immigration. Using the oud, kanun, and darbuka (traditional Arab instruments), they played Arab-style music sung with trills, but often with Hebrew lyrics. In the 1960s, acoustic guitar and electric guitar were also added, creating an eclectic sound. In keeping with the traditionalism of the music, biblical and religious texts were often used for lyrics, but as with other segments of Israel's music, Mizrachi musicians also drew on celebrated Israeli poets, such as Nathan Alterman.

The existence of a national Arabic radio station, as well as the ability to hear broadcasts from Egypt, Jordan, Syria, and Lebanon, meant that for many, Arabic music continued to live as a presence in their daily lives. For Ashkenazi Jews, Arabic and the connection of these Mizrachi Jews to Arabic culture often seemed threatening, and there was a general disgust with Mizrachi music in its pure forms. During the 1970s the Black Panther movement (civil rights activism for Mizrachim) and the involvement of Mizrachim in the success of the 1977 elections for the

Likud led to increasing political awareness about socioeconomic discrimination and highlighted racism against other Jews within Israel. Many Mizrachim responded by embracing Mizrachi culture as part of a roots movement, and a few Mizrachi singers rose to prominence, appearing not only in the traditional venues of weddings and family but also in nightclubs serving the Mizrachi population. Avihu Medina, Zohar Argov, Haim Moshe, and Margalit Tzan'ani rose to prominence, even passing into the mainstream at times. But Israeli radio continued to boycott these musicians, refusing to play their music outside dedicated programming hours.

Much of the musicians' success came about because of a change in the music industry. Cassette tapes, which could be cheaply recorded and distributed, meant that they no longer had to depend on the Ashkenazi music industry for recording facilities and contracts. Often sold at market stalls, particularly near the old bus station in Tel Aviv, *muziqa Mizrachit* was referred to as "cassette music," another label that served to denigrate it, and Mizrachi culture more broadly. However, world music was on the rise, and the interest in *muziqa Mizrachit* continued to grow. At the same time, television programs encouraged the sanitization of what were deemed the most extreme aspects of Mizrachi music so it could be aired publicly. In time it would adopt many of the influences that affected other music in Israel, including rock, eventually becoming mainstream.

Tracing the career of Zehava Ben in video clips captures the process of transformation that *muziqa Mizrachit* adopted during the 1990s and 2000s. Born to a Moroccan family in Israel's impoverished south, Ben came to prominence in the film *A Little Bit of Luck* (Ze'ev Revach, 1990) where she plays the daughter of a musician. When he goes blind she is forced to take over his singing work, and after being spotted by a talent scout she makes it big. While this film presents Ben as an ethnic singer, her numerous performances on Israeli television reveal changes in mainstream Israeli media. By the start of the twenty-first century her ethnic costumes have been replaced with a contemporary wardrobe, her hair is blond, and her dance movements no longer reflect a stylized Orient but instead capture Western rhythms. Simultaneously changes have occurred in her backing groups: the Arab instruments that characterized the start of her career gave way to synthesizers and electric guitars during the late 1990s in attempts to assimilate her into the Western mainstream. More recently she appears with full orchestration that includes both modern and traditional instruments as Israeli audiences increasingly embrace their own local variants of world music.

Along with singing traditional Mizrachi songs and even producing albums of Arabic music, in the last decade Ben's music has also included dance songs to be played in nightclubs. *Ani Shata* and *Razali* reflect Tel Aviv's own developed music scene in which trance, funk, acid house, and dance grew during the late 1990s. Large raves are held all over the country in forests, the desert, and even Rabin Square, played by international DJs as well as local musicians. In turn this transformation has affected the development of other ethnic music including Ethiopian, such as the Idan Raichel Project, whose first two albums showcased both Amharic and Yemenite cultures, mixed with strong beats and modern musical arrangements. While world music has brought rap to Israel, in the best tradition of the local Israeli scene some is still composed by beloved national authors, such as "The Sticker Song," performed by Hadag Nahash and written by David Grossman. In the twenty-first century Israeli music is richly diverse, drawing on many of the strands of its historical evolution, but it remains characterized by a tendency to prefer Hebrew lyrics, even where other languages creep in. Playing on the mix between East and West, music has not had the same international success as film, art, or television shows in recent years, but it has been and remains an integral part of Israeli life.

Dance

Israeli dance can be traced back to the earliest days of Zionist music, but it was in the 1920s that a folk tradition of Israeli dance began to be seriously established within the Yishuv. The influence of German Romanticism and the Wandervogel movement, which encouraged youths to discard the restrictions of society and return to nature, played a significant role in its evolution. The few major choreographers in Israel's early years such as Gurit Kadman, born Gertrude (Gert) Loewenstein (1897–1987), were born in Germany. Others studied there, receiving some classical ballet training, but more often spent time learning German expressionist dance. Still others were influenced by Isadora Duncan's liberated improvisation, fantasy, and return to Greek myth.

While technique and the methods of building dances drew on this formal education, the philosophy behind Israeli folk dance as an invented tradition reflected a connection to the land and the Bible. The numerous references to dancing provided authentic reference points: Miriam's dancing following the exodus (Exodus 15:20–21); David's dancing before the Ark of the Lord (2 Samuel 6:14–3); women dancing in Judges (11:34, 21:21–23); men dancing in celebration of battle victories; and numerous Psalms that depict dance as both an expression of joy and a way to worship God. Dance was connected to pleasure and celebration, it reflected the experience of freedom, and it signified a revival of the ancient Hebrews. As with music, dance was connected to the values of Hebrewism.

Accompanied by the Songs of the Land of Israel, the early dances drew on European folk tradition, central to which was the circle dance in which men and women held hands and repeated set choreographed steps. The most popular was the hora, which became so ubiquitous as an Israeli folk dance than many did not realize that it had Romanian antecedents. Influenced by Arab and Bedouin dancing, the debka—a line dance with handholding, often danced in a semicircle—was also introduced to the repertoire. These dances shared the notion that everyone was equal, no one person stood apart, and dancing was an act of collectivism. Both young and old participated, and children would learn the dances in school and youth movements. Using steps from Circassian, Yemenite, Druze, and Arab dancing, and later from the Hassidic tradition, choreographers composed new dances that were taught at kibbutzim and to youth groups that not only celebrated joyous occasions but also performed at festivals.

The secularization of Israeli culture in these early years was particularly evident in the approaches that kibbutzim took to religious holidays and the Jewish calendar. Reconstituting Passover as a festival of freedom and bringing back the biblical Omer harvest festival that had disappeared over millennia signified an emphasis on agriculture and Zionist values. The celebration of festivals such as Shavuot and Tu B'shvat (the holiday for new trees) emphasized the Zionist culture of land, labor, and agriculture. Likewise, celebratory events such as the discovery of new water sources also inspired a new dance repertoire. As part of their celebrations the kibbutzim created dances and performances using kibbutz members and amateur dancers who lacked professional training.

The circle dance "Mayim, Mayim" ("Water, Water") with its accompanying song is typical of these kinds of folk dances and their place within the Israeli consciousness. It was created in 1937 for a festival to celebrate the discovery of water in the desert after a search that had lasted several years; the lyrics were specially composed for the dance by Emanuel Pugashov Amiran and taken from the biblical verse "With joy you shall draw water from the springs of salvation" (Isaiah 12:3). For many years the myth of its creation linked it to Degania, the first kibbutz established twenty years earlier, and to an anonymous choreographer, though it was Else I. Dublin who had put it together and later choreographers modified it. Originally performed more formally, "Mayim, Mayim" moved into the folk repertoire and is commonly danced not only in Israel as part of folk dance occasions but at Jewish weddings and other celebrations both in and outside Israel.

Costumes were a distinguishing marker of the folk dance in its traditional incarnations. They were commonly blue and white; there were often simple Russian peasant blouses and work trousers for men, and blouses and skirts, or dresses, for women. Women's sleeves reflect the tensions in the creation of this new culture. While German expressionist dance (with which many of the chorographers were familiar) focused on the hands as a way to convey emotion, traditional Jewish culture had insisted on the modesty of long sleeves. The elbow length frequently chosen reveals the compromises made between the old and new worlds. Sometimes a peasant shawl or scarf tied around the waist would be used to enhance the folk impression. But it was the bare feet, simple sandals, or even light work shoes rather than ballet slippers or the high heels of ballroom dance that particularly emphasized the *ammami* (folk) style. If the bourgeois individualism of salon dancing (foxtrot, tango, waltz) seemed utterly reprehensible to the ideals of Israeli folk dance, it nevertheless offered something lacking in circle dances: couple dancing. While the folk dance was all about group participation, the need to find a way for couples to dance together and yet remain true to Zionist ideals led to the creation of specific couple dances in the folk tradition. Yet these also maintained the communal aspect and the pairs of dancers were situated within a larger rotating circle, reminiscent of the American square dance or Scottish *ceilidh*, thereby maintaining the structure of collectivism that characterized this period.

In the early years, more than anything it was the staging of dances—often performed outdoors in nature using the local agriculture or landscape to connect the agricultural pioneers with the biblical history of the place and space—that conveyed the Hebrewism of the early dance movement. Pageants that integrated an expressive dance with symbolic costumes and movements and usually created by kibbutz members, and later by special choreographers, were common. Audiences would come from many other settlements for these performances, which became significant events in the kibbutz calendar. On occasion props such as water jugs or fresh produce would be incorporated into the dance steps, and many choreographers interpreted the historical narratives of the local area in their new works.

The Kibbutz Dalia Dance Festivals began in 1944 as the brainchild of Gurit Kadman, the mother of Israeli dance. In that first year, in celebration of Shavuot, or Hag Ha-bikkurim (the holiday celebrating the harvest of the first fruits) with the biblical story of Ruth as her theme, Kadman organized, staged, and produced a pageant that brought together pieces from other kibbutz performances, as well as new dances that could be learned by the audience. The festival appealed to the masses, who learned many of the new dances, and is viewed as an early effort to understand these dances as formal performance, an issue that had already been raised within the dance world since the late 1930s. In 1945, Kadman's activities led to the creation of formal committees that in different incarnations operated under the auspices of the Histadrut and Ministry of Education into the 1980s. At Dalia, along with the specially created Land of Israel Dances, there were also displays of ethnic Jewish dancing, including Yemenite, Persian, Moroccan, and Kurdish. Thus two strands developed in this period: the Ashkenazi style of folk dance conflating both Eastern and Western European styles, and danced to the music of accordion and guitar, and the Eastern (Oriental) style of dance that was based heavily on Middle Eastern flutes, drums, and percussion instruments. Exemplary of this latter style was the Inbal Dance Company, created in 1949 by Sara Levi-Tanai (1910–2005), which derived material from Jewish heritage and tradition and evoked the Orient through costumes, music, and movement translated into modern dance.

Thanks to assistance from American choreographer Jerome Robbins, the company gained international support and traveled widely, presenting Israeli dance to an international audience.

Despite the conventions of the folk dance and its institutionalization within the Israeli imagination, there have been noticeable changes in its character from the early years. It is less common for participants to hold hands, even in circle dances, though these are often still accompanied by the traditional Shirei Eretz Yisrael. The line dances, in which people now stand apart (as in American line dancing), are often performed to foreign (non-Hebrew) music, including American pop songs or even salsa music. Moreover, the breakdown in the Zionist ethos of collectivism has reshaped the meaning and practice of this still-popular tradition among young people. At present there are more than six thousand dances, and the website www.israelidances.com offers information about music, choreographers, and steps, suggesting an energetic contemporary response to the phenomenon. However, many veterans, rebelling against the constant insistence on new moves and new dances, have created meetings or clubs whose return to the pre-1980s dances evoke a nostalgia for the glory days of the Labor movement, the kibbutzim, and the Israeli folk dance.

The formal traditions of Israeli dance developed in parallel to the informal Israeli folk dance from the 1940s onward. As noted earlier, the Inbal Dance Company, one of the first professional groups, was interpreting an ethnic style within the conventions of modern dance and innovating new compositions, moves, and interpretations that reflected the Israeli reality. Other new professional companies capitalized on what was deemed an Israeli spirit and rose to critical international acclaim. In 1964, at the instigation of Baroness Batsheva de Rothschild, the Batsheva Dance Company was founded with artistic support from renowned choreographer Martha Graham, whose influence on the development of Israeli culture was immense. Principal dancers were sent to the United States to train with her and later staged her works in Israel. For the tenth anniversary of the company, Graham came to Israel to create *The Dream*, based on the story of Jacob. However, following a break with the company over a refusal to merge with Rothschild's newer company Bat-Dor (1967), Graham withdrew her works from the company and in time they altered their style.

Bat-Dor, with Jeannette Ordman as principal dancer and artistic director, aimed to blend classical and modern techniques (a rarity at the time) to create a distinctive contemporary style. During the 1960s other companies were also founded, including the Israel Ballet (1968), the Kibbutz Dance Company (1969), and Demama (Silence), Moshe Efrati's company of young deaf dancers (1964), which amalgamated with his hearing company in 1975 as Kol 'u-Demama (Sound and Silence). By the late 1970s, Israeli dance had begun to stagnate, but in 1981 a visit by Pina Bausch with the Wuppertal Dance Theatre triggered a creative boost that inspired the creation of contemporary dance companies such as Oshra Elkayam's Movement Theater and Tmu-Na (Moving Picture). Fringe dance by independent choreographers emerged on the scene in the late 1980s and the couple Nir Ben Gal and Liat Dror, and the duo Adi Shaal and Noa Wertheim, who created the Vertigo Dance Company (1992), provided opportunities in which established dancers, often participating in traditional companies, might also appear. In addition, this period saw the creation of the Ashdod Ballet (1998), with its company members originally trained in the Soviet Union, and the Beta Dance studio inspired by Ethiopian dance. In 1989, the creation of the Suzanne Dellal Center for Israeli Dance with four performance halls, numerous studios, and a large open-air plaza in Tel Aviv's Neve Tzedek neighborhood meant the establishment of a permanent venue invested in cultivating and promoting contemporary dance. This center and the Karmiel festival in the north have ensured the creation and performance of world-class dance in Israel.

Film

Cinemas had opened throughout Palestine at the turn of the twentieth century even before there was a homegrown film industry. The association of Palestine with the Bible, which had motivated the Zionists, also inspired Christians with a taste for the exotic, and the Lumière brothers captured the landscape as early as 1896. For other foreign filmmakers, it became the setting of religious plays, silent passions narrating the life of Jesus in an area that appeared not to have changed in almost two thousand years. In the 1900s, silent movies were screened in sheds and cafés, and in 1914, the Eden cinema was built in Tel Aviv, amid protest that it was bringing decadent influences to the Zionist national enterprise. There was no stopping the hunger for foreign films that raged through the Yishuv, and cinemas soon flourished, supported by both the local Jewish population and the Arab middle class and, during the Mandate, by the British troops stationed in the region.

The first local Jewish film maker was Ya'acov Ben Dov (1882–1968), who arrived from the Ukraine in 1907 to teach at the Bezalel art school and was believed to own the first movie camera in Palestine. Celebrating the achievements of the Zionist movement, he spent the next twenty years documenting the building of the country. Often funded through the Jewish Agency, Keren Hayesod, and the Jewish National Fund, who later used these films for educational and fund-raising purposes, Ben Dov caught many of the major historical moments of his day. The films, often translated into multiple languages, such as *Springtime in Eretz Yisrael* (1928), which was distributed in fifty-six countries, brought attention to the pioneering project and the achievements taking place throughout Palestine. On his retirement Ben Dov sold his equipment and collection of film footage to Baruch Agadati (1895–1976), an artist, dancer, and choreographer who had studied at Bezalel, and in 1924 introduced the hora dance to Israel. Skillfully weaving Ben Dov's old material with new footage specially shot for the occasion, Agadati created the first sound feature film in Palestine. *This Is the Land* (1935) combined the documentary footage with dramatic sequences to tell the story of Zionist pioneering and the achievements made in the land since. Though this first film was made under Agadati's own initiative, he later turned to the Zionist institutions for funding and made informational and educational films as Ben Dov had done, for fund-raising, but also to encourage Aliya, particularly among German Jews.

This tradition was continued after World War II. Films such as *Battle for Survival* (1947), narrated by Orson Welles and documenting the concentration camps and the homeless survivors, aimed at creating sympathy for the Jewish cause in Palestine. Agadati also produced newsreels that were often screened in Palestine, but his output was inconsistent, and it was Nathan Axelrod (1905–1987) with his "Carmel" reels that ran regularly from 1935 to 1958 who became the most important source of news. By selling reels to cinemas, Axelrod was less dependent on the unpredictable funding of the Zionist agencies, and he made dramas and documentaries and even established his own laboratory for developing and printing film. In 1933, with Haim Halachmi (1902–1979), Axelrod made the first feature-length Hebrew-language drama, *Oded the Wanderer*, about a youth who sees all the glories of the land while traveling with his friends. The actors Moshe Chorgal from Hamatateh, and Menachem Gensin and Shimon Finkel from Habima, were Hebrew-speaking stage actors, but without sound, it was made as a silent film with literary Hebrew intertitles. At the same time Aleksander Ford's *Sabra* (1933), which also drew on Habima actors, was processed in Warsaw, leading to higher production values. The plot, considerably more developed than that of *Oded*, told the story of pioneers struggling against the harsh challenges of the land. Despite an Arab-Jewish romance and the final scenes of the land blooming, the violence between Arabs and Jews toward the conclusion led the British mandatory government to ban the film on the grounds that it might incite local tensions.

Avodah (1935) by Helmar Lerski, with its opening shots of feet traversing difficult terrain until with a powerful upshot we finally see the man's face as he looks out over the land he has traveled so far to find, characterized the essence of this period. Working the land and finding water to make the desert bloom would make the land fruitful, not only for crops and cattle but also for the people who worked it. The film's striking imagery, juxtaposing machinery and sweating arms with bulging muscles, points to the influence of Soviet realism that was starting to have a powerful effect on art and representation in the pre-state period. These landmark developments in Zionist cinema were halted by World War II, and it was not until the 1950s that Israeli cinema would flourish again. Some of this early footage and the publicity films can be found through the Spielberg Film Archives based in Israel (and their online database and dedicated YouTube channel).

In 1949, Margot Klausner laid the foundation stone for the United Studios and the first film processing labs in the country. She would run the company for twenty years. Along with the Geva Studios created a year later, these projects provided an infrastructure for filmmaking and a growing number of productions during the 1950s and 1960s. The USA-Israel co-production *Hill 24 Doesn't Answer* (Thorold Dickinson, 1955), dramatizing battles in the War of Independence, was the most impressive among a number of films made in this period. Its in-depth characterization, attention to detail, and combination of romance and melodrama have stood the test of time, and this marked the beginning of a period of international involvement in Israeli film, culminating in 1960 with Otto Preminger's production of *Exodus*, staring Paul Newman. The enormous success of this film (and the Leon Uris novel it was based on) persuaded David Ben-Gurion, then Israel's prime minister, that film could play an important role in representing Israel, and he introduced a law to the Knesset supporting the fledgling film industry.

The heroic period of filmmaking that followed continued to combine military heroism with ideological commitment to the project of agricultural development, creating the kibbutz-soldier as the archetypal *sabra* on screen. While the films of the 1950s had represented Israel as the world wanted to see it, often including large amounts of English dialogue, films of the 1960s reflected the Hebrewism that became important in the development of Israel's indigenous film industry. In the wake of the Six-Day War, national euphoria elevated Israeli men to mythical proportions. *He Walked in the Fields* (Yoseph Millo, 1967), based on Moshe Shamir's novel starring Assi Dayan, and *Every Bastard a King* (Uri Zohar, 1968), starring the popular singer Yehoram Gaon, created a new kind of hero. Once connected to the labor establishment, the new generation was represented as dissolute and unproductive, but in the face of war, temptations were rejected as these men found purpose and direction, reflecting the postwar obsession with security. Women during this period are minor characters and appear as girlfriends, mothers, and wives, generally marginal to the plot. *Siege* (Gilberto Tofano, 1969), the story of a widow coming to terms with her loss and grief, examined the more complex role women faced, expected to be living memorials honoring their dead, frozen in time. Gila Almagor's performance as the widow challenged women's assumed passivity, and the film's art house style signaled a new international influence in Israeli filmmaking.

Concurrently, a comic film style developed. Working with ethnic stereotypes, the *bourekas* film was born. Named for a Middle Eastern pastry widely adopted in Israel, and parodying the "spaghetti western" portrayal of 1960s American/Italian Westerns, *bourekas* films introduced music, comedy, melodrama, and tearjerkers that played on the encounter between Eastern and Western Jews. Though they featured Mizrachi Jews, they were mainly written by Ashkenazi Jews, and in some cases, Ashkenazi actors even played Mizrachi characters. Nevertheless they were extremely popular with both Mizrachi and Ashkenazi audiences. The critics frequently ridiculed this low form of culture, but they could do nothing in the face of impressive commercial success. In contrast to the high-art films that received much of their funding from the government, *bourekas* films were self-financing. Ephraim Kishon's *Sallah Shabati* (1964) sold 1.3 million tickets, in a country that numbered 2.48 million at the time. Produced by Menahem Golan, the film starred Chaim Topol in the title role as a hapless North African immigrant who arrives in Israel with his large family. The film depicts their life in the *ma'abarot* (refugee absorption camps) and satirizes their encounters with Zionist institutions, veterans, and the kibbutz. It also featured Gila Almagor and Arik Einstein as kibbutz members and love interests for Sallah Shabati's children. The film was an international triumph, winning a Golden Globe, opening and closing the Berlin film festival, and being nominated for an Academy Award for best foreign-language picture.

Music was a prominent feature of *bourekas* films, and Menahem Golan created the first Israeli musical spectacular with *Kazablan* (1974), which had started life on the stage as a play and later a musical. Yehoram Gaon, who had so often played the Ashkenazi hero, was cast in the lead role as the Mizrachi thug, Casa, named for his country of origin, Morocco. Golan was born in Israel to Polish parents and Kishon was Hungarian, but their ethnicity had no bearing on their involvement in the *bourekas* film industry, and other filmmakers such as George Ovadia, who was born in Baghdad, and Ze'ev Revach, who came from Morocco, would also go on to make many of these commercially viable films.

This light entertainment focused on the family, community and tradition, and in time a subgenre, the gefilte-fish films, developed, representing an Ashkenazi traditionalism reminiscent of Yiddish literature. In most cases the films focused on new immigrants and their encounter with Zionism and Ashkenazi culture—and though many resolved conflict through a wedding or the birth of a child, bringing the warring parties together in a final utopian vision of melting-pot harmony, cracks were already beginning in this Israeli ideal. The Jewish migrants who arrived in the 1950s and 1960s from North African, Levantine, and Eastern Arab countries had transformed the country's demographic makeup and in time would influence Israeli culture permanently. In 1977 Labor lost the general election and Menachem Begin's right-wing Likud government, supported largely by Mizrachi immigrants, offered a new vision of the country.

Two films by Avi Nesher, *The Troupe* (1978) and *Dizengoff 99* (1979), showed the changes taking place in Israeli culture during the late 1970s. They portrayed the decadence, materialism, and self-indulgence of the new Israeli/*sabra* generation. Rejecting the collective, these films celebrated individuality and the smaller intimate group. Filled with music, sexually explicit images, and biting satire about the need to compromise art to suit public taste, these films were a commercial success and gained cult status. While these films were commercial successes, their focus on sexuality and individualism were to be integral themes in the less commercially viable and "artistic" filmmaking of a New Wave known as the Kayitz Group (the Hebrew acronym for Young Israeli Cinema; *kayitz* literally means "summer"). Characterized by low-budget art films in contradistinction to the popular cinema of the 1960s and 1970s, these films focused on the problematic experience of daily life, with characters taking a psychological and introspective stance, ambivalent about the Israeli reality. For the first time political critiques were introduced to Israeli film by Kayitz directors including Dan Wolman, Avraham Heffner, Michal Bat-Adam, Yehuda Judd Ne'eman, and Dan Wachsmann, which reflected the serious and sensitive characteristics of this group's filmmaking. Clearly influenced by the French Nouvelle Vague, films such as *Iris* (David Greenberg, 1968), *My Michael* (Dan Wolman, 1976), and Moshe Mizrachi's *I Love You Rosa* (1972) portrayed loneliness and intense moods and feelings and used images and fragments in experimental ways. It had become clear that the old Zionist values were being attacked by a self-satisfied middle class in Tel Aviv, a youth disillusioned by the nightmare of war and conquest, and an ethnic sensibility in the periphery—one that was refusing to buy into labor ideology.

Dan Wachsmann's *Hamsin* (1982), the first serious representation of Arabs living within Israel's borders and the tensions over occupation; *Beyond the Walls* (Uri Barbash, 1984), a prison film in which Arabs and Mizrachi Jews come together against the establishment; and *Nadia* (Amnon Rubinstein, 1986) about an Arab girl becoming educated through the Israeli schooling system, were important steps in the evolution of cinema in Israel. These films as both art and political statements met with critical acclaim outside Israel, and *Beyond the Walls* was nominated for an Academy Award for best foreign-language film, but Israeli audiences were disinterested. In 1987, Renen Schorr's award-winning film *Late Summer Blues* captured the coming-of-age experience of army service through a group of high school students as they receive their draft notices. It was a commercial success among audiences; its antiwar protest songs included the hits "We Don't Want," with the lyrics, "We don't want you to tell us what is good and what is bad / we don't want you to tell us we have no choice / . . . . We don't want wars, orphans, and widows" and a parody of Joseph Trumpeldor's famous slogan "It is good to die for our country." Like *Ricochets* (Eli Cohen, 1986), *I Don't Give a Damn* (Shmuel Imberman, 1987), *Cherry Season* (Haim Bouzaglo, 1991) and *Cup Final* (Eran Riklis, 1991), to name but a few films, Israeli cinema had become relentless in its critical responses to war, the army experience, and the sacrifice of soldiers. At the same time, the Arab, who for so long had been invisible in Israeli cinema, now appeared in a hopeful display of the possibility of connection between two alienated peoples.

The mid-1990s saw the start of what was to become a watershed in Israeli filmmaking. Directors and filmmakers studying abroad and the growth of film schools within Israel dramatically improved the quality of films being produced. By 2000, in despair at the lack of resources available, the renamed Israel Film Fund begged the Knesset for funds to turn Israeli cinema into a serious industry again. Further collaborations with international companies, particularly the French/German Arte, British Channel 4, and the American Avi Chai foundation, and money from the new cable stations Hot and Yes led to a dramatic change in the financial backing for films. By the end of the decade, Israeli cinema had become the darling of the international community, scooping up awards at all the major festivals and being nominated repeatedly for Academy Awards for best foreign films and documentaries.

Recently many of the most high-profile films have continued to engage with questions of war and the Arab-Israeli conflict, including *Beaufort* (Joseph Cedar, 2007), *Waltz with Bashir* (Ari Folman, 2008), and *Lebanon* (Samuel Maoz, 2009). At the same time, gay cinema has become mainstream in Israel. If Amos Gutman's films portray a darker, seedier life for a gay man in Israel during the 1970s and 1980s (Gutman died of AIDS in 1993), the success of *Yossi and Jagger* (Eytan Fox, 2002) changed the place of gay discourse. This film reframed Zionism and heroism in a story about two soldiers whose sexual relationship in the battlefield seems almost an extreme form of camaraderie. Fox's other films *The Bubble* (2006) and *Walk on Water* (2004) were no less explicit and situated gay life within the day-to-day realities of Israeli society. On the back of these changes, recent films depicting gay life within the Ultra-Orthodox community, such as *The Secrets* (Avi Nesher, 2007) and *Eyes Wide Open* (Haim Tabakman, 2009), have appeared.

If gay Israeli cinema is now mainstream, it is in part due to its tendency to continue the myths of heroism and masculinity that were a feature of successful Israeli cinema in the 1960s. From the very beginning, women were featured in support roles, rarely driving the plot and with little power in the film industry. With the exceptions of Michal Bat-Adam, who became a director after starring in the Kayitz films, and Gila Almagor, the doyenne of Israeli cinema, both of whom were responsible for important autobiographical projects that reflected on the mental illness of their mothers, and in Almagor's case Holocaust trauma, rarely did women *feature* on screen. Between the depictions of the Israeli military and national concerns, the exploitatively sexual Tel Aviv films, and the comic but often misogynistic representations of women in many of the *bourekas* films, Israeli cinema's relationship to women was almost entirely dominated by sex or motherhood. In 1992, *Tel Aviv Stories* (Ayelet Menahemi and Nirit Yaron) offered three episodes that raised feminist questions about expectations for women: whether a woman could choose an independent life, a career, or her own future. The films challenged male control, including that of the religious authorities over marriage and divorce. By 1994, the rise of the chick flick, imported from Anglo-American culture, was setting a new discourse, and both on film and on television women were being given new roles and investigating feminist issues including rape, abuse, and women's experiences—prostitution, broken homes, religion, work, poverty, and family. Ronit Elkabetz, actress, writer, and director, was integral in transforming the place of Mizrachi women in the new cinema, and similarly Hiam Abbass, a Palestinian actress born in Nazareth and raised in the north of Israel, has altered the representation of the Arab woman on screen.

More recently, several films focusing on the experience of Russian Jews and Georgian Jews, including *Late Marriage* and *Gift from Above* (2003) by Dover Kosashvili, *Schwartz Dynasty* (Amir Hasfari, 2005), and *Love and Dance* (Eitan Anner, 2006), pit this newly immigrated group against the Mizrachim and the religious communities in Israel. As in the *bourekas* films, the subject is often the clash between different ethnicities, religious observance, and family values, reflecting the problems of integration within Israeli society.

The representation of the religious communities in Israeli cinema has been more diverse than almost any other group. In the early years of cinema, religion was a byword for tradition and often associated with Oriental households, but since the 1990s, filmmakers critical of women's place within the religious community, such as Amos Gitai, have made a number of films exploring Ultra-Orthodox relations, including *Kadosh* (1999) and *The Wanderer* (Avishai Sivan, 2010). The first successful cinematic ventures to represent the religious community from within the Ultra-Orthodox community were made by filmmakers who had been formerly secular and trained in filmmaking before becoming religious. *Ushpizin* (Gidi Dar, 2004) and the recent *Fill the Void* (Rama Burshtein, 2012) both received a number of international awards. In 1989, the creation of the Ma'aleh School of Television, Film and yhe Arts, with its focus on Judaism (and the intersection between religion and modern life), created a dedicated venue for filmmaking that engages with Jewish values and aesthetics. In turn this has led to a rich and diverse cadre of religious Jewish filmmakers, often interested in representing their own community.

The development of a Palestinian cinema since the 1980s has in the main been influenced by Israeli cinema. With few facilities, including studios for film processing, film sets, and the need for permits, many of the more prominent directors have collaborated with Israelis or European companies in order to realize their artistic visions. Michel Khelifi, Elia Suleiman, and the actor-turned-director Mohammad Bakri are among the best known. Their films represent not only the individual plight of the Palestinian and the absurdity of life under Israeli rule but also the tensions brought about through modernization and constant contact with Israel and Israelis. In 2013, the Palestinian documentary *Five Broken Cameras* was nominated for an Academy Award, reflecting the large strides that the industry has made in recent years. There has been a growing number of Palestinian women filmmakers, primarily working in documentary filmmaking, since 2007.

The shifts in Israeli filmmaking over the last two decades have led to rich diversity. Domestic and international audiences are again viewing Israeli cinema, which has moved away from some of the larger questions of national ideology to focus on the individual within Israel's complicated ethnic and religious map. At its low point in the late 1980s, only five or six Israeli films were produced a year, while today film festivals throughout the country, including alternative events that emphasize Arab/Jewish films, short films, and documentaries, and the Rehovot women's film festival, which ran for a decade, demonstrate an explosion in creativity. With numerous awards under its belt, and financing through international collaborations, the future for Israeli cinema looks strong.

Conclusion

The richness of Israeli culture today comes from both the diversity of mediums and disciplines and the variety of subjects being portrayed. The early years were characterized by the desire to use culture to communicate political and social ideas, to serve as educational tools for the early pioneers, and as a way to assimilate other Jews upon their immigration to Israel, including Mizrachim, Indian, Russian, and Ethiopian Jews. However, the purity of Israeli culture, as it was envisaged in the first half of the twentieth century, was under attack from multiple directions. Artists and musicians were drawn to international forms of culture, from modernism to jazz. By the 1950s, attempts to maintain Israel in cultural isolation had to be abandoned and influences seeped into local cultural productions. At the same time, the need to travel internationally in order to ensure funding affected dance and cinema, bringing positive improvements to production values in the local arena as well as introducing new styles, tools, and aesthetics.

As international music and television flooded Israel's airwaves, it became impossible to ignore the spirit of internationalism that had permeated all aspects of Israeli society. Moreover, ignoring difference within Israeli society and suppressing groups who wished to use their own cultural expression, including Mizrachim, and later Russians and Ethiopians, became an unwinnable battle. Yet despite all of these effects both from within Israel and from the international community, Israeli culture still maintained some of its Israeliness. Whether it was exporting Israeli folk dance to Jewish communities around the world, or Israeli cinema through film festivals and worldwide distribution, or whether it was the maintenance of the Hebrew language (even as it evolved) and the unique blend of innocence and satire in its humor, Israeli culture continues to reflect something that is essentially its own. The Hebrewism of an earlier generation has evolved, adapting to the changing Israeli reality, the diversity of its ethnic makeup, and the impact of international culture on local tastes and cultural products. Today, Israeli culture is a reflection of the society that both produces and consumes it. This culture is a way to view Israeli society in its entirety, historically and socially. Despite the wide range of artistic expressions, the most important remained the word, and Hebrew has permeated in every sphere. Ahad Ha'am encouraged the development of Hebrew literature and poetry, journalism, and theater, the culture of his day. He could not have envisaged the directions that art, music, film, and dance would also take over the following century, but many of his earliest principles can still be found within these fields. Behind the developments that took place over the course of Zionist history, it is text, the Hebrew language, and the creation of a cultural nucleus that have served to create Israel as a spiritual homeland, just as he had imagined.

RECOMMENDED READINGS

Almog, Oz. *The Sabra: The Creation of the New Jew.* Berkeley: University of California Press, 2000.
Gertz, Nurith. *Myths in Israeli Culture: Captives of a Dream.* London: Valentine Mitchell, 2000.
Harris, Rachel S. *Warriors, Witches, Whores: Women in Israeli Cinema.* Detroit: Wayne State Press, 2017.
Horowitz, Amy. *Mediterranean Israeli Music and the Politics of the Aesthetic.* Detroit, MI: Wayne State University Press, 2010.
Ingber, Judith Brin. *Seeing Israeli and Jewish Dance.* Detroit, MI: Wayne State University Press, 2011.
Oren, Tasha G. *Demon in the Box: Jews, Arabs, Politics, and Culture in the Making of Israeli Television.* New Brunswick, NJ: Rutgers University Press, 2004.

Regev, Motti, and Edwin Seroussi. *Popular Music and National Culture in Israel.* Berkeley: University of California Press, 2004.
Saposnik, Arieh Bruce. *Becoming Hebrew: The Creation of a Jewish National Culture in Ottoman Palestine.* New York: Oxford University Press, 2008.
Talmon, Miri, and Yaron Peleg, eds. *Israeli Cinema: Identities in Motion.* Austin: University of Texas Press, 2011.
Zerubavel, Yael. *Recovered Roots: Collective Memory and the Making of Israeli National Tradition.* Chicago: University of Chicago Press, 1995.

GLOSSARY TERMS

Ahad Ha'am
Aliya: Second Aliya
Bilu
Hibbat Zion
Histadrut
Keren Hayesod
ma'abarot
Palmach
War: The War of Independence; Six-Day War
Yishuv
Zionism: Cultural Zionism; Labor Zionism

Rachel S. Harris is Associate Professor of Israeli Literature and Culture at the University of Illinois at Urbana-Champaign. She is the author of *An Ideological Death: Suicide in Israeli Literature*; *Warriors, Witches, Whores: Women in Israeli Cinema*; and (with Ranen Omer-Sherman) *Narratives of Dissent: War in Contemporary Israeli Arts and Culture.*

FIFTEEN

Israeli and Hebrew Literature: From the Yishuv to the 21st Century

RANEN OMER-SHERMAN

Introduction

In order to grasp the revolutionary impact of Hebrew over time, we should consider not merely how Ahad Ha'am's vision of a renewed He-brew culture has been realized, both in the critical shift from *lingua sa-cra* to the lingua franca for most Israelis, and in the stirring evidence of the country's bookstores where the works of hundreds of literary figures are sold in numbers that would delight authors living in much larger societies. That is just one of the more exciting and meaningful ways in which you might encounter the startling degree to which the sacred language has become the essential tool for engaging in the rhythms of daily life. As such, Hebrew has proved fully capable of revealing both the warts and wonders of Israel's highly self-critical society. In contrast to the literature of other relatively young nations, the independent and prickly nature of some of those voices is often glaring. Perhaps because of its remarkable capacity for deep (at times searing) political and social critique, encounters with Israeli literature can be as discomfiting for readers who are not intimately familiar with the tempestuous nature of Israeli society, as it is often exhilarating. Over time, Israeli writers have opened unforgettable windows into the fraught relation between the individual and society. Their richly conflicted literature wrestles with the heavy burden of national belonging and identity, the weighty repercus-sions of the sudden reversal of Jewish powerlessness after centuries of life in the Diaspora. The exploration of these radically new circumstances culminates in a truly singular national literature; a powerful body of work that juxtaposes ancient Hebraic ethics with contemporary moral, social, and political complexities and conundrums.

Hence, the writers we examine in this chapter shrewdly measure the unanticipated distances between individuals and their claustrophobic, demanding society, raising urgent and yet often timeless questions concerning the authentic self and the burden of belonging. They address related complications with great fidelity: protagonists struggling with the stigma of some form of outsider status (whether through ethnicity or some other marginal identity deemed suspect by the insular elite), and others whose questioning of the collective mission or the national heroic ethos to which they are harnessed can prove self-alienating. Such urgent literary interventions are understandable given the extraordinary sacrifices the individual has often been called on to make. Yet to better gauge the extremely varied and sometimes surprising responses to the challenges and contingencies addressed in the literary imagination for over a century, it will be useful to place more recent exemplars of Israeli literature in conversation with some of the less familiar works of important antecedents such as S. Y. Agnon, Hayim Nahman Bialik, and J. H. Brenner. Perhaps modern Hebrew literature is as widely translated as it is because, in reverberating and morally imaginative language that can still seem to echo the prophets' voices, Israeli narratives take on a tangible universality; they explore the urgent ethical questions of what any individual owes their society and what society owes the individual. Thus, the modern Hebrew literary canon is a vibrant reflection of Israeli society's bold and creative self-interrogatory nature.

Hayim Nahman Bialik

From the beginning, early Zionist writers revived and recast biblical stories and other ancient Jewish sources, both obscure and famous, in unexpected and often provocative ways. For example, Hayim Nahman Bialik (1873–1974), the great national poet of the first generation of Zionist settlement, was drawn to an unusual Talmudic legend about the wastelands of Exodus. In contrast to Bialik's unabashedly nationalist lyrics, which were immensely and immediately influential among the readers of the day, his idiosyncratic 1902 retelling of the desert generation's experience in the biblical Exodus, "The Dead of the Desert" ("*Metei Midbar*") reads today as a troublingly ambivalent meditation on the relationship between myth and politics. Its unexpected gesture toward an ancient story of skeptical refusal seems all the more strange for its composition precisely at the moment that the Jewish people seemed to be reentering history for the first time in two thousand years by renewing their historical relation to the Land. Bialik portrays giants, who have transgressed the fixed boundaries of habitation set by divine fiat, petrified as desert boulders. Centuries later, their defiance is resurrected in an obscure legend told by the Talmud's peripatetic Arab, who intuits the hidden secrets of the Earth's rocky strata. Pious readers would anticipate the rabbinic interpretation of God's announcement ("In this wilderness your carcasses shall fall" [Num. 14:28]) as a fitting rebuke to the people's anxiety that they would "fall" by the sword of human enemies; for such readers the subversive shift from sheepish acquiescence toward political agency and refusal might seem very strange. You can readily imagine that for the Zionists of Bialik's day, this may have seemed even more troubling. Triumphantly embracing exilic existence, the immobilized but untamed dead still seem to be rising, not only against God, but against the very notion of national destiny and homecoming:

> We are the brave!
> Last of the Enslaved!
> First to be free!
> With our own strong hand,
> Our hand alone,
> We tore from our neck
> The heavy yoke.
> Raised our heads to the skies,
> Narrowed them with our eyes.
> Renegades of the waste,
> We called barrenness mother.

Bialik's warriors seem to be proud secularists, defying first Pharaoh's and later God's enslavement of the people. As they rebel against God, their human autonomy is heroically set against pious obedience to a desert deity seemingly opposed to their individuality. Like the modern Canaanite movement in early Zionism, they cast off religiosity, and their desert-preserved corpses preserve the struggle toward a radical freedom.

A popular secular interpretation often offered in classrooms during the early days of the state aligned the poem with secular Zionism: a rejection of the Talmud (and obligation to the Law as part of transcendent authority) as part of Judaism's exilic mentality that the poet sought to overcome, and the rebirth of contemporary Jews who would inhabit a more natural form of faith and relation to their homeland. However, this ideological thrust is surely complicated by the glaring fact that in their wilderness of resistance, the giants do not embrace the salvation of Zionist space. Proclaiming "barrenness mother" seemingly transforms their sterile desert into an earthly alternative to God. Moreover, Bialik further discomfits the reader by hedging in his representation, leaving open the question of whether they are truly "dead" or in a strange state of vigilant dormancy:

> The mighty phalanx awakes.
> They suddenly rouse themselves, the stalwart men of war,
> Lightning ablaze in their eyes, their faces aflame, hands on swords.

Bialik's muscular and thrilling poetic Hebrew demonstrates the rich possibilities for engaging ancient texts (the Bible, ancient *piyyutim*, Midrash) and investing them with fresh psychological and political significance. Bialik's influence in his own lifetime is of course inestimable but is also strongly felt later, insofar as the very notion of the Hebrew poet was later borne by prodigious figures such as Nathan Alterman, Yehuda Amichai, Nathan Zach, Yitzhak Laor, and Uri Zvi Greenberg.

Here you should bear in mind that among many of the First Aliya (1882–1903) generation of writers were romantic Orientalists eager to establish a bridge between the biblical Hebrews and contemporary Arabs and Bedouin. Ehud Ben-Ezer describes how that generation of writers

> saw the implementation of Zionism and of Jewish immigration as a transition from passivity in the Diaspora to action in the context of the Jewish settlement in Palestine. The image of the armed watchman guarding the Jewish settlement took on a romantic dimension and was a precursor of the nascent Israeli army and soldier. The Arab was nearly always the adversary, the enemy, in this struggle. At the same time, the concepts of courage, mastery of weapons, and power were also derived from the Arab, especially from the image of the armed Bedouin astride his noble mare. The antithesis of the feeble Diaspora Jew was the strong, forceful sabra youth, whose new image was cre-

ated in a dialectical process of assimilating the Arab's qualities while simultaneously scapegoating the Arab as an opponent. (*Sleepwalkers and Other Stories: The Arab in Hebrew Fiction*, 5)

J. H. Brenner and S. Y. Agnon

In the works of J. H. Brenner (1881–1921) and S. Y. Agnon (1888–1970), who along with Bialik constitute the greatest voices of Hebrew modernism, we find notably secular strains of skepticism toward the messianic impulses of Judaism that had been energized by the modern Zionist movement. Yet it is equally crucial to heed the extent to which, throughout his career, and here in his famous acceptance speech at the Nobel Prize Banquet in Stockholm in 1966, Agnon staunchly aligns himself with an ancient wellspring of sacred sources:

> From whom did I receive nurture? Not every man remembers the name of the cow which supplied him with each drop of milk he has drunk. But in order not to leave you totally in the dark, I will try to clarify from whom I received whatever I received. First and foremost, there are the Sacred Scriptures, from which I learned how to combine letters. Then there are the Mishna and the Talmud and the Midrashim and Rashi's commentary on the Torah. After these come the *Poskim*—the later explicators of Talmudic Law—and our sacred poets and the medieval sages, led by our Master Rabbi Moses, son of Maimon, known as Maimonides, of blessed memory.

Brenner, who immigrated to Palestine in 1909, represents a new generation of Hebrew writers who found themselves caught amid the breakdown in the stability of traditional authority and saw little on the horizon to elicit anything other than pessimism toward the viability of Jewish life in exile. Poignantly stirring autobiographic traces can be glimpsed in his drifting and unsatisfied characters. Though Brenner received a religious education, he joined the Bund (the Jewish socialist movement) as a young man, and still later restlessly gravitated toward Zionism. Hence, it should not surprise you to learn that Brenner's protagonists typically feel themselves caught between two worlds: like the unnamed protagonist of his 1904 novella *In Winter*, they seem to represent the incoherencies and vacillations of that post-Haskala malaise. He can find no consolation in any political sphere and is a classic luftmensch, unable to establish roots. Victimized by anti-Semites, he is thrown from a train.

A village lies not far away but the protagonist remains on the ground, friendless, with a winter storm assailing him. Trains have long been fraught tropes in the literary lexicon of Jewish modernism (even before the Holocaust), and Brenner's train in the narrative suggests a heightened anxiety of accelerated movement that will transport the individual irreparably beyond the safe boundaries of traditional community and identification. Here too, as with Bialik, we can perceive significant birth pangs of pessimism, self-doubt, and deep expressions of cultural unease in the self-interrogatory renderings of the early writers of the Zionist national awakening.

In his early days in Palestine, Brenner initially worked as an agricultural laborer but later taught Hebrew grammar and literature in high school. A dominant voice as critic, translator, novelist, and poet, he was the most established literary figure in Eretz Yisrael in his day and had tremendous influence in transferring Hebrew literary culture from Europe to the Yishuv. Publicly, Brenner encouraged *aliya* and envisioned exile as an abject condition of cultural and economic parasitism against which the Land of Israel beckoned as the only remedy. Yet on closer examination, his imaginative works, imbued as they are with memorable conversations, meditations, and exchanges about the nature of fate and of free will, ultimately express a radical pessimism not only toward Jewish life in Europe but even the viability of Zionism.

BRENNER AND THE ARABS OF PALESTINE

In contrast to the far more romantic representations of the indigenous Arab population in the earlier period of Zionist settlement, for Brenner, Arabs were primarily the enemy, and socialist ideals seemed enervated and thoroughly lacking realism in confronting them. Brenner's final and most famous work, *Breakdown and Bereavement* (*Shkol ve-Khishalon*, 1920), is set in Palestine during the final years before World War I. At that time, and culminating in a number of Jewish fatalities during the Arab riots of 1920, relations between Arabs and Jews were already exhibiting ominous portents of the violence and mutual suspicion of later years. This, in fact, leads to the psychic collapse of the protagonist, Yehezkel Hefetz, whose oddly messianic name combines the biblical Ezekiel of dry bones prophecy with the Hebrew word *hefetz*, "desire." Intriguingly,

Franz Kafka was one of the novel's many readers who found themselves both captivated and dismayed by its bleak sense of the pioneering reality. Brenner's hero, Hefetz, shares the unsettled condition of many of his characters, who wander in perpetual search of home, but critics widely consider this work to be the most artistically accomplished of Brenner's endeavors. Aspiring to labor in the soil and become the New Hebrew, he is humiliated by bodily ills including sexual impotence.

Even in the Holy Land, it seems, the Jew retained the recidivistic neurosis of Diaspora. Moreover, Brenner saw the Arab relationship with the Jews of the Yishuv as continuous with the ancient hostility of the Jews' host nations in the Diaspora. In her commentary on *Breakdown and Bereavement*, novelist and critic Dara Horn argues that in Brenner's acerbic vision, "the harsh reality of life in an unforgiving land appears not as a romantic challenge, but as a hopeless and debilitating burden. And the myth-smashing of the novel doesn't end there. While Zionist rhetoric taught that a return to the land of Israel and the possibility of self-determination would heal the Jewish people of the weight of centuries of sorrow and fear, Brenner's novel is peopled with characters who suffer endless mental traumas from feelings of inferiority so deeply entrenched that even their new homeland cannot cure them." Brenner, whose works were so imbued with dread and foreboding, was killed in the Arab riots of 1921.

S. Y. AGNON

When approaching the poetry and prose of subsequent years, it is crucial to understand that the bond between narrative and nation-building has been ingrained in the genesis of Israel and Hebrew fiction and poetry as in few other national literatures. And nowhere is that more evident than in the prominent work of S. Y. Agnon. Born in Galicia, Agnon (1888–1970) immigrated to Jaffa at age nineteen in 1908. After an extended sojourn in Germany (1913–1924), he returned to Jerusalem, where he lived until his death in 1970. Today, Agnon's work seems remarkable both for its complex evocation of the ordeal of traditional Jewish life struggling to cope with the contingencies of a modernity in which it did not feel fully at home, and for its exciting experiments with literary form—the embrace of symbolism, expressionism, and innovative uses of motifs and tropes. Agnon imaginatively bridges the traditional world of piety and that of the cataclysmic transformations and iniquities of twentieth-century history. No modern Hebrew writer has had greater range: ironic reworkings of folktales, satires, and richly symbolic, dreamlike fiction. Stylistically, his lucid and supple language is considered the supreme achievement of modern Hebrew prose, which in essence brings centuries of sacred and rabbinic texts into an imaginative conversation with the present. Hence, the 1940s are widely considered to mark the origin of Israel's national literary culture not merely because of the rise of the state itself but for the milestone of Agnon's 1945 novel *Only Yesterday* (*Tmol Shilshom*), which cast a wide shadow over the generations to follow. The epic novel's woeful antihero, Yitzhak Kummer, grandson to a famous rabbi, immigrates to Eretz Yisrael to redeem himself and build up the land. Yet he fails to find opportunity in the Jewish settlements, which prefer Arab labor. Instead he becomes an artist, settles in an Ultra-Orthodox neighborhood in Jerusalem (like the novel's hero, the holy city lacks any romantic qualities and is filled with squalor and disease), and marries the daughter of a rabbi. Effectively reversing his path, Kummer returns to the prayers of his father's household. In the story's grotesque denouement, he is savaged by a rabid dog and dies a miserable death.

Clearly in this novel's perversely antirevolutionary ethos, Zionism remains a dangerously quixotic if not altogether fatal endeavor. The protagonist's very name, as Ariel Hirschfeld reminds us, suggests a blighted destiny: Yitzhak Kummer "is an oxymoron: laughter (the Hebrew 'Yitzhak') and distress (Yiddish 'Kummer'). To this one must add the other Yiddish meaning of 'Kummer'—'the arriver'—and the symbolic dimension of 'Yitzhak' (Isaac) who exists, according to the Midrash, in an eternal state of being bound." You should be aware that because of the protagonist's tragic death, many other Israeli commentators have seen a prophecy of the triumph of fundamentalist religion and of the secular versus Haredi struggle being waged today. In succinct summation, Adam Rovner aptly hails *Only Yesterday* as "a powerful patchwork of the styles that have come to define modern Hebrew literature: myth, epic, social realism, psychological realism, magical realism, and symbolic parable."

S. Yizhar

There is another great literary icon of the 1940s whose influence has arguably proved even more enduring than Agnon's in terms of the topical concerns of the contemporary Israeli writer. S. Yizhar (1916–2006), who used the pseudonym Yizhar Smilansky, was born in Palestine. Yizhar would be a remarkable figure were it only for his unprecedented simultaneous immersion in the usually incommensurate realms of literature and politics. Aside from serving as a member of Knesset during Israel's formative decades, he is renowned for his searing works of wartime conscience such as the epic 1958 novel *Days of Ziklag*. The novel, set during the 1948 war, follows the struggle of a unit of Israeli soldiers to protect a remote Negev outpost and is especially distinguished by its deeply textured and loving delineation of the landscape, flora, fauna, and even sunlight of the new/old country. In shorter fiction, Yizhar wrote troubling examinations of the nation's conscience during wartime that have been read by generations of students. In the short story "The Prisoner," an Arab peasant is seized from the pastoral landscape and abused during his interrogation. Yizhar's protagonist, a sympathetic soldier observing his mistreatment, struggles mightily, but only within himself. Of Yizhar's provocative early works, Nurit Gertz astutely observes, "He is supposedly dealing with the Israel-Arab conflict but actually his subject is the conflict between Israeli and Israeli; that is, between what is revealed in the Hebrew literature of the War for Independence and what is suppressed in it." Yizhar's 1949 novella *Khirbet Khizeh* (published just months after the war's end but only recently translated into English) addressed the grim reality of Palestinian dispossession and the flawed behavior of the IDF toward civilians.

A. B. Yehoshua and Amos Oz

Tellingly, the early careers of both A. B. Yehoshua (b. 1936) and Amos Oz (b. 1939), two of Israel's most internationally acclaimed authors, are distinguished for their close examinations of their country's psyche, including nuanced attention to the historical vicissitudes and evolving identity of Israel's Arab minority. Yehoshua's early story "Facing the

Forests" (1963) gained even greater interest in the immediate aftermath of the dramatic remapping of the Middle East of 1967, whose tragic consequences for both Palestinians and Israelis continues to the present. In contemporary Israel, this work has come to be regarded as a milestone both for its representation of the figure of the Arab and for its provocative portrayal of the troubled history of the landscape itself, the violent erasures it mutely witnesses.

In retrospect, encountering this work's heavily allegorical treatment of festering political realities affords a unique opportunity to weigh the extent to which Hebrew literature, in its most liberal guise, could successfully recognize the Arab Israeli's independent identity, an uncomfortable category that might not be altogether congruent with classical Zionism's self-image or aspirations. In this story, a rootless and disaffected young academic's peers strive to correct his parasitic and listless behavior by encouraging him to accept an appointment as a fire-watcher in a remote forest south of Jerusalem. In the forest, the unnamed student finds himself alone, except for the presence of an aging Arab and the young girl who cares for him. The Arab is mute and mutilated, his tongue having apparently been cut out during the 1948 War (though it remains unclear which side committed the atrocity). Yehoshua presents the early encounters between Arab and Jew as a charade of *mutual* incomprehension, with both the charged subtext of the graduate student's thesis topic and the Arab's incapacity for language serving as a grotesque allegory of Palestinian-Israeli relations that distinguished Yehoshua's society at the time of the story's composition. By the end of the story, the forest is burned, exposing the ghostly ruins of a Palestinian village.

Oz's "Nomad and Viper" (1963) is a slyly subversive retelling of the biblical tale of Dinah, whose ostensible rape leads to the massacre of the male inhabitants of her tribe. Geula, a troubled member of a young Negev kibbutz, accuses a local Bedouin youth of rape. Juxtaposing the putative values (liberalism, egalitarianism, and democracy) of the "civilized" rational society of the kibbutz members with the "savage" Bedouins, Oz's story brilliantly deconstructs the Zionist narrative of enlightening and uplifting the indigenous population.

As these earlier works might suggest, even writers sympathetic to the plight of the country's Arab minority did not initially succeed in revealing the Arab as a fully complex character to the degree that later representations achieve. In this regard, Yehoshua's epic tapestry of a novel *The Lover* (1977) is groundbreaking, admired by generations of Israeli readers, and often singled out for its nuanced and empathic portrayal of the young Arab-Israeli boy Na'im. Set before and during the Yom Kippur War and in its traumatic aftermath, the novel quietly insinuates that the neglect of Israel's Arab minority constitutes a growing crisis for the Jewish state. Na'im, a young mechanic employed by a Jewish garage owner, finds himself constantly bemused by the disparity between his fluency in Hebrew, his education in Jewish literature and history, and the majority culture's abysmal ignorance of his people's language and culture. Because of his physical appearance he is often taken for a Jew and is torn between belonging to his village and the opportunities he believes may await him in Jewish society. Na'im falls in love at first sight with the daughter of his Jewish boss, and Yehoshua's poignant treatment of transgressive love is unforgettable. This best-selling novel has been widely taught in Israeli schools, and for generations it has been part of the shared fabric of Israeli cultural literacy. Beginning in *The Lover*, Yehoshua's fiction and polemics alike are marked by a profound disavowal of the Diaspora that he considers the epitome of irresponsibility, at best irrelevant and at worst fatal, to the perpetuation of Jewish life and an authentic Jewish culture. The novel portrays a notoriously amoral interloper, Gabriel, who has returned from abroad only to secure his inheritance and whose presence further destabilizes an already dysfunctional family. Gabriel's vague intellectualism, his history of mental illness, and his irresponsible life of aimless urban freedom in Paris vividly convey Yehoshua's misgivings toward the culture and psychology of the Diaspora. In that regard, it seems that Yehoshua has self-consciously assumed the literary mantle of Brenner. For Brenner's literary hero in *From Here and There* (*Mikan u-Mikan*, 1910), settlement in the Land of Israel constitutes heroic struggle against the *Galut* of lassitude, stagnation, and economic parasitism.

Meir Shalev and the Mythic Past

When you consider the complex ways that later generations of Israeli writers seek to comprehend the mythic achievements of the Second Aliya pioneers, no writer has proved as influential, nor as wildly entertaining, as the novelist Meir Shalev (b. 1948). Indeed, few writers have a warmer place in the hearts of Israeli readers. Shalev's birth and early years in Nahalal, Israel's first *moshav*, inspired his first novel, *Roman Russi* (*The Blue Mountain*). Ranked as the top best-selling novel in Israeli history, Shalev's richly mythic evocation of immigrant scandal and struggle easily bears comparison to Faulkner's imagined Yoknapatawpha. *Blue Mountain* encompasses the birth and subsequent decline of a *moshav* in the Jezreel Valley ("God Will Sow"), which was the geospatial center of the pioneering enterprise; the aging of its founding generation; the waning of their Labor-Zionist ideology and way of life; and the lofty ideals as well as scandalous mischief equally embodied by the second generation. Filled with intricate and exuberant storytelling, the novel frequently shifts between a reverent and playful tone to portray the tensions, contradictions, and pressures that were inherent in the struggle to create a new Jewish identity. Chronologically, the novel spans the period from the Second Aliya (the first decade or so of the twentieth century), when the village founders arrive in Palestine, charged with ideological fervor and erotic tension, to the present of the novel's contemporary narrator, roughly the time of *Blue Mountain*'s publication in the 1980s. Today you can see that this was a period in which the culture as a whole became embroiled in deep questioning about the past, and Shalev's novel contributed to a significant reworking of both the country's founding mythologies and the validity of contemporary Israeli identities. But most of all, the novel's Israeli readers were immediately struck and captivated by its singularly rich combination of biblical Hebrew and modern slang.

While by no means a pedantic "post-Zionist" work, the novel nonetheless insists that we grapple with the human cost of excessive ideals. At the same time, *Blue Mountain* strongly intimates that when you look back on the distant struggles of the pioneers from the perspective of the twenty-first century (plagued by malarial mosquitoes, tropical illnesses, poverty, and numerous other obstacles), you might well conclude that only the excessively passionate, obsessed, and nearly deranged could achieve the extraordinary transformation of lands and Jewish life that was ultimately accomplished. More recently, Shalev has brought us incisive studies of biblical narrative and the critically acclaimed *A Pigeon and a Boy*, a novel that won and broke many hearts in Israel and was later adapted for the stage by the Gesher Theater. *My Russian Grandmother and her American Vacuum Cleaner* is an intensely moving, often hilarious memoir of the novelist's grandmother, a Zionist heroine in her own mind and a deranged malcontent from the perspective of most other people in this story. Originally titled *Ha'davar Haya Kakha* (*This Is How It Was*), this plainspoken declaration is frequently and ironically iterated in the novel and ultimately undermines any possibility of locating the single authentic version of any past, especially in a family for whom "memory and imagination" were merely "different words for the same thing." The titular heroine, Grandma Tonia, who arrived in the Jezreel Valley from the Ukraine during the Third Aliya (early 1920s), labored alongside founding pioneers of Nahalal but became increasingly eccentric and estranged from her community. Shalev has always known how to spin a tale, and here he applies that dazzling vitality to a wellspring of personal and family memory. Aside from enjoying it as a genuine comic tour de force, Israeli readers gravitated to Shalev's story as a marvelous meditation on the mysterious processes of memory and the intricate tapestry of familial connections over time.

Post-Holocaust Consciousness

With the salient exception of isolated poems by Amir Gilboa (1917–1984) and others, the Holocaust did not truly transform Israeli literary culture for nearly a generation. Even a poet such as Dan Pagis (1930–1986), a child survivor, who is today considered absolutely essential to the first-generation literary canon commemorating the Shoah, wrote lyrics for two decades before he felt ready to grapple with its trauma. Today, his "Written in Pencil in the Sealed Railway-Car" (*"Katuv b'iparon bakaron hehatum"*) is one of the most cherished poems of world literature, not to mention modern Hebrew culture, where the poem is widely studied in both academia and middle-school curricula. Here, in Stephen Mitchell's stirring translation, individual readers are immediately implicated; our sense of progress in a rational world is undermined as the ominous beginnings of human community glare through present history like a murderous palimpsest:

here in this carload
i am eve
with abel my son
if you see my other son
cain son of man
tell him that i

Few works of art so successfully crystallize the problem of testimony, commemoration, and conscience; we cannot escape its call for involvement and witnessing. Moreover, as Sidra Dekoven Ezrahi memorably remarks, "lack of closure here is the absolute refusal of art as triumph over mortality" (*Booking Passage: Exile and Homecoming in the Modern Jewish Imagination*, 162). Pagis's six lines deprive us of such consolation, returning us to the shadowy silences of the dead, for whom no one can speak. Rather than a triumphal sense of having worked through and overcome loss, this spare lyric of absence paradoxically insists on its own wound as an event still to be communicated, still trapped in speechlessness. Through its insistence on unspeakability, Pagis haunts us with a Holocaust that remains an event without a witness or narrator, which urgently demands each subsequent reader's struggle—to witness and narrate.

Aharon Appelfeld (b. 1932) is one of Israel's most accomplished and prolific Hebrew-language novelists despite the fact that he did not learn Hebrew until he was a teenager, and even though he is often considered outside the mainstream of Israeli literary currents because of his relentless focus on Jewish life in Europe before and during the Holocaust. In 1941, when he was eight years old, the Romanian army invaded his hometown, where his mother was murdered. He was deported with his father to a Nazi concentration camp in Transnistria from which he eventually escaped. After hiding for three years he joined the Soviet army as a cook. After the war, Appelfeld spent several months in a displaced-persons camp before immigrating to Palestine in 1946. In his fiction, he stands apart from many other Holocaust writers in refraining from portraying atrocity directly. That indirection has enabled him to write some of the most penetrating examinations of the lingering effects of trauma, the psychology of the survivor, and especially the troubling nature of memory. After years of refusing to describe his own experience, in his late and distinctly unorthodox memoir *The Story of a Life* (1999), Appelfeld often mediates on both the capacities and limitations of language and memory:

> I say "I don't remember," and that's the whole truth. The strongest imprints those years have left on me are intense physical ones. The hunger for bread. To this very day I can wake up in the middle of the night ravenously hungry. Dreams of hunger and thirst haunt me almost on a weekly basis. I eat as only people who have known hunger eat, with a strangely ravenous appetite. During the course of the war, I was in hundreds of places—in railway stations, in remote villages, on the banks of rivers. All these places had names, but there's not one that I can remember. Sometimes I see the war years like a large pasture that blends into the horizon; sometimes it's like a dark and gloomy forest that goes on interminably; and sometimes it's like a long line of people weighed down with bundles and knapsacks. From time to time some of the people collapse onto the ground, only to be trampled by all the other feet. Everything that happened is imprinted within my body and not within my memory. The cells of my body apparently remember more than my mind, which is supposed to remember.

That seems as hauntingly representative an expression of the lingering aftereffects of trauma as can be found within the entire body of Holocaust literature anywhere.

The "Second Generation" in Israeli Literature: Nava Semel, David Grossman, and Amir Gutfreund

Nava Semel (b. 1954) is famous for an audaciously imaginative postmodern work about the Holocaust. She has written poetry and prose for children and adults as well as television scripts, much of it Holocaust-related. Semel's short story collection titled *A Glass Hat* (*Kova Zehuhit*, 1998) is a literary milestone insofar as it is the first work to voice the anxieties and concerns of the "second generation," the children of the survivors. In her introduction, the scholar Nurit Govrin describes the book's cryptic title as a metaphor for the psychic burden borne by the children of the survivors: "The glass hat, its touch is cold. It is transparent and insulated, burdensome and not isolated, vulnerable and may break into pieces at any moment. More than it protects it exposes and bears great danger."

A work of greater complexity, Semel's *And the Rat Laughs* (*Tzchok Shel Achbarosh*, 2001), was published to rave reviews and was subsequently

made into a highly successful opera as well as a film. Like the other Israeli works on the Holocaust addressed here, the focus in this multifari-
ous work is not atrocity but rather commemoration and remembrance.
Encompassing several literary genres (story, legend, poems, science fiction, and diary), the novel covers a span of 150 years in its exploration
of the uncertain and unpredictable forms of traumatic memory's transmission and the nature of storytelling itself. In the first part, the story
of a nameless five-year-old girl is related to the girl's granddaughter in
Tel Aviv who is writing a school paper. The child in the story has been
entrusted to a Polish peasant family, who hide her in a potato cellar for
roughly a year. There she is repeatedly raped by the son of the peasants;
her only companion is a rat. The second part relates the granddaughter's
diary, deepening our knowledge of her grandmother's wartime suffering, while the third part presents poetry composed by the survivor. The
fourth section leaps ahead in time to 2099. It concerns an anthropologist's struggles to make sense of the strange "Girl and Rat" myth in-
herited from the mists of the remote past. In the anthropologist's time,
the Jewish state has been divided as it was in antiquity: the citizens of
"TheIsrael," a secular, apocalyptic, ahistorical garrison singularly devoted to its survival, are uninterested in Holocaust memory or indeed
any relation to the past; the inhabitants of "Ju-Ideah" fetishize the past
as holy, are religiously intolerant, and violently reject the possibility of
any connection between a Jewish girl and a Christian hero. The novel's
wrenching concluding chapter clarifies that mystery by returning to the
events of 1943–1944 told through the personal journal of Father Sanislaw,
a priest who rescued the child after the family betrayed and abandoned
her. Struggling to restore her speech and faith in God, he discovers that
he has lost his own speech, and the diary records his personal shame and
also anguish at the moral turpitude of his congregation.

Another notable writer who takes up the question of language,
speech, and silence with memorable results is David Grossman, born in
1954, the same year as Semel. His epic postmodern novel *See Under: Love*
(*Ayen Erech: Ahavah*, 1986) has been widely acclaimed a masterpiece for
artfully weaving renderings of Tel Aviv neighborhoods circa 1950; elements of magical realism; a stunning homage to the Jewish Polish writer
Bruno Schulz, who was murdered by a German Nazi officer; and finally
the angst of contemporary Israel, into a spellbinding tapestry. Its first

section, "Momik," has long been held in such high regard in Israel that it was eventually published in a separate edition for young readers. The title character is a nine-year-old child born and growing up in Tel Aviv in the early years of statehood. Tangible traces of trauma are constantly expressed in Momik's environment, everything from his Holocaust survivor parents' eating habits to the linguistic clues that surround him. Partly because of the children's fiction he reads, Momik sees his function in life as a code-breaker and interpreter of signs. Because his parents won't let him come close to their terrifying experience, he has to engage in a project of rebuilding a past, of re-creating it for himself. He begins a search "to put together the vanished land of Over There like a jigsaw puzzle, there's still a lot of work left on this, and he's the only one in the whole world who can do it, because who else can save Mama and Papa from their fears and silences . . . which was even worse after Grandfather Anshel turned up and made them remember all the things they were trying so hard to forget and not tell anyone."

In the family's storage space Momik locates pieces of the Jewish past in Europe, such as a *Tsena Urena*, the Yiddish translation of the Bible and commentary adapted for Orthodox Jewish women, and other Yiddish texts that seem to create a bridge between exile and home, Europe and Israel, even as the child struggles to form a coherent narrative between the disparity of Zionist masculinity and the Jewish vulnerability he witnesses at home. Momik the child sees the adult world as conspiring against him to preserve its secrets, mysteries that are apparently dark and sinister. The adult Momik is a morbid and fearful parent. Yet by the end of the novel, almost in spite of himself, he is resurrected by the forces of life, creativity, and love. Of this ambitious book's work of imaginative witnessing, Grossman once remarked, "I was simply obliged to write this book. I felt that I could not understand my life as a Jew, as an Israeli, as a human being, as a father, as a man if I did not understand the life that was no longer there."

Perhaps the most critically praised novel by one of Israel's younger second-generation writers, Amir Gutfreund (b. 1963), *Our Holocaust* (*Shoa Shelanu*, 2000), winner of the Sapir Prize, portrays the fraught bridges and schisms between the generation of survivors and their children. *Our Holocaust*'s narrator happens to be a character named Amir Gutfreund, and many of the episodes and background described in the book, including the Holocaust experiences of his own father, are clearly autobiographical. The son of Holocaust survivors (both his parents were children during the war), Gutfreund portrays the novel's sibling protagonists as growing up in the domain of the "Law of Compression": with few surviving biological relatives, the most tenuous relationships transform others into their uncles, cousins, and grandparents. This powerful narrative's vividly realized cast of Holocaust survivors all live on the same street in a suburb in Haifa, and not unlike David Grossman's *See Under: Love* (Gutfreund also shares Grossman's warm affinity for the Yiddish language), a conspiracy of silence imposed by the clan's patriarch prevails among them, initially thwarting the child protagonists, a boy and a girl, from discovering what really happened "over there." Naturally, they refuse to accede to these restrictions, and their struggle to solve the mystery of the past takes them on a startling journey of transformation. Like other novelists including Meir Shalev and David Grossman, who have dabbled in magic realism, Gutfreund frequently straddles the fantastic and the everyday, including elements of whimsy in his fiction. Israeli critics frequently praise his works for their psychological and social insights and especially for their characteristic black humor. As Gutfreund himself assures us: "Even if I write an instruction manual for a washing machine, it will always contain humor, and it will always contain the Holocaust. It's part of me."

Hebrew Literature and the Akeda

For reasons both related to and independent of the Holocaust, the most pervasive biblical trope in modern Hebrew culture is undoubtedly that of the Akeda, or "the binding of Isaac." Most nascent national discourses participate in the discourse of motherland and self-sacrifice, but in the case of Zionism, historical contingencies caused this to escalate. Though the tradition was already present in early Zionist culture, its appropriations and subversions accelerated in both poetry and prose beginning in the 1940s through the 1990s and up until our own moment. Such attention seems inevitable given the increasing violence and atrocities of the twentieth century and the staggering numbers of victims of genocide, war, and terrorism. Brilliant creative works and polemics by Haim Gouri, Shulamith Hareven, Amos Oz, Moshe Shamir, A. B. Yehoshua, and others abound. Yael Feldman memorably refers to the imaginative efforts of writers and artists of this period as collectively lifting up "pens and brushes against the knife continually hovering in the air," but she also draws attention to the messy and sometimes contradictory cultural politics underlying each subsequent intervention, demonstrating that this is often a complicated, even Freudian, story of "fictionalized aggressive fathers and emasculated sons . . . filicide qua aqedah." The role of Israeli maternity in nurturing the victim/warrior and the self-conscious voices of dissenting women authors are also prevalent in this context.

An especially prominent voice in this regard is Shulamith Hareven (1930–2003), who was born in Warsaw, Poland, and whose essays (*The Vocabulary of Peace*) and fiction (most memorably in *Thirst: The Desert Trilogy*) offer stirring critiques of the policies of occupation and militarism. During the First Intifada, Hareven was one of a few journalists to enter Palestinian refugee camps, and her poetry, novels, and essays have been widely translated. Dahlia Ravikovitch (1936–2005), the most acclaimed and widely read female poet in Israel at the time of her death, was also a renowned peace activist whose empathic protest poetry presents sharp critiques of both the First Lebanon War and the politics of occupation. As Ravikovitch scholar Ilana Szobel argues, the poet "creates a space for otherness, estrangement, and inferiority. . . . The room she makes for victimhood, as well as the way her characters and speakers fail to conform or accommodate themselves to the symbolic order, creates poetic and cultural possibilities different from those established in the works of her contemporaries. . . . The way in which she confronts the issues of womanhood, manic depression, madness . . . and national identity from within and from outside . . . is one of her most influential accomplishments in terms of the construction of deviant female subjectivity in Israeli culture" (*A Poetics of Trauma: The Work of Dahlia Ravikovitch*, 132).

Another important writer whose work broaches the fragile boundaries between madness and the normative as well as the status of victims within the symbolic order in Israeli culture is the celebrated novelist Orly Castel-Bloom (b. 1960). In her postmodern comic farce *Dolly City*, Castel-Bloom's critique of the travails of maternity amid nationalist excess, a young doctor and mother becomes so obsessed with ensuring the well-being of her young son that she eventually succumbs to madness. Considered an international postmodern classic, *Dolly City* has been included in UNESCO's Collection of Representative Works and was nominated in 2007 one of the ten most important books since the creation of the State of Israel. In one of this novel's most shocking incidents, Dr. Dolly takes the place of Father Abraham and carves a map of biblical Israel onto her son's back, which remains throughout his life, though by adulthood it has somehow metamorphosed into Israel of the pre-1967 borders (without the West Bank, the Gaza Strip, and East Jerusalem). As Yaron Peleg astutely remarks of this black humor: "In this cruel upending of the biblical story, the land subjects its potential inheritor, the Jewish offspring, to its bloody and painful history, mythology or fate, rather than the other way around, as the Bible intends. Instead of a story about a brave new beginning . . . this scene describes a terrible legacy and an awful predetermination . . . this child sacrificed already in his infancy to the Moloch of his patrimony and enslaved to it." The urgent question that looms before us throughout this eminently disturbing and wildly imaginative novel seems to be whether either a happy childhood or a happy maternity is possible within such an oppressive geography.

Minority Writing in Israel: Two Exemplars

After many years of neglect, Iraqi-Israeli writers and poets (including many who self-consciously identified with the vibrant Jewish cultural past in Baghdad) began to emerge from the ghetto of Iraqi-Israeli writing into the Israeli national canon, garnering literary prizes and becoming increasingly prominent in high school and college curricula. Long one of Israel's most renowned writers of Mizrahi origin, Sami Michael, born in Iraq in 1926, still considers Arabic language and culture to be intrinsic to his own identity. As he once ruefully remarked of his transition from Iraq to Israel: "The 1950s were the most tempestuous years of my life. In 1949 I tumbled from the status of a citizen with 2,500 years of seniority in Iraq to the status of an immigrant in a world that was strange to me in its language, customs and culture." His highly acclaimed and popular novels exploring the interwoven lives of Jewish and Arab characters include *Refuge* (1977), which chronicles the activities and prejudices of Jewish and Arab members of Israel's Communist Party during the 1973 war; *Trumpet in the Wadi* (1987), a tale combining pathos and high comedy in which a Russian-Jewish immigrant courts a reticent Arab-

Israeli; *Victoria* (1993), an expansive family saga set largely in a single
courtyard in Baghdad; and *Doves in Trafalgar* (2005), a riposte of sorts
to Palestinian writer Ghassan Kanafani's (1936–1972) story "Returning
to Haifa" (1969), in which a Palestinian couple fleeing the 1948 war are
forced to abandon their child to a Jewish couple who survived the Holocaust. Michael has lived in his beloved Haifa (Israel's fourth-largest
city) for over sixty years, a city he has portrayed more than any other
writer, but Baghdad continues to play an equally important role in his
exilic narrative imagination.

Sayed Kashua is an Arab citizen of Israel and native speaker of Palestinian Arabic who chooses to write his novels in Hebrew. In this he
was preceded by earlier voices in Israeli Arab writing, including Atallah
Mansour, author of *In a New Light* (1966), and Anton Shammas, whose
transformative novel *Arabesques* appeared in 1986. Born in 1975 in Tira,
a northern village, Kashua still writes weekly for *Ha'aretz*, though in
recent years he has lived with his family in the United States. His first
novel, *Dancing Arabs* (2002), rapidly became a best seller in Israel. Its
anonymous Arab protagonist grows up in Tira and wins a scholarship
to a Jewish high school. Like Yehoshua's Na'im (discussed earlier), he
experiences a taboo, and ultimately hopeless, love with a Jewish girl.
After this and subsequent disappointments, he grows to despise himself, other Arabs, and Jewish Israelis. In his inherently stagnant life, the
protagonist seems to embody the collective condition of Israel's Arab
minority.

Let It Be Morning (2005) was written in the wake of the Al-Aqsa Intifada (the Second Intifada) and reflects the author's sense of the worsen-
ing status of Israeli Palestinians within the dominant Jewish society. It
is narrated by a Palestinian journalist with Israeli citizenship (a figure
resembling Kashua) who reluctantly leaves Tel Aviv and returns to the
village where he grew up. There he is depressed by his sense of how little
has changed. This novel moves beyond the tensions between Jews and
Arabs to examine the rift between Israeli Arabs and Palestinians in the
territories and is especially noteworthy in its chilling depiction of a loyal
village that wakes up one day bewildered to find itself under siege by the
Israeli army. A later work, *Second Person Singular* (2012), offers a more
measured assessment of the quotidian nature of Jewish and Arab interactions. A tragicomedy composed of two tautly intertwined stories about

Jewish and Arab insiders and outsiders, it offers profound psychological and cultural insights into hidden identities and the painful struggle
to create a life of meaning in the materialist culture of contemporary
Israel. To a greater extent than his earlier works, this novel portrays life
as a struggle against the destructive forces *within* the individual, even
while still bearing witness to the corrosive ethnic pressures of Israeli
society. Throughout, Kashua's novels and creative nonfiction address
the complex interplay between language, identity, and the Arab Israeli's
growing sense of disenfranchisement in the twenty-first century while
illuminating Israeli national identity as a whole.

Two Contemporary Hebrew Masterpieces

No discussion of salient developments in Hebrew literature of the first
decade of the twenty-first century would be complete without mention of
two works that have been widely deemed masterpieces by international
audiences and critics. In many ways, each marks the culmination of the
extraordinary proliferation of Hebrew literature since the establishment
of the state. In Oz's extraordinary 2004 *A Tale of Love and Darkness*
(the title does not deceive), deep personal pain and exuberant portray-
als of love and joy are both indelibly rendered. Those familiar with Oz,
whether in his guise as one of the Israeli left's most eloquent public intellectuals or as the author of probing novels into the life of the Israeli
citizen-soldier, may be startled by this exceptionally intimate window
into Oz's private losses; the familial and personal emotional archaeology laid bare here provides some truly gripping revelations into the art
of his novels.

This pastiche of memoir and the imagination recounts Oz's childhood in Jerusalem as well as his difficult and lonely early years in Kibbutz Hulda, with a few glimpses of the sleepy desert development town
of Arad he has called home since 1982. As a boy Oz experienced Jerusalem as a divided city, and he served in a tank unit in the Six-Day War
and the Yom Kippur War, so this memoir provides an exceptionally
penetrating understanding of the movement of Israeli society during
critical times of transition as well as a vivid portrait of his indelible
childhood perceptions. Indeed, the novelist's rebellion against his father's religious and politically doctrinaire Jerusalem household when he

was only fifteen mirrors the path taken by many of his alienated characters and reflects the tension between the individual and the collective that distinguishes Israeli life in each subsequent generation. *A Tale* recounts how Oz grew up with his father's sunny pioneering ethos of Zionism: secular, enlightened, rational, and militantly optimistic to the core. But equally pervasive was the diasporic influence of his mother's dark tales of European forests, demons, and Jewish mysticism. In an important sense, Oz's art has continuously strived since his first kibbutz tales to reconcile these oppositions. But here he is painfully candid in exposing the heartrending distances that can divide the members of an apparently close household. Whereas Oz was exposed to the Holocaust's shadow as well as a staggering number of other violent events and wartime deaths, it often seems as if the writer's childhood was spent in cafés where his parents and their friends passionately debated philosophy, history, and the power struggles of their day. Oz does a beautiful job of capturing the messianic fervor and intellectual fires of his parents' generation. This novelistic and multivocal memoir, so luminous in both topical anecdote and psychological characterization, is a consistently gracious, compassionate, and lyrical meditation on both personal and national history.

Finally, David Grossman's *To the End of the Land* (2011) is by turns an enthralling and harrowing intergenerational exploration of unforgettable characters whose relationships and destinies are shaped by Israel's extreme and violent reality of incessant wars. This unsparing yet compassionate exploration of wars and families features one of the most memorable heroines in Hebrew literature, a woman who in desperation flees the prospect of facing news of her son's death in battle by telling his story to a former lover who has been severely scarred by wartime trauma. Here as in earlier acclaimed novels, Grossman demonstrates the inextricable connections between personal and political realms. Israeli writers often portray the plight of mothers who bear the anxious knowledge of their son's eventual conscription into the Israel Defense Forces, knowing that they must surrender their child to the state, the reality that confirms the tragically enduring resonance of the Akeda for Israeli families. Few have done so to such searing effect.

Ora, Avram, and Ilan are children hospitalized amid the tumult of the Six-Day War in June 1967. They rapidly develop deep friendships that, years later, metamorphose into love between the men and Ora, while Avram and Ilan's intense friendship thrives until early in October 1973 when the men lightheartedly tease Ora into casting lots to determine who goes home to her on leave, a game that leads to horrific consequences for each of them in the years to come. After the Suez Canal fortifications are destroyed in the Yom Kippur War, Avram is captured and tortured, suffering lasting damage to his body and spirit in spite of Ilan and Ora's devotion. Unbearably alienated from his body, Avram is impotent until Ora lovingly seduces him and becomes pregnant with her second son, Ofer.

Years later, Ora is the mother of two sons, her marriage to Ilan in ruins, her elder son, Adam, coldly distant. Ilan and Adam are traveling abroad. Eager to celebrate her beloved son Ofer's imminent release from the IDF, Ora plans a trip to the Galilee, construing it also as "a gift for herself . . . for *her* release from his army." But at the last moment, he returns to his unit, unwilling to abandon friends called up in the latest emergency. Anguished by terrible premonitions, Ora flees her home, surrendering to the superstitious hope that if the authorities cannot reach her, Ofer will survive. Though his captivity has left Avram nearly incapacitated by depression and drug abuse, Ora forces her old lover to join her in her escape. Though Ora finds Avram barely sentient, she refuses to give up on him. In the Galilee, through Ora's fierce attention, fresh air and rigorous hiking, Avram is restored to a semblance of what he once was. He awakens to her mesmerizing stories of Ofer, the son he's never met, whose life may now be in peril.

Throughout their journey, Grossman tracks the natural world with lyrical precision; the Israel Trail itself emerges as a character, capricious and seductive, stealthily restoring the couple's bygone intimacy and arousing their passion once more. That magic is broken whenever they stumble across lonely monuments to soldiers who fell in battle. The bucolic landscape proves to be a vast graveyard, thwarting Ora's frantic quest to flee history. At one time or another, each of Grossman's sharply etched characters seems stricken by Israel's violent reality, terrified of commitment or even the ephemeral prospect of happiness. Each is shaped by the forces of war, but none is more scarred than Avram, who finds it nearly unbearable to discover that he has brought a child into such a world. Most impressive is Grossman's rendering of Ora's consciousness; the portrayal of her political and moral complexities is an extraordinary measure of his gifts. Ora's hardscrabble labors to redeem Avram from the catastrophe that has overtaken him, even as she fights off her own mounting terror, is a breathtakingly heroic battle that seizes the reader as much as the wartime travails of her men.

For his part, though kept ignorant of his real father's identity, Ofer eerily and poignantly seems to channel Avram's ordeal. As a child, he weeps at a Passover Seder ("he doesn't want to be Jewish anymore") because of the vast numbers of Arabs eager to annihilate him. Now a cynical soldier, he seems fully armored against any emotions. When he arrives home on leave, Ora rushes to embrace him, but his national-ized body and alien machismo crush her maternal spontaneity. Here is pure Grossman, contemplating the insidious ways in which the intimate spaces of domestic life become militarized zones: "Her fingers would recoil from the metal of the gun slung over his back and search for a demilitarized space on that back . . . she would sober up when he gave her three quick slaps on her back. . . . With that *thwack-thwack-thwack* he would both embrace her and mark the boundaries." The verisimilitude here is quietly damning, indelibly capturing the "situation" as it impacts ordinary Israeli life—in every generation.

Another story line (insistently interwoven, it can be compared to similar representations by Israeli Arab writers) is that of Ora's ever-shifting relation with Sami, the charmingly earthy Arab driver who has served her family for years (his "Arabesque Hebrew undermines the . . . greedy pretenses of both Jews and Arabs"). Each has steadfastly refused to allow the "situation" to threaten their affectionate bond, but now Sami resents Ora's imperious demands, which include the demand that he ferry Ofer to his base. Sami compels her to visit an underground clinic that covertly treats Palestinian workers smuggled in from the territo-ries, an encounter that transforms her perception of her society. In one memorable scene, even the car radio becomes a ludicrous ideological battleground as Sami recoils from the rhetoric of Galei Tzahal, the mili-tary station, and Ora shudders at the combative music of an Arabic sta-tion. Without ever becoming the reductive ciphers a less-accomplished writer might render, Sami and Ora, through their fragile relationship, urgently mirror Israel's deteriorating relations with its own minority citizens.

The novel's Israeli readers know that Grossman himself indulged in an Ora-like fantasy; he dared hope that writing *To the End of the Land* (more aptly titled *A Woman Flees from a Message* in the original Hebrew) would protect Uri, his youngest son then serving in the IDF. The manuscript was nearly complete when Uri was killed in the Second Lebanon War, shortly after Grossman protested its escalation. The novel exposes the intimate realm of Grossman's own raw loss. Most important, this transformative work marks the zenith of years spent scrutinizing the profound difference between survival and living. Throughout, Grossman delivers achingly beautiful observations on the strange gravitational forces binding us to one another, the strong bodily connections between lovers, and between parents and children. Rarely has the dual nature of Israel—both nurturing womb and militarized "land that devours its inhabitants"—been so stunningly realized. This haunting duality resonates in his book both metaphorically and literally, until the final wrenching scene where two figures curl together in a primal embrace, pressed tightly against the earth, momentarily immune from Israel's oppressive realities. There is tragedy in this scene to be sure, yet also perhaps the barest hint of both the characters' and Israel's open-ended destiny.

RECOMMENDED READINGS (A GUIDE TO THE ESSENTIAL IN HEBREW LITERATURE)

Books

Abramson, Glenda. *Drama and Ideology in Modern Israel.* Cambridge: Cambridge University Press, 1998. The first full-length study available in English considers Israeli drama's role at the center of public controversies on a variety of fronts: the ethical basis of Zionism, antagonism between the secular and the Orthodox, the Arab-Israeli conflict, the Jewish settlements, and the Holocaust. Israeli theater, Abramson argues, finds itself "frequently on the brink of *becoming* a social process."
Alter, Robert. *Modern Hebrew Literature.* New York: Behrman House, 1975. This is the author's selection of major developments in both Hebrew fiction and essays from the nineteenth century through the 1970s. Alter's lively critical introductory essays illuminate the weighty themes present: Emancipation, Enlightenment, nationalism, tensions between tradition and modernity, and the Zionist struggle to achieve a just and democratic society.
Ben-Ezer, Ehud, ed. *Sleepwalkers and Other Stories: The Arab in Hebrew Fiction.* Boulder, CO: Lynne Rienner, 1999. Ben-Ezer offers an important

range of representative short fiction and novels that encompass the early
romanticism of Jewish writing on the Middle East through the evolving perceptions of Jewish Israelis through wars and intifadas. He includes writers
from the early Second Aliya period (Moshe Smilansky, Yosef Haim Brenner,
Esther Raab), the 1948 generation (S. Yizhar and Benjamin Tammuz) and
contemporary writers such as Amos Oz, A. B. Yehoshua, Sami Michael,
and Etgar Keret, among others. Ben-Ezer's incisive introduction provides a
helpful survey of the major trends and developments in the Hebrew literary
entanglement with Arabs as both collective and individuals.

Ben-Zvi, Linda, ed. *Theater in Israel.* Ann Arbor: University of Michigan Press,
1996. This is a compilation of original essays, interviews, and commentar-
ies by leading international theater practitioners and critics exploring the
rich history and diversity of Israel's theater. The contributors address the
ways in which this politically committed theater mirrors the historical
and cultural forces that have shaped Israeli-Arab relations, events in the
Middle East, and the post-Holocaust experience. The book's comprehensive
scope encompasses the development of Hebrew drama from its inception in
Moscow in 1918 to the establishment of a national theater and the emergence
of a national repertoire. It also addresses the history, themes, and future of
Arab-Israeli and Palestinian theater.

Brenner, Rachel Feldhay. *Inextricably Bonded: Israeli Arab and Jewish Writers
Re-Visioning Culture.* Madison: University of Wisconsin Press, 2003.
Brenner examines Israeli identity as having long defined itself against Judaism's repressed Mizrahi Jewish Other as well as external and internal Arabs.
As a counternarrative, Brenner suggests, the cumulative impact of the writings of a significant number of Arab and Jewish authors in Israel, in spite of
their disparate sociopolitical perspectives, effectively "restores the visibility
of the Arabs in the 'empty' land and calls into question the unequivocal
Zionist claim to the land. . . . Against the doctrine of exclusion, the literary
representations reassert in the Israeli consciousness the denied histories
of the Palestinian Arab and the Diaspora Jew." Brenner argues that Israeli
Arab and Israeli Jewish writers together produce a dynamically "bi-ethnic"
rather than a narrowly "national" body of literature.

Brinner, Benjamin. *Playing across a Divide: Israeli-Palestinian Musical Encounters.* Oxford: Oxford University Press, 2009. The music Brinner examines
evolved in a historical context that oscillated wildly between a sense of
dissension and despair in the late 1980s, through a period of near euphoric
hope in the early 1990s, and on to the profound demoralization and bleak
hopelessness that has characterized relations between Jews and Arabs
in Israel and the Palestinian territories in the early twenty-first century.
Brinner argues that the linking of Jewish and Arab musicians' networks, the
creation of new musical means of expression, and the repeated enactment
of culturally productive musical alliances provide a unique model for mutually respectful and beneficial coexistence in a chronically disputed land.
Through its engaging examination of musical developments, this study

provides an important lens into key questions in the development of Israeli society, culture, and politics.

Feldman, Yael S. *Glory and Agony: Isaac's Sacrifice and National Narrative.* Stanford, CA: Stanford University Press, 2010. A comprehensive engagement with one of humanity's most ancient and consequential tropes as well as the most powerful and resonant motif in Hebrew poetry and prose is that of the Aqedah, the "binding," or near-sacrifice of Isaac. Venturing into the disparate fields of rabbinic Midrash, philosophy, linguistics, feminist criticism, and psychoanalysis, the study raises urgent and timely questions about Israeli society and literature: "How has Isaac, the *passive* survivor of a *near-*sacrifice, come to stand for the necessity for active military self-sacrifice, for a warrior's *glorious death* in battle?" and "how could Israelis have turned around a biblical scene traditionally read as a trope of obedience . . . into a trope of violence, synonymous with the oedipal conflict?" This is an essential guide to the literary archaeology of modern Israel's creative and tragic echoes and distortions of the Hebrew Bible's most disturbing myth.

Fuchs, Esther. *Encounters with Israeli Authors.* Marblehead, MA: Micah Books, 1982. The volume includes nine memorable and consequential literary interviews with authors (Amalia Kahana-Carmon, S. Yizhar, A. B. Yehoshua, Aharon Appelfeld, Yoram Kaniuk, and Yehuda Amichai, among others), reflecting on their lives as Israelis and as writers in the public sphere.

Gershenson, Olga. *Russian Theater in Israel: A Study of Cultural Colonization.* New York: Peter Lang, 2005. This study addresses the history as well as the Israeli mainstream media's reception of the Gesher Theater, which began as a marginal immigrant phenomenon and rapidly became one of Israel's most innovative cultural institutions. It tells a memorable story of the struggles of immigrant theater to gain a strong foothold in the national cultural scene, and the successful outcome of its strategic alliances with Israeli politicians and luminaries among the Israeli cultural elite. The author also addresses the theater's continued fostering of connections with the Russian immigrant community.

Hever, Hannan. *Producing the Modern Hebrew Canon: Nation Building and Minority Discourse.* New York: New York University Press, 2002. Hever provides a magisterial overview of the entirety of modern Hebrew literature, from Berdichevski and Agnon to Anton Shammas and Emile Habiby, while illuminating the ruptures and reversals that have undermined efforts to construct a hegemonic Zionist narrative. The work examines cultural and literary ferment from the early years of the emerging Labor-Zionist sensibility through Israeli state culture and the contemporary discourses of Arab dissent and otherness.

Horowitz, Amy. *Mediterranean Israeli Music and the Politics of the Aesthetic.* Detroit, MI: Wayne State University Press, 2010. This groundbreaking study explores the development of Mizrahi music and the careers of its musicians in Israel, as well as their marginalization by the mainstream. Alongside popular figures such as Zohar Argov, Horowitz examines lesser-known musicians who nonetheless significantly influenced the long journey of Mizrahi music toward wider acceptance and appreciation in Israeli society. It includes a nineteen-song CD (accompanied by commentary historically contextualizing each song in an appendix) that, in its own right, serves as a valuable guide for unfamiliar readers and listeners.

Mintz, Alan. *Translating Israel: Contemporary Hebrew Literature and Its Reception in America*. Syracuse, NY: Syracuse University Press, 2001. Delineating the reception of Israeli literature in the United States beginning in the 1970s, the author grapples with the influences that have shaped modern Israeli literature and reflects on the cultural differences that he argues have significantly impeded both American and American Jewish appreciation of Israeli authors. This study also addresses specific writers, situating them within the critical dialectic between Israeli and American culture.

Ramras-Rauch, Gila. *The Arab in Israeli Literature*. London: Tauris, 1989. This is a broad and illuminating historical coverage of the topic, from Yishuv days to the 1980s. There is much attention to early writers (Moshe Smilansky, Yehuda Burla, Yosef Haim Brenner, and more) in the Canaanite movement and the Statehood Generation as well as discussion of later figures such as David Grossman. A chapter is also devoted to Anton Shammas and other Arab writers in Hebrew.

Regev, Motti, and Edwin Seroussi. *Popular Music and National Culture in Israel*. Los Angeles: University of California Press, 2004. This interdisciplinary study addresses the three major popular music cultures that are proving instrumental in attempts to invent Israeliness: the invented folk song repertoire known as Shirei Eretz Yisrael; contemporary, global-cosmopolitan Israeli rock; and ethnic-oriental Mizrahi music. Its coauthors are a sociologist and an ethnomusicologist who bring their disparate disciplinary perspectives to bear on the book's three musical spheres.

Taub, Michael. *Israeli Holocaust Drama*. Syracuse, NY: Syracuse University Press, 1996. This major addition to Holocaust studies includes five critically important Israeli plays not previously available outside Israel: Leah Goldberg's *Lady of the Castle*, Aharon Megged's *Hanna Senesh*, Ben-Zion Tomer's *Children of the Shadows*, Motti Lerner's *Kastner*, and Joshua Sobol's *Adam*. Also included are two essays by Taub. "The Problematic of Holocaust Drama" addresses the question of Holocaust art: should artists create imaginative works about the Holocaust, and if so, what forms of narrative are appropriate? In Taub's overview of attitudes toward Holocaust art and the aesthetic reactions it creates, he draws on the scholarship of Lawrence Langer and Ellen Schiff, among others. The second essay focuses on the five plays themselves, which Taub categorizes in terms of historical trends: work from the 1950s and 1960s (*Lady of the Castle, Hanna Senesh,* and *Children of the Shadows*) that grappled with themes of Jewish resistance and the plight of survivors, and two contemporary works (*Kastner* and *Adam*) that sparked far greater controversy by raising provocative questions about collaboration and about art itself as an active form of resistance.

Book Chapters, Essays, Speeches, and Other Short Works

Agnon, Shmuel Yosef. "Address at the Nobel Prize Banquet in Stockholm, Sweden, December 10, 1966." The speech is by the only Israeli yet to be awarded the Nobel Prize for Literature. Agnon was perceived as embodying the bridge between ancient and medieval Hebrew classics and the secular language capable of expressing every aspect of contemporary life, including literary narrative. Thus, the award consolidated the status of the reborn Hebrew language even as it acknowledged Agnon, long appreciated as modern Hebrew's most important living writer. www.nobelprize.org/nobel_prizes/literature/laureates/1966/agnon-speech.html.

Avigal, Shosh. "Patterns and Trends in Israeli Drama and Theater, 1948 to Present." In Linda Ben-Zvi (ed.), *Theater in Israel*, pp. 9–50. Ann Arbor: University of Michigan Press, 1996. Avigal's comprehensive account of the prominent themes in Israeli drama presents evolving trends in Hebrew dramaturgy and staging as well as in the nature of the theater establishment.

Biale, David. "A Journey between Worlds: East European Jewish Culture from the Partitions of Poland to the Holocaust." In David Biale (ed.), *Cultures of the Jews: A New History*, pp. 799–860. New York: Schocken Books, 2002. Biale examines Zionism and other Jewish cultural and collective responses to the vicissitudes caused by emancipation, war, and revolution in the nineteenth century with attention to influential literary voices of the period.

Hirschfeld, Ariel. "Locus and Language: Hebrew Culture in Israel, 1890–1990." In David Biale (ed.), *Cultures of the Jews: A New History*, pp. 1011–1060. New York: Schocken Books, 2002. One of the strengths of this comprehensive account is its painstaking attention to how modern Zionist culture was of Ashkenazic fashioning. The new state was far more diverse than its earliest ideologues acknowledged, and the ensuing tensions between diverse cultural contact zones led to the rich Israeli tapestry of European, North African, and Middle Eastern identities, cultural forms, and resultant aesthetic expressions.

Peleg, Yaron. "Writing the Land: Writing and Territory in Modern Hebrew Literature." *Journal of Modern Jewish Studies* 12:2 (2013), 297–312. This is a critically imaginative exploration of the Hebrew language-land-ideology nexus in three distinct generations of writers: S. Yizhar, Amos Oz, and Orly Castel-Bloom.

Rovner, Adam. "Literature, Hebrew: Israeli Fiction." In Judith R. Baskin, (ed.), *The Cambridge Dictionary of Judaism and Jewish Culture*, pp. 381–384. New York: Cambridge University Press, 2011. A worthy condensed survey juxtaposing the vicissitudes of the state of Israel in relation to its literary milestones from the 1940s to the first years of the twenty-first century.

Scholem, Gershom. "On Our Language: A Confession." Letter to Franz Rosenzweig. December 26, 1926. Scholem wrote his reflections soon after the "language war" in Palestine had been waged and won, a time when Hebrew was already the accepted language of instruction at the Hebrew University and other institutions. Today his argument about the unpredictable dangers of centuries of religious tradition embedded in new secular contexts seems prophetic to many. www.jstor.org/stable/25618601?seq=1.

Szobel, Ilana. *A Poetics of Trauma: The Work of Dahlia Ravikovitch*. Waltham, MA: Brandeis University Press, 2013. Groundbreaking study (and the first of its kind in English) of various dimensions of the renowned Israeli poet, peace activist, and 1998 Israel Prize laureate Dahlia Ravikovitch. Szobel presents a richly theoretical as well as biographically grounded discussion of the poetics of trauma and the politics of victimhood, ultimately illuminating the interconnectedness of Ravikovitch's private-poetic subjectivity and Israeli national identity.

Urian, Dan. "Representations of War in Israeli Drama and Theatre." In Rachel S. Harris and Ranen Omer-Sherman (eds.), *Narratives of Dissent: War in Contemporary Israeli Arts and Culture*, pp. 281–299. Detroit, MI: Wayne State University Press, 2012. A survey of some of Israel's most sweeping ideological, social, and political influences on Hebrew drama from the 1940s to the present, the essay devotes special attention to how a plethora of Arab characters and the presence of the Palestinian narrative itself utterly transformed the Israeli stage beginning in the 1980s. Urian also focuses on the increasing tendency of Israeli dramatists to portray wars as deranged, hallucinatory realities, notably devoid of any sense or tangible mission.

GLOSSARY TERMS

Ahad Ha'am
Aliya: First Aliya; Second Aliya; Third Aliya
Canaanite movement
Haskalah
Intifada al-Aqsa (Second Intifada)
War: Six-Day War (June 1967 War); Yom Kippur War (1973 War)
Yishuv

Ranen Omer-Sherman is the Jewish Heritage Fund for Excellence Endowed Chair at the University of Louisville. He is the author of *Diaspora and Zionism in Jewish American Literature*; *Israel in Exile: Jewish Writing and the Desert*; *Imagining the Kibbutz: Visions of Utopia in Literature and Film*; and (with Rachel S. Harris) *Narratives of Dissent: War in Contemporary Israeli Arts and Culture*.

GLOSSARY

CAROL TROEN

This glossary elaborates on a selection of essential concepts and names from the essays. Items are listed alphabetically but are explained under category headings where we thought readers would find groupings such as **American Jewish Organizations, Arab Leaders, Israeli Political Leaders**, and **U.N. Resolutions** useful.

Some items are commonly called by different names. For example, the Six-Day War is also referred to as the 1967 War, the June 1967 War, and occasionally just 1967. We list such items with their various names and occasionally variant spellings of transliterations.

The Timeline (page 422) organizes the items from two categories, **Wars and Armed Conflicts** and **Peace Process and Peace Agreements**, to make the one-hundred-year span of the conflict and efforts to resolve it visible at a glance.

Abu Ala (Ahmed Querie). See under **Arab Leaders**

Abu Mazen (Mahmoud Abbas). See under **Arab Leaders**

Adenauer, Konrad (1876–1967) Konrad Adenauer served from 1949 to 1963 as the first chancellor of Germany (West Germany) after World War II. He negotiated the Jewish material claims for reparations from Germany, agreed to in 1952, and held a historic meeting in the United States in 1960 with David Ben-Gurion, then prime minister of Israel. Formal diplomatic ties between Israel and Germany were only established in 1965. See also **Reparations**

Agudat Yisrael (the Union of Israel). See under **Israeli Political Parties**

Ahad Ha'am (1856–1927) (One of the People) Born Asher Ginsburg near Kiev in the Ukraine, Ahad Ha'am opposed Herzl's Political Zionism with a vision of Jewish cultural and linguistic renewal. He called for recasting Jewish identity through a renewed secular Hebrew language and envisioned a national homeland that would be a cultural, ethical, and spiritual center of Jewish life. (See extended treatment in chapter 3, and discussion in 10, 14, and 15.)

AIPAC (American Israel Public Affairs Committee). See under **American Jewish Organizations**

Al-Aqsa Mosque; Temple Mount, Haram al-Sharif, the Noble Sanctuary; and the Dome of the Rock
- **The Al-Aqsa Mosque** of Omar ("the Farthest Mosque"), which has a silver dome, is located in the area called Haram al-Sharif (Arabic: the Noble Sanctuary) by Muslims and Har Habayit (Hebrew: the Temple Mount) by Jews. The mosque is under the protection of the Hashemite king of Jordan, and together

with the surrounding area it is administered as a Jordanian- and Palestinian-led Islamic *waqf* (religious benevolence), held in trust in perpetuity.

- **Haram al-Sharif** (the Noble Sanctuary), also called Har Habayit (the Temple Mount) This area, surrounded by a wall, is located in the southeast corner of the Old City of Jerusalem and includes more than five and a half acres. According to the Jewish tradition, this was the site of Solomon's Temple (the First Temple) some three thousand years ago and the remains of the Second Temple, including the Holy of Holies. Both Jews and Muslims identify this site with Mount Moriah, the place where Abraham came to sacrifice his son (Isaac or Ishmael, depending on the tradition).
- **The Dome of the Rock** with its golden dome is a Muslim shrine built over the stone from which the Prophet Muhammad is believed to have ascended to heaven.

Aliya Literally "going up" or "ascent," this Hebrew term refers to immigration to Israel.
- **First Aliya (1882–1903)** Mainly from Eastern Europe and fleeing pogroms but also from Yemen, in all around thirty-five thousand immigrants made up the First Aliya. About half remained in Ottoman Palestine, establishing small rural settlements of independent farmers called moshavot. (See chapter 4.)
- **Second Aliya (1904–1914)** Of some forty thousand young idealists from Eastern Europe who made up the Second Aliya, about half remained. They set the tone for the nascent state, reviving Hebrew, initiating collective settlement experiments that became the kibbutz and *moshav*, and setting up organizational structures that underlay the Yishuv. (See chapter 4.)
- **Third Aliya (1919–1923)** Like their predecessors, most of the forty thousand young *halutzim* or pioneers of the Third Aliya were fleeing anti-Semitism. Most remained in then Mandatory Palestine, encouraged by the Balfour Declaration (1917) to plan for and begin creating the infrastructure for the Jewish national homeland.
- **Fourth Aliya (1924–1929)** Anti-Semitic policies, economic hardship, and legislation that blocked immigration to the United States brought the eighty-two thousand mostly middle-class Jews of the Fourth Aliya to Palestine's cities, chiefly to the new Tel Aviv. Around 70 percent of them remained.
- **Fifth Aliya (1929–1939)** Over this ten-year period some 250,000 Jews came, 174,000 arriving between 1933 and 1936. Many of these immigrants were professionals who were fleeing anti-Semitism in Nazi Germany after 1933 and in Eastern Europe.
- **the Great Aliya, Mass Aliya (1948–1951)** In the three and a half years following the Declaration of Independence in May 1948, Israel absorbed nearly 690,000 immigrants, most of them Holocaust survivors from Europe and Jewish refugees from Arab countries. The Great Aliya more than doubled Israel's population.
- **Operation Magic Carpet** Between June 1949 and September 1950, close to fifty thousand Yemenite and other Jews were airlifted to the new State of Israel after making the arduous trek to Aden, then held by the British. The secret operation was coordinated by the Joint Distribution Committee and the Jewish Agency.

- **Operation Moses (November 1984–January 1985)** During a six-week period, around seven thousand Ethiopian Jews were flown to Israel in a covert operation before news of the mission leaked and Arab states pressured Sudan to close the borders. Almost fifteen thousand remained behind, separated from family members.
- **Operation Solomon** Beginning May 24, 1991, over a thirty-six-hour period, 14,324 Ethiopian Jews were flown to Israel in an overt rescue mission after rebel forces took control of Addis Ababa.

al-Qaeda, al-Qāʻida . See under **Palestinian and Arab Movements and Organizations**

American Council for Judaism. See under **American Jewish Organizations**

American Jewish Committee. See under **American Jewish Organizations**

American Jewish Conference. See under **American Jewish Organizations**

Americans for Peace Now. See under **American Jewish Organizations**

American Jewish Organizations (See chapter 10 for an extended discussion of the developing relationship between American Jews and Palestine/Israel.)
- **AIPAC (American Israel Public Affairs Committee)** Established in 1954, AIPAC is a bipartisan pro-Israel lobby whose self-defined purpose "is to strengthen, protect and promote the U.S.-Israel relationship in ways that enhance the security of Israel and the United States."
- **American Council for Judaism** Founded in 1942 by a group of Reform rabbis, this anti-Zionist organization held that Jews were members of a religion, not a nation, and opposed the establishment of the State.
- **American Jewish Committee (AJC)** Established by Louis Marshall in 1906, this Jewish ethnic advocacy organization acts in support of the Jewish people and Israel.
- **American Jewish Conference** Convened in 1943 and dissolved in 1949, the conference included representatives of thirty-two American Jewish organizations in an unsuccessful effort to unify responses to Nazi annihilation of European Jewry and Zionist calls for establishing a Jewish state.
- **Americans for Peace Now (APN)**, established in 1978, identifies itself as the sister organization of the Israeli peace movement's Shalom Achshav. Its mission is "to educate and persuade the American public and its leadership to support and adopt policies" leading to comprehensive peace based on a two-state solution.
- **Conference of Presidents of Major American Jewish Organizations (Presidents Conference)** was organized in 1955 to create a unified voice and action on behalf of American support for Israel. It seeks to develop consensus for collective action on relevant issues.
- **Hadassah Women's Zionist Organization of America** Founded as "Daughters of Zion, Hadassah Chapter" in 1912 by Henrietta Szold to provide for

health and social welfare for the Yishuv, the organization adopted its present name in 1914 with a mandate "to promote Jewish institutions and enterprises in Palestine and to foster Zionist ideals in America." Today Hadassah's two major medical centers and teaching hospitals at Mount Scopus and Ein Karem in Jerusalem provide care for Jews and Arabs from Israel and neighboring states in the Middle East.

- **HIAS (Hebrew Immigrant Aid Society)** was organized in the late nineteenth century to assist Jewish refugees fleeing pogroms in Russia and Eastern Europe. Its work in resettlement of Jewish refugees has been extended in the twenty-first century to helping non-Jewish refugees whose lives are at risk as a result of violent conflicts, most recently in Syria.
- **Joint Distribution Committee (JDC), also known as the Joint and the American Joint Distribution Committee,** was founded in 1914 after the outbreak of World War I. Its initial aim was to collect and distribute funds to help the Jews of Palestine who were suffering under Ottoman rule, and it soon turned its efforts to Eastern European Jews caught in the upheaval of the Russian Revolution and anti-Semitic attacks in Russia and Poland. During the Holocaust the JDC was instrumental in getting thousands of German and Austrian Jews out of Europe, and its rescue, relief, and social service programs continue to impact the well-being and welfare of Jews in Israel and throughout the world.
- **J Street** is a nonprofit liberal advocacy group incorporated in 2007 that supports American diplomatic efforts leading to a peaceful resolution of conflict between Israel, Palestinians, and Arab states.
- **National Council of Young Israel** was established in New York in 1912 to bridge Jewish tradition and Americanism for young first-generation American Jews. Today called Young Israel, it includes 146 Orthodox congregations in the United States and more than 50 in Israel. Its stated mission is to make the traditional community synagogue more central to Jewish communal life.
- **New Jewish Agenda** Founded in 1980 and disbanded in 1992, the organization gave voice to progressive values in an inclusive Jewish context, and their Jewish activism extended from supporting a wide-ranging agenda from feminism and gay and lesbian equality and the Labor movement to peaceful coexistences between Israel and the Palestinians and demilitarization and an end to the nuclear arms race.
- **UJA (United Jewish Appeal)** Formed in 1939 to coordinate fund-raising in support of European Jews, UJA became the largest voluntary philanthropy in Jewish history. In 1999 it merged with the Council of Jewish Federations (CJF) and United Israel Appeal (UIA) when the three incorporated as United Jewish Communities.
- **Zionist Organization of America (ZOA)** Initially a Federation of American Zionists convened in 1898 by Richard Gottheil, who had attended the Zionist Congress in Europe, groups like Young Judea (1907) and Hadassah (1912) merged in 1918 into the ZOA and elected Louis Brandeis honorary president and Julian Mack president. Its influence diminished after the establishment of Israel and increased among Jews on the right as it voiced criticism of the peace process and campaigned unsuccessfully against Israel's disengagement from Gaza.

Arab-Israeli Interstate War, Arab-Israeli War. See under **Wars and Armed Conflicts**

Arab Leaders
- **Abu Ala (Ahmed Querie) (b. 1937)** Born in Abu Dis near Jerusalem in Mandatory Palestine, Querie was prime minister of the Palestinian National Authority (PA) from 2003 through January 2006, when the Fatah party was defeated by Hamas in parliamentary elections. He played a key role in negotiating the Oslo Accords and in 2000 was part of the team that negotiated with Ehud Barak at Camp David.
- **Abu Mazen (Mahmoud Abbas) (b. 1935)** Born in Safed, Abbas left Palestine for Syria during the 1948 War. He was recruited to Fatah by Yasser Arafat in 1961, and only returned to the Territories in 1995. Regarded as a proponent of peace with Israel, Abbas signed the 1993 peace accord and the 1995 Interim Agreement for the Palestine Liberation Organization (PLO). Named the first prime minister of the Palestinian Authority (PA) in 2003, Arafat undermined his authority, and he resigned after four months as prime minster. Abbas has been chairman of the PLO since 2004, and following Arafat's death (2004) he was elected president of the PA in 2005. He continues to serve in both roles as of November 2016.
- **Arafat, Yasser (1929-2004)** Born in Cairo, Egypt, Arafat was a founder and later chairman of Fatah (1968-2004), which after the 1967 War emerged as the most powerful faction of the Palestine Liberation Organization (PLO). Arafat advocated and directed armed struggle against Israel. He was PLO chairman from 1969 and elected president of the Palestinian Authority (PA) in 1996 elections that followed the Oslo Accords, in which he participated along with Israeli prime minister Yitzchak Rabin and for which he was awarded a Nobel Prize. Arafat held both positions until his death.
- **Ashrawi, Hanan (b. 1946)** Born in Nablus, in Mandatory Palestine, Ashrawi is an activist and professor of English and comparative literature. She established the English Department at Birzeit University and was a participant and official PLO spokesperson at the 1991–1992 Madrid Conference and through the 1993 Oslo Accords. In 1998 she founded MIFTAH, the Palestinian Initiative for the Promotion of Global Dialogue and Democracy, and still heads the organization based in Jerusalem. The Third Way, an alternative party to Fatah and Hamas she helped form, garnered little support in the 2006 Palestinian elections.
- **Assad, Hafez al (1930–2000)** Alawite president of Syria from the Ba'th party from 1971 to 2000, Assad was Syria's minister of defense during the 1967 War when Israel conquered the Golan Heights. His attempt to win it back in a joint surprise attack with Egypt during the Yom Kippur 1973 War was unsuccessful. Assad was supported by the Soviets and was known for his ruthless suppression of dissent, as when some twenty thousand individuals were killed to end the rebellion of the Muslim Brotherhood in Hamah in 1982.
- **Husseini, Haj Amin al-, (Mufti Ḥājj Amīn al-Ḥusaynī, Husseini Muhammad Amin al-) (1893–1974)** Born in Jerusalem, Al-Husseini was a Palestinian nationalist appointed by Herbert Samuel in 1921 as Mufti and later Grand

Mufti of Jerusalem, a title given Islamic scholars whose learning gives them authority to issue a *fatwa*, or religious ruling. Samuel, high commissioner of Palestine during the British Mandate, forgave al Husseini's ten-year prison sentence for instigating the 1920 riot in Jerusalem against Zionist settlement. Despite his promise to maintain order, however, the Mufti was instrumental in the bloody 1929 and 1936 attacks on Jewish settlements, and his position was revoked in 1936. His efforts to mobilize Muslim support for Nazi Germany during World War II called for extending the policy of annihilating Jews to the Arab world, and when he met with Nazi leadership in 1941, Hitler assured him of German intentions to destroy the Jewish element residing in the Arab sphere. This explains why al Husseini's name links Palestinian nationalism, anti-Zionism, and anti-Semitism.

- **Husseini al-, Faisal (Faisal Abdel Qader al-Husseini) (1940–2001)** Born in Baghdad, Iraq, Faisal al-Husseini was a relative of the former Grand Mufti of Jerusalem, Haj Muhammad Amin al Husseini. After working for the PLO in 1964–1965 he joined the Palestine Liberation Army in 1967, was active in the First Intifada, and headed the Palestinian delegation to the 1991 Madrid Peace Conference.

- **King Hussein, (Hussein, King of Jordan, Hussein bin Talal) (1935–1999)** Born in Amman, Jordan, a direct descendant of the Prophet Muhammad (fortieth generation), Hussein became king of the Hashemite Kingdom of Jordan in 1952 following the assassination of his grandfather, King Abdullah, in 1951. He called for resolving conflicts between Israel and Arabs and among Arab states, helped draft UNSC Resolution 242 following the 1967 War supporting land for peace, and participated in the Madrid Peace Conference (1991), eventually signing a peace treaty with Israel in 1994.

- **Nasrallah, Hassan (b. 1960)** Born in Lebanon and a commander in the First Lebanon War (1982), Nasrallah has been secretary-general of Hezbollah since 1992, when the IDF assassinated his predecessor, Abbas-al-Musawi. Under Nasrallah, Hezbollah has acquired long-range missiles and fired at Israeli targets in the north of Israel, including Haifa. Nasrallah was credited with Israel's unilateral pullback from southern Lebanon but blamed for the 2006 Lebanon War. The war was ignited when Hezbollah crossed into Israel, killing three soldiers and kidnapping two, followed by Israeli bombardment of Beirut.

- **Nasser, Gamal Abdel (1918–1970)** Born in Egypt, Nasser was instrumental in the 1952 coup that deposed King Farouk I. He secretly ran Egypt until he named himself prime minister following a 1954 assassination attempt instigated by the Muslim Brotherhood. Nasser refused to recognize Israel, advocated pan-Arabism, and in 1958, joined by Syria, changed the name of Egypt to the United Arab Republic. With Soviet support he built the Aswan High Dam (1968).

- **Sadat, Anwar (1918–1981)** Born in Egypt, Sadat is remembered in Israel and the West for his courageous and path-breaking visit to Jerusalem in 1977 and speech before the Knesset calling for peace between Egypt and Israel. Vice President Anwar Sadat became president of Egypt after the death of President Gamal Abdel Nasser in 1970. He repealed some of the repressive measures put in place by Nasser, abandoned pan-Arabism, and focused instead on Egypt's needs, changing its name to the Arab Republic of Egypt. Sadat led Egypt in the surprise attack on Israel of the 1973 Yom Kippur War, hoping to win back the Sinai Peninsula conquered by Israel in the 1967 War. Later, he initiated moves to resolve the conflict including rapprochement with the United States and a break with the Soviets, and disengagement agreements with Israel that ultimately led to the Egypt-Israel Peace Treaty/Camp David Accords in 1978. Sadat served as president from 1970 until his assassination at the hands of an Islamist group in 1981.

Arafat, Yasser. See under **Arab Leaders**

Ashrawi, Hanan. See under **Arab Leaders**

Assad, Hafez al-. See under **Arab Leaders**

Balfour Declaration. See under **Pre-State Palestine**

Bandung Conference (1955) This meeting of twenty-nine newly independent Asian and African countries excluded Israel after the Arab states threatened to boycott. Intended to unify and ensure cooperation and peaceful coexistence, the conference condemned colonialism in all of its manifestations, thus implicitly condemning the Soviet Union along with the West, and adopted a ten-point declaration. However, unity was short-lived while the anti-Israel bias continued. In 2015, organizers of the sixtieth anniversary of the conference announced that all UN-recognized Asian and African countries had been invited to attend except Israel, and on the last day of the conference issued a declaration linking anticolonialism with justice for Palestine.

Barak, Ehud. See under **Israeli Political Leaders**

Basic Laws Rather than an American-style constitution, Israel has drafted Basic Laws. This legislation constitutes the values and norms of the State and defines the role and authority of government institutions and their relationships to Israel's people. (See chapter 9.)
- **Human Dignity and Liberty** (1992) Enacted by the twelfth Knesset to ensure Israel's values as a Jewish and democratic state, this Basic Law aims to preserve and protect the life, body, and dignity, property, liberty, and privacy rights of all persons and is binding on all governmental authorities.

Begin, Menachem. See under **Israeli Political Leaders**

Beilin, Yossi. See under **Israeli Political Leaders**

Ben-Gurion, David. See under **Israeli Political Leaders**

Betar. See under **Zionist (Youth) Organizations (Pre-State/Yishuv)**

Biltmore Program (1942) Issued jointly by Zionist and non-Zionist organizations attending the Extraordinary Zionist Conference held in New York because of World War II, the Biltmore Program demanded an end to restrictions on Jewish immigration to Palestine, which would serve as "a Jewish Commonwealth." As stated in article 6, "The Conference calls for the fulfillment of the original purpose of the Balfour declaration and the Mandate which recognizing 'the historical connection of the Jewish people with Palestine' was to afford them the opportunity, as stated by President Wilson, to found there a Jewish Commonwealth. The Conference affirms its unalterable rejection of the White Paper of May 1939 and denies its moral or legal validity." This was the first time non-Zionist organizations joined with Zionist groups in urging action on behalf of the Zionist cause.

Bilu. See under **Zionist (Youth) Organizations (Pre-State/Yishuv)**

Birthright Israel (Hebrew: Taglit, meaning "Discovery") was initially a philanthropic project aimed at creating experiential links between young Jews in the Diaspora and Israel. Owing to its success, the originators formed the Birthright Israel Foundation, which partners with the Israeli government, the Jewish Federation of North America, the Jewish Agency for Israel, and Keren Hayesod, and which from its founding in 1999 through 2016 has brought over five hundred thousand young Jewish adults from Jewish communities all over the world to Israel, where they spend ten days exploring Israel and their own Jewish identity along with Israeli counterparts.

B'nai B'rith International declares that it has "advocated for global Jewry and championed the cause of human rights since 1843." It is actively engaged in supporting Jewish continuity and the state of Israel, and in fighting anti-Semitism.

British Mandate for Palestine. See under **Pre-State Palestine**

Camp David Negotiations. See under **Peace Process and Peace Agreements**

Camp David Summit. See under **Peace Process and Peace Agreements**

Canaanite movement "Canaanism" was a literary, political and philosophical movement, made up primarily of Jews who had been associated with Revisionist Zionism in 1940s Mandatory Palestine and later among influential intellectuals in 1950s Israel such as Uri Avnery, Amost Kenan, and Benjamin Tammuz. They were deeply critical of mainstream Zionism and its particularistic view of Jewish nationalism, and the kinship they imagined among the ancient Hebrews (and themselves) and other indigenous inhabitants of Canaan led to a vision of a pan-Hebrew Middle East based on linguistic and geographic, not biological, religious, or racial identity, that included the Arabs.

Chabad Known also as Lubavitch, Chabad is the acronym for the Hebrew "Cho-chmah, Binah, Da'at" (Wisdom, Understanding, Knowledge), and is an Or-thodox Hasidic movement known for outreach programs established all over the world.

Chief Rabbinate The Chief Rabbinate of Israel consists of an Ashkenazi and a Sephardi Chief Rabbi, each elected for a ten-year term. The Chief Rabbinate is the head religious and spiritual authority for the Jewish people in Israel and the legal authority regarding such matters as marriage, divorce, burial, con-version, and kosher certification.

Clinton Parameters. See under **Peace Process and Peace Agreements**

Columbus Platform (1937) In significant measure a response to the alarming spread of virulent anti-Semitism in Europe, the Reform movement adopted the revolutionary Columbus Platform and its new ideological guidelines that "embraced Jewish peoplehood and leaned toward support of political Zionism."

Conference of Presidents of Major Jewish Organizations. See under **American Jewish Organizations**

Cultural Zionism. See under **Zionism**

Declaration of Independence of the State of Israel (May 14, 1948) Only 650 words long and written calligraphically on parchment, the scroll begins with a detailed historical overview of Jewish history from biblical times that includes mention of the Zionist Congress, the Balfour Declaration, and the Mandate that "gave international force to the historical connection between the Jewish people and the land of Israel and the right of the Jewish people to establish anew its national home." It concludes with the Holocaust and "the renewal of the Jewish state in the Land of Israel . . . [as] the homeland to every Jew" and the Jewish record in building up Eretz Yisrael.

The Declaration itself, in the eleventh paragraph, comes in the middle of the scroll. In larger, darker letters it proclaims the new State as "the State of Israel." This is followed by a delineation of how the State is to be governed, its policy of open Jewish immigration, and its commitment to "ensure complete equality of social and political rights to all its inhabitants irrespective of re-ligion, race or sex." Moreover, it promises to "guarantee freedom of religion conscience, language, education and culture . . . and to safeguard the Holy Places of all religions." In its last paragraphs, it calls for cooperation with the new State by the United Nations and the Jewish Diaspora, and appeals "in the very midst of the onslaught launched against us now for months—to the Arab inhabitants of the State of Israel to preserve peace and participate in the upbuilding of the State on the basis of full and equal citizenship and due rep-resentation in all the provisional and permanent institutions." It was still in draft form, edited and voted on shortly before, when David Ben-Gurion, then chairman of the Jewish Agency for Palestine and of the Provisional Council of the new state, read out the text declaring that a Jewish state in Palestine would come into effect with the end of the British Mandate for Palestine at midnight that day, May 14, 1948.

In the little notebook where he recorded his diary he wrote: "One P.M. at the Council. We approved the text of the Declaration of Independence. At four o'clock in the afternoon, we declared independence. The nation was jubilant—and again I mourn in the midst of the rejoicing as I did on the 29th of November [the U.N. vote on partition that was followed by the outbreak of Arab attacks on Jews]." He ended this volume of his diary and began a new volume as if to signal that a new page in Jewish history had been inaugurated. (See chapter 9.)

Declaration of Principles, Oslo I Accords. See under **Peace Process and Peace Agreements**

Deicide Charge This refers to the belief that all Jews were, and continue to be, responsible for the killing of Jesus. In 1964 a Vatican declaration absolved Jews of the charge of deicide and acknowledged it as a source of anti-Semitism, and the charge is now abandoned by almost all Christian denominations.

Eban, Abba. See under **Israeli Political Leaders**

Egypt-Israel Peace Treaty, Israeli-Egyptian Peace Treaty. See under **Peace Process and Peace Agreements**

Eichmann, Adolph (1906–1962) A top Nazi officer and commander of the Gestapo's section for Jewish affairs, Eichmann planned in detail how to deport millions of Jews to extermination camps and how to confiscate their property. He was captured in Argentina by Israeli agents in 1960 and brought to Israel where survivors and resistance fighters testified at his public trial in Jerusalem. This public confrontation not only brought the extent of Nazi atrocities to international attention but also marked a change in the way the experiences of the survivors and trauma of the Holocaust were apprehended, struggled with, and written about in Israel. (See chapter 15.)

Emancipation Jewish emancipation was a call to put an end to limitations and disabilities applied specifically to Jews, to recognize them as equal citizens, and to formally include them in the rights and obligations of citizenship. It originated with eighteenth-century utopian political and social ideas, and the pace and manner of implementation varied with locality.

Etzel. See under **Militias (pre-State)**

Exodus 1947 The story of the *Exodus* is emblematic of British severity in restricting the immigration of European refugees to Palestine and of the plight of the illegal Jewish immigrants during the Holocaust who were barred from other ports of refuge such as the United States. Defying the British refusal to allow immigration to Palestine, *Exodus 1947* sailed for Palestine on July 11, 1947, with 4,515 Jewish refugees on board. The British rammed the ship near the coast of Palestine and deported the immigrants to southern France and then Germany, where they refused to disembark. World opinion was so outraged that the British revised their policy, sending these and future illegal immigrants to Cyprus, where they remained in detention camps until Israel was established.

Fatah. See under **Palestinian and Arab Movements and Organizations**

fedayeen. See under **Palestinian and Arab Movements and Organizations**

Gaza Disengagement. See under **Peace Process and Peace Agreements**

General Zionism. See under **Zionism**

Geneva Conference. See under **Peace Process and Peace Agreements**

Golan Heights, the Golan, the Heights Captured by the IDF from Syria during the 1967 War, the Heights are a basalt plateau that overlooks the Hula Valley and the Sea of Galilee. The Golan has strategic importance, serving the Syrians as a convenient point from which to fire at Israeli settlements below. The Syrians tried but failed to recapture the Heights in the 1973 War, and in 1981 the Golan Heights Law imposed Israeli law and administration on the territory. Three Israeli governments under Rabin, Barak, and Olmert were willing to explore exchanging "land for peace" with Syria's President Assad, but these efforts were rebuffed and abandoned.

Green Line refers to the borders of Israel as they were between 1949 and the 1967 War. Since no peace agreement was reached following the 1948 War of Independence, an Armistice Agreement set "lines" to separate the armies of the warring parties: Israel, Syria, Lebanon, Jordan, and Egypt. References to "this side" or "that side" of the Green Line are used to designate the post-1967 territories or West Bank as opposed to the area of the State up to 1967.

Gush Emunim (Bloc of the Faithful), a movement of Religious Zionists founded in 1974, following the teachings of Rabbi Tzvi Yehuda Kook, believed that according to the Torah, the territories captured by Israel in the 1967 and 1973 Wars had been granted by God to the Jewish people. This ideology is the basis for the insistence of many in the movement that Jews should be allowed to settle anywhere in the whole of the land of Israel.

Hadassah Women's Zionist Organization of America. See under **American Jewish Organizations**

Haganah. See under **Militias (pre-State)**

Hamas. See under **Palestinian and Arab Movements and Organizations**

Hapo'el Hatza'ir. See under **Zionist (Youth) Organizations (Pre-State/Yishuv)**

Haredim This is the name given to communities of religious Jews who, in opposition to the secularization invited by emancipation and the Enlightenment, reject modern culture and live separately, strictly adhering to Jewish religious law, or Halakha. Often referred to as Ultra-Orthodox in English, a term some object to as derogatory, the Hebrew term denotes those who serve the Divine with fervor and anxiety. Initially opposed to the Zionist project, *haredim* participate in the State's political life and in recent years are slowly taking advantage of carefully crafted educational options that will allow them some degree of integration and opportunities for work in fields such as law and computers.

Hashomer. See under **Militias (pre-State)**

Hashomer Hatza'ir. See under **Zionist (Youth) Organizations (Pre-State/ Yishuv)**

Haskalah (Jewish Enlightenment) In the context of the more general European Enlightenment, for approximately a century from the 1770s to the 1880s, the Haskalah movement induced Jews to partake of secular culture and learn European languages rather than limiting themselves to Yiddish. The movement, which began in Galicia and later spread to Eastern Europe, stimulated the revival of Hebrew language and gave rise to a rich literature in both Hebrew and Yiddish. Whereas especially Western European Jews frequently assimilated in response to their encounter with secular culture and the emancipation, the resurgence of European anti-Semitism eventually led many to see Zionism as the solution to the "Jewish problem."

Herzl, Theodor (1860–1904) The originator of Political Zionism, Herzl was an assimilated Austro-Hungarian journalist and playwright. His encounters with anti-Semitism in Vienna and later in Paris, where he reported on the Dreyfus trial, caused him to reject the idea that enlightenment secular education and assimilation or even conversion would solve the "Jewish problem" and allow Jews to be accepted as equal citizens in Europe. He convened the First Zionist Congress in Basel, Switzerland, in 1897, and began a movement demanding a Jewish national home for the Jewish people in Palestine. His novel *Altneuland* (1902) describes the near-utopian state he imagined founded on modern technology and science. His statement "If you will it, it isn't a fable" became a watchword of the Zionist movement.

Herzog, Chaim. See under **Israeli Political Leaders**

Hezbollah, Ḥizbollāh See under **Palestinian and Arab Movements and Organizations**

HIAS (Hebrew Immigrant Aid Society). See under **American Jewish Organizations**

Hibbat Zion, Hovevei Zion. See under **Zionist (Youth) Organizations (Pre-State/Yishuv)**

Histadrut Founded in 1920, with David Ben-Gurion elected as secretary in 1921, the Histadrut is a still powerful organization of labor unions established to ensure social and economic justice.

Hovevei Zion, Hibbat Zion. See under **Zionist (Youth) Organizations (Pre-State/Yishuv)**

Husseini al-, Faisal. See under **Arab Leaders**

Husseini, Haj Amin al-. See under **Arab Leaders**

International Conference at Annapolis. See under **Peace Process and Peace Agreements**

Intifada, First Intifada, Second Intifada or al-Aqsa Intifada. See under **Wars and Armed Conflicts**

Irgun. See under **Militias (pre-State)**

Israel-Egypt disengagement agreement. See under **Peace Process and Peace Agreements**

Israeli-Egyptian Peace Treaty, Egypt-Israel Peace Treaty. See under **Peace Process and Peace Agreements**

Israeli Political Leaders
- **Barak, Ehud (b. 1942)** Born at Kibbutz Mishmar Hasharon, Barak served as Chief of the General Staff of the IDF from 1991 to 1995, and in this capacity he implemented the first Oslo Accords (1993) and participated in negotiating the 1994 peace treaty with Jordan. He served as minister of internal affairs under Yitzchak Rabin and as minister of foreign affairs under Shimon Peres following Rabin's assassination. Elected to the Knesset (Labor) in 1996, Barak was prime minister from 1999 to 2001. He kept a campaign promise and unilaterally withdrew IDF forces from southern Lebanon in 2000. In that same year he and Yasser Arafat met at Camp David with US president Bill Clinton in an unsuccessful effort to negotiate terms for peace. Barak later served as defense and deputy prime minster from 2009 to 2013 under Prime Minister Benjamin Netanyahu.
- **Begin, Menachem (1913–1992)** Born in Brest-Litovsk, Poland, Begin became head of Betar Poland in 1938, and after fleeing Poland at the start of World War II he joined the Free Polish Army and eventually made his way to Palestine. A Revisionist Zionist who led the Irgun, one of several military groups

of the pre-State period, Begin was founder and leader of Herut and later the Likud. He was elected prime minister in 1977. Characterized as a hawk, he nevertheless entered into agreements with Egypt on Israeli withdrawal from Sinai and ultimately, on the basis of a return of territory, signed the 1979 peace treaty with Egypt. He resigned in 1983 in the wake of serious inflation and the negative outcomes of the 1982 Lebanon War.

- **Beilin, Yossi (b. 1948)** Born in Petach Tikva, Beilin is a statesman who began his engagement with politics as a spokesman for Labor following its defeat in the 1977 election. He held a variety of positions in Labor governments, contributing to the peace process as Shimon Peres's deputy minister of foreign affairs when he secretly initiated the Oslo Process that led to the 1993 Accords and the establishment of the Palestinian Authority in the West Bank and Gaza. At the 1994 General Assembly of Jewish Federations, Beilin proposed that the Jewish people should support a free trip to Israel as a gift granted every Jewish youth, an idea that some years later was launched as Birthright Israel. (See the extended discussion on Beilin's—and Israel's—relations with American Jewry in chapter 10.)

- **Ben-Gurion, David (1886–1973)** Born David Green (Grun) in Plonsk, Poland, Ben-Gurion came to Palestine in 1906 and spearheaded Labor Zionism's efforts to lay both the moral foundations and infrastructure for the Jewish state. A leader of Ahdut Ha'avoda, he helped establish the Histadrut (1920) and served as general secretary from 1921 to 1935, and he was chairman of the Jewish Agency's executive committee from 1935 to 1948. In this role Ben-Gurion declared Israel's independence in May 1948. Widely appreciated as a pragmatic, determined and decisive leader, he was elected prime minister in Israel's first national election in 1949 as the head of Mapai (Labor), and with the exception of 1954–1955, he was prime minister until 1963.

- **Dayan, Moshe (1915–1981)** Born at Degania Aleph, Israel's first kibbutz, Moshe Dayan was IDF chief of staff from 1953 to 1958, as a member of Mapai served as Ben-Gurion's minister of agriculture until 1964, and served as defense minister during the 1967 War. He was foreign minister in Menachem Begin's Likud government and instrumental in negotiating the Camp David Accords with Egypt.

- **Eban, Abba (1915–2002)** Born in South Africa and educated in England, Eban advocated for the Zionist cause before the UN Special Committee on Palestine in 1947. As Israel's permanent representative to the UN and ambassador to the United States, he was an eloquent spokesman on behalf of the State during its first decade, and as minister of foreign affairs from 1966 to 1974 he was influential in the debates that ultimately led to the UN Security Council passing Resolutions 242 and 338 following the June 1967 War and the 1973 Yom Kippur War, respectively.

- **Herzog, Chaim (1918–1997)** The son of Ireland's Chief Rabbi, Chaim Herzog was born in Belfast and emigrated to Mandatory Palestine in 1935. He was Israel's Permanent Representative to the UN from 1975 to 1978, and when the General Assembly passed Resolution 3379, equating Zionism with racism, Herzog firmly rejected the resolution, publicly tearing it up. He served two terms as Israel's sixth president, from 1983 to 1993.

- **Meir, Golda (Golda Meyerson) (1898–1978)** Born in Kiev, Ukraine, "Golda," as she was known, grew up in Milwaukee, Wisconsin; became a member of Poalei Zion; and as a Labor Zionist made *aliya* in 1921. She was elected Israel's fourth prime minister in 1969 and resigned in 1974 following serious criticism and a general loss of faith in the government for failure to foresee and prepare for the 1973 Yom Kippur War.
- **Netanyahu, Benjamin, Binyamin, "Bibi" (b. 1949)** The current prime minister of Israel and the first prime minister who was born in Israel after the establishment of the State, Netanyahu was born in Tel Aviv in 1949. He spent part of his childhood in the United States, returning to Israel to enlist in the IDF, and served as Israel's ambassador to the UN from 1984 to 1988. As leader of the Likud he has emphasized security and a free market economic policy. Netanyahu won the 1996 elections, serving as prime minister until 1999. He was reelected in 2009 and again in 2015 to his fourth term as prime minister.
- **Olmert, Ehud (b. 1945)** Born near Binyamina-Giv'at Olga, Olmert was elected mayor of Jerusalem from the Likud and served from 1993 to 2003. Asserting that he had been mistaken when he voted against the Camp David Accords and the return of the Sinai to Egypt, he joined Ariel Sharon when he left Likud to create the new party Kadima, pledging to withdraw IDF forces and settlements from Gaza. Olmert became caretaker prime minister after Sharon was incapacitated by a stroke, and prime minister following elections in 2006. Olmert favored the creation of a Palestinian State and participated in the 2007 Annapolis Conference but resigned in the wake of criticism of his handling of the Second Lebanon War and charges of corruption on which he was later convicted. He was replaced as prime minister by Benjamin Netanyahu in 2009.
- **Peres, Shimon (1923–2016)** Born in Vishniyeva, Belarus, Peres emigrated to Palestine with his family in 1934. During Israel's first decade, as director-general of the Ministry of Defense he helped forge Israel's relationship with France; negotiated its acquisition of arms, notably French Mirage III jet fighters; and established the nuclear reactor in Dimona. Nonetheless, he played a crucial role in negotiating the Oslo Accords, for which he was awarded the Nobel Peace Prize (1994) along with Yitzchak Rabin and Yasser Arafat. He twice served as prime minister and served as Israel's ninth President from 2007 to 2014.
- **Rabin, Yitzhak (1922–1995)** Born in Jerusalem during the Mandate, Rabin served in the Palmach before and during the 1948 War, and in 1962 he was appointed Chief of the General Staff. Following a highly successful military career, he was Israel's ambassador to the United States from 1968 to 1973 and in 1974 was the first native-born son to be elected prime minister. Leader of the Labor party, Rabin was defeated by Menachem Begin at the head of the Likud in the 1977 elections, in what is known as Hamahapach (the upheaval), when, for the first time since the establishment of the State, the Labor party was deposed. In his second term as prime minister (1992–1995), Rabin negotiated the 1993 Oslo Agreements with the Palestinian Liberation Organization; was instrumental in the Declaration of Principles that, in an historic move, he signed together with PLO leader Yasser Arafat; and in 1994, reached a peace treaty with Jordan. He was awarded a Nobel Peace Prize together with Shimon

Peres and Yasser Arafat for these achievements in 1994. Yitzchak Rabin was assassinated by a right-wing Jewish extremist at a peace rally in Tel Aviv in November 1995.

- **Shamir, Yitzhak (1915–2012)** Born in Ruzhany, Belarus, Shamir became a member of Betar at fourteen, and at twenty he left Poland for Palestine. A Revisionist Zionist, he initially was a member of Etzel and later joined the more militant Lehi in opposition to the British Mandatory powers. Elected a member of the Knesset for the Likud in 1973, he became Israel's seventh prime minister after the resignation of Menachem Begin in 1983, served as minister of foreign affairs in a Unity Government with Shimon Peres from 1984 to 1986, and from 1986 to 1992 he served once again as prime minister.
- **Sharon, Ariel (1928–2014)** Born in Kfar Malal, Sharon was known as a brilliant military strategist and field commander and fought in all of Israel's wars from 1948 through the 1973 Yom Kippur War. As minister of defense under Menachem Begin, he directed the 1982 Lebanon War. He was criticized for Israel's engagement in Lebanon and was held responsible for failing to prevent the massacre of Palestinians by Lebanese Phalangist militias at Sabra and Shatila, two refugee camps. After joining the Likud, he served in a variety of positions and led the party from 2001. Although Sharon strongly advocated Jewish settlement of the West Bank and Gaza following the 1967 War, as prime minister from 2002 to 2006 he left Likud to form Kadima (Forward) and, in the face of fierce opposition, carried out Israeli military and civilian disengagement from Gaza in 2005. Following a massive stroke in January 2006, Sharon remained in a coma for eight years until his death.
- **Weizmann, Chaim (1874–1952)** Born in Motal, a village near Pinsk in Russia, Weizmann was awarded a PhD in organic chemistry from the University of Fribourg in Switzerland and became a British citizen in 1910. An ardent Zionist, he was instrumental in persuading Lord Balfour to issue the famous 1917 declaration that bears his name. Weizmann was an effective advocate of a Jewish national homeland in Palestine and became president of the World Zionist Organization in 1920. He laid the foundation stone for the establishment of the Hebrew University in Jerusalem and the Institute of Science, later the Weizmann Institute in Rehovot, Palestine. Chaim Weizmann was Israel's first president for four years, from 1948 until his death.
- **Yosef, Ovadia (1920–2013)** Born in Baghdad, Iraq, Ovadia Yosef emigrated to Mandatory Palestine with his parents when he was four. An acknowledged religious authority who also showed flexibility, he served during a particularly difficult time as Chief Rabbi of Cairo, from 1947 to 1950. Ovadia Yosef was appointed Chief Rabbi of Tel Aviv in 1968 and served as Chief Sephardi Rabbi from 1973 to 1983. He was the greatly admired leader of the Shas party from its founding in 1983 until his death.

Israeli Political Parties
- **Agudat Yisrael** (the Union of Israel) was founded in Poland in 1912 as an organization of Ultra-Orthodox (Haredi) Jews who opposed Political Zionism. Despite being avowedly non-Zionist, Agudat Yisrael has participated in Israel's governments since the establishment of the State.

- **Kadima** (Forward) was formed in 2005 by Ariel Sharon, who resigned following major disagreement in the Likud over Israeli policy toward Gaza and the peace process more generally. Headed by Sharon and Tzipi Livni, Kadima favored unilateral Israeli disengagement from Gaza, including uprooting Israeli settlements, and a return to the Roadmap as a way of ending the conflict with the Palestinians. The party won the 2006 election headed by Ehud Olmert after Sharon suffered a major stroke, and it carried out the disengagement but was unable to finalize arrangements for peace before Olmert was forced to resign in 2008.
- **Labor** Since it was established in 1968 by a union of Mapai, Ahdut Ha'avoda, and Rafi, Labor has been Israel's major left-of-center party emphasizing social and economic needs and democratic values. It has operated under different names and with evolving ideologies, and its pragmatic approach to domestic issues and the conflict with the Arabs was voted a majority from Ben-Gurion in 1948 to 1977 when Menachem Begin was elected and the right-of-center Likud party came to power.
- **Likud (Consolidation)** Like Labor, Likud was initially a consolidation. It was founded by Menachem Begin, who united the right-wing Herut, which he led with the Liberal party and others in 1973 around a platform that emphasized social equality and Jewish culture and promised a free market economy in opposition to Labor's traditionally socialist leanings and greater government control. Likud heads Israel's present government under Benjamin Netanyahu and has formed the government six times beginning in 1977.
- **Yesh 'Atid (There Is a Future)** is a new centrist political party founded in 2012 by Yair Lapid.
- **Mapai** (acronym for Workers' Party of Eretz Yisrael) Founded in 1930 with a social democratic ideology, Mapai was the dominant party of Labor Zionism. It was instrumental in laying the social foundations of the Yishuv and later of social welfare in the State, and in assembling its first defense forces, Hashomer and the Haganah. Ben-Gurion was general secretary of Mapai from 1930 to 1953, and again from 1955 to 1963. In 1968 Mapai was subsumed by the Labor Party.
- **Mizrachi** A movement founded in 1902 in Vilnius, the name Mizrachi is an acronym for the Hebrew Merkaz Ruchani, or Spiritual Center. It became a Religious Zionist political party in Mandatory Palestine and in 1956 joined with Hapo'el Hamizrachi, a religious labor party, to form the National Religious Party. (See also **Religious Zionism; Zionism**)
- **Poalei Zion** (Laborers of Zion) Groups of Jewish Marxist-Zionist workers organized in the Diaspora around the start of the twentieth century. In Palestine, as a political party, Poalei Zion split into left and right factions. The right joined in with Ahdut Ha'avoda, the party led by Ben-Gurion that became Mapai, while the left joined Hashomer Hatza'ir and became Mapam.
- **Shas** (Shomrei Sfarad, Sephardi Guardians) is a Haredi political party founded in 1984 by Rabbi Ovadia Yosef to represent Mizrachi and Sephardi Jews, many of whom are modern orthodox or traditional, not necessarily Haredi. It appeals to voters on the basis of ethnicity and by providing community-based institutions and services.

J Street. See under **American Jewish Organizations**

Jewish Agency. See under **World Zionist Organizations**

Jewish National Fund (JNF). See under **World Zionist Organizations**

Jewish Question Although it appears the "question" was first called by this
  name in Great Britain in the mid-eighteenth century, debates on the Jewish
  Question took place in public discourse and publications across Western
  Europe in the context of the Enlightenment and emancipation, with proposals to deport the Jews, allow them to convert, encourage them to assimilate,
  or otherwise deal with their presence in society. By the 1880s, and especially in Germany, the initially more neutral question became increasingly
  anti-Semitic until Hitler proposed the infamous "final solution." Jews also
  debated the question of their identity and belonging and considered such
  "solutions" as conversion, assimilation, auto-emancipation, and Zionism.
  (See chapter 3.)

Joint Distribution Committee (JDC), the Joint, the American Joint Distribution Committee. See under **American Jewish Organizations**

Judea and Samaria. See under **West Bank, Judea and Samaria (Area C)**

Kadima. See under **Israeli Political Parties**

Kasztner, Rezso (1906–1957) Following the Nazi invasion of Hungary, Kasztner
  negotiated with Adolph Eichmann and paid a substantial ransom to send
  1,684 Jews from Budapest to Switzerland instead of Auschwitz. After coming to Israel, he became a spokesman for the Ministry of Trade and Industry.
  When a pamphlet by Malchiel Gruenwald accused him of collaborating with
  the Nazis and faulted him for choosing to save a few while so many other Jews
  were sent to their deaths, the Israeli government supported Kasztner and sued
  Gruenwald for libel. The judge in the trial, which lasted eighteen months until
  1955, found that Kasztner had "sold his soul to the devil," but Israel's Supreme
  Court overturned most of the rulings against him a year later. Kasztner was
  assassinated in 1957. The trial reflected the divisiveness of the Holocaust experience in Israeli politics.

Keren Hayesod. See under **World Zionist Organizations**

King Hussein, Hussein, King of Jordan, Hussein bin Talal. See under **Arab
  Leaders**

Labor. See under **Israeli Political Parties**

Labor Zionism. See under **Zionism**

Land Day (Yom al-Ard in Arabic) commemorates one of the first mass demonstrations by Palestinians opposed to Israeli policy, when in confrontations with the Israeli army and police, six Arab citizens were killed, about one hundred were wounded, and hundreds of others arrested. Land Day has been observed annually on March 30 since 1976, when Israeli Palestinian Arabs from north to south joined in a coordinated mass protest against the government's plan to expropriate close to five thousand acres of land in the vicinity of two Palestinian villages.

Law of Return (1950) (amended in 1954 and 1970) declares the right of any Jew who so wishes to become a citizen of the State so long as the Minister of Aliya does not have evidence that he or she has acted against the Jewish people or that he or she is a danger to the health or security of the State.

Lebanon Wars (First and Second). See under **Wars and Armed Conflicts**

Lehi. See under **Militias (pre-State)**

Liberal Judaism This is the British name for what in the United States is called Reform Judaism. See under **Reform Judaism**

Liberation Theology This movement, originating in Latin American Roman Catholicism in the twentieth century, is dedicated to actively addressing the immediate needs of poor parishioners. Its ideological repudiation of "sinful" socioeconomic arrangements leading to inequalities and call for political engagement have been used by Palestinian Christians to delegitimize the Zionist project. (See chapter 12.)

Likud. See under **Israeli Political Parties**

London understanding (aborted). See under **Peace Process and Peace Agreements**

Ma'abarot Intended to provide temporary dwellings for the refugees, many from Arab lands who were arriving in the new State in great numbers, these absorption camps typically consisted of hastily built tin shacks and sometimes tents, lacked adequate sanitation facilities, and by the end of 1951 housed over 220,000 new citizens in about 125 communities. (See **Great or Mass Aliya** under **Aliya**)

Madrid Peace Conference. See under **Peace Process and Peace Agreements**

Mamlachtiyut **(statism)** A governing principle in Ben-Gurion's vision that insisted on the centrality of the state, its responsibility to its citizenry as a whole, and its obligation to forge a moral community by unifying the people around dedication to a shared sense of purpose and shared values.

Mapai. See under **Israeli Political Parties**

Meir, Golda. See under **Israeli Political Leaders**

Militias (pre-State)
- **Etzel.** See **Irgun**
- **Haganah** (Defense) Organized in 1920, this initially loose association of local self-defense groups came to include most youth and adults from the rural
  settlements and significant numbers of city dwellers as well, when the British
  failed to protect the Jews of the Yishuv during the Arab riots of 1929. In secret
  defiance of the British, the Haganah trained members and officers, solicited
  and collected arms from abroad, and undertook underground production of
  arms to be used in defense of the Yishuv. Although during the Arab Revolt
  (1936–1939) members operated as a civilian militia under the British, the organization worked against British policy in supporting the immigration of
  Jewish refugees made illegal by the 1939 White Paper. On May 26, 1948, the
  Haganah was incorporated into the regular army of the new State, Zeva Haganah LeYisrael, the Israel Defense Force (IDF).
- **Hashomer** (The Watchman) was founded in 1909 by members of the Second
  Aliya who had come to Palestine following pogroms in Russia and were de-
  termined to be able to defend themselves and new Jewish settlements in the
  Lower Galilee. With never more than one hundred members, they settled in
  Tel Adashim (1913), Kfar Giladi (1916), and Tel Hai (1918). In 1920, the Haganah
  was established and Hashomer disbanded.
- **Irgun, Irgun Zva'i Leumi, or the acronym Etzel** (National Military Organization) Ideologically aligned with Revisionist Zionism, this organization was
  founded in 1937 following a split from the Haganah by those who objected to
  the Jewish Agency's policy of restraint in the face of Arab attacks, which had
  intensified during the 1936–1939 riots. After the outbreak of World War II,
  some members fought alongside the British and eventually formed the Jewish
  Brigade, while others, who saw the British as a major obstacle to Jewish settlement, broke off to form the more militant **Lehi**, the acronym for Lohamei
  Herut Yisrael (Yisrael Freedom Fighters). Both Etzel and Lehi attacked British
  military and government targets in Palestine, tactics opposed by the Labor
  Zionist leadership of the Yishuv. From 1943 Etzel was led by Menachem Begin,
  and the group disbanded after the State was declared.
- **Lehi.** See **Irgun**
- **Palmach** (acronym for Plugot Mahatz, or Strike Forces) Established in 1941
  and closely aligned with Labor Zionism, the Palmach was the elite unit of the
  Haganah, with over two thousand young men and women members (many
  from kibbutzim) by the time of the 1948 War. The Palmach was disbanded by
  David Ben-Gurion along with other militias in 1948 to create a unified State
  army, the IDF, but its lore remains deeply embedded in the collective memory
  of the State, and the organization is remembered not only for the courage,
  commitment, and dedication of its youthful members but for their camaraderie and mutual support.

Mizrachi. See under Israeli Political Parties

Muslim Brotherhood. See under Palestinian and Arab Movements and Organizations

Nakba, al-, War of Independence, 1948 War, Arab-Israeli War. See under Wars and Conflicts

Nasrallah, Hassan. See under Arab Leaders

Nasser, Gamal Abdel. See under Arab Leaders

National Council of Young Israel. See under American Jewish Organizations

Netanyahu, Benjamin, Binyamin, "Bibi." See under Israeli Political Leaders

New Jewish Agenda. See under American Jewish Organizations

New Zionist Organization. See under Revisionist Zionism

October 1973 War, Yom Kippur War. See under Wars and Armed Conflicts

Olmert, Ehud. See under Israeli Political Leaders

Operation Cast Lead. See under Wars and Armed Conflicts

Operation Magic Carpet. See under Aliya

Operation Moses. See under Aliya

Operation Pillar of Defense. See under Wars and Armed Conflicts

Operation Protective Edge. See under Wars and Armed Conflicts

Operation Solomon. See under Aliya

Oslo Peace Accords, Oslo I, Oslo, Declaration of Principles. See under Peace Process and Peace Agreements

Oslo II, Taba 1995, Israeli-Palestinian Interim Agreement on the West Bank and Gaza Strip. See under Peace Process and Peace Agreements

Ottoman Empire Originating with Turkish tribes in Anatolia in 1299, the empire reigned for over six hundred years, and at one time controlled much of southeastern Europe, western Asia, and North Africa, including the Middle East. Its alignment with Germany during World War I created hardships for the Yishuv, then under Ottoman rule. Partition of the empire according to terms set in the Treaty of Sèvres set out the new boundaries of territories in the Middle East, including Palestine, which was placed under British Mandate in 1922 when the Ottoman Empire officially came to an end.

Palestine Liberation Organization (PLO). See under **Palestinian and Arab Movements and Organizations**

Palestinian and Arab Movements and Organizations
- **al-Qāida, al-Qaeda** is a militant Sunni Islamist terrorist network founded in 1988 by Osama bin Laden that came to world public attention when it carried out the notorious attacks on the Twin Towers in Manhattan and other locations in the United States, now remembered as 9/11.
- **Fatah** Founded in 1964 by Yasser Arafat as the Palestinian National Liberation Movement in opposition to the PLO, Fatah is headed today by Palestinian Authority president Mahmoud Abbas (Abu Mazen) and is the PLO's major political faction.
- *fedayeen* (self-sacrificers) are Palestinian militants who from the early 1950s carried out raids across Israel's borders from Syria, Jordan, and Egypt, hitting both military and civilian targets.
- **Hamas** Founded in 1987 in conjunction with the First Intifada, Hamas is a Palestinian Sunni Islamic organization associated with Egypt's Muslim Brotherhood. According to the Hamas Charter (1988), it is the Islamic Resistance Movement, one of the wings of the Muslim Brotherhood in Palestine. Opposed to Fatah and the PLO, which are secular, Hamas defeated Fatah in parliamentary elections in 2006, winning a decisive majority. Their rivalry culminated in violence in 2007, when Hamas took over control of Gaza and forced the PLO leadership to retreat to the West Bank, which is now under the control of the Palestinian Authority (PA).
- **Hezbollah, Hezballah, Ḥizbollāh** (the Party of Allah) Hezbollah is a militant Islamist Shia political party and well-armed military organization that operates out of Lebanon and is supported by and allied with Iran.
- **Muslim Brotherhood** Founded in Egypt in 1928 to encourage an Islamic revival in response to the dissolution of the Ottoman Empire and the ban imposed on the Caliphate, this movement espouses terrorist methods in the name of jihad, a holy war, typically to bring territories under Muslim control by military means.
- **Palestine Liberation Organization (PLO)** Founded in 1964 under the leadership of Yasser Arafat to liberate Palestine through armed struggle, the PLO was endorsed by the 1974 Arab Summit and recognized by some 100 UN member nations as the "sole and legitimate representative of the Palestinian people." Because of its terrorist activities it was labeled a terrorist organization, and both the United States and Israel denied its authority until the United States brokered negotiations between Israel and the PLO at the 1991 Madrid Conference. In 1993 the PLO recognized Israel's right to exist and in accordance with UN Resolutions 242 and 338 rejected violence, while Israel accepted the PLO as the legitimate representative of the Palestinian people.

- **Palestine Authority (PA)** Following the 1993 Oslo Accords, the Palestinian (National) Authority became the interim governing body of the West Bank and Gaza Strip of a future autonomous Palestinian state (1994). The PA lost control of Gaza when Hamas defeated Fatah, the major PLO party, in the 2006 elections, and its leadership was forced to retreat to the West Bank, where it has authority over Areas A and B and shares responsibility for maintaining security with the Israel-governed Area C. (See also under **West Bank.**)
- **pan-Arabism** This ideological movement originated around World War I and was influenced by socialist and Marxist ideology. Associated with early Arab nationalism, it imagined an extraterritorial union of all Arab countries making up the "Arab world." Egyptian president Gamal Abdel Nasser became a strong proponent in the 1950s, and this led to renaming Egypt when he joined with Syria in 1958 to establish the United Arab Republic.

Palestine Authority (PA). See under **Palestinian and Arab Movements and Organizations**

Palmach. See under **Militias (pre-State)**

Pan-Arabism. See under **Palestinian and Arab Movements and Organizations**

Partition Plan. See under **Pre-State Palestine**

Peace Process and Peace Agreements The items in this set are listed alphabetically. A chronological view is provided by the Timeline (page 422) that includes both **Peace Process and Peace Agreements** and **Wars and Armed Conflicts.** (See chapter 6 for an extended discussion of the peace process.)
- **Camp David Negotiations and Accords (1978)** These accords between President Anwar Sadat of Egypt and Prime Minister Menachem Begin of Israel were facilitated by US president Jimmy Carter. After twelve days of negotiations at Camp David, they agreed on conditions for returning the Sinai territory that Israel had conquered during the 1967 War in exchange for peace with Egypt.
- **Camp David Summit (July 2000)** This summit took place July 11–24, 2000, when President Bill Clinton convened Ehud Barak, prime minister of Israel, and Yasser Arafat, Palestinian Authority chairman, to follow up on the Oslo Accords (1993) and proceed from an interim peace to a final peace settlement. No agreement was reached.
- **Clinton Parameters (December 2000)** Representatives of the Palestinian Authority, Israel, and the United States convened. President Clinton read aloud the remarks, outlining his understandings regarding the terms for a possible and fair peace agreement, at the White House; no printed copy was given to the parties.
- **Declaration of Principles, Oslo I Accords (1993)** A follow-up to the Madrid Conference (1991), the accords were negotiated in Oslo, Norway, and the declaration signed in 1993 in Washington, D.C. by Mahmoud Abbas (PLO)

and Shimon Peres (Israel) in the presence of President Clinton, PLO chairman Yasser Arafat, and Israeli prime minister Yitzchak Rabin. The principles follow from an agreement to end the Israel-Palestinian conflict and include specifications regarding the establishment of an interim Palestinian Self-Governing Authority; a council to be elected in a free political election by the Palestinian citizens of the West Bank and Gaza; and such details as arrangements for the elections, jurisdiction of the interim body, and provision for a transition to negotiations on a permanent settlement and security.

- **Gaza Disengagement (August 2005)** Israel implemented Prime Minister Ariel Sharon's plan by unilaterally withdrawing IDF forces from the entire Gaza Strip and dismantling all settlements, in addition to uprooting four settlements in North Samaria in the West Bank.
- **Geneva Conference (1973)** and an attempted **Geneva Conference (1977)** The 1973 conference in Geneva held under joint US and Soviet Union auspices was intended to produce direct negotiations for a comprehensive Middle East peace. In fact, it served as decoy for Egypt and Israel, who had been negotiating their post–1973 War disengagement, and the conference was adjourned a week after it began. Despite stated intentions, it never reconvened, and President Carter's efforts to resurrect it in 1977 were unsuccessful.
- **International Conference at Annapolis (2007)** US president George W. Bush in the presence of representatives of forty other countries, including the Quartet, urged Palestinian Authority president Mahmoud Abbas and Israeli prime minister Ehud Olmert to implement the Roadmap (2003).
- **Israel-Egypt disengagement agreement (1974)** Following the 1973 Yom Kippur War, US secretary of state Henry Kissinger helped broker an agreement between Israel and Egypt. It committed them to observe a cease-fire and specified the details for the initial disengagement of forces. While in the agreement both asserted this was not a peace treaty, they also stated that it was seen as a first step toward peace as provided in UN Security Council Resolution 338 and the framework of the Geneva Conference.
- **Israeli-Egyptian Peace Treaty, Egypt-Israel Peace Treaty (1979)** This historic treaty following President Sadat's visit to Jerusalem and negotiations leading to the 1978 Camp David Accords included mutual recognition, an end to the state of war that had existed since 1948, and access to the Suez Canal in exchange for Israeli withdrawal from the Sinai territory it had captured from Egypt.
- **London understanding (aborted) (1987)** This secret plan, signed in London by Prime Minister Shimon Peres and King Hussein of Jordan, intended for Israel to negotiate with a joint Jordanian-Palestinian delegation that did not include the PLO. The plan never materialized.
- **Madrid Peace Conference (1991)** Attended by delegations from Israel, Egypt, Syria, Lebanon, and a joint Palestinian-Jordanian delegation, the conference was an effort by President George H. W. Bush to engage the parties in direct negotiations of a comprehensive peace for the region. The comprehensive approach did not result in regional peace. However, secret talks between the Palestinians and Israelis in Oslo led to the 1993 Oslo Accords, and Israel and Jordan signed a peace treaty the following year, in 1994.

- Oslo I Accords, Oslo Peace Accords (1993). See **Declaration of Principles**
- **Oslo II, Taba 1995, Israeli-Palestinian Interim Agreement on the West Bank and Gaza Strip** Signed in Taba, Egypt, by Israeli prime minister Yitzchak Rabin and PLO chairman Yasser Arafat, Oslo II was intended to facilitate further negotiations leading to a comprehensive peace agreement.
- **Peace Treaty between Israel and Jordan (1994)** "The Treaty of Peace between the State of Israel and the Hashemite Kingdom of Jordan" was signed by Israeli prime minister Yitzchak Rabin and Jordanian prime minister Abdelsalam al-Majali in October 1994, near the Arava border crossing to Jordan.
- **Quartet (2002)** An initiative to support negotiations and bring an end to Arab-Israeli conflict, the Quartet was established in Madrid after the outbreak of the Second Intifada and includes the United Nations, the United States, the European Union, and Russia.
- **Roadmap (2003)** "A Performance-Based Roadmap to a Permanent Two-State Solution to the Israeli-Palestinian Conflict": "The U.S. State Department April 30 released the text of the 'roadmap' to a permanent solution . . . [that] specifies the steps for the two parties to take to reach a settlement, and a timeline for doing so, under the auspices of the Quartet—The United States, the European Union, the United Nations, and Russia."
- **Rogers Plan (1969)** Under the Nixon administration, US secretary of state William Rogers sought to resolve the impasse between Israel and the Arabs during the War of Attrition, but his plan was rejected by the parties, as were subsequent proposals in 1970 and 1971.
- **Sadat's historic trip to Jerusalem (1977)** The first Arab leader to visit Israel, President Anwar Sadat of Egypt came to Jerusalem on November 19, 1977, and there made a rousing speech before the Knesset calling for an end to war between Israel and Egypt. The hope felt in Israel in response to his visit can hardly be exaggerated.
- **Second Sinai disengagement (1975)** Like the first, this second agreement was also arranged through the shuttle diplomacy of US secretary of state Henry Kissinger. It called for further Israeli troop withdrawal from Sinai, with a UN buffer zone to take their place.
- **Wye River Memorandum (1998)** Palestinians and Israelis agreed to an immediate return to negotiations and a serious effort to reach a permanent agreement.

Peace Treaty between Israel and Jordan. See under **Peace Process and Peace Agreements**

Peel Commission Report of 1937. See under **Pre-State Palestine**

Peres, Shimon. See under **Israeli Political Leaders**

Poalei Zion. See under **Israeli Political Parties**

Political Zionism. See under **Zionism**

Pre-State Palestine
- **Balfour Declaration (1917)** The first recognition of the Zionist aim of reestablishing the Jewish national homeland in Eretz Yisrael/Palestine by a world power (United Kingdom), the declaration was in a letter by Foreign Secretary Arthur James Lord Balfour to Lord Walter Rothschild. It states, "His Majesty's Government view with favour the establishment in Palestine of a national home for the Jewish people, and will use their best endeavours to facilitate the achievement of this object, it being clearly understood that nothing shall be done which may prejudice the civil and religious rights of existing non-Jewish communities in Palestine, or the rights and political status enjoyed by Jews in any other country."
- **British Mandate for Palestine** The British were made trustees and administrators of the territory between the Jordan River and the Mediterranean Sea by the Mandate for Palestine. The Mandate is a legally binding document unanimously approved by the fifty-one member countries of the League of Nations in 1922 that recognized "the historic connection of the Jewish People with Palestine and ... the grounds for reconstituting their national home in that country."
- **Peel Commission Report of 1937** This report was issued by a royal commission of inquiry into Arab-Jewish violence (1936–1939) headed by Lord Robert Peel. In light of its findings in Palestine, the commission recommended ending the Mandate and partitioning Palestine. The proposal was endorsed by the British Parliament, hotly debated but accepted by Zionists, and rejected by the Arabs.
- **Partition Plan (1947)** Resolution 181 was put forward by the United Nations Special Committee on Palestine (UNSCOP), which convened after the British declared their intention to end the Mandate. It recommended partition into two independent states, a Jewish and an Arab state "joined by economic union," with Jerusalem and Bethlehem as an international zone. The vote on November 29, 1947, in the UN General Assembly approved partition 33 to 13, with 10 abstentions. The plan was accepted by the Jews and roundly rejected by the Arabs. It was never implemented.
- **Two-State Solution** The two-state solution has been the widely accepted paradigm calling for partition, with an independent Palestinian state coexisting with the Jewish state of Israel. UN Resolutions from 1947 have proposed two states with recognized borders, but so far, diplomatic efforts beginning with the Madrid Conference in 1991 have not led to agreement.

Prisoners of Zion This epithet refers to Jewish Zionists trapped behind the Iron Curtain after the establishment of Israel. Beginning in the 1950s, Romanian Zionists were persecuted and often tried and imprisoned for their activities. Significant pressure led to the eventual release of those who survived the persecution and immigration to Israel. Requests from Jewish Zionists to emigrate from the Soviet Union in the 1960s and 1970s similarly met with rejection and resulted in persecution and hardship. Their determined activism along with pressure on the Soviets from across the world, not least from Jewish organizations, effected a change in Soviet policy, and the "Refuseniks" were allowed to leave.

"Protocols of the Elders of Zion" First published in Russia in 1903, this anti-Semitic pamphlet purports to record minutes of a meeting by Jewish leaders in the late nineteenth century and their plans for dominating the world. The document was disseminated around the world and is still available despite having been exposed as a malicious and unmitigated fraud. It epitomizes both the persistence of anti-Semitic caricatures and opinions and their apparent immunity to factual rebuttal.

Quartet. See under **Peace Process and Peace Agreements**

Rabin, Yitzhak. See under **Israeli Political Leaders**

Reform Judaism Originating in nineteenth-century Germany, the proposed reforms emphasized the ethical prophetic teachings of Judaism compatible with emancipation and full civic participation in the life of society at large, and deemphasized the ritual observance and personal practice that were necessarily more restrictive. Defining Jewishness as a religious choice, and Judaism as a religion like all others, Reform Jews did not identify themselves with Jewish peoplehood and initially rejected the Zionist call for a Jewish homeland. This changed with the revolutionary 1937 Columbus Platform.

Religious Zionism. See under **Zionism**

Reparations In 1952, Israeli prime minister David Ben-Gurion argued that the German government was responsible for paying material claims to Israel on behalf of the five hundred thousand refugees it was in the process of absorbing, "so that the murderers do not become the heirs as well," benefiting from both forced labor and goods and property confiscated from survivors and the six million Jews who did not survive. A fierce public debate ensued about accepting reparations. Opponents rejected relations with Germany and protested that money must never be imagined as compensation. These views spanned left and right, and the arguments were ideological, ideational, and emotional, with mass riots against the government decision. Nevertheless, Israel and West Germany signed an agreement in September 1952 on reparations to be paid to the Jewish state.

Revisionist Zionism. See under **Zionism**

Replacement Theology. See under **Supersessionism**

Roadmap. See under **Peace Process and Peace Agreements**

Rogers Plan. See under **Peace Process and Peace Agreements**

Sadat, Anwar. See under **Arab Leaders**

Sadat's historic trip to Jerusalem. See under **Peace Process and Peace Agreements**

Second Sinai disengagement. See under **Peace Process and Peace Agreements**

Secular Zionism. See under **Zionism**

Shamir, Yitzhak. See under **Israeli Political Leaders**

Sharon, Ariel. See under **Israeli Political Leaders**

Shas. See under **Israeli Political Parties**

Six-Day War, 1967 War. See under **Wars and Armed Conflicts**

Socialist Zionism. See under **Zionism**

Status Quo Agreement (1947) Outlined in a letter sent by David Ben-Gurion, Jewish Agency chairman, to the leadership of the World Agudat Yisrael organization, the Status Quo Agreement responds to their "request to guarantee marital affairs, the Sabbath, education and kashrut in the Jewish state to arise in our day" with the Jewish Agency's position on these matters. Ben-Gurion points out that "the establishment of the state requires the approval of the United Nations, and this will not be possible unless the state guarantees freedom of conscience for all its citizens and makes it clear that we have no intention of establishing a theocratic state." At the same time, he acknowledges the concerns not only of Agudat Yisrael but also of other Jews about the relationship between law and religion in the future Jewish state. Finally, he presents the position of the Jewish Agency on each of these matters. The document illustrates the contrast between the US system separating church and state and the Israeli system, which must maintain a difficult balance between their competing needs. (See chapter 8 and an extended discussion in chapter 11).

Supersessionism, Replacement Theology A theological position that persists among Christians that the New Testament superceded the Old, and that the Christian religion supplanted Judaism, essentially bringing the history of the Jewish people to an end and making a Jewish state unnecessary. (See chapter 12 for further discussion.)

Two-State Solution. See under **Pre-State Palestine**

UN Resolutions (See chapter 7 for an extended discussion.)
- **Resolution 181 (November 29, 1947)** Also known as the Partition Plan, Resolution 181 calls for Palestine, then under British Mandate, to be partitioned into a Jewish and Arab State. The date in 1947 when the General Assembly voted to pass the resolution 33 to 13 is still memorialized in Israel. (See also under **Partition Plan**)
- **Resolution 242 (November 1967)** This United Nations Security Council (UNSC) resolution, adopted following the 1967 War, affirms that "a just and lasting peace" should include both Israeli withdrawal from the territories it

occupied and "respect for and acknowledgement of the sovereignty, territorial integrity and political independence of every State in the area and their right to live in peace within secure and recognized boundaries free from threats or acts of force." This resolution is still referenced in diplomatic efforts to implement the conditions it sets forth.

- **Resolution 338 (October 1973)** In the later days of the 1973 War, after Israel had succeeded in pushing back the Syrian assault on the Golan Heights and occupied a bridgehead on the Egyptian side of the Suez Canal, UNSC Resolution 338 called for a cease-fire and for negotiations to begin immediately based on Resolution 242.

- **Resolution 3376 (November 1975)** This resolution of the UN General Assembly expresses concern for the lack of progress by the Palestinian people to achieve its "inalienable rights in Palestine" including "their inalienable right to self-determination without external interference and the right to national independence and sovereignty . . . and their inalienable right to return to their homes and property from which they have been displaced and uprooted." The resolution ends with the decision "to include the item entitled 'Question of Palestine' in the provisional agenda of its thirty-first session."

- **Resolution 3379 (November 1975)** Sharply and unequivocally rejected and denied by American ambassador to the United Nations Daniel Patrick Moynahan, Resolution 3379 defined Zionism as racism and a form of racial discrimination. Seventy-two states voted in favor, 35 against, and 32 abstained. Despite sustained objection, the resolution was not revoked until 1991.

UJA (United Jewish Appeal). See under **American Jewish Organizations**

War of Attrition. See under **Wars and Armed Conflicts**

Wars and Armed Conflicts The wars are organized chronologically. The various names for each war are listed together, separated by commas. The Timeline (page 422) shows **Wars and Armed Conflicts** along with **Peace Negotiations and Agreements** taking place at around the same time. (See chapter 5 for an extended discussion of the Arab-Israeli conflict; see chapter 6 for the peace process.)

- **War of Independence, 1948 War, Arab-Israeli War, Arab-Israeli Interstate War, 1948–1949 War, al-Nakba** The different names for this war reflect its complicated historiography. Armed conflict, the War of Independence, began immediately after the UN vote on November 29, 1947, to partition Palestine into an Arab and a Jewish state. On May 15, 1948, the day following Israel's Declaration of Independence, the new State was attacked along all its borders by Egyptian, Jordanian, and Syrian forces, reinforced by Iraqi troops. For this reason, it is also known as the Arab-Israeli War. The fighting lasted for ten months with occasional cease-fires. Palestinians refer to the war as **al-Nakba**, the Disaster or Catastrophe. Initially a lament by Constantine Zurayq of the catastrophic failure of the combined Arab armies to eliminate the Jewish State (*The Meaning of the Disaster, al-Nakba* (Arabic, 1948)), al-Nakba has come to refer to the flight and expulsion of Palestinians and the loss of Palestinian homes and villages within Israel. In 1998, when Israel celebrated its first fifty years of independence, Palestinians observed their first Nakba Day on May 15, on the fiftieth anniversary of the Nakba, a memorial day declared by Yasser Arafat.

- **Six-Day War, 1967 War, 1967 June War, June 1967 War** This war pitted Egypt, Syria, and Jordan against Israel. Egypt's President Nasser had proclaimed the Arab states' intention to eradicate Israel. In May 1967, he moved Egyptian forces into Sinai close to the Israeli border, ordered the United Nations emergency forces stationed in Sinai since 1956 to withdraw, and announced that he was closing the Straits of Tiran to Israeli shipping in and out of Eilat—in other words, imposing a blockade that would preclude the import of Iranian oil, which was Israel's main supply. Syria had been attacking Israeli kibbutzim from the Golan Heights and announced its readiness for a battle of annihilation. The Arab forces mobilized over 400,000 soldiers, with some 2800 tanks and 800 aircraft poised for battle. In response, on June 5, 1967, Israel sent almost its entire air force to bomb Egyptian airfields, and shortly thereafter airfields in Syria, Jordan, and Iraq. This was followed by huge tank battles between Israeli and Egyptian forces in Sinai; a rebuff of Jordanian troops that attacked Jerusalem, including the recapture of the Old City and Western Wall by Israeli paratroopers; and bloody battles where Israeli troops were finally able to wrest the Golan Heights from the Syrians. The fighting lasted six days, hence the name the Six-Day War. Israel more than tripled its territory, retook the Old City or East Jerusalem lost to Jordan during the 1948 War, and captured Sinai, the Golan Heights, the Gaza Strip, and the territories of the West Bank.
- **Yom Kippur War, 1973 Yom Kippur War, 1973 War, October (1973) War, and referred to by Arabs as the Ramadan War** Egyptian and Syrian forces surprised Israel by a coordinated attack across Israel's southern and northern borders on Yom Kippur, which coincided with the Muslim month of Ramadan in 1973, hence the names. While Israel succeeded in repulsing the attacks, in the aftermath of the surprise, it contended with its unpreparedness and vulnerability. And although neither the Syrians nor the Egyptians were victorious, their success in inflicting losses restored their reputation and self image as forces to be reckoned with.
- **War of Attrition (1967–1970)** The policy of the "Three No's" adopted by the Arabs in the Khartoum Resolution of September 1, 1967, was absolute rejection: no recognition of Israel, no negotiations, and no peace. Given this policy and the absence of diplomatic pressure on Israel to return territory captured during the June 1967 Six-Day War, Egyptian president Gamal Abdel Nasser allied with Jordan and the PLO to initiate artillery attacks on Israeli positions. These escalated to include bombing and commando raids and continued for nearly three years. A cease-fire in August 1970 ended the War of Attrition, though without any exchange of territory or talks of peace.
- **Intifada, First Intifada, Second Intifada or al-Aqsa Intifada**
  - **First Intifada (December 1987–1992)** During this Palestinian uprising, Palestinians directed violence at both Israeli soldiers and civilians. Significant numbers of Arabs were also killed "for political and other reasons" by PLO death squads. The uprising appears to have been orchestrated by the PLO.

o **The Second Intifada or al-Aqsa Intifada (2000–2005)** was initially claimed to be a response to Likud leader Ariel Sharon's visit to the Temple Mount (Haram al Sharif); however, there is substantial testimony, including from Palestinian sources (e.g., Imad Faluji, then PA communications minister) that the violence had been planned well in advance, following the failure of the Camp David Summit, and was encouraged by the PLO leadership. This period was marked by repeated terror attacks and suicide bombings.

- **Lebanon War, 1982 War in Lebanon, First Lebanon War (also Peace for Galilee)** The IDF crossed the border into southern Lebanon in June 1982 following repeated cross-border attacks and shelling by the Palestine Liberation Organization (PLO) on settlements in northern Israel. The operation succeeded in forcing Yasser Arafat and the PLO leadership to evacuate and reestablish themselves in Tunis. However, the IDF became mired in southern Lebanon, and the government's defense policy and its consequences for Lebanese civilians lead to open criticism and gave rise to the Peace Now movement. Israeli troops were unilaterally withdrawn from southern Lebanon by Prime Minister Ehud Barak in 2000.

- **Second Lebanon War (2006)** This war, lasting from July 12 through August 14, was between Hezbollah, heavily supported and backed by Iran, and Israel. Preceded by repeated Hezbollah rocket attacks on cities along Israel's northern border and an attack and abduction of Israeli soldiers on patrol on the Israeli side of the border, the IDF attacked Hezbollah positions in Lebanon and targeted strategic sites such as the Lebanese airport. Israel complied with UN Security Council Resolution 1701 by withdrawing troops from Lebanon; however, Hezbollah has not been disarmed as called for by the resolution.

- **Wars with Hamas, Gaza Wars: Operation Cast Lead (2008–2009); Operation Pillar of Defense (2012); Operation Protective Edge (2014)** These three military operations followed Israel's unilateral withdrawal from the Gaza Strip and the victory of Hamas over Fatah (PLO) in the 2006 elections in Gaza. Each was preceded by persistent mortar shelling and particularly firing of rockets often supplied by Iran from Gaza into Israeli settlements. Initially aimed at settlements near the border, the increasingly advanced rockets were aimed at Israeli cities and by 2014 even Tel Aviv was under fire. The Hamas policy of embedding rocket launchers and other ammunition in densely populated civilian areas has led to debates about proportionality, human rights, and Israel's right to self-defense following IDF incursions into Gaza, as even carefully targeted bombing of rocket launchers results in destruction and human casualties.

Wars with Hamas, Gaza Wars. See under **Wars and Armed Conflicts**

Weizmann, Chaim. See under **Israeli Political Leaders**

West Bank, Judea and Samaria (Area C)
The West Bank is the area West of the Jordan River. After the 1948 War the West Bank including East Jerusalem fell to Transjordan, which occupied and administered the territory and annexed it in 1950. The 1947 UN Partition Plan

designated "the hill country of Samaria and Judea," including the territory
now known as "the West Bank," as part of the new Arab-Palestinian state. The
"East" Bank was part of Jordan. In the 1967 War, Israel captured the territory
on the other side of the Jordan, including East Jerusalem. "West Bank" has
been used to refer to the area that is supposed to become an important part of
a future Palestinian state, with rural villages, towns, and cities such as Ramallah and the new planned Palestinian city of Rawabi, and Israeli settlements
and cities, like Ariel. The territory was divided by Oslo II into Area A (18 percent) and Area B (22 percent) that include about 2.8 million Palestinians and
are primarily administered by the Palestinian Authority. Area C (60 percent)
which has some 300,000 Palestinian residents and 350,000 Jewish settlers, is
administered by the Judea and Samaria Area administration, and is under full
Israeli control.

World Zionist Organization (WZO). See under **World Zionist Organizations**

World Zionist Organizations
- **Jewish Agency** The operational arm of the World Zionist Organization (WZO),
  the Jewish Agency was established in the British Mandate for Palestine granted
  by the League of Nations and was responsible for governing the Yishuv during
  the Mandate and for *aliya* and absorption of immigrants. David Ben-Gurion
  was chairman of its executive committee (a post he had filled since 1935) when
  he proclaimed Israel's independence on May 14, 1948.
- **Jewish National Fund (JNF) (Hebrew Keren Kayemet)** The JNF was founded
  in 1901 at the Fifth Zionist Congress to collect funds for purchasing and developing land in Palestine for Jewish settlement, and its mission was quickly
  disseminated when the now iconic Blue Box was distributed in Jewish institutions and homes beginning in 1904, a "pushke" where individuals could
  collect funds to help buy land and make it fit for settlement in a future Jewish
  homeland by planting trees and draining swamps.
- **Keren Hayesod** Dedicated to raising funds for the Jewish State outside the
  United States, Keren Hayesod was founded in 1920. It saw to the transport of
  thousands of Jewish refugees to Palestine and then Eretz Yisrael and contributed to the social and economic infrastructure necessary for their absorption. In addition to recent projects such as building mobile shelters for Israeli
  settlements under fire from Gaza, Keren Hayesod supports Zionist and Jewish
  education in the Diaspora.
- **World Zionist Organization (WZO).** Originally named The Zionist Organization (ZO), the organization was founded by Theodor Herzl in Basle in 1897
  at the First Zionist Congress. Its stated goal was "to establish a home for the
  Jewish people in Palestine, secured under public law." In 1960 it was renamed
  the World Zionist Organization (WZO). Initially it had responsibility for
  aliya, absorption of immigrants and the establishment of settlements, but its
  present focus is on Jewish life and education in the Diaspora.

Wye River Memorandum. See under **Peace Process and Peace Agreements**

Yesh 'Atid. See under **Israeli Political Parties**

Yishuv This Hebrew term, which comes from the root that means to sit and to settle, refers to communities of Jewish immigrants who settled pre-State Palestine with the intention of building and being rebuilt in the land, reconstituting a Jewish homeland, and reviving the Hebrew language and culture. The **Old Yishuv** refers to pre-Zionist, pre-1881 Jewish communities in Palestine.

Yom Kippur War, 1973 Yom Kippur War, 1973 War, October War, and referred to by Arabs as the Ramadan War. See under **Wars and Armed Conflicts**

Yosef, Ovadia. See under **Israeli Political Leaders**

Zionism
- **Cultural Zionism** Promulgated by Ahad Ha'am in contrast to Herzl's Political Zionism, cultural Zionism assumed that most Jews would remain in the Diaspora but that Jewish cultural and linguistic renewal in Eretz Yisrael were fundamental and would strengthen Jewish spiritual and ethical identity everywhere. (See the extended treatment in chapters 3 and 14.)
- **General Zionism** Initially this designation referred to the general commitment to a Jewish homeland without affiliation to any particular faction or political party. In 1922 it was institutionalized as the Organization of General Zionists, splitting into two factions in 1931 over issues relating to Palestine including social affairs and attitudes to the Histadrut, and reuniting in 1945. A majority of Israel's Liberal movements and parties originated within General Zionism and resulted from mergers in and secessions from the movement.
- **Labor Zionism** Socialist Zionism, founded by Nachum Syrkin, sought to fuse Zionism with socialism and held that "the Jewish problem" would not be solved by a socialist revolution in the Diaspora but by Jewish emigration to their own homeland. Only Zionism would allow for restructuring the class system to liberate the people and the Jewish proletariat. David Ben-Gurion, Yitzchak Ben-Zvi, and Berl Katznelson were all important leaders of Labor Zionism in the pre-State years, a movement that later gave rise to the Labor party.
- **Political Zionism**, associated with Theodor Herzl, emphasized the political means necessary for gaining international recognition for the Zionist program and support for Jewish sovereignty.
- **Religious Zionism** When the Fifth Zionist Congress (1902) included cultural activity in the Zionist Program, Merkaz Ruchani (Spiritual Center) with the acronym Mizrachi organized and focused its 1904 platform on the observance of commandments and Jewish religious life in Zion. While Ultra-Orthodoxy considered Zionist activity blasphemous and a misguided human effort to undertake Divine prerogative, Rabbi Abraham Yitzhak Hacohen Kook endorsed the program, declaring Jewish "settlement in the Land of Israel as the beginning of Redemption."

- **Revisionist Zionism** began as an effort, led by Vladimir Ze'ev Jabotinsky (1925) to revise Herzl's Political Zionism, taking a more assertive stance toward Great Britain with demands for open immigration and a Jewish majority in Palestine, a state on both sides of the Jordan, and military training. Leaving the WZO to form their own New Zionist Organization. They rejoined in 1946 when the Biltmore Program declared the Zionist commitment to a Jewish Commonwealth in Palestine. In Palestine, more militant Revisionist Zionists joined the pre-State military organizations Etzel and Lehi, and the Revisionist movement merged with the Herut movement in the Herut party, later part of the Likud.
- **Secular Zionism** is the category name given to the various forms of Zionism that are not Religious Zionism. The term emphasizes the contrast between their various ideological and political positions and those of Religious Zionism for which adherence to commandments is primary.
- **Socialist Zionism.** See **Labor Zionism.**

Zionist (Youth) Organizations (Pre-State/Yishuv)
- **Betar** Founded in Latvia in 1923, this activist Zionist youth movement takes its name from the acronym of B'rith Trumpeldor, the covenant of (Joseph) Trumpeldor, the legendary one-armed Jewish soldier who died in 1920 defending Tel Hai in the Galilee. Born in Russia, Trumpeldor saw significant action during World War I, and in 1918 on a visit to Russia he founded Hehalutz, a youth organization to prepare youth to settle on the land.
- **Bilu** began as an initiative of Russian Jews who declared a fast and gathered to discuss possibilities in January 1882 following pogroms of April to December 1881. The name is an acronym from the Hebrew "Beit Yaakov Lekhu Venelkha" ("House of Jacob, come and let us go," Isaiah 2:5) and represents a shift from assuming assimilation would solve the Jewish problem to an adherence to Jewish nationalism. The group aimed to regain political independence in Palestine, and the first Biluim arrived in July 1882. Of the estimated fifty-three Bilu members who came to Palestine, few remained, but they set an important early example, taking action and making Palestine a real option.
- **Hapo'el Hatza'ir** (The Young Laborer) (1905–1930) was a pacifist and anti-militarist socialist Zionist group during the Second Aliya that sought to conquer the land through labor. To avoid duplicating efforts, around 1920 its members joined with Ahdut Ha'avoda to form the Histadrut, but the groups remained rivals until 1930, when Ben-Gurion united them to form the Mapai party.
- **Hashomer Hatza'ir** (The Young Guard) originated in Galicia in 1913 and is the oldest Zionist youth movement still in existence. It was also a political party in the Yishuv that called for equality with the Arabs and a binational solution. Hence they voted against the 1942 Biltmore Program declaring Zionism's goal as a Jewish Commonwealth. The first members settled in Palestine in 1919, and in 1927 its four kibbutzim formed the Kibbutz Artzi (National Kibbutz) federation.

- **Hibbat Zion, Hovevei Zion, Chibat Zion, Chovevei Zion** (Lovers of Zion or Love of Zion) was a pre-Zionist movement organized in response to Russian pogroms in 1881 and became an official entity at an 1884 conference led by Leon Pinsker, author and advocate of Jewish auto-emancipation. Members founded Rishon Lezion, the first Zionist settlement, in 1882.

TIMELINE: A CENTURY OF WARS AND CONFLICT AND PEACE NEGOTIATIONS AND AGREEMENTS, 1917–2016

PRE-STATE– 1948	1950–1956	1957–1970	1973–1975	1977–1981
1948 War, War of Independence, referred to by Arabs as al Nakba	1956 Suez Campaign	1967 War, Six-Day War, 1967 June War, June 1967 War 1967–1970 War of Attrition	1973 War, Yom Kippur War, referred to by Arabs as the Ramadan War	**1981 Assassination of President Anwar Sadat**
1917 Balfour Declaration 1922 League of Nations agrees to the Mandate for Palestine 1937 Peel Commission Report recommending partition 1947 UN vote on partition 1948 Israel Declaration of Independence		1969 Rogers Plan	1973 Geneva conference 1974 Israel-Egypt Disengagement Agreement 1975 Second Sinai Disengagement	1977 Sadat's historic visit to Jerusalem 1978 Camp David Negotiations and Accords 1979 Israeli-Egyptian Peace Treaty

1982–1987	1988–1998	2000–2005	2006–2016

1982
First Lebanon War
 	
1987
First Intifada begins
 	
1987
London understanding (aborted)
	1988–1992
	First Intifada continues
	
	1995
	Assassination of Prime Minister Yitzchak Rabin
	
	1991
	Madrid Conference
	
	1993
	Oslo I/Declaration of Principles signed by Yasser Arafat and Yitzchak Rabin
	
	1994
	Treaty of Peace between the State of Israel and the Hashemite Kingdom of Jordan
	
	1995
	Oslo II/Taba/Israeli-Palestinian Interim Agreement on the West Bank and Gaza Strip
	
	1998
	Wye River Accord
		2000–2005
		Second Intifada, al-Aqsa Intifada
		
		2000
		Unilateral Israeli withdrawal from Lebanon
		
		2000
		Camp David Summit
		
		Clinton Parameters
		
		2002
		Quartet (USA, UN, European Union, Russia)
		
		2003
		Roadmap for Peace (Quartet)
		
		2005
		Gaza Disengagement
			2006
			Second Lebanon War
			
			Wars with Hamas, Gaza Wars:
			  o Operation Cast Lead 2008–2009
			  o Operation Pillar of Defense 2012
			  o Operation Protective Edge 2014
			
			2007
			International Conference at Annapolis

Note: Text in gray denotes events related to wars and conflict. All other text denotes events related to peace negotiations and agreements.

CPSIA information can be obtained
at www.ICGtesting.com
Printed in the USA
BVOW06s0718090317
478199BV00001B/1/P